The Family

The Family

The Story of Charles Manson's Dune Buggy Attack Battalion

by
Ed Sanders

E. P. Dutton and Co., Inc. | New York | 1971

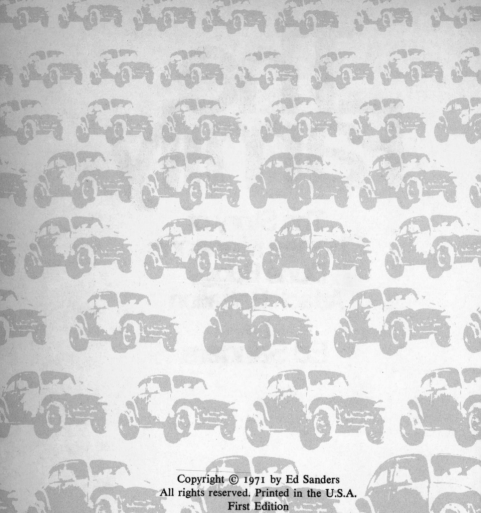

Published simultaneously in Canada by
Clarke, Irwin & Company Limited, Toronto and Vancouver
Library of Congress Catalog Card Number: 77-125906
SBN 0-525-10300-7

For my friend
Paul Fitzgerald

Introduction

I first heard of Charles Manson and his family, so to speak, around October 20, 1969, when I received in the mail an issue of an ecology newsletter called *Earth Read-Out*. The newsletter had reprinted a story from the *San Francisco Chronicle* dated October 15, 1969:

The last survivors of a band of nude and long-haired thieves who ranged over Death Valley in stolen dune buggies have been rounded up, the sheriff's office said yesterday. A sheriff's posse, guided by a spotter plane, arrested 27 men and women members of the nomad band in two desert raids. Deputies said eight children, including two babies suffering from malnutrition, were also brought in. Some of the women were completely nude and others wore only bikini bottoms, deputies said. All the adults were booked at Inyo county jail for investigation of charges which included car theft, receiving stolen property and carrying illegal weapons. Six stolen dune buggies were recovered, deputies said.

Deputy Sheriff Jerry Hildreth said the band lived off the land by stealing. He said they traveled in the stolen four-wheel-drive dune buggies and camped in a succession of abandoned mining shacks. The band previously escaped capture by moving only at night and by setting up radio-equipped lookout posts on the mountains, he said. "It was extraordinary the way they covered up their tracks and would make dummy camps to throw us off," Hildreth said. "They gave us a merry chase. . . . This is probably one of the most inaccessible areas in California."

Six weeks after I read those two paragraphs in *Earth Read-Out,* the front pages of newspapers were filled with glaze-eyed pictures of Manson, the accused murderer. He was depicted all at once as a hippie satanist car thief cult-leader sex-maniac bastard butcher. His followers—a few young men and around twenty girls—were depicted as "Satan's slaves," willing to do anything anytime anywhere for him. Out of all of the headlines and stories no consistent set of facts seemed to emerge that explained in any depth how a group of young American citizens could develop into a commune of hackers.

Accordingly, in January of 1970, I began to gather data about the family, as a matter of personal curiosity. Then I decided to write a book about the family, thinking it would take only three or four months, after which I could return to a quiet life of poetry and peace. Almost at once, upon my first flight to Los Angeles, I dipped into a frenzy of continuous day and night activity that would last for a year and a half, resulting in this book.

At the beginning of my research I prepared an elaborate plan for securing information so that my personal safety would be insured and so that I would have to make as few deals as possible with anyone. That is, I wanted to have information that I could feel free to use in any way I saw fit. Quite often, people would want anonymity in exchange for supplying data. Only in a few instances when I knew the information was true and was vital to the book did I agree to anonymity. In several cases, when it seemed that the person's life might be in danger if I printed his or her name, I have left it out.

There was a lot of information—particularly related to the occult—concerning the private lives of various murder victims that I have left out in respect for the memory of the innocent slain. Accordingly, this book deals in the main with the growth and development of the family of Manson and the murders they committed, and deals only in brief with the lives of the deceased.

Every assertion in every sentence of this book is based upon information received from official documents, court records, trial transcripts, taped and written interviews with witnesses to events described herein, personal observation, maps, photos and public officials.

For a year and a half, I wrote down literally everything I heard or saw related to the so-called Manson family. I carried with me at all times a tape recorder and recorded at least one hundred hours of interviews, confrontations and comment. Each day I wrote a report on the day's activities. Nothing was too trivial to escape my jotting Rapidograph. Often a strange bit of information that seemed to have no meaning would, a year after I received it, turn out to be important. With me at all times during my peripatetic data-collecting was an Instamatic camera and a Polaroid camera with which I snapped hundreds of pictures. Day and night I roamed Los Angeles gathering data. I became a data addict. I ran ads in underground newspapers for information about Manson's group which brought forth a lot of data.

In addition to daily data-reports, I established files on selected subjects. For instance I put together separate files on the L.A. occult scene, on Manson's relations in Hollywood and on each aspect of the history of the family, around fifty files in all. In addition, I transcribed important taped interviews and inserted the data into the appropriate files. In regard to each subject file I compiled vast lists of unanswered questions which in subsequent interviews and data-forays I sought to answer. In this way interviews spawned interviews and continuous examination of my data horde was necessary in order to isolate unanswered questions. After a few months, I was traveling around with about 10,000 pages, literally, of data.

From my daily reports and subject files, I created monthly data files covering the years 1967–68–69. These monthly files contained the week-by-week history of the family. It was from these chronological files that I wrote this book.

The 25,000 or so pages of the Tate-LaBianca trial transcript, of which I read a large part, were invaluable in determining in many cases where an event fitted into the chronology. The same is true of the transcripts of the trial of Robert Beausoleil for the murder of Gary Hinman. I obtained considerable information by compiling a chronological set of newspaper clippings, totaling several thousand, from all over the United States and Europe dealing with the Tate-LaBianca homicides and the Manson family.

Occasionally my research required the adoption of a persona to secure data, as when I posed as a New York pornography dealer with Andy Warhol out-takes for sale during an elaborate two-month caper in which I attempted to purchase certain famous porn-films of Manson and the family and citizens of Hollywood. On other occasions I posed as satanist, drooling maniac and dope-tranced psychopath.

Over the period of a year I wrote about twenty-five articles for the *Los Angeles Free Press* covering the Manson trial and the ongoing existence of his family of followers. Without the friendship of the Staff of the *Free Press,* this book could not have been written, for the *Free Press* office was a zone of sanity where I could escape after a day of gathering insane data about corpses, rituals and weirdness. I want particularly to thank Paul and Shirley Eberle, Brian Kirby, Judy Lewellen, brave publisher Art Kunkin, John Carpenter and Kitty for their help and friendship.

Part of this book was written in the Hall of Justice in downtown Los Angeles where I attended about four months of the trial of Susan Atkins, Patricia Krenwinkel, Leslie Van Houten and Charles Manson. I also attended Robert Beausoleil's second trial for the murder of Gary Hinman and numerous court hearings pertaining to other trials and murders involving the family. It was necessary to maintain a considerable correspondence with individuals all over the United States and Europe.

It was necessary to spend several weeks reading microfilm in the New York Public Library where I had the pleasure of reading the greater part of the *Los Angeles Times* and *San Francisco Chronicle* for 1968 and 1969. It was necessary to study maps of murder houses, to see photos of death, to read autopsy reports and to recreate in written form acts abhorrent.

I divided the Los Angeles area and indeed all of California into investigatory grids. Each grid had its own problems regarding information, because Manson and his group tended to have different relationships with different areas. Thus the "image" of the family was vastly different in Topanga Canyon than it was in Death Valley and required different investigation techniques. I visited the Spahn Movie Ranch over twenty times to try to understand exactly what this group of humans known as "the family" really believed and practiced. I even trekked up into Devil Canyon to check out obscure campsites of the family.

Four times I went on overnight trips to Inyo County and Death Valley, where I camped out and talked to miners, officials, etc. I rode up the treacherous Goler Wash waterfalls in one of the family's abandoned vehicles to see what it was like. I hung out at the Ballarat Ghost Town, I walked over Mengel Pass, I visited the Barker and Meyers Ranches, old mine shacks, obscure springs, following the routes of Helter Skelter.

During the last six months of my investigation, I was aided considerably by a private investigator, Mr. Larry Larsen, an intrepid sleuth whose persistent, resourceful collecting of data was amazing. Together we conducted an intricate investigation of various occult societies in Los Angeles concentrating on cruelty-freaks, satanists, and other partisans of pain-magic. We had quite a few adventures. One moonlit night we staked out a beach in Ventura County where we thought a group of occult corpsoids were going to conduct an animal sacrifice. On another occasion we scraped what we thought to be animal blood off a ritual altar at an abandoned movie set on an obscure mountaintop fire road above Topanga Canyon.

It was to be expected that there were quite a few psychopathic liars encountered during the four or five hundred interviews necessitated by the investigation. In the majority of anecdotes in this book, there were two or more versions received from separate individuals regarding the same event. Each interview required sort of a "truth analysis" where everything was checked against the main chronology of known facts. One of the biggest problems is the fade-out that human memory experiences with the passage of time. For instance, the memory of a human for the first week of November 1967 is usually very vague. Add elements of damaged minds, use of psychedelics, fear, etc., and the recollection of many was pretty tattered.

Naturally my path crossed many others whose activities were not directly involved in family life and death but who were nevertheless weird beyond weird. Particularly in the areas of occult groups I encountered the spiritually wounded: drinkers of dog blood, the video-bugger crowd, people who hang rotting goats' heads up in their kitchens, people who rent corpses for their Bel Air parties, victimizers of every persuasion.

daring

There were problems of a scary nature that hampered my investigation, particularly the problem of the body in the car trunk. Several business friends of Jay Sebring have been murdered. I was trying to locate one of them, a man named Rostau, from whom I wanted some information, when news came in the fall of 1970 that he had been found dead in a car trunk in New York. Another associate was found murdered in Florida around Christmastime 1970. These events caused me to swerve my investigation to safer areas of inquiry. No book is worth permanent meditation next to a tire.

It is not the intention of this book to solve any murders although there are plenty to be solved. Accordingly a number of homicides were not brought into the narrative. The probability that uncaught murderers—plus groups who commit human sacrifices and from whom the family drew ideas and support—were running loose in California also crimped investigation. One encountered several nomadic hippie Cassandras whom no official seemed to believe and who told ghastly tales of sacrificial rituals in the mountains and beaches of California.

There is no pretense that this book is the final work on the Manson family. A scientific, scholarly study, for instance, is needed on techniques of psychedelic brainwashing and criminal behavior under complex hypnotic suggestion-patterns. Young people need to know the techniques a guru or so-called leader might use to entrap them in a web of submission so that they can keep a constant vigil against it.

Manson and his associates now live condemned to die in the cyanide gas chamber in San Quentin Prison, Tamal, California. I am opposed to capital punishment because I believe that killing killers only perpetuates the vengeance and violence. There must be an existing facility wherein Manson can be kept during his life and from which he would be unable to direct any further violence through his disciples, many of whom, in my opinion, are crazed with the willingness to murder. In fact they are all crazed: Manson, Susan Atkins, Tex Watson, Patricia Krenwinkel, Leslie Van Houten and many others in the family. Psychiatric examination has revealed that when certain of the family are alone by themselves in cells they seem to enter into a state of deep psychosis. When they are together they seem bound by iron bands as if connected to the same body and will. And that is the story presented in this book, how a group of young Americans became welded together into a war-like clan that killed.

Contents

13

Section II

The Murders
July 25, 1969–August 15, 1969

Section III

Manson Captured
August 16–December 1, 1969

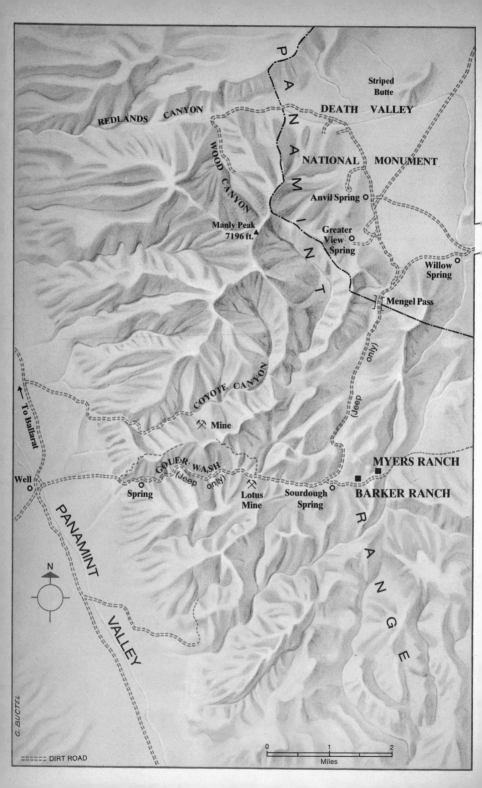

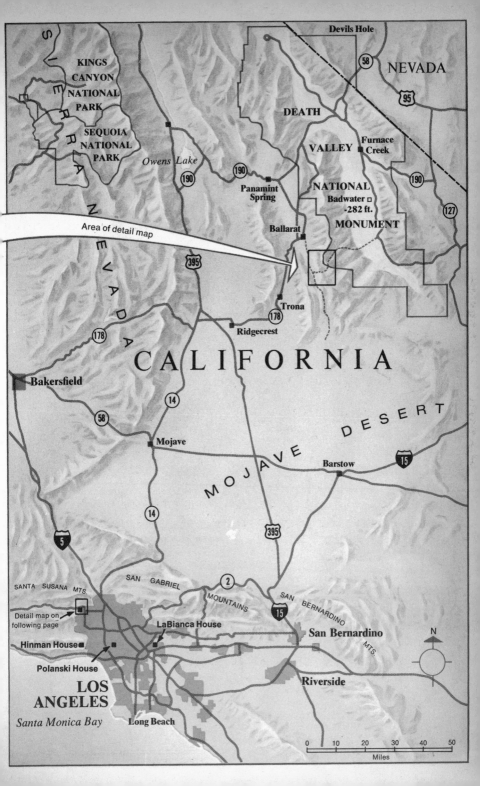

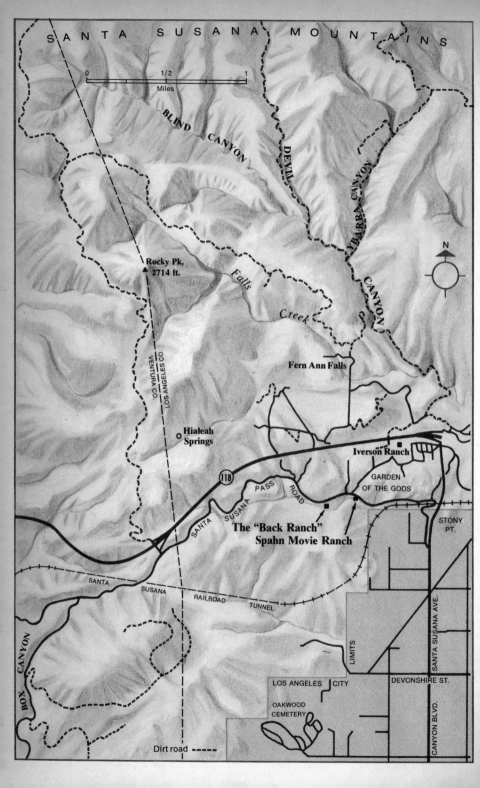

Section I

The Family
From the Beginning to mid-1969

One

A Poor Risk for Probation

Around July 22, 1955, Charles Manson drove a stolen 1951 Mercury from Bridgeport, Ohio to Los Angeles, bringing with him his seventeen-year-old pregnant wife Rosalie. All was.

In September he was arrested and pleaded guilty on October 17, 1955. The psychiatric report prepared after Manson's arrest stated that he was a "poor risk for probation" but, on the other hand, it was felt that married life plus incipient fatherhood, which calms down juvenile delinquents everywhere, might put him onto the direct path of the American Way. So on November 7, 1955, Manson was sentenced to five years probation. Manson had been on parole since May 18, 1954. He was twenty-one years old. He had been in prison since he was sixteen and in various corrective institutions before that since he was thirteen.

After his arrest Manson made the mistake of admitting to the Feds during interrogation that in 1954, the year previous, he had taken a hot auto from the strip-mine area of West Virginia down to Florida.

As a result of this self-snitch, on January 11, 1956, Manson appeared before the Federal Commissioner in Los Angeles regarding a complaint filed in Miami, Florida charging violation of the Dyer Act.

Released on his own recognizance, Manson was told to return to court on February 15. Shortly thereafter he fled Los Angeles, evidently accompanied by his heavily pregnant wife Rosalie. They drove back home to Appalachia.

On February 29 the chief probation officer in Los Angeles requested the court to issue a bench warrant because Manson had not reported in to his probation officer. He was arrested on March 14, 1956, in Indianapolis, Indiana and transported back to Los Angeles for trial.

In March of 1956 a son Charles, Jr., was born.

On April 23, 1956, Judge Harry C. Westover revoked probation and imposed a three-year federal prison sentence for Manson at Terminal Island Penitentiary in San Pedro, California.

For almost a year during the first part of his Terminal Island sentence, Rosalie, his wife, stuck by him—living with Charles, Jr., the son, and Manson's mother Kathleen in Los Angeles. Early in 1957 Rosalie discontinued her visits and according to a Federal probation report, was living with another man, which upset Manson greatly. On May 24, 1957, Manson tried to sneak away from Terminal Island and was indicted under the United States Code Title 18 Section 751, Escape from Federal Custody after Conviction. Manson pleaded guilty on May 27, 1957, and on June 10, 1957 was given a suspended sentence by Federal Judge William Mathes and placed on probation for five years.

Shortly thereafter Manson's West Virginia wife sued for divorce. A summons was served on Manson on July 15 at Terminal Island in San Pedro. Affidavit of final judgment of divorce was filed August 30, 1957. Adios, wife.

Manson served from April 23, 1956, until September 30, 1958: two years, five months, five days of so-called rehabilitation. In prison the young, 125-pound man played on various basketball teams and evidently boxed a bit. He continued his sex life in the only way possible in jail—by hand, by mouth and by buttock.

For two and one-half years Manson was exposed to the endless discussions of schemes and crimes and psychopathy out of the mouths of older, so-called seasoned criminals. At Terminal Island there was a lot of what might be called "pimp talk"—about the devices to be used in controlling a bevy of prostitutes. Charlie listened avidly, according to people interviewed from Terminal

Island. A friend who knew him then writes: "We'd rap a lot about whores, especially how to control them. We talked about Main Old Ladies—a pimp's number one girl who controlled all the others; stables—more than one girl working for you; and we talked mostly about how to turn chicks out."

Time passed for young Charlie Manson and "Subject was released from the FCI, TI on 9–30–58 and is on CR till 10–24–58"—noted his federal parole office on October 1, 1958, in what are called chrono notes.

Manson announced that he was going to live with his mother on Harkinson Avenue in Los Angeles. This was the first of twenty addresses Manson would have in this particular year and eight months' stretch of freedom.

The parole office gave him some employment leads. His employment pattern for the following months reads like a struggling novelist's. But Manson was just struggling, working as a bus boy, bartender, frozen-food locker concessionaire, canvasser for freezer sales, service station attendant, TV producer and pimp.

On 1–16–59 an irate father complained to the Los Angeles police department that Manson was making attempts to turn his daughter Judy out onto the streets to hustle. Manson also ran around with Judy's roommate, a wealthy UCLA student named Flo from Baker, California, who drove a white Triumph.

On May 1, 1959, Manson was caught running from a Ralph's Market in Los Angeles having attempted to forge and cash a stolen government check for $34.50. Earlier in the day he had cashed another stolen check at a Richfield service station. He was to be severely spanked for this. Impounded at the scene of the crime was a blue 1953 Cadillac convertible evidently belonging to Manson's mother.

After the Los Angeles police department had turned Manson over to the federal authorities, the Feds while questioning Manson made the mistake of leaving the forged check lying out in an open dossier. Manson appears to have seized and gobbled down the check when the secret service agents turned their backs for a moment. In any event, the check disappeared and Manson soon begged to go to the bathroom in order to void the contents of his stomach due to gobbled check nausea.

On June 19, 1959, an attractive, according to the parole officer, nineteen-year-old female Caucasian named Candy Stevens visited Manson's parole officer and announced that she was pregnant by Manson and that he and she were going to get married if only the mean old federal authorities wouldn't salt him away. In reality, she was not pregnant but was a strumpet currently working for Manson. In fact, Manson may have been the first to turn her out.

On September 4, 1959, another psychiatric examination was given Manson by the same doctor who had examined him four years previous. The report concluded:

> He does not give the impression of being a mean individual. However, he is very unstable emotionally and very insecure. He tells about his life inside the institutions in such a manner as to indicate that he has gotten most of his satisfactions from institutions. He said that he was captain of various athletic teams and that he made a great effort to entertain other people in the institutions. In my opinion, he is probably a sociopathic personality without psychosis. Unfortunately, he is rapidly becoming an institutionalized individual. However, I certainly cannot recommend him as a good candidate for probation.

Charlie Manson was twenty-four years old.

Manson had a hearing on September 28, 1959, with the young lady Candy beseeching and weeping in court before the judge in behalf of Manson—and the judge relented and suspended sentence of ten years, placing Manson on probation for five.

In November of 1959 Manson met an eighteen-year-old girl from Detroit named Mary Jo who had been suckered out to Los Angeles by a magazine ad for an airline stewardess school. When the girl reached Los Angeles the school turned out to be a fraud and she couldn't get her money back. She talked her parents into letting her remain in Los Angeles and moved into an apartment with a girl friend named Rita.

In late 1959 Manson hooked up with a Tony Cassino forming something called 3-Star Enterprises, Night Club, Radio and TV promotions, Suite 306, 6871 Franklin, Hollywood. (This address was just a couple of doors away from the apartment where a decade later Manson would gun down the black dope dealer Bernard Crowe.) Manson was president and Tony was VP. Allegedly Manson obtained some money from Detroit Mary Jo for three of his so-called promotions. The reality of 3-Star Enterprises seems to be that Manson was dealing female sex objects out of the Hollywood Roosevelt Hotel.

In October Charlie's mother moved back to West Virginia and alleged that she was going to stay there.

On 12–4–59 Candy Stevens, the girl who cried in court, was arrested in Beverly Hills for prostitution. Manson raised money and bailed her out, but a short time later she was given a jail term. In the meantime, Manson caused pregnancy to occur within that girl from Detroit, Mary Jo.

On December 24, 1959, Christmas Eve, Manson was arrested and was accused of sending a person named Harold in a stolen car with Candy and a girl named Elizabeth to Needles, California in order to deal out bod. He was soon released for lack of evidence. On New Year's Eve Manson was picked up on charges of stealing credit cards but was released on January 4, 1960.

On January 5, 1960, Manson was summoned to court as a witness regarding theft of American Express and Bank of America credit cards. Things were heating up for the young Manson, "this weak, tricky youth"—as his parole officer called him. The FBI began an intensive investigation of Manson, and February 15, 1960, was the last date that Manson reported in to his parole officer.

On February 20, 1960, the pregnant Mary Jo from Detroit became very ill. Her pregnancy became ectopic—i.e., the fetus was growing in the Fallopian tube, a serious condition—and the girl began to bleed and was taken to a hospital. Manson called the girl's father, an insurance executive in Detroit, who flew immediately to Los Angeles where he was met at the Los Angeles

International Airport by Manson and Mary Jo's roommate Rita.
On the way back Manson announced that he didn't have a driver's
license and that he was a federal parolee. Mary Jo's father,
according to a Federal probation report, was shocked at the
sudden flash that his daughter had been knocked up by a convict.

Mary Jo seesawed through her crisis, then quickly recovered.
Her father hustled her away to a private recuperation home.
Manson somehow found her phone number and began to call
her. Mary Jo told her father that she was deeply in love with
Manson. The girl's father began to snoop around Hollywood
and discovered a few people who alleged that Manson had been
doing a bit of pimping. To quote the parole officer's report of
that era, the father was "sick with the thought that this subject
planned to have his daughter and Rita work for him." Then to
the father's horror, he discovered that the man his daughter
loved, on the very night that Manson had taken Mary Jo to the
hospital in serious deathly condition, this man Manson had
seduced Mary Jo's roommate Rita.

On February 29, 1959, the father visited Manson's federal
parole officer to complain. The father, a skilled insurance investigator already, had really burned up the roads getting the
data on Manson. He was angered over Manson's refusal to
hand over Mary Jo's luggage. The father even had tried to get
the Pasadena police to arrest Manson, but they refused.

In the afternoon after seeing the parole officer, the irate father
drove to Manson's rooming house in Pasadena and found that
Manson had abandoned the pad but not Mary Jo's luggage which
Charlie took with him. Father was horrified to find semi-nude
girlie photos left behind. A police officer neighbor in the rooming
house described Manson as a "sex maniac" and hinted that
Manson may have been taking beaver photos for sale out of
state.

It was all over for Manson. The machinery of justice began
to gobble up his trail.

In April of 1960 Candy Stevens snitched to a federal grand

jury and on April 27, 1960, an indictment was handed down charging Manson with violation of Title 18 Section 2421, Transportation of Women in Interstate Commerce for Purposes of Prostitution. Evidently he himself transported the young ladies, Candy and Elizabeth, on December 12, 1959, from Needles, California to Lordsburg, New Mexico in a stolen Triumph convertible.

On petition of the federal parole office, Judge Mathes revoked parole on the previous check forgery charge. On May 23, 1960, bond was set at $10,000. On June 1, 1960, a week after the issuance of the bench warrant for his arrest, Charlie was picked up in Laredo, Texas, evidently on a separate matter, charged with violation of the Mann Act, aka (also known as) White Slave Act. A few days later, on June 16, Manson was returned to authorities in Los Angeles.

On June 23, 1960, Judge William Mathes sentenced Manson to serve ten years at McNeil Island Federal Penitentiary in the state of Washington. On July 10, 1960, the federal pimp charges were dropped but Manson had already been sentenced for parole violation.

Manson had been free for one year, eight months and two days. He appealed the ten-year sentence and remained about a year in Los Angeles County Jail on the top floors of the Hall of Justice where a decade later he would be tried for murder.

In June of 1961 he gave up after losing a court appeal, and allowed himself to be shipped to McNeil Island Penitentiary.

In December of 1963 Manson's mother, evidently remarried and living in Spokane, Washington, wrote a letter to Judge Mathes offering to put up her house as security for Manson's release. The judge had his clerk write her back that after ninety days the judge had no jurisdiction to alter terms of sentencing.

For most of the 1960's Manson sat in jail. Through the tumult of the various liberation movements outside in America, through riots, through assassinations, the beginning of Vietnam, peace rallies, sexual liberation, rock and roll, the Beatles For Sale, the Beach Boys, napalm, Hare Krishna, and the growing refusal of women to be victimized—a movement of which he had little awareness—through all this sat Manson monitoring reality through magazines and hearsay conversation.

It was while counting the days at McNeil Island that Manson began studying magic, warlockry, hypnotism, astral projection, Masonic lore, scientology, ego games, subliminal motivation, music and perhaps Rosicrucianism.

Especially hypnotism and subliminal motivation. He seemed determined to use it to effect control over others, to his benefit.

One prison mate of Manson at McNeil Island recalls vividly the great Charlie Manson Headphones Caper.

Utilizing the prison radio station, Manson planted what his cell partner called "posthypnotic suggestions" in all the prisoners at McNeil Island Penitentiary.

Each prisoner had access to the station by means of headphones hanging on the bunk beds in the cells. Manson set up a clandestine scheme whereby the radio station would broadcast messages at 3 A.M. over the earphones. The message or instruction was repeated over and over.

The prisoners were required to hang their headsets at night on the bedsteads so that the messages were picked up by the sleepers but were not loud enough to attract the guards.

The story continues that McNeil Island had a basketball team that rarely won any games. Manson beamed messages to the sleeping inmates urging them to get out and to root for the McNeil Island team.

Charlie then placed bets with the zealous new fans that the opposing teams would win and quickly won himself two hundred packs of cigarettes, the medium of exchange in U.S. prisons.

Another was the applause caper: he planted suggestions over the earphones that everyone should keep applauding for Manson when he sang at a particular prison talent contest. Manson won the contest earphones-down, evidently receiving a standing ovation of some duration.

Of irony, Manson seems to have become a protégé in prison

of prohibition gangster Alvin Karpis, a member of the evil Ma
Barker gang, which left fourteen victims dead.

Alvin "Old Creepy" Karpis taught Charlie to play the steel
guitar and seems to have been a general counselor to the young
man, although when interviewed after Manson's arrest, Karpis
said that he had considered Manson the last man on earth "to go
into the mass murder business."

"Charlie was hooked on this new thing called 'scientology,' "
says Karpis. "He figured it would enable him to do anything or
be anything. Maybe he was right. The kid tried to sell a lot of
other cons on scientology but got strictly nowhere."

Scientology is a reincarnationist religion that claims to train
individuals to experience past lives, to leave their bodies—i.e.,
"exteriorize"—and to achieve great power and immortality, among
other things. Manson learned about scientology from one Lanier
Raymer, from Gene Deaton and from Jerry Milman, who was
Manson's roommate at McNeil Island Penitentiary.

Lanier Raymer, according to Manson's followers, had been
active in the study of scientology and had become a Doctor of
Scientology, an early rank in the movement, now abolished.

Raymer broke away from scientology and formed his own
group. He was apprehended for a shotgun holdup and was sent
to McNeil Island.

Manson has told a jail house visitor that he received 150
sessions of "processing" in jail, evidently from Lanier Raymer.

Manson has contended that he learned scientology methods
very quickly because his "mind wasn't programmed." But Manson was not a "product" of scientology in any way; he merely
borrowed a few ideas from it. The scientologists call it "squirrel-
ing"—that is, borrowing and mutating scientology practices or
methods.

Manson picked up a fair number of scientology phrases,
neologisms and practices which he put to his own use when he
began to reorganize the minds of his young followers.

Phrases like "to mock up" and "cease to exist" and "to come

to Now" and the concept of "putting up pictures" all seem to
have their origin in Manson's McNeil Island sessions with Lanier
Raymer.

Manson also studied Masonic lore and picked up some knowledge of Masonic hand signals (which later he would flash to
judges during court appearances).

He evidently learned something about scientology recognition
signals also. Later, in the era of creepy crawlie, Manson would
develop his own complex system of hand and body signals—
really a whole language of chop-notation—among his followers.

For someone so unskilled in reading and writing, Manson took a
high interest in certain books on hypnotism and psychiatry. According to a friend, he was interested particularly in a book called
Transactional Analysis by Dr. Eric Berne, the author of *Games
People Play.* Charlie, ever the proselytizer, urged his friends to
read his discovered books.

From his study of *Transactional Analysis,* Manson may have
developed his perverse doctrine of Child Mind. Certainly he
borrowed lots of ideas from the pioneer work in group therapy.

He had a friend, one Marvin White, who appears to have
been released from McNeil Island and then to have made arrangements to mail Charlie books on black magic and related subjects.

Another book that helped provide a theoretical basis for Manson's family was *Stranger in a Strange Land* by Robert Heinlein,
the story of a power-hungry telepathic Martian roaming the
earth with a harem and a quenchless sexual thirst while proselytizing for a new religious movement. Initially, Manson borrowed a lot of terminology and ideas from this book—not, hopefully, including the ritual cannibalism described therein.

Manson was, however, to identify with the hero of the book,
one Valentine Michael Smith (Manson's first follower's child
was named Valentine Michael Manson)—a person who, in the
course of building a religious movement, took to killing or "discorporating" his enemies. Smith, in the book, ultimately was
beaten to death by an angry mob and ascended to the Sky.

To this day Manson's followers hold water-sharing ceremonies where Manson, in jail, magically takes a long-distance hit off a glass of water which is being stared at by a circle of sitting adepts.

What he seems to have known most intimately though was the Bible, which he was able to quote at great length.

Singing and songwriting began to occupy his time also. The idea of becoming a performer seemed to interest him. Manson at some point, appears to have been allowed to own a guitar. "A Mexican taught me the guitar," Manson has written. One young lady who owned a boutique in the Silverlake area of Los Angeles remembered Charlie, after he was released from jail, coming to her shop with his guitar and singing her "beautiful love songs in Spanish"—songs probably learned in jail.

The Beatles attracted Manson's consciousness early in their career, even during the Wanna Hold Your Hand mania of 1963–64.

Alvin Karpis of the Barker Gang remembers it: "He was constantly telling people he could come on like the Beatles, if he got the chance. Kept asking me to fix him up with high-power men like Frankie Carbo and Dave Beck; anyone who could book him into the big time when he got out."

After five years at McNeil Island, several friends of Manson, "prison lawyers"—prisoners with legal expertise—worked out a legal maneuver whereby on June 29, 1966, Charlie was transferred from McNeil Island, Washington, to Terminal Island prison in San Pedro, California near Los Angeles. Probably it was felt that he stood a better chance of early release at Terminal Island.

At Terminal Island Manson really began to prepare for operation superstar. He spent the better part of a year there. Friends remember him as being fanatically dedicated to music and singing.

One person, Phil Kaufman, in jail on a federal marijuana charge, was impressed by Manson's musical abilities and offered him certain connections on the outside whenever Manson should be set free. Kaufman, whom the police believe to have possession of the legendary Manson video-porn, evidently gave Manson the name of a person at Universal Studios in Hollywood where Manson, in late '67, would record his songs.

Manson made many friends during this last seven years in prison. Some cellmates say that Manson planned all along to collect an army of outcasts operating "beneath the awareness" of the mother culture. Others say he was an out-and-out creep, but a few remember him with affection and seem almost dazed that he became the leader of a kill-coven.

But it is safe to say that when he was released, he had a chance. A complex, long-term tragedy had been punching Charles Manson in the face all his life. But now in the year 1967, love had caught the attention of war-crazed America and the streets were paved with acceptance for a troubadour and a peripatetic collector of walking wounded war children.

Two

Out of the Slams

With thirty-five dollars and a suitcase full of "clothes," Manson walked out of jail on March 21, 1967, after serving six years and nine months of punishment. He was thirty-two and a half years old.

The legend is that Manson actually tried to re-enter the prison, or balked at leaving the front gate. Once on the street, however, he began two and a half years of ceaseless wandering.

At first, Charlie walked around and rode buses in Los Angeles for about three days after leaving Terminal Island. Then he went north to Berkeley to visit some friends he had met in prison.

Manson was anxious to impress as a minstrel/wandering singer. He spent time at the University of California Berkeley campus with his guitar.

Guitar in hand, he began to scrounge around the streets of Berkeley. One spring day he was sitting and singing in the open-air mall near Sather Gate on the University of California campus when he met slim, red-haired Mary Brunner of Eau Claire, Wisconsin, a recent graduate of the University of Wisconsin who was working at the library at the University of California. Also working in Berkeley then, at the University of California Art Museum, was Abigail Folger, heiress to the Folger Coffee Company fortune.

Right away Manson and Brunner became friends and evidently he moved into her apartment with her.

As a federal parolee, Manson was required to keep close
contact with a federal parole officer, informing the officer of
his whereabouts, employments and activities. Manson was assigned to a federal parole officer, a man named Roger Smith, who
befriended him. Charlie was heavily into using many Heinleinian
words like Grok and Thou Art God and Share Water and other
Strange Land terminology, so Manson and the girls renamed
Roger Smith Jubal after the fatherly protector Jubal Harshaw
in the novel, *Stranger in a Strange Land*.

Parolees are supposed to find gainful employment so Manson
sought or was offered work as an entertainer. He actually played
at a club in San Francisco's tenderloin district. He also may have
played a club in North Beach. His parole officer says he was
offered a job in Canada to sing.

It is nearly impossible to follow the peripatetics of Manson
in early 1967 because he began his roaming at once and who
indeed really can remember the specifics of a given week in early
1967?

Manson made definite attempts to locate his mother Kathleen.
He secured permission from his federal parole officer to travel
out of state several times. Once he went north to Washington in
search of her. Another time, east to West Virginia.

A young redhead named Lynn Fromme joined Mary Brunner
as addition number two to the inner circle of ladies. She was
picked up near the beach in Venice, California where Charlie
coaxed her off a curbside as she was sitting, crying. Legend
has it that she had just been thrown out of her father's pad in
Redondo Beach following a quarrel.

She was initiated. "I am the god of fuck" were his words.

Manson and girls moved to San Francisco where they evidently
lived near Haight Street with a beautiful ex-nun named Mary
Ann. Manson spent some time on the streets of the Haight,
meandering among the flower children. A sixteen-year-old flower
waif, perhaps a boy, perhaps a girl, it doesn't matter, homeless
and alone, offered Charlie his or her friendship. It was amazing,

to the man who'd spent his youth in jail, that this young boy was sleeping in Golden Gate Park located near Haight-Ashbury.

There are hundreds of anecdotes floating around about Manson in the Haight—a lot of which are glorified. The reality was that he was a glib grubby little man with a guitar scrounging for young girls using mysticism and guru babble, a time-honored tactic on the Haight.

According to Manson, he became a sort of hostel-keeper for runaways. At the start, he ran into a runaway girl whom he put up at a friend's house and as he was walking out of his friend's house he found still another young girl with flowers in her hair who became his housekeeper.

When Manson first took acid the story goes that it changed his life in that he went into a heavy stations-of-the-cross trip where he experienced the crucifixion of Jesus Christ—a common enough LSD experience but one that he really grooved with since it gave form to his chaos. Charlie Manson, the Son of Man, you dig.

The essence of the Jesus rap for the family was that Jesus and his original followers were much like Charlie and the girls. For this is what they believed about Jesus: that ninety years after Christ, priestly creeps killed off the loving sensual-sexual Christians, thus annihilating the original Christian impulse; and substituted for the original their own black-robed sexless death-breaths.

On the Haight, Manson encountered the entire collection of subcultural currents that had been building up in the United States during the previous decade. Acid music. Dope. Sexual freedom. Turn on, tune in, drop out. The politics of free. Peace rallies. Provos. Guerrilla theater. Communes. Long hair. The concept of the underground superstar. Astrology. The occult. Underground newspapers. Crash pads. Dayglo art.

At a Grateful Dead concert at the Avalon Ballroom Manson curled up into a fetal position right on the dance floor while the strobe lights blinked him into a trance.

He seemed to be a familiar darting figure on the Haight. He claims to have hung around with the Diggers as they distributed their daily food in Panhandle Park. He may have even stayed a while in a house behind the Digger crash pad on Waller Street. This Waller Street house, later, in the era of psychedelic satanism, was to be renamed The Devil House.

Charlie had a tremendous effect on those he met. Open. An incredible talent for using one part of a personality against another. For spotting weaknesses—for creating confusion and appearing therein as a source of leadership. He had a quick, glib but seemingly complicated answer for everything. Even though he told everyone to do their own thing, to be themselves, his own personal magnetism, combined with a constant process of selection, attracted those who thirsted for a leader. Control was what Charles was into all along, in spite of the claims of liberation and freedom.

"I'm a very positive force. I'm a very positive field. I collect negatives," he later told a lawyer friend.

The guy had experienced nothing but ugliness, strip mines, jail, poverty and boredom for most of his life. Now he could have his own universe. He was terribly insecure, and the praise from his followers was no solace.

One day, perhaps in July of 1967, Manson and gang were down in San Jose, California where they met a minister named Dean Morehouse and his wife and fourteen-year-old daughter RuthAnn aka Ouish. Manson's tale of meeting Dean Morehouse contends that Reverend Morehouse, driving a pickup truck, picked Charlie up and that Manson blew him, thus kicking off a friendship of great duration. Until Morehouse a year or so later would be sent to prison for forking over LSD to a thirteen-year-old girl.

Manson's parole officer visited the family when they were visiting Dean Morehouse in San Jose, and he played the very piano in Morehouse's residence that Charlie would soon trade for a Volkswagen camper. Morehouse gave, it seems, the beautiful piano to Charlie, who traded it for a 1961 Volkswagen microbus, bearing the license plate CSY 087.

At the end of July 1967 the troupe traveled to the Mendocino coast north of Frisco where Mary Brunner became pregnant.

The pregnancy of Mary Brunner seems to be the only verifiable instance during the history of the family of a pregnancy caused by Manson. Which is strange. Because if one calculates, with data supplied by Manson intimates, an average of three orgasms a day for a total of something like three thousand fornications in two and a half years, one would expect a greater number of pregnancies.

On July 28, 1967, Manson was arrested in Mendocino County for trying to come to the aid of a runaway being apprehended by the police. He received a suspended sentence.

One almost had to live there to understand the frenzy that engulfed the Haight-Ashbury district of San Francisco in the spring and summer of 1967. The word was out all over America to come to San Francisco for love and flowers. California was flooded with what *The New York Times* labeled hippies.

But all over the United States, in hundreds of cities, in the spring and summer of 1967, there were love-ins, be-ins, share-ins and flowers. However, once again, as in the beat generation of the late 1950's, the nerve center was San Francisco. Potentially, flower-power was one of the most powerful forces of change ever seen in recent history. Through the work of the San Francisco Diggers, the Free Clinic in San Francisco, the San Francisco music scene, the *San Francisco Oracle,* its underground newspaper of that time—through these enterprises and others, things came into focus in San Francisco. It was a noble experiment. It was the politics of Free. The Diggers served free food in Panhandle Park each day. The Haight-Ashbury Medical Clinic gave free medical care. There were outdoor free concerts held all the time in the park. People lived and loved in the streets and parks. It was Free. There were no rules. But there was a weakness: from the standpoint of vulnerability the flower movement was like a valley of thousands of plump white rabbits surrounded by wounded coyotes. Sure, the "leaders" were tough, some of them geniuses and great poets. But the acid-dropping middle-class children from Des Moines were rabbits.

The Haight attracted vicious criminals who grew long hair. Bikers tried to take over the LSD market with crude sadistic tactics. Bad dope was sold by acne-faced methedrine punks. Satanists and satanist-rapist death-freaks flooded the whirling crash pads. People began getting ripped off in the parks. There was racial trouble. Puke was sold as salvation. Ugliness was.

And Manson took his children away from it. Because by the end of the summer of flowers, the streets of the Haight were griseous and filthy, psychedelic weirdburger stands were springing up in mutant profusion. As Charlie roamed up and down the California coast, he warned all the hitchhikers and runaways he met not to go to the Haight.

Two jail buddies of Charlie from Terminal Island lived with Charlie on the Haight during the summer of love, 1967. One of them was the legendary Danny M., a skilled counterfeiter. Family members would brag that Danny's twenty-dollar bills were 96 percent perfect, on the average, whereas the U.S. Treasury's were only 94 percent on the simulacral scale.

These guys were mean and rough-tough but when they came under Charlie's influence—just like a wind that blows first one way then another—they grew their hair long and began to groove with flower-power.

One anecdote from the summer of love deals with the ritual of the Golden Gate gun-drop. It goes that at the end of the summer Charlie and the flower girls were set to hit the bricks and roam the void. His dear friends, the two ex-cons, one of whom was the 96-percent-perfect twenty-dollar-bill counterfeiter, evidently were going to remain behind. Charlie asked the guys for the guns he knew they had. He received the weapons, wrapped them up in a cloth, held some sort of ceremony over them, then carried them to Golden Gate Bridge where he dropped the cloth-wrapped guns into San Francisco Bay several hundred feet below.

At the end of the summer of love the group set out to roam the coastal highways.

They survived by odd jobs and cleaning service stations, anything. Another legend swift growing was of Charles Manson the master panhandler. He could get things with ease. He would walk up to a house and people would seem to give him things, the legend being that it was because of his Christ vibes.

Sometime, perhaps in August '67, Charlie and Lynn Fromme aka Squeaky and Mary Brunner acquired a residence at 705 Bath Street in Santa Barbara, California, 334 miles south of San Francisco.

On or around September 8, 1967, Charlie, Lynn and Mary Brunner visited a former jail buddy named Greene who had an apartment in Manhattan Beach near Los Angeles. Visiting Greene also was one Patricia Krenwinkel, a lonely, searching girl from Los Angeles with an endocrine problem—an excess of bodily hair. She was the girl, as her early diaries note, that the men seemed to neglect at the high school dances.

Patricia Krenwinkel of Inglewood, California was eighteen years old, a former Sunday school teacher and a Bible freak— she would really get into the acid Bibleland of Manson, quoting and counterquoting with abandon from the scriptures.

Patricia Krenwinkel was living with her sister Charlene in an apartment in Manhattan Beach, and while the girls drove the microbus north Manson remained with Miss Krenwinkel at Manhattan Beach for four days.

Then Squeaky and Mary returned. Patricia Krenwinkel had been unhappily employed as a process clerk for the Insurance Company of North America. On the night of September 12, 1967, she abandoned her car in a service station to become a clerk in the Process of Charles Manson. Most popular accounts of the Manson story are careful to note that Krenwinkel dared to leave behind uncollected her final paycheck from the Insurance Company of North America. The point being, indeed, what true American would abandon a paycheck?

Patricia Krenwinkel was able to present to the budding family— then known, of course, only as "Charles' girls"—besides her soul, the gift of gifts: a valid Chevron credit card backed by her father who loved her enough to pay the bills. Also she gave a telephone credit card number.

They drove north through Santa Barbara to San Francisco, financed by Patricia Krenwinkel's father's credit card. Then on September 15, 1967, they proceeded into Oregon. The Volkswagen van spent two weeks shuttling back and forth between Washington and Oregon, spending a considerable time in the Seattle area. One of the purposes of this trip in the northwest probably was to locate Charlie's lost mother.

It was on this trip north that Manson et al. met a twenty-five-year-old man from Monroe, Louisiana named Bruce Davis, soon to be a prime male follower of Manson. Davis had been the editor of his high school yearbook in Kingston, Tennessee, had attended the University of Tennessee for three years, then had gone through a series of odd jobs until November of 1966, when he dropped down from America and became a transient undergrounder.

On October 1, 1967, the microbus passed through Carson City, Nevada, on the way to San Francisco. The group spent about ten days in the San Francisco-Berkeley area, then hit the bricks, proceeding toward Sacramento where they stayed for a couple of weeks, possibly at the Sacramento residence of the beautiful ex-nun Mary Ann, with whom they had stayed in the summer of flowers.

On October 6, 1967, residents of the Haight held a funeral for hippie, son of media, in Buena Vista Park in San Francisco. It was more than symbolic for it marked the end of a noble experiment and the beginning of the era of pig.

Invitations were sent out reading as follows:

FUNERAL NOTICE

HIPPIE
Haight-Ashbury District
of this city,
Hippie, devoted son
of
Mass Media

Friends are invited
to attend services
beginning at sunrise,
October 6, 1967
at
Buena Vista Park

Manson's group was growing. There were too many to sleep, much less grope, comfortably in the Volkswagen. And winter was oozing onward.

So the opportunity arose to acquire a school bus for their further travels.

It was Ken Kesey and his band of Merry Pranksters, including the wonderful Neal Cassady, who popularized in 1964–65 the concept of the traveling school bus, painted and decorated artistically, full of decorous wanderers.

It was they who experimented in group acid trips and, more importantly, group mystical experiences under LSD. They were into filmmaking during wandering. Kesey's group, however, was essentially good.

Manson carried this onward, making it evil, slowly changing the colors, the red tempura becoming dog blood, the acid test turning to psychedelic satanism, the filming of happiness turning to the filming of hapless murder of female Caucasians on the beaches of southern California. But it was a slow change. Such weirdo warping takes months and years to put together.

It was in Sacramento where they seem to have traded the Volkswagen bus as down payment for an old yellow school bus, large enough to hold the growing youth-pack.

On October 16, 1967, at the Stuart E. Miller Standard Chevron station in Sacramento, they outfitted the school bus with a thirty-nine-dollar battery and two sets of 825-20 tires costing $216.20.

They removed the seats from the back of the bus to create an area in which to live. On top of the bus they built a large rectangular storage compartment. Inside the bus, as time oozed by, they emplaced an icebox, a stereo set, a floating coffee table sus-

pended by wires and pillows aplenty. Gradually the walls became
painted with Early Acid-American Dayglo whirlings of color.
God's eyes, peacock feathers and musical instruments gave the
dope-mobile cheer. At first, the bus remained school yellow in
color, but the police began to stop them for violation of laws
governing school buses. At a beach somewhere they acquired a
quantity of black spray paint and some bikers sprayed the bus,
even the windows, black. They meant to paint the bus with white
letters, "Hollywood Productions," but a French girl did the painting and spelled it as she pronounced it, "Holywood Productions."

The scam was to come on like a roving film crew—to avoid
the obvious problems that a thirty-three-year-old man with a bus-
load of mini-skirted teenage girls might pose, particularly to the
police.

In November, Manson's parole supervision was transferred from
San Francisco to the Los Angeles office indicating that he intended to shift his base of operations to southern California.
Around November 7 or 8, 1967, Manson drove to San Francisco where he met a pretty young female named Susan Atkins
at an apartment on Lime Street possibly belonging to Sandra
Good, a future Manson follower.

Susan Atkins was an impressionable nineteen-year-old from
San Jose, California with a background of strife and bad news.
There was fighting and drinking aplenty at home. Her mother
died of cancer when Susan was thirteen and Susan led her church
choir in a religious serenade outside her dying mother's bedroom
window. After the death of Susan's mother, Mr. Atkins had to
sell their house to pay the medical bills for the high cost of dying
of cancer.

When Susan was fifteen she quit school and then, age sixteen,
she headed for San Francisco. It was 1964. There she dwelled.

In 1966 she was a waitress, living alone, so to speak, in a hotel
in San Francisco. She met a couple of men who were into armed
robbery.

In August of 1966, when she was eighteen, Sue met a human
named Al Sund in San Francisco. Al and another human, Clint

Talioferro, took Susan along on a trip north in a stolen Buick Riviera to Salem, Oregon.

They hid in the woods when they learned the fuzz were after them, snuffing food from other campers—just ordinary outlaws in the wilderness.

On September 12, 1966, she was arrested by the Oregon State Police. She languished in the slams for three months till December of 1966 when she was placed on two years probation. She hit the trail, returning to San Francisco where she worked as a waitress, a knocker-trembler at a topless bar, and as a domestic on Muir Beach.

She returned to San Francisco, resuming a career as a topless dancer and cocktail waitress. She took LSD and began to experiment with life styles. She had a succession of men friends who used her. Then she met God.

The day before she met Manson she told a social worker she was hot to pursue a career in dancing. When they met, Manson sang songs to her and accompanied her to her apartment where they lay naked together. He asked her to pretend he was her father while they made love. She did. Later she claimed that it was the most ennobling experience of her nineteen years.

The story goes that after this initial encounter, Manson went back to Sacramento and brought to San Francisco the newly bedecked school bus.

He scooped up his waifs preparing to travel south.

He asked Susan if she was ready to accompany them. Yes she was. Later he blessed Susan Atkins with a new name, Sadie Mae Glutz.

Around November 10, 1967, Susan Atkins checked in with her probation office in San Francisco all excited about some roaming preacher named Charlie. She did not know his last name. Susan stated that there were seven girls, two of whom were pregnant, who were going to accompany this Charlie on a trip to Los Angeles and on to Florida.

The probation officer was unenthusiastic about the venture. Forthwith the official fired off a letter to Oregon authorities requesting that Miss Atkins be hauled into court for a revocation of probation hearing. But Sadie/Susan was already in the bus whizzing down 101.

Through credit card data, it is known that on November 10, Manson called Universal Studios in North Hollywood, seemingly to arrange for a recording session to kick off operation superstar.

There was a man at Universal Studios in Los Angeles named Gary Stromberg who was a close friend of Manson's jail pal, Phil Kaufman. Through Kaufman, Manson met or contacted Stromberg and a routine was arranged whereby Manson would record a session or so for Universal Records, the company evidently agreeing to pay for the recording costs.

Down the coastline toward an appointment with fame drove the bus. They stopped in San Jose where they snarfed up Dean Morehouse's fourteen-year-old daughter, RuthAnn, adding her to the pack. Morehouse went into a rage. Three days after Manson had left with his defiant daughter, Morehouse, traveling with the man who'd given Manson the original Volkswagen microbus, located Manson near Los Angeles and was prepared to kick ass.

"I'm just doing to her what you want to do"—was what Manson is supposed to have said to the raging father. Charlie also slipped him some LSD. Morehouse's wife, subsequently divorced, was amazed at the effect that Manson had on her husband during that trip to get Ruth back. Ruth stayed with Charlie but Dean returned to San Jose a changed man. He had left foaming with anger; he returned a near-convert to the Way of the Bus.

On November 12, 1967, Manson was thirty-three years old.

The family stopped for a couple of days in Santa Barbara, then drove to Universal Studios in North Hollywood for a recording session. Manson recorded only one three-hour session for Universal Records, then hit the breeze, off to the Mojave Desert though Mr. Stromberg was eager to record more sessions with this barefoot little minstrel. Later on Charlie would help a group of writers to prepare a film script for Universal Studios.

Charlie Manson, biblical quote-freak and living Christ figure, was hired as a "technical advisor" off of whom the writers were to bounce ideas. The script was to be a "what-if" story of Christ returning as a black man in the South. The white Southerners, of course, would be the drool-lipped Romans.

Universal never made the Jesus as a Black Man movie because the executives higher up couldn't buy the concept. Working on this Jesus project may have made a strong impression on Manson. Indeed the idea of a Second Coming with the current money-waving Christians starring as the jaded Romans soon to join the rubble of history lay heavily in his later lectures.

Submission was always a key factor in Manson's rap horde. Once during the idea flagpole sessions for the film, Charlie and the twenty-year-old callipygian Squeaky aka Lynn Fromme performed a reciprocal foot smooch, she bending down to kiss his feet and he hers.

All through 1967 and '68, foot kissing, mutual submission and love were very much in vogue with the M brigade. It wasn't until 1969 that Charlie got into kissing people's feet after he shot them.

There had been some gossip about Manson's supposed commingling with certain prestigious people at Universal so Manson was asked about it and he wrote back that he couldn't remember their names but said this: "I knew lots of people at Universal Studios."

Right around the time that Manson was making that demo tape at Universal Studios, Roman Polanski was finishing up the final work on *Rosemary's Baby,* living on Malibu Beach on the Los Angeles coast. Soon he would return to London for the world premiere of the satanoid epic and he and Sharon Tate would marry.

The family stayed for about a week in the Los Angeles area, then hit the road. They took a swing up into the Mojave Desert, then back to Los Angeles on November 26, 1967. The next day they were in Santa Barbara, then they went to San Francisco, and then back across the state, across the Mojave Desert, then to Las Vegas, Nevada where they spent four days in early December. They passed through Arizona and New Mexico and arrived in El Paso, Texas on December 6, 1967. They backtracked into New Mexico for about a week then went into the deep South, into Mississippi and Alabama. Patricia Krenwinkel visited her mother in Mobile, Alabama on December 14, 1967. The black flower bus drove back to Los Angeles, arriving about December 19, 1967. They stayed for four days in Topanga Canyon, then left for Arizona. Out, demon, out.

Topanga Canyon winds and twists up from Topanga Beach on the Pacific Ocean to a high point overlooking the San Fernando Valley. There is a creek that runs its pleasant boulder-strewn and cabin-sited way down the Topanga Canyon into the Pacific. Following along the creek is Topanga Boulevard, which runs from the ocean up over the top of Topanga into the San Fernando Valley and north a few miles in a straight line to Santa Susanna Pass Road, the home of Helter Skelter.

Woody Guthrie once lived in the canyon and his cabin still stands. In spite of the mutant condition of Los Angeles, the canyon maintains a form of rustic beauty and its inhabitants are among the most knowledgeable to be encountered anywhere.

It was in the Topanga Canyon/Malibu Canyon area in December 1967 that the family was first to establish vertical roots in Los Angeles. It became necessary—because of the hordes of adepts—to put down roots, to camp near a friendly house, to set up tent cities, to spread out.

In the summer of love Manson had met a lady named Gina who lived in Topanga Canyon near the beach. She invited him to come down to Los Angeles sometime for a visit. This lady, Gina, had an ancient famed two-story house located on Topanga Canyon Lane behind the Raft Restaurant at the mouth of the canyon.

Because of a large spiral staircase the house, since torn down, was known merely as The Spiral Staircase. It became a scrounge-lounge for the family. They stayed on and off there for several months parking the black bus there. All kinds of people congregated at the spiral house including an occasional starlet driving a Rolls Royce.

At one "light show party" at The Spiral Staircase one Robert

K. Beausoleil, a young twenty-year-old actor-musician from Santa Barbara, wearing a pointed beard and smoking a hand-carved skull pipe, arrived and found Charlie and the girls singing together. He joined in and began playing along with Charlie. A few days later, Charlie, wearing an old tweed jacket, a tweed cap and a walking stick, came to see Beausoleil then living at Gary Hinman's house. Hinman was a thirty-year-old music teacher from Colorado with a Master's degree in Sociology.

Beausoleil was a young man who possessed some skill in music and songwriting and more than a passing interest in devil worship and magic. In 1967 he was associated with famed author and weir-warped filmmaker Kenneth Anger in San Francisco. Beausoleil evidently lived with Anger in an old house in San Francisco called the Russian Embassy, where Anger introduced him to the universe of magic, not to mention the cruelty-streaked universe of Aleister Crowley. Anger was involved in making an occult movie called *Lucifer Rising* in which Beausoleil played the role of Lucifer. At that time Beausoleil has said that he was on an all-meat diet and believed himself to be the devil. Beausoleil was the lead guitarist and sitarist for The Magick Powerhouse of Oz, an eleven-piece rock ensemble formed by Kenneth Anger to perform the music for *Lucifer Rising*.

On September 21, 1967, the Magick Powerhouse of Oz played at a gathering at the Straight Theater on Haight Street to celebrate the so-called Equinox of the Gods. The film *Lucifer Rising* was supposed to be nearly completed so the night was one of celebration. Anger filmed the event that night but Beausoleil remembered later that Mr. Anger flipped out during the proceedings and smashed a priceless caduceus-headed cane that had once belonged to the king of sex-magic himself, Aleister Crowley.

Things went awry between Beausoleil and his mentor Kenneth Anger shortly thereafter. Beausoleil seems to have ripped off Anger's automobile, some camera equipment and, more importantly, some of the footage of *Lucifer Rising*. Then he split. Beausoleil claims that he only took what already belonged to him.

The rip-off may have occurred in late October 1967 when

Kenneth Anger, during the famed Exorcism and March on the Pentagon, was in Washington, D.C. conducting a notable magic ritual beneath a flat-bed truck parked in front of the Pentagon.

While various Diggers and exorcists were standing atop the flat-bed truck screeching "Out Demons Out," Anger, bare from the waist up, revealing what appeared to be a tattoo of Lucifer upon his chest, burned a picture of the devil within a consecrated pentagram, shouting oaths and hissing as he flashed a magic ring at inquiring reporters thrusting microphones at him hunched down in the gravel.

When he discovered that Beausoleil had ripped him off, Anger thereupon fashioned a locket, the face of which bore the likeness of Bob Beausoleil. The obverse contained the likeness of a toad, with the inscription "Bob Beausoleil—who was turned into a toad by Kenneth Anger."

Beausoleil moved down to Topanga Canyon in the fall of '67 following his break with Anger. He became friends with Gary Hinman. When he met Manson, Beausoleil and a girl friend Laurie were living at Hinman's small hillside house at 964 Old Topanga Canyon Road. Hinman had a tendency to allow people in transit to use his home for temporary crashing, and several times members of the family would cop zzz's there.

Beausoleil and Charles Manson would have a difficult relationship since Beausoleil had his group of girls and Charlie his group. There was a bit of friction between the two because of Charlie's Second Coming hangup. Beausoleil would tend to keep himself separate and that was a sin. There were striking similarities in the two. But only Manson had the Rommeloid passion for the fine details of government.

Another convert, Diane Lake, a red-haired, fourteen-year-old with hip parents, met Charlie and the girls at The Spiral Staircase house of flickers. Diane and her parents had been living in the Los Angeles area with the Hog Farm, an important seed commune later to roam the continents as a world peace brigade. Somehow, the fourteen-year-old Diane was impressed enough to join up with the family bus. Squeaky and Patricia Krenwinkel asked her if she wanted to accompany them to the desert and off she went. In fit time, Miss Lake was renamed Snake, evidently in tribute to the transverse ophidian wiggles she made during intercourse.

Diane Lake's parents both highly valued their daughter's freedom to develop on her own. They allowed Diane to travel with the family, although later Mrs. Lake would visit the Spahn ranch to try to reclaim her daughter, only to to be rebuffed, according to Diane, by one of Charlie's chief disciples, Squeaky. The story has it that the mistress of The Spiral Staircase house, Gina, apologized to Snake's parents when she left with the Manson dope-bus. After all, Snake was fourteen and Manson was thirty-three.

But the bus was very persuasive. There is general agreement that the family was neat, orderly and extremely clean in physical appearance, during these early days prior to snuff. So Diane's parents, just like RuthAnn Morehouse's, let their daughter do her thing.

On December 22 the family took the barely pubescent Snake Lake touring through Arizona and the deserts of New Mexico. Five days later, on December 27, 1967, the bus broke down near Winslow, Arizona and had to be towed to a Chevron station. Some people hitched back to Topanga Canyon, and after repairs the bus itself proceeded back to Los Angeles where the family would stay, more or less, for three and a half months until early April of 1968.

The people of the black bus lived in a profusion and confusion of places in Topanga Canyon. One night one place, one night another—but the numbers were growing. They proceeded to try to settle in various abandoned homes and canyon crash camps, but they kept having to move. For a few weeks they parked their bus at The Spiral Staircase.

Strange doors open to the floweroids. There was no telling where a man with a black bus full of girls might end up for the night—in a cave or castle, by a hot springs in the wilderness or by a heated pool in the Malibu hills. Doors opened all over Los Angeles to Charles Manson and the family.

The police in Malibu became aware of Manson. They saw the bus parked at The Spiral Staircase on Topanga Canyon Lane behind the Raft Restaurant. They noted that the family was doing odd jobs for various residents in the Malibu-Topanga area.

In December of 1967 the Beatles released their album *Magical Mystery Tour* and their corresponding movie. The Beatles to the rescue. This seems to be the first Beatles album from which Manson drew philosophical guidance. The whole black bus trip came to be called "The Magical Mystery Tour." They were into such a trip of mystic transformation that the family evidently believed that there was an archetypal core personality in each human that could be discovered through acid-zap, mind-moil, role-playing, bunch-punching, magic, blasting-the-past and commune-ism. This was the Magical Mystery Tour.

For most of the early part of 1968 the family stayed in the Los Angeles area. They continued to spew out in quick trips here and there. In early 1968, evidently on such a voyage, Susan Denise Atkins, aka Sadie Glutz, was made pregnant by a human named Bluestein in New Mexico.

In February 1968, through a service attendant named Jerry, Manson met a lady named Melba Kronkite who owned a luxurious ranch in the hills between Malibu and Topanga Canyons, near the old Malibu sheriff's substation. Evidently the lady had been wealthy but had fallen into impecunious times. She was amazed at the brigade and became a close friend. Unmentionable and secret were the encounters around her heated Malibu pool. She became so friendly with the family that she was used as a character reference when family members got busted later on.

Off and on the family would visit Malibu Melba. They worked for her. Manson claims to have given her some money. Manson also gave to Melba a 1967 Ford Mustang which a New Yorker named Michael, divesting himself of worldly goods, had given to Manson.

Mrs. Kronkite had huge stables and an exercise track on her property. Once the family, (like Heracles cleaning Augean stables,) spent a week cleaning an incredible mountain of horse dooky from several hundred stalls in her stables.

Sometime in February '68 Manson and crew were left temporarily homeless. After his stay with Gary Hinman, Robert

Beausoleil had moved into his own house on a steep hillside at 19844 Horseshoe Lane, above Fernwood Pacific Road in Topanga. This property was a citadel of porn, consisting of a burnt-out basement dwelling, below which lay a crude swimming pool. Beausoleil said, "Sure, come on up and live here," so a gypsy tent scene was set up down the hillside and the family filled the pool with archeological refuse picked up over later during research for books. They stayed at the Horseshoe Lane property for about six weeks and this seems to be the first known time they got into making movies—or, as they say, allowing people with cameras to film their activities.

Around this time the family added to itself Brenda McCann of Malibu and one Little Patty aka Madeline Cottage aka Shirley Amanda McCoy aka Linda Baldwin. Both girls would cling to the thrill until the end, one and a half years later. Also oozing into the acid mosaic at this time was a lovely girl named Ella Beth Sinder aka Ella Bailey aka Yeller, whom a biker named Danny De Carlo describes as a slim shapely Greta Garbo type.

Various others, gone now, and nameless, lived with the family. There are a hundred or so whose names are known but who flitted away into the void. This account deals with those who passed the process of selection and remained with the family.

One of the jewels in Charlie's barely pubescent pack at this time was the twelve- or thirteen-year-old Didi Lansbury, the daughter of actress Angela Lansbury. To ward off possible jail-bait charges, the young Miss Lansbury carried around with her a to-whom-it-may-concern letter from her mother, OK-ing association with C.M. Manson has said, however, that he only met Angela Lansbury herself once or twice.

Manson seemed to seek out encounters with the children or relatives of entertainment personalities. In Los Angeles famous sons and daughters often form close associations with one another. This was okay with Manson in that, like one of his beloved coyotes stalking a nestling, he zeroed in on the fame children in order to scarf up free credit cards, money, hospitality, fame-grope, connections and, most important, acceptance and adulation.

While the family was camped on Horseshoe Lane, Bob Beausoleil and Manson formed a six-piece electric rock band called The Milky Way. Manson played guitar and Beausoleil was on guitar and bass clarinet. The Milky Way was short-lived, though it did have one weekend of public performance.

While The Milky Way was rehearsing one day, a man from the Topanga Corral, a country and western night club in Topanga Canyon, came to hear the group and thought they were "tight" so he hired them for a weekend gig.

During the weekend the group was fired. When asked why, Beausoleil said that the group was too far out, that the potheads came to the club but not enough beer drinkers. Adios Milky Way.

Sometime in late March of '68, the family traded houses with someone living on the other side of Topanga Canyon at the top of Summit Trail and High Vale Trail. The dwelling lay above a maze of trails in the woods. There they parked the black bus and set up camp.

Manson's jail friend, Phil Kaufman, was released from prison in March. A couple of weeks later he went out to Topanga to check out the family. Kaufman stayed around for a while but found theocracy a bit overbearing, though he remained a "sympathetic cousin."

Phil Kaufman had a friend named Harold True who came out to Topanga to visit him in March '68. Harold True lived in an opulent house located at 3267 Waverly Drive near the Silver Lake area of Los Angeles. Next door to True's house was a home owned by the family of Leno and Rosemary LaBianca at 3301 Waverly Drive.

Harold True met Manson and the family through Kaufman. Before True moved out of his Waverly house in August '68, Manson visited Waverly Drive four or five times during the summer, sleeping over twice. True himself went out that spring to Topanga approximately ten times to check out the lair of dope-grope.

Danny M., the ace counterfeiter from the summer of love, drove onto the set bearing some fresh sheets of twenties, just off the press. Charlie talked him into printing up some i.d.'s and driver's licenses for the family. Danny, according to Topanga gossip, later went into business in Woodland Hills, got caught and was sent to jail.

On April Fools eve, President Lyndon Johnson abdicated, announcing he would not seek another term in office.

The next day, April 1, 1968, in the woodsides of Topanga, Valentine Michael Manson was born to Mary Theresa Brunner in the shack on Summit Trail. To relax during the birth she filled her lungs with dope. She was attended by her friends.

On the night Mary gave birth, Sandy Good, twenty-four-year-old daughter of a San Diego stockbroker, flew down from San Francisco with a friend in a private plane, rented a car and sped toward the family. Charlie drew her aside and they clinked bodies near the High Vale bus camp. She marveled out loud after they made love at Charlie's continuing permarigid condition. Boy, other girls didn't know what they were missing.

Although a bright, well read college graduate who was active in civil rights causes, Sandy was ready to submit herself. It became an item of gossip among her friends back in San Francisco that she had "joined somebody's harem." Sandy was also to acquire great skill at coaxing money from her wealthy father, a skill ever cherished by Manson.

One Paul Watkins, a short, sixteen-year-old baby-faced drifting dropout, became another addition to the family's lair on Summit Trail. He was wandering through the hills and spotted the black bus and six naked girls. Needless to say it was paradise to the young boy Watkins, soon dubbed Little Paul, evidently a name chosen by the girls.

That night everybody took LSD and experienced a group encounter involving indiscriminate apertural-appendage conjugation. It can be seen that LSD was the wafer. Conceivably, the family provided the first instance where a man, believed to be Christ, ever dispensed LSD as a sacrament, before an act of group sexual psychodrama and after a garbage run.

In early April, a few days after Mary Brunner gave birth, the Magical Mystery Tour decided to leave Topanga Canyon. They were around twenty in number, maintaining the four girls to one guy ratio that was pretty constant throughout the history of the family.

Citizens in the area remember how the heat from the fuzz was severe in the Topanga and Malibu Canyon areas in early 1968, a year of great unrest everywhere in the United States. And Manson and his friends received their share. Arrests, particularly for stupid laws regarding marijuana, create hatred. It had to be a factor in the family's switch from flowers to knives. And then there was also the baleful hate-spell cast by the war.

The Vietnam war lay like a curse upon America in 1968. In March, unknown to millions, Calley and friends creepy-crawled a village called My Lai and blew off the head of a white-robed Buddhist monk stooped to his knees in prayer. Such was the curse.

On April 14, 1968, a drifting racist hick, probably under contract, snuffed Martin Luther King in Memphis, Tennessee.

The Panthers had been calling the police pigs for some time. The Hog Farm's main force, a gentle leader named Wavy Gravy, proposed to run a porcine animal for President. The idea caught on. The Yippies, preparing to pull aside the bandages placed atop the unattended sickness of the Democratic presidential convention, adopted the piggie-for-President proposal. Pig was born.

Somewhere in England, probably in the summer of '68, one George Harrison of the Beatles wrote a song called "Piggies." Nobody had heard the song yet, but it was there, to be released in December 1968. Pigs appeared in ecology ads on television, gobbling garbage at the beach. Respected citizens, long accustomed to calling the police fuzz or cops, switched to pig.

Sometimes happy, sometimes blue, Sergeant Charlie's dope-troupe wandered up the coastline.

They camped for a while on the beach at Leo Carillo State Park, setting up tents. Leo Carillo Beach is just south of the L.A./Ventura County line, the location of the famed dog-blood beach where L.A. satanists later sacrificed dogs and animals and drank the blood.

Bruce Davis, whom the family had encountered some months

previous, perhaps in Washington state, showed up on a motorcycle about this time and became an avid member. Bruce Davis
began to listen so carefully to Manson's speeches on religion and
philosophy that he could repeat them word for word with an
easy exactness, even imitating Manson's voice. Observers in the
canyon, however, noted that when Charlie was around, Davis
talked in his own Tennessee dialect.

They broke camp at Leo Carillo Beach sometime around the
second week of April '68, and drove further north up the coast
to a wooden area near Oxnard, California in Ventura County.
This was the location of the great Oxnard bust, which occurred
on April 21. The black bus got caught or broke down in a ditch
so the family evidently set up camp in nearby woods. Ventura
County sheriff's deputies stopped to investigate and were shocked
to find a bunch of nude hippies sauntering in the woods.

Charlie and Sadie and several others were arrested, evidently
for possessing those homemade driver's licenses from the counterfeiter. The next day each was fined ten dollars. Mary Brunner
also was arrested, as a result of felonious breast-feeding in a
ditch. Family legend has it that the police were upset over the
casual and shameless public feeding of Pooh Bear aka Valentine
Michael Manson.

The Oxnard bust made the second page of the *Los Angeles
Herald Examiner,* something about "Nude Hippies Found in
Woods"; and, of course, the local radio stations made mention
of it in the latest up-to-the-minute news bulletins.

After the arrests in the Oxnard ditch, the family drove back
to the encampment on Summit Trail in Topanga Canyon. There
they dwelled for a few days until around May 2, 1968, when
police raided and arrested a bunch of them, including Manson,
Sandy Good, Snake, Patricia Krenwinkel, for possession of marijuana. They were held in jail for a couple of days, then they were
released. The charges were eventually dropped.

This seems to be the time that musician Gary Hinman bailed
Snake and Sandy out of the slams and then they accompanied
Hinman to his house for a couple of days of rest and rehabili-
tation. At that time Hinman's house on Old Topanga Canyon

Road was one of the few semi-crash pads in the canyon housing young transients. Hinman never entirely would "die in his mind" and join the family but was one of those "sympathetic cousins." Until they made a poster with his blood.

Around May 6, 1968, the black bus drove for the first time to the scroungy, dilapidated Spahn Movie Ranch in Chatsworth, California. The family went to consult with a person named John, a friend of Sandy Good, who occupied the so-called "back house," a corroded, wooden building removed about a half mile down a bumpy dirt trail from the main Western movie set.

John had an arrangement with the then eighty-one-year-old George Spahn to pay for his rent by keeping in repair the various Spahn Ranch automobiles and trucks.

They stayed about four days while John helped to repair the black bus. Manson continued to give. He sent a couple of the girls out with a credit card to purchase some retreads for an old Chrysler belonging to one Richard Kaplan, from whom Manson was going to secure possession of the back ranch house of the Spahn Movie Ranch.

Around this time, Bob Beausoleil was acting in an X-rated hat-in-lap film called *Ramrodder* shot near Happy Trail in Topanga Canyon.

Beausoleil had been working at a restaurant, since snuffed by fire, called the Topanga Kitchen, located at the Topanga Shopping Center. The producers of *Ramrodder* offered him a job at a dollar per hour building sets for the flick. Beausoleil accepted and began to live in a tepee at the movie location with his girl friend Gail.

While shooting the movie, Beausoleil met a girl named Cathy Share aka Gypsy aka Manon Minette aka etc. who was acting also in the movie. Beausoleil played the foreboding part of an Indian who murdered and tortured a white man who had sexually assaulted an Indian girl.

Gypsy, Gail and Bob became inseparable and lived together in the tepee on the movie set. Gypsy, playing Earth Mother, became part of a two-girls-one-guy triangle which was to serve as a model for nighttime deportment in the family.

Beausoleil was a fierce person in the canyon, with a hooded

falcon on his shoulder and a huge black dog. Like Manson, he
gave off the dual love-hate vibes. Beausoleil evidently had a grope
scene with the wife of the producer of *Ramrodder* and had to
split. He struck his tepee camp, scarfed up Gypsy into his group
and went to live again at Gary Hinman's house for a few days.

After a while he went to the Spahn Ranch and got employment
there, such as it was, for a few days, then Beausoleil and his
followers drove north to the San Francisco area, driving an old
Dodge powerwagon that George Spahn gave them.

Meanwhile, the Manson group had left the Spahn Ranch,
traveling north in the black bus to San Francisco and to Mendocino County before returning to Los Angeles. They seem to
have spent a few days back in Topanga Canyon, parked by The
Spiral Staircase.

Around this time the family moved to a luxurious home on
Sunset Boulevard belonging to Dennis Wilson, a member of the
Beach Boys, an enormously successful singing group of that era
which had sold tens of millions of albums to fans around the
globe.

Wilson, drummer and singer for the Beach Boys, was living on
a three-acre estate at 14400 Sunset Boulevard near Will Rogers
State Park. Opinion is divided, even in the family, about how
the family barnacled in on Mr. Wilson. Some say that somehow
wig-hawker Tex Watson had a hand by picking up Dennis Wilson who was hitchhiking. An unlikely story. Another recension
has it that Garboesque Ella Beth Sinder aka Yeller was picked
up by Wilson as she hitchhiked, and she introduced Wilson to the
family. Manson at one time seems to have claimed that he met
Wilson in San Francisco.

Whatever happened, one day, after he had already met parts
of Manson's magnetic field, Wilson came home from a Beach
Boys' concert tour to discover the black Hollywood Productions
bus parked outside and twenty-five people in his living room, the
majority of which were nubile caressing females.

On Sunset Boulevard Manson plugged into the restless world
of successful rock musicians and continued his adventures inside
the interlocking circles of young sons and daughters of figures in

the motion picture and music industries. It was a sociopath's
paradise. Like a dowser's wand, the little hypnosis addict homed
in on two American symbols:

A. The Beach Boys—America's perfect singing group with their
    clear excellent high harmonies and their enormously popular
    songs about surfing, hot rods, good vibrations and fun, and

B. Terry Melcher—son of virginity incarnadine.

Terry Melcher was born Terry Jordan on February 8, 1942. Doris
Day, at the time, was a singer with Les Brown and his Band of
Renown. She was married to a musician named Al Jordan. After
his parents were divorced, he was raised in Cincinnati by his
maternal grandmother.

D.D.'s third husband Marty Melcher adopted Terry. He attended
Beverly Hills High School, class of 1960. For a year he attended
Principia College in Illinois. Melcher attempted to become a
singer himself but after a short atonal period wound up pro-
ducing groups for Columbia Records. He produced some of
The Bird's early and excellent records and then recorded the
hype-ridden Paul Revere and the Raiders, a group from Washington that was quite successful in the late 1960's.

In 1966 he rented a secluded L.A. house at 10050 Cielo Drive
and was living there when he met Manson in the summer of 1968
at Dennis Wilson's Pacific Palisades home. Melcher's father Martin had died in April of 1968 and Terry had been the co-executor
of the estate, inheriting great wealth in hotels, oil and real estate
in California, Texas and Oklahoma, not to mention the helm of
his mother's then upcoming comedy series for CBS, plus various
music-publishing and TV enterprises.

Manson also met Gregg Jakobson, a songwriter and colleague
of Melcher who was evidently working at the time for one of
Melcher's music-publishing companies. Jakobson was to become
quite intimate with the family. He recorded Manson singing several times and was privy to non-lethal family affairs for several
years.

Manson was singing when Melcher first met Manson and the
girls. Manson went to Melcher's home several times and even

on occasion borrowed Melcher's Jaguar. On one occasion when
Melcher visited Dennis Wilson, Dennis and Gregg drove Melcher
home to 10050 Cielo Drive while Manson sat in the back of the
Rolls-Royce singing and strumming the guitar.

The relationship between the family and Melcher is much more
extensive than has been known. What William Burroughs calls
an "area of silence" has been created about the matter. People
can't really be blamed because a strong relationship with Manson
could chop points from a TV series.

Dean Morehouse, the white-haired former minister, arrived
in Los Angeles evidently still trying to regain possession of his
fourteen-year-old flowering daughter, RuthAnn. He sought help
from people at the Wilson residence in gaining back RuthAnn but
was unsuccessful. Somehow he too began to live with the family
at Wilson's estate. Morehouse lived in the guest house and secured
some sort of employment from Manson and Dennis Wilson as the
gardener and groundskeeper.

The rest of the Morehouse story is acid. Dean became the most
devout of Charlie's occult changelings. He was to become an
obsequious embarrassment to Manson because Morehouse himself
went on a Jesus-identity trip under LSD. And how many Jesuses
can one cult contain? Morehouse became a daily dope gobbler,
his thin white hair growing long, declaring himself both the Christ
and the devil as he made himself happy at the parties that summer
at Melcher's home and Wilson's residence.

Dean was such an apostle of lysergic acid that once in the
mountains before he broke up with his wife he dropped a few
tabs on the sly into her orange juice, leaving her alone in the
wilderness to have her own trip. Thanks a lot, Dean.

Morehouse brought with him a young man from Texas named
Brooks Posten, a musician who later would create family legend
by being able, on command, to put himself into a trance. Posten
forked over to Manson a credit card belonging to his mother
which was used extensively in family travels in 1968.

Posten too grew quickly to believe Manson was Jesus. He

stayed most of the summer with the family at Wilson's house, helping Dean Morehouse with the "gardening."

Manson's greatest work of magic, however, was the transformation of Charles Denton Watson. When they met Watson in the spring of 1968 at Dennis Wilson's house, Watson was a swinger dating a stewardess from Chicago. The family was proud that it could create a change in Tex Watson, the holder to this day of a Texas high hurdles track and field record. Watson dressed mod. He looked mod. He had a wig shop. He was strictly now. But they erased the swinger from him. Years later, when he was down to 110 pounds, weeping in his cell, covered over with a blanket, just before they shipped him to the Atascadero nut hatch, he was truly now. No past—time burnt—books burnt— past burnt. All bridges melted with dope and fervor. All time factors in the now. The now of Charlie.

Tex Watson was born in Copeville, Texas on December 2, 1946. He lived a normal life for a boy growing up in the agricultural cotton-raising areas of central Texas. People in Copeville remember him riding his bicycle, working in the cotton fields, helping his father at the family grocery store-gas station in Copeville. They were stunned that he had turned into a murderer.

He wore a flat top and modified duck-tails in high school in Farmersville, Texas where he was an ace high hurdler and a star halfback.

For a couple of years he attended North Texas State College where he studied Business Administration and joined a fraternity. He was an American.

Watson dropped out of college after 1966 and in early 1967 moved to Los Angeles. He attended college for a semester or so in Los Angeles in 1967, then dropped out again. He lived at residences on Glendale Boulevard, Wonderland Road, Dracena and North Larrabee—a street famed for dope-dealing.

Before Manson, he began to work as a wig dealer, opening a popular hair store called Crown Wig Creations Ltd. at the mouth of Benedict Canyon. He and a buddy from Denton, Texas were in partnership. The shop was located at 9499 Santa Monica Boulevard, near Beverly Hills.

At the time he met Manson, Watson seems to have been living at a beachhouse at 18162 Pacific Coast Highway. He drove an elegant 1935 Dodge pickup truck.

Among three billion possibilities, Watson chose to become Charlie. "I am Charlie and Charlie is me," went a tune of the day. They were his replicas. Watson has complained that he actually thought he *was* Charlie. He even used Manson's name. Once in Mendocino County he signed Manson's name when buying gas with Terry Melcher's credit card.

Tests at the University of Southern California Neuropsychiatric Institute have shown that as a result of his trip in Manson's void, Watson's IQ dropped thirty points, probably through use of drugs like telache or belladonna. If the Pentagon ever formulates the Manson secret, the world's in trouble.

The Wilson house was a great address to use with his parole officer. In fact, Manson used the Sunset Boulevard address on his i.d. long after he moved out of the place. Manson was really cooking in his Jesus image—kissing feet and granting immortality as never before. "Are you ready to die?" he'd say, and if the answer were yes, he'd say: "Then live forever."

He was always finding places for people to crash. He'd send Squeaky with a carload of sleepy crashers out to Topanga Canyon or to the Spahn Ranch to find beds for the night.

Wilson possessed a rock star's booty: two Ferraris, a Rolls-Royce, a house in Benedict Canyon, a fabulous rock-star wardrobe, a boat equipped with radar. He was rich.

The girls went on garbage runs in the Rolls-Royce. It must have looked weird to see them loading the discarded supermarket produce into the back seat.

But Dennis Wilson let it happen. Once during that summer, he took Snake, Lynn and Ouish with him when the Beach Boys performed at a music festival in Colorado. Later, during a Beach Boys' English tour, in an interview with a rock magazine called *Rave* he would call Charles Manson "The Wizard" and said that Manson would probably issue an album on Brothers Records, a label owned by the Beach Boys. Manson brought Robert Beausoleil out to Wilson's house for a swim at the palatial pool after meeting him in Topanga Canyon one day.

It was strictly a locust scene as far as Wilson's personal property was concerned because the family evidently managed to give away the substance of Wilson's immediate wealth in the course of two or three months. But it was the year of the Maharishi and transcendental meditation so Wilson seemed to groove with Manson's millenarian material detachment, and later came to live in a state of poverty himself—when that fall he moved into a penurious one-room basement apartment at Gregg Jakobson's house on North Beverly Glen Drive.

It was summer 1968 at the Wilson estate when it first became apparent that Manson had some sort of prostate problem. Part of the legend eagerly spread abroad by the family then was that Charlie made love seven times a day: once before and once after each meal or snack and once in the middle of the night, when he awakened with desire. Each new girl shared with Manson an extensive multi-hour lovemaking session using the picture-me-as-your-father routine plus lots of perv. And perv is what the L.A. music scene eats for breakfast. The word must have gotten around. It could be called an exhaustion grope. It seems that Charlie felt that it was only after the first three or four hours that the sex really got good—when the woman "gave up," lost her ego entirely, then the act was of the Soul. And it was true. Out of many, many oral depositions taken from ladies in the Los Angeles area, there was only one who claimed that Manson waxed unable in eros.

Most girls thought Manson was very young, even in his early twenties. Which was okay with Charlie, because his scene really was prepubescent girls. They couldn't get young enough.

But he didn't fool everybody. His face when seen inches away revealed incipient biological phasing.

"His face seemed very young but close up he was wrinkled," recalled one lady friend of 1969.

Three

Sleazo Inputs

People remember that Sadie particularly was eager for people they encountered to go to Los Angeles "to meet Charlie." Everything oozed past. Sometime, probably in late May '68, Charlie made a decision to send a scouting expedition north to Mendocino County in the black bus to look for a permanent place to settle. Susan Atkins aka Sadie Glutz was the leader of the journey and driver of the bus.

Charlie, buttressed by a chosen core of followers, stayed behind for fun and games at the Wilson house. Malibu Brenda, Sandy Good, Ouish, Squeaky Fromme and Snake Lake were the girls picked by Charlie to keep close at hand during those easy months on Sunset.

Before going north to Mendocino Susan Atkins' group resided temporarily at a commune at 532 Clayton a couple of doors up the hill from the Haight-Ashbury Free Medical Clinic. Mary Brunner's seven- or eight-week-old baby, Pooh Bear, was treated for a yeast infection at the Free Clinic.

The bus bearing the family, without Manson, attracted considerable sympathy. There had been that pattern of harrassment from the police and the idiotic marijuana arrests. And the girls were eager proselytizers, according to observers. They were zealous, these girls, and when they resided in Mendocino became known as the Witches of Mendocino.

The officials of the Haight-Ashbury Clinic certainly had already heard of them since Manson's former federal parole officer, Roger Smith, had left the parole scene and in January of 1968 had established a drug counseling treatment program associated with the Haight-Ashbury Medical Clinic.

The clinic was housed in a three- or four-story house just off Panhandle Park on Clayton Street. Several of the staff of the clinic began to spend time observing the group. Al Rose, the administrative head of the clinic, gathered data on the girls when they were placed in a Mendocino jail and later visited them when they were at the Spahn Ranch. He and Dr. David Smith, the medical director, later wrote a formal paper entitled "The Group Marriage Commune: A Case Study" about the family of 1968, which was published replete with footnotes and scientific terminology in the November 1970 issue of the *Journal of Psychedelic Drugs,* a slick but interesting publication analyzing the so-called drug culture.

The Haight-Ashbury Free Clinic had opened just prior to flower-power in late 1966. It struggled bravely to survive through 1967 when it treated the countless children.

Once in 1967 it closed briefly for lack of funds but soon re-opened. The need to be perpetuated meant becoming chummy with the foundations to get grants to continue its deserved existence. Also, in previous years, the rock and roll groups of San Francisco occasionally performed benefits to aid the Free Clinic.

To focus briefly on the Free Clinic: There had been a mild furor in the papers during the spring of 1968 over a benefit rock and roll concert the Free Clinic was proposing to present on Easter Sunday, April 15, at the prestigious Palace of Fine Arts in San Francisco. The affair would raise a needed twelve or thirteen thousand dollars for the clinic.

Big Brother and the Holding Company, featuring Janis Joplin, and Quicksilver Messenger Service were scheduled to play at the benefit. Certain San Franciscans complained that the elegant Palace of Fine Arts should not be used for an affair featuring rock and roll especially if it was to benefit clap-suffused hippie slime. They won and at the last minute the concert had to be moved to the Carousel Ballroom.

It was sometime in the spring or summer of 1968 when Mrs. Inez Folger, the mother of Abigail Folger, began to help the Haight-Ashbury Medical Clinic. She worked as a volunteer aiding Dr. Roger Smith's drug treatment program. Mrs. Folger helped the clinic receive a grant from the Bothin Foundation and $25,000 from the Merrill Trust, according to a high official at the clinic. She held several fund-raising parties during the year she worked at the clinic. Abigail Folger, as well as Colonel and Mrs. Tate, attended one such benefit party given by Mr. and Mrs. Folger and it appears that one or more members of Manson's family, perhaps Manson himself, attended that fund-raising cocktail party.

At least one official at the clinic recalled that fund-raising party on the day when he read in the newspapers that Manson was arrested for the murders.

Sometime in the first two weeks of June, the girls drove north of San Francisco into Mendocino County looking for a home. They lived for awhile in a commune-type house located off Route 128 near Philo, northwest of Ukiah, in dope country.

A little while after midnight on June 21, 1968, one Mrs. Rosenthal of Booneville, California phoned the resident deputy sheriff of Mendocino County and requested that an officer be sent to her house because someone had given some dope to her 17-year-old-son. When the police arrived they found young Allen Rosenthal speaking of his legs as if, in fact, they were snakes and he was having color hallucinations.

He told the police that the Witches of Mendocino of the Philo "hippie" house had laid a small blue tab of dope on him.

That night the sheriff's deputies raided the hippie lair occupied by five females (the Witches of Mendocino), three males and an infant, Pooh Bear. The police searched the house and surroundings and in a woodshed next to the house came up with a small film can containing cannabis and also a plastic bag with some blue kernels of acid inside. They caught the commies with dope. Arrested were Ella Beth Sinder aka Yeller, Mary Brunner, Patricia Krenwinkel, Sadie Glutz, someone named Mary Ann Scott, Robert Bomse, Peter Kornbuth and Eugene Nagle plus the eleven-week-old Valentine Michael Manson aka Pooh Bear.

After the arrest one of the girls phoned Dennis Wilson's house down in Los Angeles to tell Charlie about the bust.

The next day, June 22, 1968, Sadie Mae Glutz et al. were charged with violation of Section 11910 of the California Health and Safety Code, possession of a dangerous drug with a prior conviction, Section 11913 of the California Health and Safety Code, felonious implacement of dope into the mouth of a minor, and Section 11530, possession of the herb marijuana.

Katie was booked under the name of Katherine Smith. Evidently Mary Brunner was afraid that she would be the one to be convicted so they told the police that the young Sunstone Hawk aka Pooh Bear was Katie's baby because they thought Katie had a good chance of getting off. And the girls were afraid that the state would take Pooh Bear away when they found out that Mary Brunner had recently been arrested for felonious breastfeeding in a ditch down in Oxnard, California.

Naturally, the girls were unable to raise bail. Pooh Bear was taken away from his mother and placed in a foster home. Mr. and Mrs. Roger Smith of the Free Clinic were somehow chosen to serve as foster parents for the child.

It was discovered, horror of horrors, that not only had the baby no birth certificate, but that it had not been circumcised. Both were accomplished in rapid time.

So the girls languished in jail until at a hearing on July 2 some of the charges were dropped but the Witches of Mendocino were rearrested right in court on what was designated as "an amended complaint." The girls continued to be held in jail.

While the Witches of Mendocino remained incarcerated up north, Manson spent most of his time in June and July '68 in Los Angeles.

The small misogynist was busy dominating women and making contacts.

One of his greatest tricks was talking his followers into the worship of infant consciousness. Somehow, the infant was the ideal. Children were not cursed by the Culture but acted spontaneously, from the Soul. It must be remembered that the family believed in reincarnation and in the possibility of monitoring past lives. So the child was the sum culmination of the life-chain of evolution.

Charlie encouraged childbirth. Rubbers, pills, i.u.d.'s, diaphragms and, Lord forbid, vasectomy were not allowed. Women, according to the Manson hype, had no souls but were superaware slaves whose duties were to whelp and to serve men. Ironically, there were actually very few pregnancies in the family, a fact, according to Sandy Good, that used to upset Charlie.

In a place where twenty women love one man the attention paid each one by the man becomes an issue. Manson had a quick mind and maintained an intimate disarming relationship with each of his followers—and somehow satisfied them all.

As a flip-side of the jealousy question, Manson had the greatest scam of all. He'd tell the girls that if they really loved him they'd go out and bring him back a girl prettier and younger than they were—and he got away with it. He seemed really to dote upon short, skinny masochistic redheads with superstitious minds. And he loved to find kids who'd been stomped on by their parents.

They came and went. "If you fit in, you can stay," was the formula and some of them did their damndest to fit in.

This is the image his followers would present the world.

But Manson's life wasn't merely spent compiling a harem and gearing for stardom.

There was another Manson, a Manson with years of connections with a seamier side of Los Angeles. Manson seems to have maintained contacts with criminal types for years. It will be remembered that he came to Los Angeles in 1955 and operated in Los Angeles throughout his fourteen-year career in California as prisoner, pimp, bartender, forger and robber and then as minstrel and guru.

Manson was a guy that claimed thousands of friends. For

instance, there was a person named Pete who lived in Sacramento with whom in late 1967 the family visited for several days during their wanderings. Pete and Manson evidently had worked together at a bar in Malibu in 1958. He kept up his friendships.

Manson used to hang out on the Sunset Strip using the name Chuck Summers. There were a bunch of sleazo bars and cafés on or near the Sunset Strip with names like the Galaxy Club, Omnibus and The Melody Room that Chuck Summers frequented in 1968. Bikers, prostitutes, petty criminals and porn models flocked to these clubs.

The Galaxy Club was a favorite of Chuck Summers. Manson, as Summers, used to come around in the mornings according to the club manager of that era. The manager was also a stage hypnotist who later opened something called the Hollywood Hypnotism Center. He and Manson used to talk about hypnotism. The Galaxy Club was located up the street from the Whiskey A Go-Go. Manson probably met the bike club, Jokers Out of Hell, at the Galaxy. Some of Manson's lesser-known girl friends, with names like Mouse and Venus, were also frequenters of these establishments.

Sunset Strip seems to be where Manson first made contact with the satanic variety of bike groups, with names like The Satan Slaves, The Jokers Out of Hell, The Straight Satans, The Coffin Makers and other snuff-oriented groups of young men. It is undeniable that an increasing contact with some of these clubs with hellish names would create great violent "reflections" in Manson. With some of the groups like Straight Satans and particularly The Satan Slaves Manson had deep associations during the following year of violence.

There had been a year of flowers. But sometime in the summer or spring of 1968 a change occurred in the family. Into the mix of flowers, sex, nomad-communality walked Satan, devil-worship and violence. Perhaps it was the will to change—the need to maintain that magnetism—that caused Charlie to groove with gore.

Something happened. After all, Patricia Krenwinkel didn't

just jump upon command, aroused from sleep, and drive to the Polanski residence, as some would like to think, because of sex, drugs and communes.

It was a continuing claim of Manson that he was merely a reflection of those around him, that he was "dead in the head" and therefore acted from the Soul. There is no doubt that he borrowed his ideas from plenty of sources. He was ever the avid listener and he prided himself on a vast range of weird information.

But what was it that caused Manson's death-trip? The factors that seem to have fed the violent freak-out shall be termed here sleazo inputs.

Gazing about Los Angeles, it is possible to discern at least three death-trip groups that must have provided powerful sleazo inputs into Manson and the family. It is significant that there exist in Los Angeles occult groups that specialize in creating zombi-like followers. These are groups that have degrees of trust and discipleship, that use pain and fear and certain drugs to promote instant obedience.

These three groups are:

1. The Process Church of the Final Judgment, an English organization dedicated to gore, weirdness and End of the World slaughter. The Process, as they are known, was active in Los Angeles in 1968, when Manson abandoned flowers, and in the summer of 1969—when murder reigned.

2. The Solar Lodge of the Ordo Temple Orientis, a loony-tune magical cult specializing in blood-drinking, sado-sodo sex magic and hatred of blacks. The Solar Lodge of the O.T.O. was run by one Jean Brayton, a vicious middle-aged devotee of pain who attracted a crowd of groveling worshipers.

3. an obscure occult group of forty or so which we shall here call the Kirké Order of Dog Blood.

All three cults certainly were aware of one another, and the similarities and connections between them and the family cannot be avoided. They will be described in subsequent chapters.

It was the Process that Manson probably encountered first.

One family member has claimed that the head of the Process, one Robert DeGrimston aka Robert Moor, was hanging out at The Spiral Staircase in Topanga Canyon. Whatever the case, Manson had to have run across them on Sunset Strip where Processoids dressed in black capes went around hawking their cult magazines and books.

One of the stories the Process would dream up to explain its connections with Manson was that somehow Father Christian of the Process sold a copy of the *Process* magazine number 4, the sex issue, to Manson somewhere on the Sunset Strip in the spring of 1968.

Manson was cooking. It was June 1968.

While Manson was scrounging on the Strip and singing and kissing feet at 14400 Sunset Boulevard, just a couple of miles away to the northeast, Sharon Tate and Roman Polanski were moving into a house at 1600 Summit Ridge Drive located in the hilly fameland above Beverly Hills.

Four

The Polanskis

"Characters and utmost fear
are the most important thing in cinema."
—Roman Polanski

Sharon Tate was born on January 24, 1943, in Dallas, Texas.
Her father was a career army officer and the family subsequently
lived in various parts of Europe and the United States. Her family
entered her in a Tiny Tots beauty contest in Dallas and she won.
As she grew older her parents continued to move, living in San
Francisco, Washington state, Washington, D.C., etc. She was Miss
Autorama in Richmond, Washington.

Her family moved to Verona, Italy where she attended something called Vincenza American High School. She was Home-
coming Queen and Queen of the Senior Prom. How many tens
of thousands of American girls crowned queen of the prom have
hungered for Hollywood? When she was living with her family
in Verona, Italy, she met Eli Wallach, Susan Strasberg and
Richard Beymer who were shooting a movie there.

Mr. Beymer encouraged Miss Tate with the old "you ought
to be in pictures" and it seems to have led to her resolve to become an actress.

Her father was transferred back to the United States and the
Tate family was stationed in San Pedro, California, just a few
miles from Hollywood. From San Pedro, she made her move.
She used to hitchhike to the various movie studios where the
soft-voiced eager Miss Tate was known as the girl from San
Pedro.

There is one memorable interview about her start in Holly-
wood that she gave on the set of a movie about vampires, *The
Fearless Vampire Killers.* She said: "I used to hitchhike in Los
Angeles to all the studios because I couldn't afford the cab fare.
The men were so generous, especially the truck drivers; they all
gave me lifts. My first experience was doing TV commercials.
"I convinced Daddy that I'd be safe in Hollywood."

Miss Tate acquired an agent, Hal Gefsky, and in due order
began to make automobile and cigar commercials. In 1963, when
she was twenty years old, her agent sent her to New York to
audition for a bit part in *Petticoat Junction,* a CBS-TV series in
preparation and produced by one Martin Ransohoff and his company, Filmways.

Ransohoff arrived on the set, checked out the beautiful young
girl, then called her over. According to columnist Lloyd Shearer,
in a London newspaper story, Ransohoff spoke to Sharon these
formuletic words:

"Sweetie, I'm going to make you a star." With emphasis on
the *I'm.*

Mr. Ransohoff was the producer, also, of a yuk-yuk TV comedy
series called *The Beverly Hillbillies.* Not since Troy II-a, known
in archeological circles as the Slob Culture, had there been anything like *The Beverly Hillbillies.* Ransohoff signed Sharon to a
seven-year contract. For two and a half years he kept her as his
own. Like a beautiful date-palm, she was watered into stardom.
She was given singing and dancing and acting lessons. She was
given tiny training roles, wearing wigs, in *The Beverly Hillbillies,
Petticoat Junction,* plus several films produced by Ransohoff, including *The Americanization of Emily* and *The Sandpipers.*

She spent a considerable amount of time in the Big Sur area
of California, a beautiful coastal region she grew to love. She
stayed there with Ransohoff while he filmed *The Sandpipers* starring Elizabeth Taylor.

Sometime in 1963 Jay Sebring, hair stylist for male movie
stars, met Sharon Tate in a Hollywood restaurant. They became
friends and lovers quickly and sometime later became engaged

to be married. Jay Sebring was an eager, successful entrepreneur, rapidly establishing himself as the king of the haircut.

If you are a public performer, you pay a lot of attention to your face and hair—that's all there is to it. You do. In many cases, the face and hair of a talent is just about all he has to donate to his career. Sebring had a way that commanded the respect of many of the famed and wealthy of Hollywood. He was almost a magician at keeping hair from disappearing down the shower drain. And he came along in fit time to aid the transition in hair styles from Marine Corps to mod.

Right around the time they met, Sebring purchased a remarkable home in Benedict Canyon where he lived until his death. Sebring's house at 9860 Easton Drive had a certain grim fame in that it was once the hideaway of actress Jean Harlow and it was there Harlow's husband Paul Bern snuffed himself with a bullet in 1932.

After two years of preparation, the starlet was ready. In late 1965 Ransohoff gave her her first "major" role opposite David Niven and Deborah Kerr in the movie *13* aka *Eye of the Devil*. *13* was the story of a hooded religious sect which worshiped the devil and committed sacrificial murders.

The movie was made in London. Jay Sebring came to London and they lived together in an apartment at Eaton Square, but pressures of his own career caused him to return to Los Angeles.

When Ransohoff made *Eye of the Devil (13)* in London, the company hired an English magician called Alex Saunders, the so-called "King of the Witches," as technical advisor. Alex Saunders aka the High Priest Verbius claims that Aleister Crowley tattooed him as a tenth birthday present. He claims to have initiated and trained people in two hundred covens of witches in the British Isles. He also claims that he became friends of Sharon Tate on the set of the devil movie. Before filming ended, Saunders claims he initiated Miss Tate into Witchcraft. He has photos purporting to show Miss Tate standing within a consecrated magic circle.

In early 1966 Martin Ransohoff hired one Roman Polanski

to direct a film written by Polanski called, at various times, *The Fearless Vampire Killers* or *Dance of the Vampires* or *Pardon Me, But Your Fangs Are in My Neck,* or something. Mr. Ransohoff was eager for Sharon Tate to be in the flick so he made arrangements for Roman Polanski and Sharon to meet.

A number of Polanski films notably *Knife in the Water, Cul-de-Sac* and *Repulsion* had achieved great success. *Repulsion* has the grim distinction of being one of the most horrifying films ever made.

Roman Polanski was born in Paris of Polish parents on August 18, 1933. In 1936 his family traveled back to Poland and settled in Krakow. Five years later they were taken away to the Nazi concentration camp, where his mother died in the gas chamber. Shortly after incarceration, Polanski's father, armbanded with the Star of David, took his young son to the barbed wire surrounding the Krakow ghetto. He cut the wire and the young boy escaped, living on his own with various families till Hitler was beaten out of Poland.

During the horror of the war, movies became a refuge to him. When he was still very young, he became an actor and a moviemaker. He attended the Polish State Film College in Lodz, Poland for the five years, and there he seems to have met Voityck Frykowski.

His earliest works were short, bleak Beckettoid films. In 1960 Polanski went to France for eighteen months where he directed and acted in *The Fat and the Lean.* In 1961 he divorced his wife, Polish actress Barbara Lass. In 1962 he returned to Poland where he made an eleven-minute film called *Mammals.* Also in 1962 he created a feature-length movie, *Knife in the Water,* which made him famous in the West.

Knife in the Water won the Venice Film Festival Critics Award in 1962. In 1964, when it finally arrived in America, it was nominated for an Oscar as best foreign film.

In 1963 he went to Holland where he directed an episode for a movie entitled *The Best Swindles in the World.* He also that year wrote the scenario for *Do You Like Women?* which is a movie about a "society of cannibals" in Paris who like to cook and eat pretty girls. Oo-ee-oo. *Fade in electronic soundtrack from Rosemary's Baby.*

In the early '60's, Roman Polanski collaborated with Girard Brach and turned out scripts for three movies: *Repulsion, The Fearless Vampire Killers* and *Cul-de-Sac.* Producer Gene Gutowski, an admirer of *Knife in the Water,* brought Polanski to England where in 1965 he made his first film in English, *Repulsion.*

Repulsion is the story of a beautiful manicurist, played by Catherine Deneuve, who suffers horrific violent hallucinations and winds up hacking and pummeling two male acquaintances to death. *Repulsion,* horribile dictu, was a success and Polanski was able to raise the money to make *Cul-de-Sac,* a story of murder and weirdness in a seaside castle.

Polanski gained a reputation as a meticulous and thorough craftsman. The success of his blood-suffused movies and his obvious skill attracted Martin Ransohoff, who agreed to produce Polanski's script *The Fearless Vampire Killers* for MGM. In it, Sharon Tate would play a vampire.

One story always told is that on the night Roman and Sharon met they were alone in an apartment together. Mr. Polanski excused himself and left the room. Then he crept up behind the unsuspecting Miss Tate wearing a Frankenstein mask and pulled a boo! scene, throwing her into hysterics.

Vampire Killers is a comedy about a university professor and his servant, played by Roman Polanski, who travel into Transylvania to brick out a castle full of vampires. Sharon Tate played Sarah, an innkeeper's daughter who is abducted to castle necksuck by the head vampire. There she is turned into a vampire herself. Etc. On the set of *The Fearless Vampire Killers,* she posed for publicity pictures, flashing her vampire bicuspids, shiny and fanglike.

In April of 1966 Jay Sebring complained to friends that he'd been bird-dogged by Roman Polanski, who seemed to have scooped the lovely Sharon Tate into his life. Sebring traveled to

London and returned in the early summer of 1966, announcing
that it was all over between him and Sharon.

Her public statements during that time regarding her breakup
with Jay Sebring were almost self-deprecating.

"Before Roman I guess I was in love with Jay. It was a fine
relationship but the truth is I was no good for Jay. I'm not
organized. I'm too flighty. Jay needs a wife and at 23 I'm not
ready for wifehood. I still have to live, and Roman is trying to
show me how."

Sharon returned from England in 1966 to play a role in *Don't
Make Waves,* with Tony Curtis and Claudia Cardinale. During
this stage in her career her father, Lieutenant Colonel Paul Tate,
was doing his thing in Vietnam, capping a career in army in-
telligence.

In the March 1967 issue of *Playboy* magazine there appeared
a photo series called "The Tate Gallery" featuring Sharon with
bared bosom, shot by Roman Polanski.

In '67 Sharon Tate gained notice for her role as Jennifer in
the movie *Valley of the Dolls.* Jennifer was a young starlet who
commits suicide in the flick.

Somewhere in the chronology, Martin Ransohoff, the producer
of *The Beverly Hillbillies,* and Polanski had a feud over *The
Fearless Vampire Killers.* Mr. Ransohoff cut footage out of the
film before its release in the United States. This film-cut caused
Polanski to demand that his name be stricken from the movie's
credits. Ransohoff also bought U.S. rights to *Cul-de-Sac* and
altered the movie extensively, angering Polanski. Sharon subsequently severed relationships with Mr. Ransohoff, reportedly
purchasing her contract back for $175,000.

His continued triumph made it possible for Polanski to become
the first filmmaker from a so-called Iron Curtain country to
direct a picture in Hollywood. Lucky Roman.

The head of Paramount Pictures offered Polanski the opportunity to direct and write the screenplay for *Rosemary's Baby,*
a novel by Ira Levin. *Rosemary's Baby,* a saga of satanic
chauvinism, is a story about the big-league affluent hail-Satan

crowd and their evident success in getting Satan to make pregnant an innocent female victim, played by Mia Farrow.

Mr. Polanski flew to Hollywood and stayed up all one night reading the galleys of the book, and the deal was made. Veteran moviemaker William Castle produced the film.

The studio wanted Mia Farrow to play the lead so Polanski was shown reels of the TV series *Peyton Place* wherein Miss Farrow acted, and he okayed her role in *Rosemary's Baby*. The Polanskis and Miss Farrow, according to most accounts, became close friends.

Rosemary's Baby had a shooting schedule of around 56 days. There were around 10 days spent filming in New York at the elegant Dakota apartments off Central Park West. The Dakota was transformed into a lair of Satan during the filming. Editing and dubbing evidently were done in Los Angeles, occupying the latter part of 1967.

Jay Sebring and the Polanskis maintained a friendly relationship. Some friends claim that Sebring still loved Sharon. While *Rosemary's Baby* was being created, some of Polanski's friends threw a party at Sebring's house on Easton Drive. Evidently the party was a mock-up magical mass where guests wore white robes. One English journalist was invited and blindfolded, whereafter Jay, robed in white, offered him, hopefully in jest, the choice of two antique goblets, one containing wine, one containing rat poison.

San Francisco satanist Anton La Vey was a "consultant" for *Rosemary's Baby*. La Vey played the role of the devil in the movie. There are rumors that the real-life black-mass freaks were angered with Polanski for making such a movie. At the completion of the film, the cast gave Polanski an engraved 45-caliber Colt revolver, perhaps as a bit of amuletic humor because of the grumblings of the hail-Satan crowd. *Rosemary's Baby* has been called the greatest advertisement for satanism ever concocted. And Los Angeles possesses more than one lady moon-yodeler who claims to have given birth to children of the devil.

On January 20, 1968, following the completion of *Rosemary's*

Baby, Sharon Marie Tate and Roman Polanski were married in London. He was attired in what the press described as "Edwardian finery," she in a white mini-dress. They moved into a mews house off Belgrave Square. The world premiere for *Rosemary's Baby* was held in London and it became obvious that the film was a smash success.

Polanski and his bride moved to Los Angeles where they evidently occupied a suite at the Chateau Marmont Hotel. With the success of the film, Polanski was a popular man—the cooers and backscratchers as usual, attending the man of the hour. The Polanskis were part of an energetic, liberal group of actors and actresses and businessmen at the heights of Hollywood success. They were all airline nomads, always packing, always on the move. But always working and planning.

Both admitted in print that they tried LSD. Polanski was bummered by it but his wife said, "It opened the world to me," although she was hesitant to trip again.

In May '68 Roman Polanski attended the Cannes Film Festival. At the same time, the students of France revolted and nearly toppled the government. Polanski, in solidarity with the students, resigned from the festival jury.

On June 5, 1968, Roman and Sharon and friends dined with Robert Kennedy at a beach house in Malibu. After dinner, Senator Kennedy was driven to the Ambassador Hotel where he was shot.

June 15, 1968, was the date of the West Coast premiere of *Rosemary's Baby.* "Pray for Rosemary's Baby" was the legend in the newspaper ads. The film was so popular in Los Angeles that extra showings were added to the theater's schedule. It opened in San Francisco on June 19, where it began a smash engagement. The film was on the track to a ten to twenty-million-dollar gross.

Mr. Polanski's screenplay was nominated for an Academy Award. Mia Farrow received the Best Actress award at a film festival in Rio de Janeiro. Ruth Gordon received an Oscar for Best Supporting Actress for her role in the film.

In the summer of 1968, Sharon Tate and Dean Martin and

Elke Sommers starred together in a movie called *The Wrecking Crew*. In June of that year, Roman Polanski rented a house at 1600 Summit Ridge Drive in the Hollywood Hills. The house was owned by young actress Patty Duke with whom Sharon had become friends during the filming of *Valley of the Dolls*. The Polanskis hired a housekeeper named Winifred Chapman who worked for them during the following year, first on Summit Ridge and then on Cielo Drive. It was she who was picked by fate to discover the tragedy.

Sharon and Roman gave a housewarming party to celebrate their new rented house on Summit Ridge Drive. There was a strange occurence at the party, according to a friend of Sharon Tate, involving Roman Polanski and some vicious dogs from down the hill.

The Polanskis had agreed to take care of Patty Duke's sheep dog while they rented the house. The sheep dog had the habit of running away. On the night of the party, the sheep dog bounded away down the hill, in the direction of the old John Barrymore mansion located at 1301 Summit Ridge Drive.

Polanski went after the dog and somewhere down the hill seems to have encountered a group of vicious Alsatian dogs belonging to a group of English occultists who were in America to promote the end of the world. Mr. Polanski got locked in a garage, evidently to try to escape the demi-wolves of the cult's dog pack. He had to batter himself out of the garage.

Five

The Process

"My prophecy upon this wasted earth and upon the corrupt creation that squats upon its ruined surface is: THOU SHALT KILL."   —from *Jehovah on War*
                                    by Robert DeGrimston aka Christ

The black-caped, black-garbed, death-worshiping Process Church of the Final Judgment arrived on the Los Angeles scene in early 1968. They stayed in public view till a few days after Robert Kennedy's assassination in June of '68, after which they dropped from sight in Los Angeles.

And for what purpose were these noble Englishmen journeying to the United States? Gore and world-end.

They had made a decision to travel around the world to make converts and plant the seeds of their cult. They had spent quite a bit of time in a remote beach lagoon on the Yucatan peninsula and there they had discovered Satan and sacrifice—full moon frolics in which they paid obeisance to gore. From there the Process moved into southern California to collect violence-prone adepts—a form of human that just loves southern California, the home of weird cults.

And now it was the spring of the Year of the Pig 1968 and they were swarming the streets of Sunset Strip, trying to convert psychedelic merchants, seeking out movie stars and especially they doted on the hell-oriented bikers and bike gangs that frequented Hollywood.

The Process really grooves with war. Among their many publications, founder Robert DeGrimston has published three books on the subject of war, *Jehovah on War, Lucifer on War* and *Satan on War,* alleging that the words are from the three gods themselves as operating through the mouth of Robert De-Grimston. It is interesting to note that as things got hot for the Process, they toned down some of the violent language in later editions of the same books, particularly *Jehovah on War.*

In *Satan on War,* for instance, Robert DeGrimston urges humans to:

> Release the fiend that lies dormant within you, for he is strong and ruthless and his power is far beyond the bounds of human fraility.

It is necessary, unfortunately, to devote a few words of description to this depressing unsalvation army, these black-garbed DeGrimston-zombies, in order to describe yet another sleazo input which warped the mind of Charlie Manson.

The Process Church of the Final Judgment is an English occult society dedicated to observing and aiding the end of the world by stirring up murder, violence and chaos, and dedicated to the proposition that they, the Process, shall survive the gore as the chosen people. Sound like Manson?

It was formed by two fierce occult death-freaks, Mary Anne Maclean DeGrimston Moor and Robert Sylvester DeGrimston Moor. At his wife's suggestion, they dropped the name Moor, except when they want to travel incognito, and do so using the surname Moor. She is now around forty, if she is still alive, and he is around thirty-six years of age.

Mary Anne DeGrimston is a baleful lady who dotes on groveling followers. She has assumed various names such as Hecate and the Oracle and possibly Circe.

Both are devout reincarnationists. According to one account, Mary Anne DeGrimston believes she is the reincarnation of Goebbels. But in the era of Manson she was known as Hecate, an apt appellation. Hecate in ancient lore was the queen of ghosts and magic, she haunted crossroads, she was attended by hellhounds, she was the protectress of enchanters and witches.

Robert DeGrimston is thought by the cult to be Christ. He

was born on August 10, 1935, in Shanghai, China. Before waxing weirdo, DeGrimston studied architecture.

Bob and Mary Anne met at the Hubbard Institute of Scientology on Fitzroy Street, London in 1963 or 1964. They had been training to become scientology auditors or instructors. They were married in 1964 and left the Hubbard Institute a few months later, to seek some sort of spiritual salvation together.

At the time, Robert DeGrimston was powerfully built, tall, blond with a well-cut beard. He was known as a sharp dresser. He had been educated at Winchester and had received preliminary architectural training at the Regent Street Polytechnic.

Mary Anne DeGrimston worships spank-spank. She was born on November 20, 1931, in Glasgow, Scotland, an illegitimate child. In her youth, she was slapped into reform school. At some point she moved to the United States, where she became engaged to the former boxing champion Sugar Ray Robinson. After breaking up with Sugar Ray Robinson, she went back to London, where she was a dance-hall hostess and a prostitute. She set up hooker headquarters at 31 Lesusington Street in London where she was a kept woman for several influential men, including one gentleman who was later to become the lawyer for the Process. She was energetic during the Christine Keeler era at sado-sodo in London.

Mary Anne, in the manner of all occult ladies who dote on worship, possesses that fixed gaze of imminent punishment. Her hair has been in the past coppery red in color. Her vehement fingernails have been known to be long and painted silver. Process members are trained to fawn and grovel at the very thought of her. And, of course, none but the most trusted are ever allowed to see her in person.

Together Robert and Mary Anne DeGrimston formed something called "Compulsions Analysis." The purpose of this group was to study the reasons behind compulsive behavior, to remove the need for such behavior and to set people free from such behavior. A key point in the group was that an individual is totally responsible for his acts, that even birth defects were chosen by an individual, including any characteristics held over from alleged prior lives. Mary Anne was always saying that Jews died in the Nazi camps through free choice.

Their charismatic and diligent efforts created around them a circle of followers, mostly young and perturbed English youth. They specialized in attempting to attract wealthy people, for they charged considerably for trying to find the causes of various neurotic behavior. And the two founders, as they are known, just loved to fly first class and gobble up that hotel room service.

In March of 1966 they secured the lease on a luxury mansion on Balfour Place in the exclusive Mayfair district of London. Twenty-five young followers were required to leave their homes at once and move into the mansion. In addition, they were required to turn over all their money and worldly possessions to, guess who, Bob and Mary Anne.

Mr. and Mrs. DeGrimston encouraged complete emotional dependence from their group of followers. The Founding Couple, as they were called, established themselves in the top apartment of the Balfour Process Palace, to which only the inmost group was admitted.

"When Bob and Mary Anne came down, they descended like gods. She was the resident deity, he her consort." So deposed an acolyte of that era.

Mary Anne DeGrimston took care never to be seen alone, but always as the center of a crowd, always as the magical matriarch.

One day, after she and Bobby DeG. moved into the Balfour mansion, they each got a large, vicious Alsatian dog, a variety of German shepherd. Other member puppets also acquired the Alsatians, to the point where a dog pack was assembled.

It was decided to go abroad with the full membership of the burgeoning cult. So, on June 23, 1966, having sent out an advance party to prepare their arrival, Mary, Robert, eighteen Processans and six Alsatian dogs went to Nassau in the Bahamas.

They encountered some difficulty there, so they looked around for a more suitable location for their group. In August of 1966 they secured a large property in Xtul, Mexico, a village on the

Gulf of Mexico on the north coast of the Yucatan peninsula, near Mérida. There they acquired an estate for $175 a year, which included four miles of seashore, a palm tree jungle, a lagoon and the roofless, gutted, stone remains of a salt factory, plus various wooden huts. It was desolation alley.

Because of the tendency of the DeGrimstons to attract the young sons and daughters of wealthy, aristocratic Englishmen, several parents hired lawyers to attempt to get their children back from Mexico. So in November of 1966, lawyers, representing the parents of converted adepts, flew to Xtul, Mexico, to bring back several young people. The *Sunday Telegraph* of London, a newspaper, printed an article entitled: "The Mind Benders of Mayfair," dealing with the return of the youth-pack from the jungle lagoon.

It was at Xtul where the Process got into satanism. Up to then, their "gods" were Lucifer and Jehovah. They added Satan, evil Satan, the god of human sacrifice, bloodshed and rip-off.

At Xtul they coined a word "xtummie," evidently an adjective denoting a satanic state of preparedness. A "good" satanist exists in periods of depravity, periodically "exploding in dynamic action" i.e., cruelty. Oo-ee-oo.

Even though many of the Process members returned to London, some stayed behind or returned to Xtul to continue experiments in the new modes of psychedelic satanism.

The concept of a Process Church was also formed in Xtul. This formative period was recounted to all new converts.

"Xtul . . . was a place of revelation. It was a time of revelation. The basic church formed itself at that point," recalled Brother Ely in an interview.

The grim experiences of Xtul had more or less divided the Process group. The issue seemed to be whether to proselytize or to become a very inner-directed group. One of their members had inherited a considerable amount of money, so evidently they used about $80,000 of it to buy a yacht in Greece, in order to criss-cross the seas in secret comfort between the Mayfair mansion and the Satanic Lagoon in Mexico.

In London, in the spring of 1967, the Process was into fixing up their stately mansion in Mayfair. They had opened up an all-night coffee bar, where they showed art movies to attract the intellectuals. They made forays into the pop field, attempting to attract the Beatles and Mick Jagger of the Rolling Stones. They held lectures, demonstrations, telepathy classes and outdoor soap-box rant sessions in Hyde Park. They opened up a book store. They began to publish expensively produced tracts and philosophical works. They began to put out a magazine called *Process* that, gradually as the issues oozed out, became more and more murderous. The magazine eulogized Hitler, slaughter and carnage, adorning itself occasionally with pictures of battlefield death. Somehow, they managed to attract for a while Marianne Faithful, the singer and actress, into their circles. In *Process* magazine number 3, they showed Marianne Faithful lying down, holding a rose, as if she were dead. The story goes that Mick Jagger was instrumental in weaning Miss Faithful away from the cult.

In the latter half of 1967, the DeGrimstons seem to have made a tour of the Far East and Turkey.

In October of 1967, perhaps during his travels in the East, Robert DeGrimston recorded or wrote a book called *As It Is*. On the front page of *As It Is* is a seven-sentence gibberish plexus, declaring the unification of Christ and Satan, in order to snuff the human universe. It is this:

> Christ said: Love thine enemy. Christ's Enemy was Satan and Satan's Enemy was Christ. Through love, enmity is destroyed. Through love, saint and sinner destroy the enmity between them. Through love, Christ and Satan have destroyed their enmity and come together for the End. Christ to judge, Satan to execute the judgment.

They have printed this statement in several of their subsequent publications, although, to soften it a bit, they have added, after the final word "judgment," the words: "Salvation or doom."

The title, *As It Is,* and the last line of the thirteen-page tract, "So be it," became a sort of hosanna of the cult, which they would repeat over and over to each other when they met each other in the corridor or halls or streets: "As it is, so be it," almost like a "hello" and "good-by."

From Xtul or the Far East or somewhere, DeGrimston and Hecate arrived from their proselytizing travels and the Process celebrated their return by printing a handbill for a meeting called "Christ Has Returned," which was held on November 24, 1967. Shortly thereafter, the Process ran into trouble with the police. They kidnapped a recalcitrant follower and zapped him with some shock treatment and/or torture. There was a fall 1967 freak scene, since which Robert DeGrimston and Mary Anne DeGrimston have not been seen in public, except in shuttling anonymously back and forth from airport to airport in their world travels.

From this point forward, it was a go-ye-forth and convert scene.

There is a picture published in an issue of their magazine in late '67 showing eleven Processors sitting around a table, dressed in black, all looking intently at their leader Robert DeGrimston aka Christ. A globe of the world sits in the center of the table, perhaps indicating a meeting to plan where on earth to send their cult's spores.

It was the game of the gods. Here is Brother Ely talking:

> "The gods set up the game a long time before the players came onto the scene. And part of the way, the gods have set up this game, as if there are certain beings who are the gods (Lucifer, Jehovah, Satan), beings who are servants of the gods, whether they know it or not, consciously or unconsciously, they serve and do their part. What the Process did was sweep through the whole world and when they went into each area, those beings who were of the gods, those beings who were serving their purpose . . . those beings that were in the service of the gods came magnetically attracted to the Process in that area. So in going through the world systematically, they've picked up those people who are of the gods, who are servants in the destiny of things. And they've picked those people up.

Some stayed with the Church, some were taught, and in that way, the seeds were planted."

The Process had now become firmly subdivided into three groups, the Luciferians, the Satanists and the Jehovans. The Luciferians were of this world; they were fun-loving, they celebrated tranquillity, harmony, order, peace and sensuality. The Jehovahs were uptight, narrow-minded, rectitudinous, anti-sex, zealous and austere. They beat each other as punishment and were into self-flagellation according to a girl who once was associated with the group. And Satanists—well, the Satanists were both cold and calculating, and cruel, and violent; they were the goons.

According to his desires, an individual could become an advocate of any of the three. It didn't really matter because all were going to unite at the End—i.e., for the world-wreck.

In late 1967 the Process spores spewed out to America. They also sent a contingent to Germany, always a fertile ground for death-freaks.

The Process, or members of it, visited Los Angeles late in 1967 around the same time as the DeGrimstons sent Process members to San Francisco. In Los Angeles they spent several weeks at a house operated by the Diggers on North Highland just south of Sunset Boulevard, then they headed north.

Meanwhile, an advance party of Jehovans consisting of Father Alban aka Christopher Alfred Fripp and Father Aaron Tubal-Cain, with his dog Lucifer, voyaged to the Haight-Ashbury district of San Francisco, arriving in November 1967, just about the time Manson was driving his school bus full of girls toward Hollywood.

Father Aaron, once called Hugh Mountain, had given over a hundred thousand dollars to the Process. He was a founding father.

Eager were they to win over the Haight. They visited the offices of the *San Francisco Oracle,* the underground newspaper of the Haight, wearing their black capes and their black suits and their silver crosses, but were hooted off the set.

Father Alban gave a lecture on the Berkeley campus of the

University of California sometime in that fall of 1967. For his
lecture, there was an advertisement in the Berkeley campus newspaper.

Attending the Process recruiting meeting was a former dental
student, Victor Wild, a twenty-seven-year-old dropout from Los
Angeles. Wild had been attending dental school in Chicago and
had experienced a vision on LSD that involved a Christ-figure
telling Wild to gather up a group of followers and go to California. Later he associated this vision-wraith of Christ with
Robert DeGrimston.

He went to San Francisco in 1967 where he found employment servicing artificial kidney machines. He had been graduated
in 1964 from UCLA with a degree in zoology.

Evidently Wild lived at 407 Cole Street near Panhandle Park.
He was living in a commune where other ripe plums for the Process also lived. He saw the ad for the Process meeting on the
Berkeley campus and decided to attend. It was the answer to
his prayers.

After the meeting Wild brought Father Alban back to meet
the members of his commune on Cole Street. Process members
have claimed that Father Alban almost wept at the sight of such
a large group of people waiting for the word. He went Jaweh-batty
with happiness.

Victor Wild turned over his followers and his possessions including almost a thousand dollars to the Process. In due time,
after proper instruction, Wild was renamed Brother Ely.

And no one was as gung-ho for the Process as Victor Wild aka
Brother Ely.

In quick order, Processans began to flood into San Francisco.

At first the Process stayed at 407 Cole Street. But they were
eager to set up a "processcene"—a center where they might
have church "services" and proselytize. The cult acquired a
house at 1820 Oak Street where they ate and slept and did their
thing. Members would rise at 6 A.M. in silence. There was a morning invocational service of obeisance to Jehovah and Satan. Internal members of the Process wore black robes, silver crosses

and what was known as a "Mendez goat," a triangular red magical sign, the goat symbol of Satan, sewn on their cult-capes. As for a church, they located a basement at 2416 Geary Street where they poured pillars and painted the walls red and black and set up lighting as befitting a chapel.

Bob and Hecate sent Luciferans to proselytize in New Orleans, Louisiana. There is indication that the Satanists continued to operate on the beaches of Xtul, Mexico. They tried to incorporate in New Orleans as the Church of the Process of Unification of Christ and Satan, but they weren't allowed to use the name Satan.

Instead at 1:35 P.M. on January 29, 1968, under the name "The Process Church of the Final Judgment," the Process incorporated in New Orleans as a non-profit religious scam. Their address listed on the corporation papers was 1205 Royal Street.

In New Orleans, the Process rented a large house in the French quarter. The eight Luciferans from the London home church, with Alsatian dogs, began to run a coffee house and serve home-made brownies, attempting to relate to the hippie community. One night a week they ran telepathy sessions. They talked about the Gray Forces of moderation which needed to be annihilated. They also talked about some of the Process "work" on the Yucatan peninsula. There is some indication that while in New Orleans they became interested in voodoo.

In early 1968 Processans left New Orleans for California. Reports from two people, one a former Processan, say that they encountered trouble with the local authorities in New Orleans. In any case they were summoned by Robert and Hecate to San Francisco.

There developed in San Francisco considerable strife between the dope-loving, sensual Luciferans and the austere sexless self-flagellating Jehovans, according to witnesses. There was talk among the Luciferans of gang-banging the "prissy Jehovan bitches." People were accusing one another of being anti-Christ—the ultimate sin in a cult whose leader is thought actually to be Christ.

It was decided by Hecate and Christ to abandon, at least publicly, San Francisco.

Meanwhile, the DeGrimstons were in Los Angeles where they located a real estate operator named Aarons with offices on Robertson Boulevard who showed sympathy for the group. Father Christian aka Jonathan dePeyer claims that it was John Phillips who located Artie Aarons for them and that Philips, a songwriter and pop singer, offered them aid and comfort.

Once a week the Process would go around and clean up and do repairs and small construction jobs at the various properties owned by Mr. Aarons. In exchange for this work service, the real estate operator agreed to permit the Process the use of a large, two-story house at 1882 Cochrane in south central Los Angeles. It was a fifteen- to twenty-room house which now is a rest home for the aged. At that time, it was far from a rest home.

One night in early March 1968, DeGrimston called from Los Angeles and gave the Process two days to pack up and come to Los Angeles. Around March 10, 1968, a convoy of seven Process automobiles containing thirty people and fourteen Alsatian dogs journeyed toward Los Angeles. The Process moved into the South Cochrane house with all their dogs and their black turtlenecks and black pants and black capes with pictures of the devil sewn on them. In the following week they went around to various mansions, cleaning them up, in order to pay for their rent. One such mansion that the Process work group visited while working for Artie Aarons was the John Barrymore mansion, located at 1301 Summit Ridge Drive. It is a large, four-story mansion located several blocks down the hill from where Roman Polanski rented his house at 1600 Summit Ridge.

Early in 1968, a young man from Baton Rouge, Lousiana named Kirn was living at 1882 South Cochrane with a few friends of his from Louisiana. He was employed in some capacity by Artie Aarons, the owner of the property at 1882 South Cochrane.

In February of 1968 Lawrence Kirn, because of the heavy freakiness-ratio at the house on South Cochrane, got permission from Artie Aarons to move into the so-called John Barrymore mansion at 1301 Summit Ridge Drive, in the Hollywood Hills.

A few days later the Process Church of the Final Judgment moved into the house owned by Artie Aarons on South Cochrane.

Kirn remembered that Processans would come to see Aarons. "They were trying to get him to move them over to a Pasadena property he had because it was a lot bigger and they were expecting more of the followers in or something." He already had a caretaker for that property, a woman and her son, so he was loath to turn it over to the Process.

The Process spent some time at the Barrymore mansion, and may have attended parties there for show business personalities. Mr. Aarons did not actually live at the Barrymore property but rented parts of it out, and there were parties aplenty there.

In March '68, the Process held public meetings to recruit dupes at the former Digger house on North Highland. They flooded the streets to whisper about the end of the world and to hawk their magazines.

At the time, there were approximately six grades or degrees of status in the Process. The first and lowest was that of acolyte, which was the status of a person just joining up with the group. The next step was that of initiate, which lasted for about six weeks of intensive training for the nascent cultist. The next step was that of messenger, where one acquired his or her cult name. The next step was that of prophet and then priest, and finally the highest rank in the order, that of master.

The cult used the family unit as a model. Those of the degree master were called Father this and Mother that. After a few months of intensive training with the group the Founding Couple (Christ and Hecate) chose a cult name for new converts, such as Sister Sarah or Brother Reuben, and they left their legal names far behind.

Like any cult, information was not shared. Practices of the upper grades were not known by the lower punks. How convenient.

It is known that in the early phases of the initiation sexual celibacy is practiced. Further on, however, in the trek toward higher ranks, all sorts of bunch-punchings take place.

At one stage the Processans are required to enter into a pro-

longed worship of Satan, involving satanic ceremonies and blood
sacrifice. They engage in various telepathy meditation sessions
and are into psychometry, a form of group telepathy. They sit in a
circle and exchange personal objects in order to scan each others'
personal vibes and to communicate via telepathy.

Mary Anne liked giving rings to people for the psychometric
effect—a practice used by Manson, who once gave Dean Martin's
daughter a ring at Dennis Wilson's beachhouse.

Every night at midnight the inner Processans hold a worship
service for Satan, Jehovah and Lucifer. Twice a month on Wednesday nights, the Processans sit in a circle and summon the gods
Satan, Jehovah and Lucifer, who talk through the mouths of the
cult members. Oo-ee-oo.

Their vicious Alsatian dog-pack accompanied the group. It is
interesting to note that the dogs were considered members of
the group and were given special names and even oaths to bind
them to the group.

They pimped the psychedelic merchants. For instance, the
Brother Joshua and Brother Reuben, a recent convert from New
Orleans, came into a psychedelic shop on North Cherokee called
Stick It in Your Ear and tried to convert the proprietor, Ron
Mathes. They backed off when they discovered he was a prac-
ticing Gurdjieffan.

Doubtless you ask, what publications were they hawking on
the streets of Los Angeles? The main publication at that time
was issue number 4 of the *Process* magazine, the so-called "sex"
issue, which depicted on its front cover a ceremony involving
an inverted cross and a naked girl upon an altar surrounded by
hooded snuffoids, one bearing what appears to be a sword. In
another part of the front cover a long-haired young man raising
a sword is walking across a beach or a desert toward the full
moon, perhaps a reference to Process full-moon beach ceremonies. On the back cover of the *Process* magazine a large
winged skeleton is hovering atop a mound of shrieking suffering
naked bodies evidently dead or in hell. Inside the magazine contained a hodgepodge series of articles about sex, an article about

black masses and corpse violation, and various pain-streaked items of confused writing.

One place that spring where the Process distributed their literature was at the Omnibus Restaurant on North LaCienega Boulevard. A lot of the bikers that later associated with Manson hung out there. Rick, "a biker," brought in Process material to the Omnibus. Rick worked at a Shell station on Sunset across from Whiskey A Go-Go.

The Process tried to deal with the Satan-oriented bike groups but had to be content with stirring them up. One girl associated with the cult then said this: "They tried, you know, getting them [the bikers] to come to meetings and you just can't do nothing with a motorcycle rider. So they decided to use them and it would be easier to sort of incite them and get them to do what they wanted done. That is the thing, you know, figuring they were the forces of Satan."

They, or at least Brother Ely, had great visions of the bikers becoming Process assault squads. Sound like Manson?

"When it really gets going, we'll have a mobile conversion unit with messengers in jack boots on black Harleys, wearing black leather jackets with the Process symbol [an inverted swastika] in studs on the front and the cross in studs on the back." This is what a dropout from the Process says that Brother Ely told him in the summer of 1968, following the breakup of Process activities in Los Angeles.

It was the message of the unity of Christ and Satan that Manson grooved with.

"Christ and Satan through love dissolved the enmity that existed between them and the unity of Christ and Satan is what the Process is all about. They've come together to usher in the end of the world," said Brother Ely to a reporter from an English occult magazine.

The unification of Christ and Satan is exactly what Manson was getting into at that time, when the family was roaming Hollywood in the black bus.

The Process decided to make it big in the entertainment business, so they formed a rock and roll group called The Black Swan. Some Process members claim that the rock group was actually called the Voice of the Process. The Black Swan consisted of Brother Joshua on guitar—Brother Joshua had been in a pop group in London for quite a while—and Brother Benedict, the satanist, on drums. Brother Ely on flute and Brother Barnabas on string bass. Says Father Ely: "Brother Barnabas was a really good string bass player. You know, he was doing lounge shows in Las Vegas. Very professional bass player.

"We never made much money. We used to pass the hat. Sometimes we'd get a couple of bucks, but that's about all." The Black Swan, the world's only rock group that believed in human sacrifice, at least publicly, would play in various clubs and bars, generally filling in between the main acts.

"We went into a biker bar one time. They took up a collection for us. They really liked us," said flutist Ely. The biker bar was on Sunset Boulevard near the Strip.

The Process sought out rich and successful people. Father Christian of the Process has claimed, for instance, that the Process managed, in addition to John Phillips, to meet Warren Beatty and Cass Elliott. To understand this phenomenon, all anybody has to do is create a hit record or a successful film and watch the money-grubbing psychopaths come aswarming.

They approached Terry Melcher right around the time Melcher was meeting and grooving with Manson at Dennis Wilson's house on Sunset Boulevard.

It is known that the Process tried to make an appointment to see Joey Bishop who then had a talk show on ABC-TV.

It is interesting to note that there was an employee of the Joey Bishop show living at the Barrymore mansion at the time the Process was above ground in Los Angeles.

The Process members, most of whom were English citizens, had been allowed into the United States on three-month visitor's permits. Apparently they tried to get permission to stay by saying that they were students of the Church of Scientology. There was talk about a $100,000 bond that the group was going to have to put up in order to stay in the country.

In the third week of May 1968, the U.S. Immigration office in Los Angeles forwarded the Process files to New York for deportation proceedings.

At the house on South Cochran they scraped possessions together and held a garage sale to raise money. Artie Aarons, the owner of the house, complained that they sold some of his stuff also in the sale. They moved out. Some of them seem to have gone to New York to work on their immigration problems. There was talk of going to Toronto.

Others went into hiding. Some may have been staying at the Barrymore mansion on Summit Ridge when the vicious dogs went after Roman Polanski.

On Monday, June 5, an official for the Church of Scientology —evidently an English citizen—went to apply for an immigration permit to the United States. The scientology official's application was refused because "Twelve members of the Church of the Process of Scientology" had been ordered to leave the country by June and supposedly had fled the set. The Church of Scientology waxed miffed and evidently made attempts to locate the Process because as long as the Process got away with posing as scientologists, things would be grim for scientologists trying to come to America.

It is possible that the Process had a baleful influence on Sirhan Sirhan since Sirhan is known, in the spring of '68, to have frequented clubs in Hollywood in the same turf as the Process was proselytizing. Sirhan was very involved in occult pursuits. He has talked several times subsequent to Robert Kennedy's death about an occult group from London which he knew about and which he really wanted to go to London to see.

There was one Process member named Lloyd who was working as a chef for one of the large Los Angeles hotels, either the Ambassador or the Sheraton. Lloyd was around fifty years old and was always complaining of the penurious life of the Jehovans while Bob and Hecate cruised the world in jet comfort.

It is probably a coincidence that Sirhan seems to have visited a friend who worked in the kitchen of the Ambassador Hotel the day before he shot Senator Kennedy.

Sometime in mid or late June, the Process was holding internal meetings at a Hollywood motel. Some people interviewed claim that the gatherings were public recruiting meetings for new followers. But others say it was for internal Process members only. The motel may have been the Yucca Motel, a known Process haunt on Hollywood Boulevard. This may have been the motel where Robert DeGrimston caused a Process member to freak out and require sedation, merely by being in the same hotel as the member.

It will be remembered that the ace selling point of the Process, besides being the "chosen few," was that DeGrimston was Jesus Christ snuffing the world. The DeGrimstons were never seen by the underlings of the cult. Cult members were expected to have the attitude of fawning dogs wetting in fear.

This is what our trusty informant tells us about the event: "They were not allowed to see Robert because they were on the bottom floor of this one hotel and he was on the top floor and they were just all shaking and crying because he was so powerful. One of the men happened to see him and just ran back into the room and had hysterics and they had to sedate him."

"We discovered the Process group staying in a Hollywood motel . . . and reported it to immigration authorities," said Reverend Gordon Mustain, a Deputy Guardian of the Church of Scientology. Some sort of raid ensued but the wily Processans had already hit the bricks.

Some members of the Process, including Robert and Mary Anne DeGrimston, went to New York, where they set up a church there for a while. Others went underground and traveled north to San Francisco and to the Santa Cruz Mountains and evidently to King City and points here and there. Their subsequent activities will be recounted later.

Brother Ely aka Victor Wild went to San Francisco and then to San Jose, where he opened up a leather shop and became rich.

Six

The Spahn Movie Ranch 1968

Sometime that summer of '68 Manson recorded his songs at the recording studio located in the home of head Beach Boy, Brian Wilson, Dennis Wilson's brother and the producer of their albums. In Los Angeles, it was a heavy status symbol among the nouveau chart-toppers to have a fully equipped recording studio in their homes.

The Beach Boys, as is common in many rock groups, were quarreling, so Manson claims that he wrote a philosophical song for them to heal their schisms. The song was called, believe it or not, "Cease To Exist" and it was put on the album that the Beach Boys were then working on. It has subsequently been a key family song. It was the song Gypsy was singing when first this writer encountered the family.

The key words of the song "Cease To Exist," were changed by Wilson to "Cease To Resist," as if the song had to do with sexual submission. The title was also changed to "Never Learn Not To Love." The song was given a full Beach Boys' production job with those excellent back-up harmonies. Nevertheless, it was upsetting to Manson, who hated more than anything for someone to tamper with his words.

When the song was released on the B-side of a Beach Boys' single, it did not sell so well. Manson believed the song would have been a smash if only they'd left the words intact. As payment for the song Manson evidently got some cash and a BSA motor-cycle which he gave to Little Paul.

Tex seems to have been the one to hang out at Terry Melcher's house that summer of 1968. Tex and the former minister, Dean Morehouse. Dean Morehouse was a familiar sight at the parties at Melcher's house where he was well known as a dirty old man.

Manson has said that he was at the Cielo Drive house about five times and that he used to wheel around Melcher's Jaguar.

Rudy Altobelli, Terry Melcher's landlord at the house at 10050 Cielo Drive, was a successful show business talent manager. He testified at Manson's murder trial how Terry and Gregg Jakob-son were always talking about Manson and his philosophy. They were anxious for Altobelli to meet Manson, perhaps having in mind that Altobelli might guide Charlie's career. That summer Altobelli met Manson at a party at Wilson's residence on Sunset Boulevard. He listened to a tape of Charlie singing.

"They talked to me on many occasions about Manson. They wanted Dean to come and talk to me." Altobelli expressly ex-pressed to Gregg and Dennis and Terry that he didn't want to be philosophized by Manson and his group. "They were telling me about his philosophy and his way of living and how groovy it was." But Altobelli didn't dig it and was not interested in managing Manson and his crowd.

John Phillips of the Mamas and Papas recording group was ap-proached. Says he: "Terry Melcher and Dennis Wilson and the people who were living with Manson at Dennis Wilson's house used to call me all the time, you know, and say come on over, it's incredible. I'd just shudder every time. I'd say no, I think I'll pass."

Others say that Manson and some of the family in fact met Phillips, not a hard task to accomplish actually, and one witness claimed that Manson's blue bus was parked for a while in the fall of '68 at Phillips' house on Bel Air Road. It is not surprising, because if Phillips indeed came to the aid of the Process and helped them find a house, would he not have aided Manson and friends?

Things got weird for Manson on Sunset Boulevard. The family, like the hairy locusts they later admired in the Book of Revelation, had pretty much devoured the scene. Dennis Wilson's fabulous rock and roll wardrobe became community property and Manson gave away Dennis Wilson's gold records, which are given to a group whenever an album grosses over a million dollars in sales. One gold record wound up in the possession of the lady who owned the Barker Ranch in Death Valley. Another gold record evidently wound up in the hands of George Spahn's brother. This was evidently distressing to Wilson.

Around August 1, Dennis Wilson and Gregg Jakobson abandoned ship and moved to a house near the beach on Pacific Coast Highway. They left the house on Sunset open for anybody who wanted to crash, according to Jakobson.

Shortly thereafter, Dennis Wilson's manager threw Manson and crew off the Sunset Boulevard property.

Off and on throughout that fall, people showed up at the Sunset Boulevard crash-estate to pick up belongings left there. New owners purchased that property and hired a guard to defend the house and grounds from crashers in the night.

Sometime around the first week of August, homeless Charlie drove to the Spahn Ranch and asked the people who were living at the back ranch area at the time if it was okay for the family to use the outlaw shacks nearby. The so-called "outlaw" shacks, small movable huts looking like tornado-devastated motel units from the 1920's, were located near the back ranch. These shacks were evidently used as props during the heyday of the good guys versus the bad guys kind of movies shot at the ranch. Several of the residents were reluctant to let Manson stay but it was agreed to let Charlie and the guys and gals stay "for a few days," as one person remembers. The possibility of gourmet garbage, family cooking, housekeepers and the use of the family credit cards weighed heavily in the decisions to let the brigade remain. John, the previous occupant of the back ranch, had moved out but the family knew the people who had moved in. They stayed this time at the Spahn Ranch about two and a half months.

After a couple of days at the outlaw shacks near the back

ranch, Charlie, backed up by some of his silent harem waifs, approached blind George Spahn and conned Spahn into letting the family stay for a while at the front ranch on the Western set itself. They spent the first few days living in the wooden barred jail.

The deal that Charlie worked out was that the family was to cook, bale hay, help rent horses, help keep the barn, corral and grounds clean. Ultimately Charlie set up a near-nude geriatrics care squad for the elderly owner, cowboy-hatted George Spahn.

There were sixty or so horses to tend, many of them headed for the Jello factory, that were rented out for about three dollars an hour to weekenders. On the ranch, almost like a mental affliction, were thousands and thousands of Spahn Ranch horse flies which were a devouring menace, especially to vulnerable lovemakers.

George Spahn had bought the ranch in 1948. It had once belonged to silent movie actor William S. Hart.

Spahn's eyesight was failing over the years as he pursued a career owning the movie ranch and renting out horses to high school classes, etc. He had a long-time associate named Ruby Pearl who managed his ranch affairs. Ruby, according to family gossip, was a former animal trainer and dancer. She was in her late forties during the Manson era when she was seen overseeing the activities wearing a cowboy hat and riding clothes. With the family she had a wavering relationship because the family at all costs wanted to keep on George's good side. Ruby Pearl had George's ear and was constantly observing what the family was up to, except at night when she went home. Which was okay with the family, because night is when it *was*.

Ruby Pearl is rumored to have a great autograph book containing the signatures of all kinds of entertainment figures who have visited the Spahn Ranch over the years.

The Spahn Movie Ranch, as it was called, was located at 12000 Santa Susanna Pass Road, running west of the northernmost section of Topanga Boulevard in the northwest of the San Fernando Valley.

The ranch was located midpoint between the wilderness and the

city so that it was at the same time a thirty-five minute ride to
Sharon Tate's living room and also a fifteen-minute dune-buggy
ride out into the wilderness of Devil Canyon into the Santa Susanna Mountains. It was also located in heavy dope traffic country. The communes of the northwest San Fernando Valley at that
time were warehouses for the L.A. dope trade just as on the out-
skirts of any big city there are wholesale grocery and merchandise
terminals.

The Spahn Ranch was situated just in front of a creek which
cuts down from the northwest and oozes and trickles down along
Santa Susanna Pass Road behind the Spahn Ranch. There are
waterfalls in the creek which were the bathing spa of Helter
Skelter. The Spahn Ranch is backed up by bouldery hills which
climb sharply north and south. It is Grade B Western movie turf
from the 1940's. The ghosts of Tim Holt and the Durango Kid
yodel in the mountain crags.

The Western set, where movies were made, was located just off
Santa Susanna Pass Road. It was a ramshackle collection of buildings in a straight row. A boardwalk extended the length of the
set. Sleazy awnings held up by crooked posts ran the length of
the mockup cowboy main street. There was a mockup restaurant
called the Rock City Café; a jailhouse with wooden-barred cell;
the Long Horn Saloon complete with mirrors and room-length
bar and juke box; a carriage house full of old carriages; an under-
taking parlor and several other buildings including George Spahn's
small house which lay perpendicular to the right of the movie
set. All these were built in the manner of a Kansas town of the
early America. A dirt driveway connected the movie set with the
reality of Santa Susanna Pass Road. Painted movie props often
were strewn about, leaning against the haystack or corral.

It was fantasy land. But the era of the formula Western was
over, and the ranch needed horse rentals to keep it going. On
holiday weekends the ranch sometimes took up to $1000. In the
case of the Spahn Ranch, an occasional beaver movie, TV commercial, sci-fi or monster movie brought in additional amounts
of money.

Across the road from the Spahn Ranch was a bouldered, hilly

area called the Garden of the Gods. And in a slit which ran for miles up into Santa Susanna Mountains were Devil Canyon and Ybarra Canyon, which would come to be a favorite helter-skelter haunt of the family. There were several little ranches in the area. In the Garden of the Gods was something called Wonderland Movie Ranch where, after Manson got arrested for murder, the owners kept a caged jaguar in the front yard for protection from the family.

At the Spahn Ranch, the salary for the ranch hands was food, a place to sleep and a pack of cigarettes a day. Some of the ranch hands, like Randy Starr, worked as stunt men in films. Randy Starr specialized in neck drags, horse falls and various gravity-defying stunts and fancied himself a performer of high quality. Others worked the rodeo circuit. Some like Larry Cravens were attempting to be stunt men. Murder-fated Shorty Shea was a Spahn Ranch stunt man and actor who eagerly pursued a career in the movies until they killed him. The stunt men used the Spahn Ranch as a business address.

The family met a sixteen-year-old Spahn ranch hand from Simi, California, Steve Grogan aka Clem aka Scramblehead, who crashed Wilson's red Ferrari into a barn near the Spahn Ranch, trying to see how fast he could take a curve. Smasho. Ater crunching up and down the hills of Santa Susanna Pass the $15,000 machine was abandoned.

Clem became one of Charlie's righthand men. He was able to copy Charlie's guitar style almost exactly and even copied Manson's voice. Clem is now in jail, accused of decapitating Shorty Shea, the stunt man.

Manson met a young muscular Panamanian ranch hand named Juan Flynn who had been working for the Spahn Ranch since 1967 after he had fought in Vietnam. Juan Flynn would have a great effect on Manson because of Flynn's excruciating bloody battle experiences. Under the influence of LSD Juan Flynn would relive the Vietnam blood bath and scream and shriek describing in shocking detail sitting three days trapped in a trench beneath the blown-up bodies of his comrades.

On a typical day at dawn George Spahn arose and clanged the Spahn Ranch dinner bell, whereupon the hippie horse wranglers awoke to feed the horses and put them out to pasture. They gobbled breakfast and then saddled horses in preparation for possible rentals. Some were positioned in the front to guide the riders down the various riding trails. Then they had to clean the stalls and prepare the oats and hay for the horses.

The story is told how some of the family, evidently as part of the program to experience everything, reveled in horse excrement. They walked barefoot as they cleaned the dilapidated Spahn Ranch barn, shovels in hand, grokking the fullness of the green horsemush between their toes.

The family, after staying in the jailhouse barn, quickly branched out to the Long Branch saloon and the nearby Rock City Café, a mockup restaurant. These buildings shared the same boardwalk as the movie set. Charlie set up an "office" in a small building that lay on the extreme east of the Western set, a building which during the era known as Helter Skelter, became a repository for weapons.

Like a Dayglo mosaic, the family began to spread out over the woods and streams and fantasyland buildings of the Spahn Ranch. They built lean-tos, they set up tents in remote clearings in the woods. Manson would roam about supervising the construction. "All my women are witches and I'm the Devil," he told the people at the back ranch house.

Evidently they fashioned occult items for the decoration of the ranch. For instance, one person recalled seeing in a gulch by the back ranch a steer skull residing atop a stake, the skull painted with arcane emblems. Manson's very own tent was painted with an occult host of eyeballs, sun symbols and loony-tune scrawls.

The ranch hands were meat eaters but the family was more or less vegetarian, and usually ate communally in a large circle with communal bowls passed around counterclockwise. After dinner, dope was brought forth and Manson would whip out his guitar and lead the singing.

The bulk of the choff was garbage. Part of the "rent" the

family paid at the ranch was the preparation of food. To the west of the Spahn Ranch, in Simi Valley, and to the east in Chatsworth, and in fact all over the San Fernando Valley, the family made daily garbage runs. At the San Fernando Valley supermarkets they throw away fruits and vegetables that in the slums of New York would be sold as Grade A.

Even the car the killers would drive to the various murders, Johnnie Schwartz's 1957 yellow Ford, would have the back seats removed in order to receive more readily fruit crates full of throwaway food.

For instance, several miles away from the Spahn Ranch, at the edge of the concrete loading platform in back of the Market Basket supermarket in Chatsworth, lay two four by four by six-foot salmon-colored wheeled garbage bins. On a typical day, the bin on the left was packed solid with wooden crates tossed askew, cardboard boxes, celery, lettuce, sliced display melons, slightly mutant bell peppers, corn husks, pink unripe tomatoes, raggedy squashed balls of lettuce. In the right bin were hunks of fatty tissues cut from the steaks of dead cows, old peach boxes and pink-brown wavy blobs of suet. To test the edibility of much of it the only known test was the sniff test.

And there was no hesitance on the part of the soul-driven girls to get down and grovel in the gunge of large bins of rotting animal and vegetable matter in order to sort out the good from the less good.

The girls were in to using their witchiness even in preparing for the daily garbage run when they would "get a picture" in their minds as to what store would have the best gourmet garbage. That is, they would scan the void with witch-rays to locate the location of the most food-filled bins. Then they would drive there.

There were always parts of movies being shot at the Spahn Ranch. The karma of the Marlboro man cigarette commercials, some of which were made at the Spahn Ranch, must have lingered on. So they played games, the family. They played, believe it or not, Cowboys and Indians, Mexican knife fighters, flatlanders versus the hill people, Charlie Manson as Mexican bad-ass raping the stockbroker's daughter from San Diego. Be what you don't want to be; free your mind.

These games were part of the so-called Magical Mystery Tour. They were carried out like encounter group games designed to liberate the psyche. The master game was to find the real personality amid the maze of traits handed down through reincarnation and the traits given by parents and society. Whatever role the person "got stuck in" in his various game-roles, that was his real archetypal personality. Charlie called it "getting stuck in one part." Paul Watkins, for instance, got "stuck" in the part of playing the Apostle Paul—and also an entity called "daddy's boy."

Manson, over the years, has taken a more cynical attitude about his relationship with his followers at the Spahn Ranch. He said he would "play around with the kids at the ranch" and pick up a beat-up old truck at the Spahn Ranch and drive to Dennis Wilson's house all dirty. He would shower, don a few expensive clothes, grab up some money and head out for a few laughs in the luxury hills.

One girl, named Roberta, who left the group shortly thereafter, said this about Manson in the summer of 1968: "He was very beautiful in many ways and gave out lots of love." They were always hugging and kissing and making love. Ceaseless was the lovemaking. And with the remote, seemingly safe fantasyland location of the Spahn Ranch, the word really went out and people began to flock in.

Like any other youth movement, the greatest number of recruits appeared in summertime. Charlie was upset at the throngs appearing at the ranch so he threw matches to see who split.

Recalled Roberta: "Charlie was uptight cause so many people came down to the ranch, so he was doing the thing about . . . like how many of us would stay. . . . He took matches and he threw them out . . . and the direction . . ." would evidently determine who would stay or leave. "It meant that a certain amount of girls would leave and boys would stay."

Charlie would imitate someone's facial expressions if he didn't like them around. Or worse, he would sing songs about them.

The girls, with that trump card that men fear, would cut them off of the grope list.

And then there was the gorilla problem for Charlie—guys kept coming around merely for the sex. Some of the girls like Ella and Sadie, who liked to hang out on Sunset Strip downtown, were always bringing home what Charlie termed "gorillas"—guys who did not fit in.

One of the girls (Manson always accused Sadie) brought in the vehement Vietnamese clap to the ranch in summer '68. It got so bad that Charlie had to bring in a doctor to wipe it out. Juan Flynn had such a bad case of it that it took three months to clear it up.

Books were banned by Manson, the semi-illiterate prophet of doom. Manson was heedless of Revelation 1:3—"Blessed is he that readeth." But that didn't stop him from getting the girls to read to the hairy-chested pasha, books such as *Siddhartha* and, of course, the Bible.

Charlie also deprecated what he called "black slave music" and wouldn't allow Jimi Hendrix records to be played. This did not prevent Charlie from trying to sing like Nat King Cole during some of his recording sessions and from borrowing blues riffs and chord progressions for his songs.

Charlie impressed everybody with his drum-playing ability. He was "mean at the drums" according to Richard Kaplan. But his sense of pitch seemed fallible. "Let me hear a note, man," was often heard during pauses to tune, during "family jams." "It is a test of enlightenment how far you are into the drums," Charlie told Richard Kaplan.

Not only books and Jimi Hendrix records but even glasses were put on the nicht list. Charlie did not believe that George Spahn was blind. In fact, that was one of Charlie's raps: about how George was conditioned by his former wife over the years so that he slowly became blind, evidently through some sort of shrewing on the part of the wife. In fact, Charlie did not cooperate with any form of ocular disease. Mary Brunner was supposed to have possessed as many as fourteen pairs of glasses, according to Danny De Carlo, but these were banned by Charlie. No glasses.

Charlie was also out to impress with his power over animals. Picking up snakes and zapping them with the stare, allowing the Spahn Ranch horse flies to land on his mouth and swarm upon his lips. The girls claimed he conjured them not to bite him.

Later on, it was always amazing to see unconcerned family members with horse flies on their lips—horse flies that can really chomp into a lip, should they decide it.

But Charlie hankered to obtain the remote back ranch for his growing family of friends. The back ranch was a ramshackle dive consisting mainly of one large room with a stone fireplace and a large five by eight multi-paned window. The back ranch was powered by a clandestine tapping of county power lines. And for water it had the rather yucky creek water from a homemade dam created upstream. A small water pump pumped the water to a tank up on the hillside. From the hillside, a green plastic water hose brought water to the bathroom, and another green water hose stretched across the living room into the kitchen.

Like any edge-of-desert location, the Spahn Ranch seemed to gather rusty ancient hulks of various pieces of automotive and industrial equipment. It was cluttered, dusty, creepy, tarpapered metal-roofed, rusty-posted, broken-windowed, tawdry, tarnished ramshackle plexus of buildings that Charlie saw to overrun with his hemp horde. But it was remote and more importantly it was run by a weak, confused old blind man who was beleaguered on all sides by relatives and associates, some seeking to burn him, and all delivering advice gratis.

Manson finally ran the people out of the back ranch and took over.

A biker from Topanga that some of the family probably met downtown at the Galaxy Club, gave Richard Kaplan some LSD which turned out to be p-c-p animal tranquilizers, or steam, as it is known in dope-land. It is a weird mind-zapping drug. Kaplan, freaked out on the steam, stumbled into Charlie's office at the end of the boardwalk and found Charlie and the torrid twenty listening to a tape of guess who, singing. Charlie then took him

on a tour of the family camp and asked him if he would fork over
the back ranch to the family because Charlie sorely needed it.
Charlie offered to trade his witchy painted tent for it. So, tranced
on dope, Kaplan gave up the ranch. That night the family had
an orgy of celebration when they moved from the Western set
down the trail to the back ranch. To this day, Kaplan possesses
the witch tent as a Manson-mania relic first class.

As befits book-haters, the family burnt all his books including
his magical library and the young man fondly remembers seeing
his books on alchemy and Nietzsche's *Beyond Good and Evil*
going up into flames in the back ranch stone fireplace.

Meanwhile, back up north in Mendocino County, the witch
girls were finally released on August 16, 1968, on their own recognizance after fifty-five days in the slams. Charlie sent Brenda and
Squeaky north to Ukiah to bring the rest of the recently freed
girls back to the Spahn Ranch. Eagerly they fixed up the back
ranch so that the girls released would have a place to prepare
themselves for upcoming court dates, which were to occur several
weeks later in early September. When Brenda and the girls were
driving the black bus back they passed through San Jose where
the bus broke down, leaving people stranded.

Somewhere around August 20 or so, Bob Beausoleil, traveling
with his girls in northern California, called the Spahn Ranch.
There was something afoul with the pink ownership slip to the
truck George Spahn had given him so he called to clear the
matter up. It was then that Beausoleil was told the bus had
broken down in San Jose.

In June of 1968 an eighteen-year-old girl named Leslie Van
Houten was living with some girl friends at the Kalen Ranch
near Victorville and Apple Valley, California. Along came Bob
Beausoleil, who freaked the group with his throwing of knives.
He scooped up Leslie Van Houten, leaving in a 1962 blue Volkswagen offed from Leslie's roommate's stepfather. Later the VW
was de-wired and dumped in San Francisco.

Throughout the summer, Gail and beautiful Gypsy the Magna
Mater embodiment and Leslie and Beausoleil and two unknown

female Caucasians from San Francisco drove in the environs of northern California in the old black Dodge powerwagon formerly belonging to George Spahn.

Born in Cedar Rapids, Iowa, Leslie Van Houten had been the freshman class treasurer at Monrovia High School in California. She was in the Job's Daughters service organization and was active in her church choir. She was mystically inclined, became involved in the Self Realization Fellowship, became a dropout, met Beausoleil and slowly became enmeshed in the agreements and submissions and mutations that led to murder.

When Beausoleil called the Spahn Ranch around August 20 and learned that the black bus had broken down in San Jose, he drove to the rescue. Beausoleil and friends went to San Jose and towed the broken bus to a plum orchard. Data regarding events are confused at this point. Beausoleil evidently secured a new bus for the family, abandoning the old one. The new bus also was painted black.

After Beausoleil and the girls drove to the place where the family was stranded, in San Jose, there occurred some sort of jealousy squabble among Beausoleil's girl friends so he was forced to cut loose Gypsy and Leslie from his thrill pack. "About one in a hundred of the girls I'd make love to we'd go through our changes and I'd add her to the pack," he said. Little Paul and Gypsy and Leslie then drove to the Spahn Ranch from San Jose.

While the family was still in San Jose, a schoolteacher named Joan Wildbush aka Juanita picked up four hitchhikers, T. J. Walleman aka T.J. the Terrible, Tex Watson, Ella Sinder and Clem aka Scramblehead, while she was driving her shiny new 1968 Dodge van near Palo Alto, California; or so she said later to the police. She was a schoolteacher on a summer vacation, an eager young lady of Rubenesque frame. She took the four to San Jose where evidently she was persuaded to drive down to the Spahn Ranch to meet Charlie. Juanita was, in the language of police reports, a female Caucasian, height five foot four inches, blond/blue, weight 150 pounds, d.o.b. 1-21-44.

Manson must have singed her soul with the love beams during

one of those all-day love sessions because Manson drew her forthwith into the fold of the followers. She withdrew $11,000 from a
trust fund which was set up for her by her father, a New Jersey
lawyer, and turned it over to Satan. The family was overjoyed.

Around this time in South Topanga Canyon Manson located
a great new bus, a 1956 White or GMC school bus owned by
a lady in South Topanga Canyon named Mitzi. They saw the
school bus one day when Manson and Kaplan and Ouish were
whizzing through the canyon on an errand. The price was $600.
Manson used some of the newly acquired Juanita booty to pay
for the bus.

The family painted the bus light green in color and began to
outfit it for possible trips.

Dean Morehouse recalled seeing Tex and Mary Brunner driving to 10050 Cielo Drive in the new green bus, looking for Terry
Melcher, but he wasn't at home.

Another input into the mind of Manson was provided by a
religious cult, The Fountain of the World, located west of the
Spahn Ranch in Box Canyon near the Santa Susanna fire department. He was very impressed with the Fountain and spent a
lot of time visiting it.

The Fountain of the World, a religious sect dedicated to
"Peace through Love and Service" or so the sign on the hill
above the cult corner reads, was an apocalyptic Christian cult
that held public meetings every Saturday night. Several of the
Spahn ranch hands, including Shorty Shea, were associated with
The Fountain of the World. Ranch hands would attend the
Fountain's religious meetings and group song sessions. Manson
and the family occasionally attended these meetings. A black
guy named John was involved in the leadership of The Fountain
of the World and Manson several times hungered to take the
place over. The cult members wore robes and practiced celibacy.
Charlie assigned some of the girls to try to seduce the priests
of the order, evidently to no avail.

The Fountain was formed by a holy man named Krishna
Venta who died by violence. The family grooved with the violent

history of the Fountain. The religious retreat occupied subterranean chambers and caves wherein they did their thing. As the
cult progressed, dissension ensued and parties unknown blew up
the founder, Krishna Venta, and nine of his followers—with
forty pieces of dynamite placed in the catacombs. This occurred
on 12–10–58, whereafter the Fountain struggled onward and
was still thriving when Manson discovered it.

Charlie seems to have gotten the idea for his crucifixion ceremony from The Fountain of the World. There was a large rock
at The Fountain of the World that looked remarkably like a
huge skull. At the top of the "skull" was a wooden upright
cross. Fountain members, so one is told, were wont to strap
themselves up on the cross for penitential meditation sessions.
Far out.

Not far from the Spahn Ranch the family discovered an almost
secret clearing guarded by a natural surrounding wall of large
boulders. On one side of the clearing was a hill, The Hill of
Martyrdom. For upon this hilly boulder-shrouded secret clearing
was performed perhaps the world's first outdoor LSD crucifixion
ceremony.

There they snuffed Charlie, in role as Jesus, strapping (not
nailing) him to an actual rustic cross, while others, acting as
tormenters and apostles, jeered or weeped. One chosen female
was Mother Mary cloaked and weeping at the foot of the cross.

Then they fucked, evidently after some form of resurrection
service.

In August of 1968 part of the family spent about a week living at The Fountain of the World. There is talk that Manson
gave about $2,000 of the money given to the famliy by Juanita
to the Fountain.

At some point in its development, the family—particularly the
girls—began to say "Amen Amen" whenever Charlie spoke, as
if his words were divine.

Manson began to formulate obedience tests for his followers
as when he once told Sadie Glutz during a meal to go get him a
coconut, even if she had to go clear to Rio. She executed an

about-face and she trotted off to Rio. However, after a few steps he called her back. Another time, at a meeting at The Fountain of the World, when he was trying to impress the Fountain members with the obeisance of his followers, he instructed Little Paul to go spend a week on the cross—which Little Paul darted off to do but the Wizard showed mercy and called him back.

On August 20, 1968, the very pregnant Sadie Mae Glutz aka Susan Denise Atkins had a hearing in the Mendocino County Supreme Court and pleaded guilty to the 11530 H. and S. possession of pot charge. She was ordered to reappear in court on August 30 for sentencing, pending a probation report ordered by the court. An arrangement was made whereby Susan (Sadie) agreed to cop out to the pot charge and to take that guilt upon herself and Mary Brunner decided to take the acid charge so that the others then would go free.

Sadie managed to pull off a charm job on the deputy probation officer up there, one David Mandel, because he wrote a sympathetic probation report which might be called the damaged soul document. It concludes, "Your Honor, it is our opinion that incarceration for this defendant would be of little or no use to society or to herself.

"Even while she was still a minor, she was well on her way to a career of minor confidence-style operations, high styled prostitution and prostitution of herself in the more general sense, as an object of entertainment and vicarious satisfaction for other damaged souls."

The Witches of Mendocino were able to spend only a couple of days at the Spahn Ranch before they had to go to their dope trials.

Around the last part of August the girls prepared to drive north to the Mendocino County trials from the Spahn Ranch in the new green and white family bus. They drove up the coast highway through Big Sur to Mendocino County. Sadie was the driver of the bus.

On August 30, 1968, in Mendocino County Superior Court in Ukiah, California Sadie Mae Glutz was found guilty by reason of plea of guilty on violation of Section 11530 of the California

Health and Safety Code aka pot bust. And the pronouncement of sentence of sixty days in the slams was suspended and she was placed on three years' probation.

Evidently she waited around until the others had their trials on September 6, 1968. On that day Mary Therese Brunner aka Mother Mary pleaded guilty to Section 11910 of the Health and Safety Code aka LSD bust and Judge Robert Winslow sentenced her to sixty days in jail with time credited already served. Though Mary Brunner also had a favorable probation report, she was carted away to jail.

The rest of the defendants, Susan Scott aka Stephanie Rowe, Katherine Patricia Smith aka Patricia Krenwinkel aka Katie and Ella Sinder, beat the rap in Department Number 1 in Mendocino County Superior Court before Judge Winslow. Another human, one Robert Bomse, was convicted for possession of the herb.

This exercise in justice, the smashing of a cabal of hippie witches, cost the county of Mendocino considerable money. The fees for the court-appointed lawyers alone cost the taxpayers $2,999.50.

After the court hearing on September 6, 1968, Susan Atkins aka Sadie Glutz and the girls drove back down and spent a few days visiting San Jose. Susan was heavily gravid, the child due in about six weeks. Susan's father contends that Manson and Susan and several of the family spent a few days then, staying at his house. Quite a few family members also were scrounging around in San Jose in September of 1968.

One day in September '68, Manson came to Dennis Wilson's Malibu Beach house and Charlie told him and Gregg Jakobson in the style of a psychedelic Billy Graham that it was the hour of decision. It was time for them to join, or not to join. You were with him or against him. He wanted Jakobson and Wilson to choose. The family was with them, but were they?

Tex Watson of Copeville, Texas, the former sports editor for his high school yearbook, joined the family forever that fall. He gave up his wig shop on Santa Monica Boulevard and he gave to Manson his 1935 Dodge pickup truck.

Manson met quite a few interesting people at Wilson's beachhouse. One was a wealthy young lady named Charlene Cafritz. Mrs. Cafritz took some motion pictures of Manson and various of the girls at Wilson's house. Later in the fall Manson visited her for two weeks at a luxury dude ranch in Reno, Nevada, about which more later.

While Manson was in San Jose during those days after the Mendocino trials, he ran into a man named Patterson, evidently an employee of a local underground newspaper. Manson told Mr. Patterson an interesting anecdote that gave tribute to Manson's trigger temper.

Manson told Patterson, in fact astounded Patterson—because Manson seemed so much a part of flower power—that one time a few months previous Manson had chased a father and his daughter down a street with a knife in his hand prepared to cut them up and that Manson ascribed this homicidal urge to a toothache where the poison from the inflamed tooth had seeped into his brain.

Meanwhile Brother Ely of the Process had opened up a leather shop at 74 East San Fernando Street in San Jose, California with a girl friend and another couple.

Ely aka Victor Wild had, by every account, been a gung-ho Processan but evidently had found the sexual celibacy required by the Jehovan wing of the Process to be unacceptable. He drifted into the spirit of the Luciferans, where dope and sex were allowed. When the Process was forced to flee Los Angeles, various members went underground and carried on ceremonies in secret. According to various police sources and individuals interviewed, Wild maintained a group that was, in fact, a Process organization. Several friends and associates of Manson's family became a part of Brother Ely's group.

Wild still communicated with the main Process force operating in New York as the months passed, according to one of his girl friends, nameless here because of fear for her safety.

A close associate of Wild at that time said that Patricia Krenwinkel and others from the Manson family came into the leather shop and bought some sandals.

Important in terms of sleazo inputs is to remember that Brother Ely was and is, to this day, one of the most gung-ho members of the Process. Who knows how much information and Process ideas he imported to Manson and the family?

The leather shop was located in the head shop area near San Jose State College. Wild made "leathers," i.e., leather pants and jackets, for the bike clubs. Members of the Gypsy Jokers began to hang around the leather shop. One Gypsy Joker was interested in one of the girls associated with the shop and connections with the club sprouted.

Brother Ely aka Wild became so involved, in fact, with them that he was "flying the patch" of the Gypsy Jokers, i.e., wearing a jacket bearing the club's emblem, according to the San Francisco police department.

The Manson family stayed with some of the Gypsy Jokers in San Jose. Charlie told one Straight Satan that the family stayed in several houses that September belonging to the Gypsy Jokers. Later the family had Victor Wild make some leather outfits for Manson and Watson, etc.

The Gypsy Jokers were extremely violence-prone. They were among the elite of the 1 percenter bike clubs. According to his onetime friends, Wild liked to watch the violence committed by the group.

The Gypsy Jokers lived in the world of aliases, using such names as Theo, Dago, Dirty Doug, Gypsy Jack, the Thumper, Frenchy, Big Rich. Included in the group were a terminal cancer sufferer who decided to die freaky and a one-legged person named Garbage Can who had a shotgun built into his wooden leg. In September of 1968, on the Labor Day "run" to Mendocino County, Brother Ely went along and observed with dispassion according to a witness a violent sadistic "turnout," which is biker terminology for a violent gang rape. Only this girl was nearly killed—punched, slugged, gagging and puking with mouth rape, while four men held her down, punching her in the face whenever she wouldn't obey. Later, they picked her up, put her clothes on and dumped her at a road near the location of the biker frolics.

Evidently Brother Ely envisioned the bikers as being the brown shirts for the Fathers of the Process.

In August of 1968, Brother Ely and his girl friend casually watched some members of the Gypsy Jokers slam a car door repeatedly upon the head of a middle-aged man who had called one of the bikers a punk in an obscure bar in San Jose.

In December of '68, police shot and killed a member of the Jokers while twenty or thirty of the club were burning down a house on Sunnyvale Road in San Jose.

There was an interesting article which appeared in a Berkeley newspaper authored by a person named Blaine. The article purported to tell of the involvement of Charles Manson in a "death-cult" in the summer and fall of 1968 which operated out of the notorious Waller Street Devil House in the Haight district. The Devil House, it will be recalled, was formerly, during the era of flower-power, a crash-house run by the Diggers. Manson claimed to have lived there briefly.

The article describes a "trial" conducted by the cult, called the Final Church of Judgment (perhaps a garbled version of Church of the Final Judgment), wherein a person was accused of putting a curse on the Haight-Ashbury.

It is interesting to note that people who lived at the Waller Street house had, in fact, been associated with the Process. One man named Green and his wife had lived there until they accompanied the Process Church of the Final Judgment down to Los Angeles in March of '68.

It is known that there had been a group on the Haight that had set up sort of a pseudo-Process group that broke up when the actual Process arrived to set up operations. Perhaps the cult of which Manson was part was such a pseudo-Process group.

Or it is also possible that this is an actual account of an actual Process inner meeting as filtered through the memory, months later, of a magic-oriented witness.

In any case, the story is internally consistent enough with known facts to be recounted here, numbered from one to thirty.

This is what Blaine alleges:

1. He first heard of Manson in 1964 when he was a prisoner in the U.S. Medical Center, where a guy named Richard was sent, transferred from McNeil Island Federal Penitentiary in Washington. Richard had been a gobble-mate of Manson, but alleged that after Manson spurned his affections, Richard tried to kill himself, an act for which he was sent to the U.S. Medical Center.

2. Blaine met this Richard in the Medical Center prison library where Richard allegedly babbled a lot about his "lost lover" Charles Manson—referred to evidently by name and as a convict from West Virginia. Blaine remembered that Richard said this about Manson: "Charles will be a great man some day." Why? "Because he knows all about magic."

3. Blaine, after release from prison, went to the Haight-Ashbury love scene in 1967. He met Manson in the I-Thou coffee shop in 1967, not knowing who he was. He talked with Manson, Manson mentioning that he, Manson, just got out of the slams. Blaine claims then to have discovered, in the course of the conversation, that Manson was Richard's lost lover, so to speak. Manson evidently said that now he was into girls, allegedly saying: "Boys aren't where it's at. Out here it has to be girls. You can control girls easier than boys." And "Hey, I know where all that's at. And it's this way: two scorpions together would only sting one another to death." A person named Sam Tela was also involved in this conversation at the I-Thou coffee house. Manson left the shop and the two didn't meet for about a year.

4. Blaine and Manson met again in summer-fall 1968, again on the Haight.

5. Blaine claims to have become involved in a "death-cult" called The Companions of Life or The Final Church of Judgment. "The Final Church is the name Manson chose for the church he eventually founded," Blaine wrote. The church was operating in the Waller Street Ashram or Devil House.

6. Cult members would talk about Manson, saying that he was living down in L.A. on a "movie lot"—evidently the Spahn Ranch.

7. The cult evidently was led by one Father P. the 66th (666?)

aka Carl who claimed to be an M.D. and Ph.D. and a magician, and wore a mustache and was said to have been expelled from pre-Castro Cuba, to have set fire to some church in North Carolina for which he was run out of town, and to have recently returned from Damascus, Syria.

8. The cult was homosexual. There was a "crash room" where girls could sleep but women could not venture into the adyta or inner rooms of the homo-thanatos cult.

9. Manson supposedly showed up at a "medieval trial" in late summer 1968 wherein it was to be decided whether or not to put to death a former cult member named Sadyi for "committing crimes against Haight-Ashbury, against nature and for crimes against Pussycat." They accused him of (1) cursing the Haight, (2) consorting with a woman, (3) causing a demon to enter the body of Father P.'s kept cult-boy, Pussycat.

10. They said, in regard to Pussycat, that Sadyi, after leaving the cult, had re-entered the cult house one night and somehow caused a demon to possess the body of Pussycat. So, evidently, part of the ceremony required trying to drive the demon of Sadyi out of Pussycat. Poor Pussycat.

11. Manson showed up with a female Caucasian, maybe Sadie Atkins-Glutz, who had to remain in the "crash room" and could not come into the trial room. A man named Smith, a former college teacher, allegedly alleged to Blaine that Manson had been called in "to sit in" on the trial, since Manson himself had been a magical understudy of Father P. Evidently Manson was forgiven his interest in young ladies, as long as he did not bring them before the holy of holies.

12. Charlie talked about being his "own master soon." Charlie sat next to a person referred to as D.K., upon a mattress.

13. Father P., to begin the trial, donned a brown tunic and prepared his religious relics, for purification.

14. Pussycat began to fight, calling Father P. an arsonist, so that they tied Pussycat, a twenty-year-old youth, hand and foot and gagged him.

15. Father P. then started running around the room scream-

ing: "I'm God! I'm Satan! I'm Jesus!" while Pussycat on the floor was moaning behind his gag.

16. Father P. proclaimed him, Pussycat, again possessed by Sadyi so he, Father P., sent Manson and D.K. out to steal holy water from a nearby church.

17. Blaine and Smith stood guard over the trussed cult-lad while they went for the holy water.

18. Manson and D.K. returned and Father P. sprinkled the holy water on Pussycat's face.

19. Pussycat calmed down. Father P. motioned for them to untie Pussycat, but as soon as the gag was off, Pussycat began to scream. So Manson and Father P. retied Pussycat.

20. Father P. then supposedly ran to the altar, seized a large wooden "stolen" crucifix and began to beat Pussycat across the face with the crucifix.

21. Blaine then claims to have run to his microbus and grabbed a small tape recorder and carried it within the ashram to record the ceremonies, secretly.

22. Pussycat was yelling, "Help! Police!"

23. Father P. threatened to retie the gag, kicking the trussed victim.

24. Evidently it really got freaky for a while, where they got into plans to sacrifice the lad. "If you must die, Sadyi will die with you," Father P. said, allegedly.

25. D.K. got a stake and began to carve it, saying: "He must die."

26. People came to the door, stopping the action inside. Father P. then tried to remove the influence of Sadyi from the lad: "Sadyi, go away or I will take your body and destroy it with great pain. I will burn it piece by piece and I will chop it up in little pieces." Evidently he would also have had to destroy Pussycat.

27. Blaine alleges that Manson left the next day to drive back to the Spahn Ranch in the hot bus.

28. Blaine says that Father P. went down to L.A. subsequently, to see Manson.

29. Blaine alleges that later, after the death of a member of the Final Church, he, Blaine, drove Father P. and Pussycat down to the Topanga Canyon area and dropped Father and Pussycat off.

30. And as for Sadyi and his pregnant wife, they picked up on the bummer vibes and left the Haight, so at least part of the story has a happy ending. Oe-ee-oo.

The Manson Family seems to have oozed back to Los Angeles where they spent the latter part of September and October occupying the Spahn Ranch. The old black bus, the Love Bus, Charlie gave to a person named John, that friend of Sandy Good who at one time had rented the back ranch. John gave Charlie in return a pickup truck. John took the black bus and drove it to a commune called the Commune of the Sacred Heart in Oregon.

As for Beausoleil, in the early fall he and his girl-friend-wife Gail spent time in Santa Cruz, then went to Santa Barbara where Beausoleil traded his truck for a boat in which he began to live in Santa Barbara harbor. Gail split and went back to San Francisco while Beausoleil remained, living in his houseboat. Later, Manson came to the houseboat, according to Beausoleil, and asked him to come away and help to prepare the music for a record album. This he did.

Sometime in early October during a group acid trip, the family members began to fight and growl and whip one another and tried to throw each other into the burning fireplace. Further family legend has it that they finally succeeded in throwing one another into the flames and even threw a cat into the flames but the soul was so strong among them that no one got burned.

On October 7, 1968, Susan Atkins aka Sadie gave birth at the back ranch to a premature baby boy whom she named, by the eyebrow of Ra, Zezo Ze-ce Zadfrak aka Zezo. When Sadie announced to the happy family that she was about to give birth, Charlie sent Sadie to boil some water. He sent Katie to fetch a razor. Upon the arrival of the water and the razor, even with labor coming on, Charlie proceeded to shave, thus giving a lesson in cool and calm to his idolators. This was almost like a koan to the family, this "breaking the fear force"—as they termed it.

It was a breech delivery. When first the arm and then the body of the little Zezo emerged from the laboring mother, Manson, according to legend, seized the moment by halting the singing, tearing from his Spanish guitar a guitar string and tying off the umbilical cord with it.

Evidently the family sang songs to relax the atmosphere as Sadie gave birth. The family had a particular form of relaxation mantra which they sang during times of tension. This relaxation mantra was added by the Beach Boys as a coda to "Cease To Exist/Resist" during the fadeout at the end of the song.

The week following, Tex Watson and kourephile Dean Morehouse drove to Ukiah in Terry Melcher's Jaguar to pick up Mary Brunner's baby, Pooh Bear aka Valentine Michael Manson. There is an area of silence around the matter because of uptight individuals, but it is known that producer Terry Melcher allowed family members to use his Jaguar and his Standard Oil credit card. The family ran up a large bill on the credit card, using it for their important travels.

Mrs. Roger Smith, as will be remembered, had been appointed as foster parent for Pooh Bear during Mary Brunner's trouble with the law in Mendocino. Her husband had been Manson's parole officer and was then operating a drug abuse program for the Haight-Ashbury Free Clinic Annex.

On the day Tex and Dean drove to Mendocino, Mrs. Smith brought the baby to Ukiah evidently for a custody hearing, to give it back to its mother.

Seven

Death Valley 1968

Sometime in the evening of October 13, 1968, two ladies, Clida Delaney and Nancy Warren, were beaten and strangled to death with thirty-six-inch leather thongs about six miles south of Ukiah, California on U.S. Highway 101. The thongs were left tied around the necks of the victims.

Mrs. Warren was eight months pregnant and the wife of a Highway Patrol officer. Mrs. Delaney was her sixty-four-year-old grandmother who operated an antique store next to a house trailer where she lived.

This double homicide is mentioned because it is the first of a series of unsolved murders that occurred strangely enough when various family members were in the vicinity of the killings. Two of those convicted to die for the so-called Tate-LaBianca murders were in Ukiah, California for hearings of some sort the afternoon of these two hideous events, according to Officer Bob Richardson of the Mendocino County sheriff's office.

Sometime in the middle of October 1968, the family left the Spahn Ranch. Manson decided to take a trip all of a sudden to "Grandma's place" in Death Valley, California.

With the usual satins and silks and pillows and Arabian tapestries, they fixed up the new bus in the style of Manson Moorish.

The family had learned of the place in Death Valley in the remote vastnesses of the wilderness from one Cathy Meyers aka Cathy Gillies aka Patty Sue Jardin. Cathy Gillies had been raised on a ranch or piece of patented mining land located high in the bordering mountains of the Death Valley National Monument. The ranch was known as the Meyers Ranch after Cathy's grandparents who still own the property. The Meyers Ranch was located about a quarter mile east of the Barker Ranch in Goler Wash. Goler Wash, formerly a gold mining area but now an unused wasteland, is a narrow treacherous slit in the Panamint Mountains that connects the Panamint Valley to the west with the hilly high desert area near the Meyers Ranch to the northeast. She had met Manson at a ranch in Topanga Canyon and was highly tuned in to the Los Angeles music scene where she had been an ardent Buffalo Springfield groupie.

The green bus traveled somewhere for a few days, then drove to Grandma's place in Death Valley, arriving around Halloween. They proceeded north several hundred miles to a small desert town called Trona, a town plagued by crusty fallout from a potash plant. Trona is located a few miles south of the Death Valley National Monument. From Trona they proceeded north on Highway 28 about twenty miles to a long thin salt lake where they turned right and crossed over the salt lake to the Ballarat ghost town, the home of the only retail food source in the area, the Ballarat General Store.

The ghost town Ballarat—a mining settlement from the late 1800's—serves as a supply center for the local miners who still search avidly for gold. It lies on the edge of a thin, twenty-five mile salt lake at the junction of Ballarat Road and Wingate Road, two roads of the bumpity-bump variety. Having driven up the west side of the salt lake, the bus drove south on the east side of the salt lake of mushy selenite, a good salt source protected by law against encroachment or mining.

It is fourteen miles on Wingate Road from Ballarat to the slim mouth of famed Goler Wash. The bus passed an old Spanish arrastre, a burro-driven ore-munching machine from the previous centuries, but now little more than a rusted metal shaft jabbed up from the hill void.

In the distance, on the left as the bus headed south, up against the Panamint mountainside, lay the Cecil R. mine, a little man-made greed gouge in the hillside. The bus bounced past South Park Canyon, then past Redlands Canyon and then Redlands camp where Harry Briggs' Schultag Mine is located.

The salt lake ends about ten miles south from the Ballarat General Store and several miles south of the lake's ending is a white pole stuck in the dirt on the right side of the road, which marks the almost hidden access road to Goler Wash.

There the bus hung a left and began the bumpity-bump climb east toward the narrow mouth of Goler Wash and the dry water-falls which mark the way into the Meyers-Barker Ranch area.

The road at that point is impassable to normal conveyance, especially to an old bus full of hippie wanderers. The road up Goler Wash used to be the main road between Las Vegas and the Panamint Valley during the heyday of the Goler Wash gold strikes early in the twentieth century. But devastating floods in the winter of 1941 washed out the road leaving a series of sheer waterfalls. According to the local miners, Cathy Meyers' grand-father dynamited the falls so as to allow at least some sort of conveyance to pass up and down the Goler Wash road.

The bus drove past the rusty hulk of a Model T Ford and the old rear window lying near it in the dust until it reached the first waterfall where it burnt out one of its brakes and was backed down and abandoned.

The family walked the seven and a half miles from the begin-ning of the waterfalls to the Meyers Ranch, up the long, very narrow, steeply cliffed gash in the mountain where barrel cacti stick out from each cliffside like big green fingers.

Immediately the family hikers encountered the first dry water-fall. Climbing up it they reached a second waterfall and crossed a big curve to the right and encountered the third waterfall. Then, grabbing a boomerang curve to the left they came to the treach-erous fourth Goler Wash waterfall, then the fifth, sixth and seventh. Then they had to hang along some sort of sheer cliff. After that it's merely two or three miles of rollercoaster creekbed travel, whereupon they arrived in the vicinity of the Barker and Meyers Ranches.

In the journey up Goler Wash there are several cabins in which travelers may stay. All cabins in the area are always kept open. There is the Newman cabin, which is the first cabin to be encountered upon coming up the wash. There is something called the Lotus Mine, which is owned by Warner Brothers, of all people, on which there are two houses and a mine shaft perched up on the mountainside.

After about five miles, the road forked at Sourdough Springs. The left fork proceeds up north over Mengel Pass in the direction of Death Valley. And the fork straight ahead leads directly first to the Barker and then the Meyers Ranches. The Barker Ranch consists of two small cabins and a third larger main ranch building. The Barker mine itself exists further down Goler Wash high up on a precipice which is reached only by risky footpath. Scrap iron junkies have long since hauled away the cable and metal for the hopper and the mine car which lowered the ore down to the wash.

Proceeding further east on Goler Wash they encountered the Meyers Ranch, which is a well-kept series of buildings, including the ranch house, a trailer and several outbuildings. The watered ground grows all kinds of wild fruits, grapes and wild vegetables. The plants are watered by a spring shafted into the hillside. They stayed for a couple of days at the Meyers Ranch but were unable to secure permission from Meyers' grandmother to remain so the family established headquarters at the dilapidated Barker Ranch just a quarter mile west of the Meyers Ranch down Goler Wash.

A gentleman named Ballarat Bob, a local miner, had been prospecting out of the Barker Ranch for about three and a half years and was more or less in charge of the upkeep of the place. Ballarat Bob trained several wild burros for use in his prospecting expeditions. Shortly after the family arrived at the Barker Ranch, around Halloween 1968, Ballarat Bob showed up with a friend and found nude hippies ensconced in his pad. But there was nothing much he could do about it because this remote area was never patrolled by the police.

The Barker Ranch is encircled by a fence. Inside the fence is deposited forty or fifty years of desert detritus. There were several old collapsed trucks, a chicken coop, plus, upon the hill in back, an old pear-shaped concrete swimming pool.

There was part of an old mining-ball grinder on the property, the body of an old World War II plane, wing tanks and bits of ejected cockpits. There was a huge tire which Ballart Bob used to drag the wash with in order to make it a more serviceable entrance road. Constant use of Goler Wash, especially by dune buggies, sometimes made it impossible to negotiate the wash even with four-wheel drive because the spinning tires would throw all the gravel out, exposing the boulders.

The main Barker ranch house is an L-shaped building with a kitchen equipped with stove and refrigerator. The electricity was not working at the time. A generator was necessary to supply electricity because the remote ranch is fifty miles from the nearest power lines. There was a concrete bathtub and shower and a small medicine cabinet over the lavatory. Beneath was the twenty-two-inch cabinet in which Manson would be found hiding a year later. There was Ballarat Bob's bedroom in the main ranch house and a haven of mattresses to accommodate the family.

The only transportation they had was Juanita's Dodge camper and a jeep belonging to Gregg Jakobson that Dennis Wilson had given them.

It was a paradise for Manson. He could do anything in this wilderness where park rangers so seldom patrolled. It was as remote as Xtul, Mexico.

Manson became friendly with the gold prospectors who continually comb the Death Valley highlands looking for the Mommie Mine. Manson would pick up rocks from various quartz veins and show them to the prospectors. In Death Valley there are a few younger miners, some of whom smoke pot and some have long hair. It is strange on a summer night in a prospector's camp to hear conversation about rock music and gold mining and

minerals and the Grateful Dead. Some of the older miners also
knew Manson and they asked him the locations of the various
places where Manson had found promising rocks. Manson has
said that he showed some miners the sites of possible mining
claims and that they had offered him percentages of any gold
profits therefrom.

In Hopi Indian legend there was a myth called the Emergence
from the Third World wherein there was a reference to a large
underground world from which the Hopi nation emerged to dwell
on Earth's surface. Manson believed that there was some geological possibility for the existence of The Hole.

Sometime in the fall of 1968, Manson grew zealous about The
Hole. He thought The Hole was a large underground city where
he could live with his family and escape from the profligacies
of the mother culture. "I found a hole in the desert that goes
down into a river that runs north underground, and I call it
a bottomless pit because where could a river be going north underground? You could even put a boat on it. So I covered it up and
I hid it. I called it . . . The Devil's Hole."

It is not known who or what inspired him to believe that a
subterranean paradise was waiting for him and his followers.
Perhaps it was a vision on an acid trip. Who knows? There
evidently have been claims made in the past that there is a huge
city-sized cave under Death Valley fed by the underground
Amargosa River.

Death Valley, the claim goes, is a geological "graben" developed along formations that could conceivably house a large
open underground area. But not certainly a place with chocolate
fountains and food-trees and a race of people already living there,
as they came to believe.

The family claimed even into 1970 that there are places on the
edge of Death Valley where there are openings to the Amargosa
River. The family would go out on Hole patrol to try to find hidden openings to The Hole because they felt there was some sort
of occult conspiracy to keep secret the entrance to their paradise.
Manson seems to have claimed that he had personal access to The

Hole and was able to go down there, or so he got his followers to believe.

One such entrance to The Hole was thought to be the so-called Devil's Hole in the northwest triangular corner of the Death Valley National Monument where the monument extends briefly into Nevada. Devil's Hole, fenced off from potential visitors, is a baleful pit full of water, and inhabited by blind fish according to the family. A couple of skin divers had drowned several years previous trying to touch bottom.

For anyone interested, to get to Devil's Hole you proceed to Death Valley on Route 127. Then drive north to a town called Death Valley Junction. Hang a right there and proceed to Ash Meadows Rancho. Then grab a northish county road across the California-Nevada line to The Hole. Manson considered that this Devil's Hole was the key to *The* Hole.

For three days, abject and humble, at the edge of The Hole, Manson meditated and contemplated the meaning of this bottomless well-pit. Then it dawned on him that the water in Devil's Hole must be the door or the blocking mechanism preventing entrance to the Underworld, so that, were the water sucked out, the Golden Hole of chocolate fountains would be revealed.

He consulted a pumping company to see about pumping The Hole dry and supposedly received a bid for the job of $33,000.

Manson received, on the metaphysical plane, further guarantees of the existence of such a hole in key passages of Revelation. Wasn't the world hip to references to locusts proceeding from the bottomless pit—the *puteum abyssi*—as foretold in Chapter 9 of the Book of Revelation?

There was a new persona developing for Charlie: The Devil from the bottomless pit beneath Death Valley. Oo-ee-oo.

Sometime in the desert that fall Manson undertook a prolonged nude meditation period in the high desert chill, discovering death. Indeed it was a legend among Manson's followers that he experienced his "final death" when he picked up a live rattlesnake in Death Valley National Monument. Paul Watkins tells how he and Charlie encountered a rattler one day and Charlie persuaded

Watkins to sit right down in front of it, beam it out with a snake.

In his wilderness revelation, Manson seems to have suffered a typical experience that thousands have encountered, say, on psilocybin: that of the experience of submission to Death.

Charlie always talked about a final flash he received while meditating in the desert:

"Once I was walking in the desert and I had a revelation. I'd walked about forty-five miles and that is a lot of miles to walk in the desert. The sun was beating down on me and I was afraid because I wasn't willing to accept death. My tongue swoll up and I could hardly breathe. I collapsed in the sand.

"I looked at the ground and I saw this rock out of the corner of my eye. And I remember thinking in this insane way as I looked at it, 'Well, this is as good a place as any to die.' "

Then he started to laugh. "I began laughing like an insane man, I was so happy." Then he got up "with ease" and walked ten miles forthwith and reached safety.

Manson developed in Death Valley a great fondness for the coyote, the predator's predator. Nothing is more vicious and overbearing in the pursuit of varieties of food than the coyote.

He began to applaud a state of mind called here coyotenoia. Here is the basic Manson quote on coyotenoia: "Christ on the cross, the coyote in the desert—it's the same thing, man. The coyote is beautiul. He moves through the desert delicately, aware of everything, looking around. He hears every sound, smells every smell, sees everything that moves. He's always in a state of total paranoia and total paranoia is total awareness. You can learn from the coyote just like you learn from a child. A baby is born into the world in a state of fear. Total paranoia and awareness. . . ."

Gregg Jakobson wanted back his jeep that Wilson had given to Manson. So on November 24, 1968, Jakobson and Dennis Wilson drove to Death Valley to retrieve the jeep. Jakobson's jeep was broken down somewhere in the vastness of Goler Wash so they

towed it out to Trona to be fixed, taking Manson with them.
While driving in Goler Wash, Jakobson ran over a spider, which
made Manson angry. Better a human, he contended, than a spider.

Jakobson and Wilson took Manson with them out of Death
Valley to L.A. perhaps to celebrate the impending release of the
song written by Manson.

Two weeks later Jakobson returned to Goler Wash in a
motorcycle to visit and broke his bike on the treacherous terrain.
So he went back to Trona, picked up his jeep which had just
been repaired and threw his motorcycle in the back and went
back to Los Angeles.

On December 8, 1968, Capitol Records released the Beach
Boys' single, "Bluebirds Over the Mountain" "Never Learn Not
To Love (Cease To Exist)." Charlie Manson was on the charts.

A more important event occurred, however, on December 7,
1968. Capitol Records released the white-jacketed Beatles double
album containing among the thirty songs, such gems of snuff as
"Sexy Sadie," "Rocky Raccoon," "Blackbird," "Revolution 9"
and "Helter Skelter"—all found by Manson to foretell his con-
quest of the World.

Manson felt able to twist and interpret the lyrics and production of these Beatles' songs as if they were holy writ. After Wilson
and Jakobson took Manson out of Death Valley in late November
1968, Manson seems to have stayed on Topanga Lane at the
mouth of Topanga Canyon by the ruins of The Spiral Staircase.

The Spiral Staircase house where Manson and crew had stayed
a year previous had subsequently been demolished. Manson was
living in a blue bus parked by the ruins.

Manson was seen at a Thanksgiving dinner at Layne Wooten's
house in Topanga Canyon on November 28, 1968.

In early December 1968, Manson sent ace-acidassin Bruce Davis
on a trip to England where he spent around five months, including
considerable time at the London headquarters of the Process.

Little Paul described it as being a go-to-Rio-and-get-me-a-coco-
nut scene where Manson told Davis to take a trip around the
world and report back. Whatever the case, Bruce Davis, with two

traveling companions, journeyed to England by way of North Africa.

There is also a story flitting about that Davis took a collection of 500 silver dollars over to England to sell. People that have intimate knowledge of the Tate-LaBianca case will see an interesting possibility if in fact, Davis did transport the silver to Great Britain.

In London, Davis approached the Church of Scientology to pursue courses of study. He was employed by the Church of Scientology for a short time, working in their mail room. The Church of Scientology fired Davis after a couple of weeks when he wouldn't stop using drugs, they say.

According to a homicide investigator extremely close to the case, Bruce Davis then began to hang out with the Process Church of the Final Judgment at their Mayfair townhouse. Later, when he returned from London to the Spahn Ranch, Davis was talking and whooping about the Hitler-loving satanic organization.

In the summer of 1968, Processeans flooded the New York underground where they sought out writers, editors and musicians as potential converts. They hounded Paul Krassner, editor of the Realist for days trying to get Tim Leary's home phone number for a conversion attempt. They claimed to Krassner that they only had to be physically present in a street scene to cause street riots.

For a while, Robert and Mary Ann DeGrimston aka Christ and Goebbels-Hecate, lived for a while with a lady named Godard in Brooklyn while the main body of caped Process members lived in a building on 12th Street in the Lower East Side.

The Process set up a chapter of their so-called "church" at 28½ Cornelia Street in Greenwich Village where they held more or less public meetings. With their black capes and black garb they flocked about on the streets near the Fillmore East. Once poet Allen Ginsberg was attempting to purchase an egg cream at the Gem Spa luncheonette at 2nd Avenue and Saint Marks Place when several Processoids approached him, giving forth the there is no good/ there is no evil routine. When Process members were encountered they usually announced that they were on the way to California.

In August 1968, Robert DeGrimston-Moor dictated his book, *A Candle in Hell.*

The Process continued their feud with the Church of Scientology. Once Father Aaron Tubal-Cain interrupted a scientology meeting in N.Y. to try to hold an auction of E-Meter parts. An E-Meter is a form of electrogalvanometer used by the Church of Scientology in the training of their converts. In the early period of the Process, they also used the E-Meter but later abandoned its use.

In the summer of 1968, the Process told at least four people interviewed by this writer that they were traveling to California, yet in interviewing people up and down the state of California, there is only the faintest indication that they were there.

It is known that the Process had, among its "chapters" three closed chapters, the locations of which are kept secret. In California there were Process activities in Marin County, Santa Barbara, The Santa Cruz Mountains and the Santa Ana Mountains.

It is regarding activities in the Santa Cruz Mountains south of San Francisco beginning in late fall 1968, that ghastly reports of occult sacrifices have been received. The same people indicate that the Process stopped using the name Process and began to use other names.

Police began reporting finding exsanguinated animals and decapitated animals, in the remote Santa Cruz wilderness. One human has recounted witnessing ritual executions in a grove on Route 17 south of Santa Cruz. The ceremonies involved use of a portable crematorium to dispose of the bodies, a wooden altar adorned with dragons and a wooden morgue table. There were as many as forty people in attendance at these sacrifices. The instrument of sacrifice was a set of 6 knives welded into a football shaped holder. The heart was eaten.

The group was called the Four Pi movement, and was dedicated to the "worship of evil." Later, the group moved ceremonies to the Santa Ana Mountains south of Los Angeles where they continued their barbaric abhorrencies. The leader of this human sacrifice group, a large man, held the cult title Grand Chingon. It was not Manson.

However, at least five times in this writer's presence Manson has been called The Grand Chingon or the Head Chingon by members of his family.

According to interviews with individuals in New York who had contact with the Process chapter in New York in late 1968, part of the Process returned to England in December and others spread out across America on the sly, and open activities in New York were ceased. By early 1969, the Process was operating in New Orleans openly. For secret activities in the Los Angeles area, there are indications that the sacrifice group was running pre-arranged obscure ads in the personals sections of underground newspapers to inform members of upcoming nocturnal assemblies.

Eight

From Death Valley to Canoga Park

Voityck Frykowski and Roman Polanski went to school together in Lodz, Poland.

Evidently Mr. Frykowski's father financed Polanski's first film, *Two Men with a Wardrobe.* He also served as an assistant on several of Polanski's productions. He had been married twice, once to a well-known writer Agneski Osiecka. He had a son Bartyke Frykowski, now fourteen and living in Poland. He was an educated, intelligent man who formed part of an energetic circle of artists and intellectuals, some of whom defected to the West.

Sometime in the latter half of 1967 Mr. Frykowski split from Poland and moved to Paris where Roman Polanski encountered him and gave him some financial help and encouragement.

Polish writers and intellectuals who have fled the confining atmosphere of the homeland help each other considerably. They keep in touch, aid one another's careers and even celebrate Polish holidays together.

Voityck Frykowski was thirty-seven years old when he died.

In early 1968 it was arranged that Voityck Frykowski come to the United States to live. He was diligent in his study of the American language and kept daily notebooks learning the nuances of American-speak. He was interested in poetry and evidently was writing verse during his stay in America. He was viewed by his writer friends such as novelist Jerzy Kosinski as a perceptive critic of their work.

Sometime in January of 1968 Mr. Frykowski met Abigail Folger at a party in New York City. Miss Folger was born in 1943 and was raised in the closed tradition of San Francisco society. A talented pianist, she was also interested in art and painting. She was educated at the Catalina School for Girls in Carmel, California and at Radcliffe College. After graduation from Radcliffe, she did graduate work at Harvard.

Her father was the chairman of the board of the Folger Coffee Company, now a subsidiary of Procter and Gamble. Miss Folger's private fortune was extensive. A close friend estimates that her personal income after taxes was around $130,000 per year.

In 1967 she was employed by the University of California Art Museum in Berkeley. In the fall of 1967, Miss Folger came to live in New York City. After working for a magazine she worked one of the best avant-garde bookstores in the world, the Gotham Book Mart on Forty-seventh Street.

Miss Folger met Jerzy Kosinski at a party when she was working at the Gotham Book Mart. Subsequently, Mr. Kosinski introduced her to Voityck Frykowski. They were both fluent in French and he was eager to learn the American language.

In the fall of 1968 Abigail Folger and Voityck Frykowski drove a Drive-a-Car across the United States to the West Coast. They moved into a house at 2447 Woodstock in Los Angeles, a residence located off Mulholland in the Hollywood Hills.

She was involved in the struggle for racial equality. Miss Folger worked as a volunteer social worker for the Los Angeles County Welfare Department from sometime in fall 1968 till March 31, 1969. Her place of employment was south central Los Angeles, where evidently she aided black ghetto children.

In Los Angeles, Miss Folger and Voityck Frykowski stepped into the world of movie actors and actresses, friends of Sharon and Roman. They also acquired friends of their own, including friends of Charles Manson and the family, one of whom, a lady singer who later starred in a video-bugger film classic, lived on a nearby hilltop.

Miss Folger's money attracted people. More than one aspiring film producer approached her to contribute money to film projects. She met hair tycoon Jay Sebring and he persuaded her to invest in his empire of barber shops and hair-care products. Through Mr. Sebring, they met others in the interlocking circles of film-fame.

In late December 1968, Miss Folger made arrangements to purchase around $3500 worth of stock in Sebring International.

In December of 1968 Charlie and three girls drove in an old Studebaker to an exclusive dude ranch near Reno, Nevada where they spent two weeks as guests of Charlene Cafritz, whom Manson had met the previous summer at Dennis Wilson's beach home. Mrs. Cafritz was in Reno logging enough time to get a divorce.

Manson seems to have had a great effect on the young lady in terms of material detachment. As a result of her divorce settlement, the lady was left with a fortune in excess of two million dollars. This sum she spent in something like ten months, aided in early phases of her spend-frenzy by guess who.

Sometime toward the end of December, a friend named Warnick drove the young divorcée back to Los Angeles from Reno. In January '69 Mrs. Cafritz visited New York where she spent $92,000 during that month.

At one point, Manson told the young lady that he wanted a blue Fleetwood Cadillac. The young lady erred and purchased instead a fire engine red Cadillac and he told her to take it back. She also evidently purchased a number of thoroughbred horses which Charlie gave away for her.

She bought him a number of items, including a chain saw which he gave to some people who were cutting wood for a livelihood and even a quantity of fly spray to help snuff the huge horde of Spahn Ranch horse flies.

Mrs. Cafritz took numerous motion pictures of Manson and the family in Reno which no one seems to want to discuss. Mrs. Cafritz was a friend of Sharon Tate and Terry Melcher and many others associated with the oncoming tragedy.

There is great confusion about where certain family members

were living in the late '68 and early '69. They seem to have been scattered here and there, some in Death Valley, some in Topanga Canyon, one or more with the Process in England, and some in Laurel Canyon in the Hollywood Hills.

One former Manson family associate claims that a group of four to six family members lived on Laurel Canyon Boulevard in the log cabin house once owned by cowboy-actor Tom Mix. They lived there for a few weeks, in late 1968, in a cave-like hollow in back of the residence.

At the end of the year there was a savage, hideous murder in the Hollywood Hills of a young girl who may have been associated with the family.

Marina Elizabeth Habe, seventeen years old, was home for a vacation from the University of Hawaii where she was a student. On Sunday, December 29, she had a date with John Hornburg, age twenty-two and an old family friend. Later that night Eloise Hart, her mother, at 3:30 A.M. heard noises in the driveway of their home. She looked through the window and saw a man standing beside Marina's red sports car. A black sedan was in the driveway, Mrs. Hart remembered.

The man said "go"; he got into the sedan and drove quickly away. There seemed to be two people in the car. John Hornburg told the police this: "That among other things they visited a club on the Sunset Strip; that after their evening Miss Habe returned with him to his parents' home, changed from evening dress into capri pants, a white turtleneck sweater, brown coat and drove home in her car."

She was found on New Year's Day in thick underbrush off Mulholland Drive, 100 feet west of Bowmont Drive. Only maniacs could have wreaked such hatred upon a human. Contusions in eyes, slashes in throat and heart, burns inflicted, raped, nude, except for a shoe. According to one former family associate Marina Habe was known by members of the family.

Manson seems to have attended a New Year's Eve party thrown for the cast of *Hair* by John and Michelle Phillips at their home in Bel Air.

Meanwhile, back on Cielo Drive, Terry Melcher began to

move his belongings out over the holidays, and in January of 1969 he moved into his mother's beachhouse at 22126 Malibu Beach Road in Malibu, California.

Manson returned to Death Valley in January 1969. Early in January 1969, Little Paul Watkins led a deputation into Las Vegas, Nevada from the Barker Ranch in order to trade Juanita's red Dodge van, which was unsuited for traversing through the wilderness terrain, for a 1953 four-wheel drive International Scout jeep.

While Watkins and Juanita were in Los Angeles Charlie was having the green and white bus towed out of the mouth of Goler Wash by a local fireman to have a brake shoe fixed. They had learned of a long, looping route of a couple of hundred miles which would lead them into the Barker Ranch from the north. So Charlie drove the bus full of nascent creepy crawlers north through Emigrant Pass and around Stovepipe Wells, up around the Tucky Mountain area and down the middle of Death Valley where they stopped off at the small town of Shoshone. The towns-people remembered them with some amazement at the thought that anyone could drive a school bus into the wilderness.

Out of Shoshone the bus drove west past vast pile-hills that looked like giant oblong loaves of millions of huge burnt match heads. They drove past Salisbury Pass, Jubilee Pass to the dry Armagosa River. They drove past Ashford Mills and turned left going northwest on the first gravel road passing a sign "Warning: Road Not Patrolled Daily." (Gurdjíeff said not to trust maps of wilderness roads.) One's map of Inyo County indicates that the turn-off is east of Ashford Mills whereas in reality the turn-off is west of the Mills. Although by now the road may have been changed, for a road in those voidal stands is whatever the county road grader creates in his quarterly scraping of the roads.

From the Death Valley floor, the bus climbed up a long ribbon leading up the east side of the Panamint Mountains.

The bus made another left at the Wingate Jeep Trail past a sign "Warm Springs, 4 miles, Anvil Springs, 18 miles."

The bus was, from that point on, as it oozed into the mountains, inside the Death Valley National Monument, passing a sign with white letters on a black background: "Firearms prohibited."

"Charlie could drive like a mother fucker," Clem commented when he was crossing the same road a year and a half later. It was on this trek over the wilderness down to the Barker Ranch that several miracles were alleged to have been performed by Charles Manson.

The green and white bus had to go over unbelievable creek-bed roads, twisting and creek gravel. At one point they broke a wheel. They ripped the bottom of the bus. Clem claimed that Charlie levitated the bus over a creek crag. And the girls, naturally, often had to bridge road pits with rocks and planks.

Gradually as the road headed up into Warm Springs Valley it began to coincide with the creek bed. Four miles in lay a cluster of talc mines, huge mounds of baby powder on the hillside. At the warm water springs, the bus passed a cluster of trees, gasoline pump and trailers for the miners.

The road got worse immediately as the bus passed the talc mines, evidently because the trucks hauling the talc to market used the road out rather than the road in toward Mengel Pass, so only prospectors and campers used the road which passed the black and white Striped Butte.

Bounce bounce was the experience for the family as it entered the strewn chaos. The road forked and the sign, "Jeep Road— Butte Valley" pointed to the left. To the right the road curved around to more talc mines. Packs of wild burros roamed the Striped Butte Valley and coyotes prowled openly, their thin noses rising above the greasewood bushes.

The bus rose from the high valley floor over Mengel Pass somehow, and then bumped another five miles or so down sacred Goler Wash to the Barker Ranch. There they dwelled.

Somehow, as of a miracle, the bus arrived at the Barker Ranch where to this day, its engine removed, it reposes at an angle facing Ballarat Bob's chicken coop. Upon its back fender some sardonic individual had placed a red and white sticker saying, "America. Love it or leave it."

Meanwhile, in sacred Goler Wash, things started getting brrr in the high desert. A chill swept upon nudism. Winter was creeping in.

Manson left to find more suitable habitats, taking "quite a few people with him"—as Brooks Posten recounted it.

Apparently there was a housing problem in early 1969. Something was preventing their return to the Spahn Ranch.

Susan Atkins spent some time living at a house on the Buchanan Ranch in Topanga Canyon. She lived with a man named Rory. This may have been the time when Manson threw Sadie-Susan out of the family and took baby Zezo Ze-ce Zadfrak away from her.

Friends of Sadie at the Buchanan Ranch were scheming how she might reacquire Zezo. It was interesting that, according to observers, Sadie was actively putting Manson down and asserting her independence. Until one day Manson appeared at the top of a ridge above Sadie and yelled "Sadie!" motioning her to come, whereupon Sadie Glutz immediately returned to the family.

Somehow Charlie obtained a house at 21019 Gresham in Canoga Park, California in the San Fernando Valley, not too far from the Spahn Ranch. They occupied the house and a small guest house to the rear of the property where they set up their musical equipment and their commune.

21019 Gresham is a sleazy red-roofed house with columned porch and a small little green "guest house" behind it. To the left are some horse stalls or stables behind a double garage.

Down the dirt road toward Devonshire Street are the Island Village apartments where various associates of Manson lived.

Cutting down San Fernando Valley from the hills to the north is Brown Canyon wash, more like a huge paved storm sewer. This wash ran just to the west of the house on Gresham, and Manson used to drive his dune buggy down the wash to the Gresham house from the Devil Canyon area, the home of Helter Skelter.

Because Manson allegedly was living in the Death Valley Hills, his federal parole supervision was shifted from Los Angeles to

San Bernardino. On January 17, 1969, Manson's new federal parole officer attempted to pay him a visit in Death Valley. He got as far as the Ballarat General Store and there he learned from an old miner that he would have to walk seven miles up the waterfalls if he wanted to visit the family camp. No thanks.

After a week or so at the Canoga Park house on Gresham Street, Manson sent a squad up to the Barker Ranch to remove the rest of the family. These people were left behind at the Barker Ranch to take care of things: Brooks, Juanita and Gypsy the violinist.

A week later, the International Scout jeep, for which Juanita and Watkins had traded her Dodge camper in Las Vegas, arrived in Goler Wash to pick up the remaining three and took them to the house on Gresham Street in Canoga Park.

From around February 1 to 20, 1969, they all stayed at the sleazo cottage on Gresham.

Specific inputs to specific activities of the group at this time are scant but there are ample depositions concerning the famous "Death Mockup Party" that occurred at the house on Gresham Street on the day that Brooks, T.J., Juanita and others returned from the desert in the new jeep.

That was the time that the people arrived from the desert, attired in leather, tanned and trim of form. And they were all sitting around "mocking up snuff," postulating the event of their own death so as to experience it mentally. Sound like fun?

A part of the group was stoned and were sitting in the middle of the room. They had begun to write a song and had left off the project. Charlie was sitting in the midst of the gathering and the topic was the ever-present subject of snuff. Charlie said, "Die," so all lay down and pretended they were dead. Bo started screaming "Charlie"—and then "Oh-h-h-h-h!" Paul Watkins testified to the following concerning this famous party: "I was listening to Charlie say die." Watkins testified that he tried to think of a way to die but he couldn't so when Charlie said, "Die," Watkins lay down and "acted like I was dead." Everybody else did and Bo was screaming and Charlie was sitting in the middle of the room moving the fingers, talking about the confusion in the air, how fine it was.

Evidently Brooks Posten was able to go into a trance on command and Charlie commanded him to die. So he died. He went into a trance that lasted three or by some accounts five days. As he lay wasting on a couch in the living room the girls would clean up after his natural functions and even Charlie would try to pull him out of it but he couldn't. So on the fifth day, lo! Charlie commanded that his very own sacred embroidered gray corduroy vest be placed beneath Brooks as a symbolic diaper. Horrified with the prospect of Jesus' very own vest being used as a diaper, Brooks revivified himself from his trance. Or so it is told.

During this three-week stay at the house on Gresham occurred the famous Manson gobble-miracle. Zonked on lysergic acid, Manson was being blown by a hysteria-prone young adept named Bo. Bo was a small masochistic girl with thyroid eyes and long black hair, one of Charlie's favorite pain-targets.

The legend continues that during the gobble the girl went nuts and, all in one incision, bit in twain Manson's virility. Then, through the miracle of magic, Manson, they claim, at once healed his tragic amputation and continued onward.

Meanwhile back in the Hollywood of reflections, on February 18, 1969, Charles Manson checked in with his parole officer and announced that he was living in Los Angeles. His parole supervision then was changed back from the San Bernardino office to Los Angeles. He told his parole officer that when the snow melted in the high mountains, he would be returning to the wilderness.

Also, on February 18, 1969, a DC-3 "Gamblers' Special" loaded up with a drunk pilot and thirty-five gamblers crashed into the snows of Mt. Whitney near Bishop, California in a flight from Hawthorne, Nevada to Long Beach, California. According to the tale, the plane remained buried in deep snow until summer when the snow melted. The plane and dead occupants were located but supposedly all valuables and cash had been stripped from the gamblers, booty valued at a quarter of a million dollars or so.

The finger of blame has pointed naturally at Manson and his dune buggy battalion. One defected family member says, though it is hard to believe, that pieces of the crashed airplane were used by the family to adorn their dune buggies.

Around February 20, 1969, Charlie sent a force back to Death Valley consisting of Brooks, Juanita, T.J., Bo, Mary Brunner and a female Caucasian named Sherri, probably Simi Valley Sherri.

There were heavy rains in Goler Wash during these days, causing a flash flood, and the water rose up to the ranch buildings. Shortly after the floods, Sherri and Juanita and others went into Shoshone, California and perhaps to Las Vegas to get supplies. On the way back they stopped in Shoshone where occurred the notorious dope-smoke involving the local deputy sheriff's daughter.

The Inyo County sheriff's deputy stationed in Shoshone, California lived in a trailer camp near the town. The deputy had a teenage stepdaughter. She seems to have become friendly with members of the family. When Sherri and the others came through the town, they stopped at the trailer and were entertaining themselves visiting the deputy sheriff's young daughter. Little Paul remembers the event like this: "She was up there in the bushes with the family, smoking a joint and the sheriff comes up and asked, 'What are you doing?' His stepdaughter replied, 'Oh, smoking a joint, Daddy.'" Waxing furious, the deputy went into action. He sent his stepdaughter away forthwith to live with relatives and then mounted a raid against the Barker Ranch, the alleged dope source.

Somebody called Charlie down in Los Angeles and he immediately sent a big van up to the Barker Ranch and took everybody out except Juanita and Brooks, who were ordered to pretend to be married. Evidently the thinking was that appearing as a married couple would ward off any form of arrest.

Sure enough, the deputy and another deputy and some Death Valley National Park Rangers came to the Barker Ranch asking about marijuana. No, no, they didn't know anything about marijuana. So they beat the bust.

Juanita and Brooks had enough food for a one-meal-a-day scene for two weeks. When the rest of the family left they told Juanita and Brooks that they would send for them shortly. Manson et al. were not to return to Death Valley for six months, after the murders.

Nine

Helter Skelter

Around the first of March 1969, two miners named Paul Crockett and Bob Berry arrived at the Barker Ranch to find Brooks Posten and Juanita living there following the marijuana raid. Bob Berry had visited the Barker Ranch area the preceding autumn and evidently had enjoyed himself. Crockett, an articulate gentleman in his fifties filled with the lore of scientology, left his home in Carlsbad, New Mexico to come to Goler Wash for the purpose of discovering gold.

In the ensuing weeks, Bob Berry and Juanita began to have an affair, culminating in their marriage and her leaving the clutches of Manson.

Bob Berry and Paul Crockett began to stay in the small tar-roofed cabin to the left of the main Barker Ranch house. The two began to scour old mining sites in the Panamint Mountains, Wingate Wash and south into Dora Canyon, in order to hook into the mother lode. By night Berry and Crockett would sit and chat with Brooks and Juanita, and later Paul Watkins when he returned from Los Angeles. One thing that struck the miner/metaphysician, Paul Crockett, was the enormous fear that Paul Watkins and Juanita and Brooks had for this mysterious Charlie.

It came to pass that Paul Crockett hired, for board, Brooks Posten to help haul ore down from the hillsides. It is common for miners to engage someone to bring weekly shipments of supplies via jeep to their claims or their camps from supply depots such as the Ballarat General Store. Crockett upped his food order to accommodate the thin young trance-prone Texan Posten.

They would go out by day to inspect old mine sites, old diggings and outcroppings, hauling ore samples back down to the ranch when they returned at dusk. They would crunch up the samples in a rock-breaking machine that could chew the mineral into forty pieces per cubic inch. Then they would pan the gold out to see how much was in the samples.

Sometime in the spring Little Paul Watkins traveled to Death Valley where he visited Juanita and Brooks and met Crockett. Little Paul returned to the Spahn Ranch to announce the horrible news that "scientologists" had taken over the Barker Ranch— news which triggered off a fearful reaction within the family.

Watkins persuaded Charlie to let him go back up to the Barker Ranch, perhaps to keep an eye on the so-called scientologists, looking for the mother lode. Several times during these spring months of 1969, Manson and the others tried to drive up to the Barker Ranch, but it always seemed that something went wrong. Witch-beams were thwarting them? Or were the so-called scientologists keeping the family away? Paul Crockett certainly didn't do anything to dispel this illusion that he was preventing the family from coming up there by means of his mental powers. In fact, he was promoting the idea that he could establish a magical warp to prevent Manson from returning to harm those remaining in Death Valley. The family seems to have begun to believe that occult beams and powers were attempting to prevent them from returning to holy Devil's Hole. Even Manson, ever a beam-phobe, evidently held some belief in Crockett's power.

Paul Watkins, so he claims, decided at the advent of various murderous schemes to get out of the family. So he placed himself in the tutelage of Paul Crockett: "He [Crockett] knows how Charlie set up his whole thing and I went to Paul, 'Paul, help me out of this!' Blam! Just, like, I was hung right up in it. And using processing, and looking at what is, I was able to be free from it. But old Clem, Sandy, Lynn and Gypsy, there ain't no way they can get free from that. I mean they could snuff Charlie out, and they're still stuck to him."

"Is the power that great that held you there?" he was asked.

"It's by agreement," he replied. "You see I can't do anything to you without your agreement, without your saying it's okay. But to someone who's so asleep, and so unconscious, they'll agree to anything—" Then it's a different story.

"I got unhooked from the family with just a few simple words. I got Charlie to agree to a few things and then just walked right out."

Once that spring Sadie and a member of the Straight Satans motorcycle club tried to go up to the Barker Ranch and met with failure. Another time, Charlie Manson himself, the Devil, loaded up the GMC truck and trailer with two dune buggies, but the truck broke down not far from the Spahn Ranch and the mission was aborted. So the legend grew that this guy Crockett up there was using freak-beams to prevent the family from returning to the Barker Ranch.

By the middle of January 1969, the new Beatles' white double album had already grossed twenty-two million dollars in the United States alone. The white double album was the first cultural instruction from the Beatles since the album *Magical Mystery Tour* a year previous. Even its all white cover was symbolic to the family—all white, dig it?

Something freaked Manson out in early 1969 enough for him to prepare for the end of Western civilization. He had already talked about an impending Armageddon of some sort but he had always preached "submission is a gift, give it to your brother." That is, walk humble beneath the violence.

Along oozed Helter Skelter.

Manson had a hypnotic rap about how the modern blacks were arming themselves, how he, Manson, had talked to blacks in prison and he had learned of heavy arms caches here and there.

He had a way of stirring up paranoia that was legendary. Goose

bumps shivered the back of the arms during his whispered superstitious lectures on karma and imminent doom. With language
as flawed as a President's announcing an invasion of a South
Asian country, he announced that the blacks would rise up, kill
a few million whites, take over the reins of government.

Then, the story continues, after forty or fifty years the blacks
would turn the government over to Manson when they supposedly found themselves unfit to run the world. Oo-ee-oo.

It was the pig Christian wealthy Americans that were going
to get cut. He, Christ, he, Devil, was going to pull off the Second
Coming. "Now it's the pigs' turn to go up on the cross," he
would say.

On a metaphysical plane, Manson linked the impending Helter
Skelter with the concept of The Hole. For inside this mystic
Hole in Death Valley, Manson and his family would live and
dwell while the blacks and the whites in the cities would fight
to a bloody end and then the blacks would take over.

From The City in The Hole, Manson would make forays to
sack cities with his hairy locusts of the Abyss. And the blacks,
through their "super awareness"—in the words of the family—
would know that Charlie was where it was at, and nod him into
power.

On a higher level, if higher is any word to be used, Manson
taught that the family bringing the seven holes on the seven
planes into alignment would be the ones to squirt through to the
other side of the universe. And The Hole was to be the magic
paradise—magic, because where else can you find subterranean
chocolate fountains?

He even over-dubbed a weirdo exegesis atop the chapters and
verses of the Book of Revelation, to back up his claims.

The dune buggies were the horses of Helter Skelter with those
"breastplates of fire," described in the Book of Revelation of
St. John the Divine, Chapter 9. And the Beatles, unknown to
them, were the "four angels" who would wreak death upon a
third part of mankind. And Manson found a scriptural basis for
announcing that the Beatles were destined to have a fifth mem-

ber or "angel"—the angel of the bottomless pit, otherwise known as guess who.

One of Manson's favorite passages from Revelation 9 was: "Neither repented they of their murders, nor of their sorceries, nor of their fornication, nor of their thefts"—words he would quote over and over again, preparing his worshipers to kill. And did not the family have "hair as the hair of women, and their teeth were as the teeth of lions"?

And was not Manson the king of the pit?

"And they had a king over them, which is the angel of the bottomless pit, whose name in the Hebrew tongue is Abaddon, but in the Greek tongue hath his name Apollyon." When they translated the Bible from Latin to English, the translators left out another name in the text besides Abaddon and Apollyon, for the angel of the bottomless pit. The name in Latin is Exterminans.

Exterminans—what a word to sum up Charles Manson.

The correlations that Manson found between the Book of Revelation and the Beatles and his own crazies could be continued in moonfire profusion but the reader will be spared.

Manson began to listen to the song "Helter Skelter" off the new Beatles' album with earphones and somehow, as of a miracle, he began to hear the Beatles whispering to him urging him to call them in London. It is unfortunate that Manson evidently did not know that a helter skelter is a slide in an English amusement park.

The girls say that at one point Manson placed a long-distance phone call to London to try to talk to the Beatles. There is no doubt that the song "Helter Skelter" on the white Beatles double album is a masterful, insistent, rock and roll number—and it is very weird sounding, especially the long final section which fades out twice at the end, sounding like a universal march of wrecked maniacs.

"Charlie, Charlie, send us a telegram" was what he thought lay beneath the noise plexus of the composition "Revolution 9." It was felt that if one were to listen closely on headphones, one could hear the Beatles softly whispering just that. As it is, so be it.

"Rise! Rise! Rise!" Charlie would scream during the playing of "Revolution 9" (which Manson associated with Revelation, Chapter 9). Later they wrote *Rise* in blood on the LaBiancas' wall.

It is necessary to listen to the white Beatles double album to understand what Manson was hearing and seeking to hear. The album, as a whole, is of confusing quality. It has flashes of the usual Beatle brilliance but it was produced at a time that the Beatles were locked in bitter quarrels and it is reflected in the album.

The album has the song "Piggies," of course, and, more creepily, a song called "Happiness Is a Warm Gun." Other songs like "Blackbird," "Rocky Raccoon," etc., were interpreted strictly as racist doom-songs.

The song, "Sexy Sadie," must have sent Susan Atkins aka Sadie Mae Glutz, into spasms of happiness. "Sexy Sadie, you came along to turn everybody on," the song croons, and "Sexy Sadie, you broke the rules, you laid it down for all to see."

While the family was still at the house in Canoga Park, Manson began to encourage members of various motorcycle clubs to hang out with the family. The two gangs closest to the family were motorcycle groups with the initials S.S., the Satan Slaves and the Straight Satans. He wanted the bikers to join in his group to supply a needed military wing.

The family was also associated with the Jokers Out of Hell, a group whose members were into the occult and one of whom had a record store in Santa Monica. According to people interviewed, the Jokers had houses in the San Fernando Valley near family headquarters.

Manson used his girls to entice the motorcycle riders to hang around the family. He would order a girl to strip and suck. Forthwith the zippers zipped and the mini skirt hit the ground. The bikers loved it. Manson also set his followers to work on the bikers in terms of material possessions. They would peel the wristwatches from the bikers' arms while one girl would coo in his ear, "You don't need time. What's time?" And sometimes a biker would try to move into the ranch with a wife and the girls would say, "Why do you need an old lady?" and they would deprecate the "old lady's" jealousy.

Manson put on a whole public relations project to attract the bikers. He loaned them money. They were encouraged to fix and park their bikes there, and after the family had reacquired the Spahn Ranch, there were plenty of horses to ride and girl-objects and there was always food. Bands of brigands always have flocked on the edges of desert wilderness. The deserts ringing L.A. carry on this distinction, with rip-offs, clandestine shipments of dope and stolen automotive parts, and weird magic ceremonies abounding.

In many ways the Manson family became like a bike club: the incredible male chauvinism, the outlaw attitude, the "death-trip," the satanism, the rituals. The new girls of the family even wore ownership ankle chains like some bike club mamas.

The bikers are famous for their elaborate funerals with single-file lines of motorcycles forming the funeral procession. The woman's "colors"—her club garb—are often buried with the colors of "her man" in the grave. Sometimes there are mourning periods for the woman, with periodic observances at the gravesite such as pouring wine on the ground.

One Straight Satan who lived with the family for a while was a tall handsome man named Joe. Joe came to the family's house on Gresham Street looking for directions to a house he was going to rent. So enticed was he by the family, particularly Sexy Sadie, that he stayed on. He had a girl friend who was hooked on reds at the time.

Joe the Straight Satan fulfilled an important role in the helter-skelter preparations: he was the architect of the secret escape route to Death Valley.

Joe's stay with the family cost him about $2600. He gave up his watch, a revolver, a microbus and even his motorcycle to the common kitty. He lived with the family on Gresham Street for about a month, at the Hollowberry Hill Ranch of Satan for a couple of weeks, and then at the Spahn Ranch till Mother's Day, 1969.

A short, black-haired mustached Straight Satan named Danny

De Carlo had the longest and strongest known relationship of any of the bikers with Manson.

In March, Danny De Carlo came around to fix a bike. Charlie invited him to stay, proffering an endless supply of women. De Carlo was soon dubbed, by the girls, Donkey Dick Dan due to abundance in down-scope.

A lot of the Straight Satans spent passing time at the various houses in which the Mansonists lived. The Satans had those colorful aliases like Droopy, Dirty Old Man, 86 George, Stickman, Philadelphia John and others.

De Carlo's wife Marian was around for a while but De Carlo beat her up and she fingered out Manson instead as the culprit and Charlie was arrested on March 30, 1969. But the matter was quickly cleared up.

De Carlo was born in Canada and had been in the U.S. since the early '50's. He had served in the United States Coast Guard. His father owned a machine shop in Inglewood. In August of 1965 Danny De Carlo, his brother Laurence and a couple of others were busted for smuggling dope at the Mexican border coming back from Tijuana. He was given a five-year sentence which he was still appealing when he came to live with the family.

De Carlo had a son Dennis, over a year old, the same age as Pooh Bear. Dennis was handed over to be raised at the Spahn Ranch creepy-crawl nursery.

De Carlo was one of the first "gun-freaks" to be associated with Manson. De Carlo worshiped guns. He is an authority on many kinds of rifles and firearms.

After the family had conned themselves back onto the Spahn Movie Ranch, he quickly set up a small munitions factory in the "Undertaker's Parlor" on the Western ranch set. The undertaker's parlor was renamed the gun room. It was from the gun room that they sallied forth to murder.

The gun room had equipment for making four or five different types of bullets. It was a repository for all kinds of knives and bayonets. De Carlo slept there and parked his bike there. Among De Carlo's weapons were a 303 British Enfield, a .22 caliber rifle, a .20 gauge shotgun, a .30 caliber carbine, a .12 gauge riot gun, an M-1 carbine and a submachine gun (a spizer MP 40 SH). De Carlo obtained one machine gun from a gun collector in a Hollywood rock and roll group.

De Carlo and various of the Straight Satans used to visit the house occupied by the rock group. The gun collector in the band was on an LSD Spirit of Nonviolence trip and decided to throw away his machine gun so he gave it to Donkey Dan.

Manson and the family really put down alcohol so there was a conflict with some of the bikers, notorious juicers, especially De Carlo. The girls used to get miffed also at Danny listening to black jazz programs on the radio. They were horrified by the Aphrosheen commercials. "They thought we were listening to 105 [on his radio dial], listening to jazz was . . . eh . . . was plastic," he said. It offended their Okie-Aryan racism.

Anxious though Manson was to please the bikers, not all of them passed the race test. For instance, Joe of the Straight Satans once brought a guy to the ranch that was one-half Indian, a guy named Sammy. Charlie would not allow him to make it with the girls. A person named Mark who was only one-quarter Indian was not allowed commerce with the Aryans at the Spahn Ranch.

In conjunction with plans for Helter Skelter, Manson began to work on an escape route to Death Valley. He wanted to forge a secret trail over the Santa Susanna Mountains and over the Mojave Desert so he could travel with his chosen band when the blacks were sacking the L.A. Civic Center, clear to Death Valley without crossing a major highway.

He decided to begin to build a fleet of helter-skelter dune buggies with which to transport the family back and forth from the Spahn Ranch to Death Valley, up into the Santa Susanna Mountains by means of Devil Canyon and across the Mojave Desert.

From his experience in the rough terrain of Death Valley, Manson decided that dune buggies were the vehicles for his mobile snuff squad. They were great for outrunning cops in the abyss. They were light enough so that two or three of the gore groupies could lift them over boulders and precipices. Motorcycles, on the other hand, were scorned as being inadequate in the wilderness.

But dune buggies, ah sacred dune buggies—they were like battleships. He would later outfit dune buggies with huge gas tanks giving them a 1000-mile assault field. They put machine-gun mounts on them and Manson's command dune buggy was fixed so that it could be slept in. There could be food dune buggies, ammunition dune buggies, dope-supply dune buggies, etc.

Manson met a young man whose family owned the Steele Ranch on the other side of Santa Susanna Pass Road from the Spahn Ranch. There were a series of dirt fire roads that connected the Steele Ranch with Devil Canyon. So it came to pass, as it is/so be it, that the Steele Ranch was chosen as the beginning of the Armageddon trail.

Manson kept cutting the locks on the gates and substituting his own so finally the foreman just gave him duplicate keys. There was an old World War II weapons carrier and a water truck at the Steele Ranch that Manson coveted for his helter-skelter hardware. For the first time the family was into gathering possessions.

At first, Manson actually bought units for his flotilla of dune buggy assault vehicles. Later they would steal Porsches and strip off the bodies to make buggies. On March 6, 1969, Charlie, Bill Vance and Little Patti moved into the Butler Buggy Shop on Topanga Canyon Boulevard near the Spahn Ranch. Charlie had a big thick roll of hundred-dollar bills and purchased two rail-job dune buggies for $1300.

The Butler Buggy Shop was owned by two brothers, one a Los Angeles police officer.

The family subsequently had quite an interesting relationship with the Buggy Shop, as did the Satan slaves who, according to police reports, claimed that they got free Volkswagen parts from the shop. The L.A. sheriff raided the Spahn Ranch and seized some dune buggies that were purchased with money stolen by Linda

Kasabian.

Anyway, to pay for the first two dune buggies, Charlie forged and cashed a $700 check which had come in for Juanita from an insurance company. The other $600 came from some stock that slim blonde Sandy Good sold.

One day late in March, a member of the Satan Slaves named Joey C. arrived at the Gresham Street house looking for a place to live. Manson asked him where he had been living and he replied that he had been staying at a large house out west on Mulholland in the remote Malibu Hills near Agoura. The place had about ten bedrooms and a swimming pool and the owner was evidently away. The house was further noteworthy in that a descendant of the outlaw Jesse James lived next door.

Since the owner was gone—a fact that created possibilities— Manson pulled tent pegs and moved the family to the Malibu mansion where they overran the place for about two weeks.

It was from the ten-room Malibu house that they plotted a helter-skelter escape route down through the fire roads to the sea.

Joe of the Straight Satans knew the fire roads in the area from serving on the county work gangs when incarcerated. In Los Angeles County there are several work camps where prisoners work on fire roads and fire prevention because of the high incidence of fires in the mountains surrounding the city.

Somehow the family obtained keys or a master key to the fire roads in the area.

While the family was at the Satan Slaves' house in Agoura, Joe charted a helter-skelter freak-road from the house in Agoura down to the sea. All they had to do was clear out about a hundred feet of brush and the road was perfect.

Patricia Krenwinkel purchased a couple of hundred dollars' worth of United States topographical maps of the mountainous area between the Spahn Ranch and Death Valley, in order to plot the master helter-skelter escape course. They plotted supply-cache locations along the way. They laid out all the various topographical maps one day in the driveway and taped them together so that all of southern California from sacred Goler Wash to Malibu Beach was one.

These helter-skelter maps later were found buried in Death Valley.

Most of the plotting was done by map although they did check out some of the trails with the buggies. But, according to the person who plotted the helter-skelter snuff-route, the family never did travel the route all the way to Death Valley.

In all its glory, the helter-skelter escape trail led from Malibu Beach up Castro Fire Trail to the Hollowberry Hill Ranch in Agoura. From Agoura it led by fire road and creek bed to the Steele Ranch, north of the Spahn Ranch. From there it sliced up Devil Canyon and oozed across the Mojave Desert and on to sacred Goler Wash, crossing only two major highways (Highway 99 and the Antelope Freeway) on the way.

There is a rumor that Manson or someone in the family stole a half-track from an auto salvage lot in Chatsworth near the Spahn Ranch which was used, and perhaps burned out, in digging part of the helter-skelter escape road over the Santa Susanna Mountains.

There was one heavy problem facing Helter Skelter. By early 1969, the West Valley Station of the Los Angeles sheriff's department had in use Bell-65 two-man helicopters with powerful searchlights installed that could light up a city block from 1000 feet in the air.

Manson had various plans to deal with these helicopters. One was to attack the helicopter with magic. Another method was to thwart the helicopters at night by taping the headlights of the dune-buggy battalion with black tape, leaving only a small slit in the tape to allow a thin ray of light to escape, hopefully undetectable from the air.

Manson added a murderous ingredient to the concept of Helter Skelter—that is, the possibility of a trigger that would set it off. Manson somehow came to believe that the big race war would begin with blacks murdering some white families in their homes.

"The karma is turning," he said, meaning that "to complete the karma of the world," such a collision was inevitable.

Helter Skelter was a dream project for ambulatory schizo-phrenics. There was something in it for everybody. Those who had had creepy childhoods looked upon Helter Skelter as a means of "saving the children." Others had a more racist point of view in that Charlie put up a picture of a white elite ultimately ruling over a black population.

People who liked violence looked upon Helter Skelter as a chance to engage in warfare. People into robbery and chase dug it for its plunder and looting. End-of-the-world freaks could really rejoice in Helter Skelter.

It was the Satan Slaves—that secretive aloof motorcycle club with occult proclivities that lived and operated in the Malibu-Topanga Canyon areas—which seems to have provided another impulse for family violence. The previous year, members of the Satan Slaves club had been seen at a Ku Klux Klan rally in the valley, complaining that black people were scarfing up welfare benefits that belonged to good white folk like the Slaves, accord-ing to a reporter who attended the rally.

They hung out sometimes in Hollywood. The Satan Slaves used to come into the Compleat Enchanter, a shop on Los Palmas, to purchase medallions.

About four of the Satan Slaves were linked with an obscure satanic cult of around 40 members that held outdoor ceremonies —a cult called here the Kirké Order of Dog Blood. The cult is headed by a woman whom the members worship. They believe her to be the reincarnation of Circe, or in the Greek, Kirké, but she seems to take on names of other Greek goddesses also. Circe or Kirké is thought to be red-haired and to be English.

Adepts of the Circe/Kirké cult carve the so-called Star of Circe, a fourpointed star emanating from a rectangle, into their chests, evidently as a mark of adoration of Circe. The Circe group held outdoor ceremonies twice a month, on the new and full moons, perhaps on the secluded beaches of L.A. and Ventura Counties, where they sacrificed black dogs, black cats, black roosters and probably also goats. Animal vampirism is supposedly involved.

There are grim hints that some of these blood sacrifices were filmed and that members of the family were involved in the filmings. There is some indication that some members have the letter "K" tattooed on them and wear "K's" around their necks. The cult is supposed to have elements of voodoo in its rituals, including belief in werewolves. Because of the Manson family's very close relationship with the Satan Slaves there is no doubt the Circe group provided another sleazo input into Manson's mind.

One of the headquarters for the Circe group or the Kirké group was a house not far from the Spahn Ranch in the Granada Hills area.

Manson got into studying what would cause group freak-outs. Around this time an Indian came to the Ranch and showed Charlie a plant called telache, believed to be belladonna. Charlie tried it and was in a coma for three days. They collected leaves and stewed them, placing the coffee colored brew in water jugs. This was to be dropped into water reservoirs. Anybody who was stupid enough to try belladonna in the beatnik belladonna craze of the early 1960's, will understand how grim telache was.

Danny De Carlo remembered it vividly: "It drives you insane where they see little people and goofy things like that and you bang your head against the wall. It drives you mad. They had jugs of this stuff because the girls would take all the leaves and they put them in water and boil them and it comes out a coffee color—brown and really rank tasting stuff."

Manson even planned robberies through the use of telache. The theory was to sneak into a house where a party was going on and put belladonna into the water.

Again, De Carlo: "All their drinks were going to have belladonna in it and right away—going to drive them nuts. While they're in there going through all these contortions and don't know what the hell is happening to them, they [the family] just walk on in and take what they want to take and do anything they want to do and just sneak on out."

Manson used to talk about pouring LSD into the L.A. water supply. They believed mass acid use would cause citywide violence.

Around this time Charlie and the girls made a pornographic movie by the swimming pool at 2600 Nicholas Canyon Road in the hills above Malibu. The producer, according to Los Angeles homicide officers, was Marvin Miller. The owner of the property, Mrs. Gibson, after receiving numerous complaints from her neighbors, inspected her house in the company of her lawyer and found a bloody machete which police say Manson used during the filmmaking to slash somebody's arm.

After a couple of weeks living at that mansion on Mulholland near Kannan, the family talked 82-year-old George Spahn into letting them return to live at the Spahn Movie Ranch.

They stole an intercom from the swank Kannan Ranch house and some other items which they stored in back of the Spahn trash dump, the site of the upcoming dune-buggy assembly line.

It may have been while the family was staying with the Satan Slaves at the Hollowberry Hill Ranch in the hills above Malibu Beach near Agoura that they began to associate with the occult group known as Jean Brayton's gang or the Solar Lodge.

It is thought that a few of the bikers that Manson met were part of Brayton's outlaw Solar Lodge of the Ordo Templi Orientis, and that they turned him on to it.

There certainly were quite a few family credit card forgeries out in the Blythe, California area during that time. North of Blythe is where the Brayton gang had its blood-suck initiation ranch.

At least five separate individuals have claimed that they were told by a member of Brayton's rebel O.T.O. Lodge that Manson was involved with the Lodge, both at the Lodge's desert ranch near Blythe, California, and at one of the cult houses in L.A., near the USC campus.

Two family members, one of them Susan Atkins aka Sadie Glutz, have said that the family participated in ceremonies involving the drinking of dog blood and the sacrifice of animals.

This was alleged to be a sexual tonic. Readers, however, should not take that possibility seriously. The blood-drinking of the family forces contemplation of the hideous possibilities of a new form of psychedelic vampirism, i.e., getting hits off of blood while on dope.

According to testimony at the Brayton gang's trial, the Brayton gang was into drinking the blood of sacrificed animals.

More important to the study of the Manson family is the fact that the Brayton cult also believed most vehemently that there was an imminent black-white bloodbath to occur.

And that it was going to happen in the summer of 1969. Sound like Manson?

Ten

The Solar Lodge of the O∴T∴O∴

Georgina Brayton aka Jean was born on December 29, 1921. Her husband, Richard M. Brayton, age fifty-nine, was a teacher in the philosophy department at the University of Southern California.

Jean Brayton and her O.T.O. Solar Lodge operated right at the gates of the USC campus with a network of cult houses and a bookstore. They also owned various houses in the desert near the Colorado border in Riverside County, California.

Like Mary Anne DeGrimston of the Process, Jean Brayton had, or has, collected circles of fearful, brain-washed followers, many of them young, but a significant number also older and in the professions. There were around fifty known followers in the group, with many more probably undetected at this time.

Her magic organization, the Ordo Templi Orientis (O.T.O.) was founded in 1902 in Germany. The cult purported to continue the work, so to speak, of the Order of the Knights Templars.

Aleister Crowley formed his own O.T.O. "chapter" in England in 1911. It has been around ever since, with current world headquarters in Switzerland.

Crowley had problems in the field of sadism. His books hinted at human sacrifice. His aphorisms such as "Know! Will! Dare! and be silent" betokened violent encroachment. Crowley took peyote 60 years before beatniks gobbled it in North Beach. He was into using drugs to pulverize the personality a half-century before the advent of brain-wash cults like Manson or the Brayton gang or the Process.

In California there are evidently two O.T.O. jurisdictions—one for northern California and the other in the south. The Southern lodge was overrun by Jean Brayton's group.

The O.T.O. is another occult society where initiates proceed upward through degrees of initiation, so that slowly the acolytes are sucked into a weirder and weirder scene. It is pyramidal, with the Ipsissimus (Jean Brayton) occupying the position of the eyeball atop the pyramid.

The hype was similiar to other groups including Manson's: tearing down the mind through pain, persuasion, drugs and repetitive weirdness—just like a magnet erases recording tape—and rebuilding the mind according to the desires of the cult.

Get this: Brayton's Solar Lodge would hold magic meetings where they would try to summon and radiate hate-vibrations into the Watts ghetto in order to start riots. The Solar Lodge believed that a heavy race war similar to Manson's Helter Skelter was imminent.

To venture ahead of the Manson story, in late spring 1969, Brayton sent followers around to various desert locations to find places to stay when the race-blaze would occur. She sent some to Utah and others went to Taos to hunt.

And the conflagration was imminent.

Everyone, all her followers, were to be out of Los Angeles by the summer solstice, June 21, 1969—prepared for the brick-out.

Brayton doted upon John Symonds' book on Crowley, *The Great Beast*. From reading the book, *The Great Beast,* Brayton came to believe that Aleister Crowley, while operating his Abbey of Thelema in Sicily, drank the blood of freshly snuffed animals as part of the higher rituals of his cult. The first two grades of the Brayton Hollywood cult, the so-called Minerval grades, didn't have to drink blood. But the upper levels reveled in sacrificing cats, dogs, chickens, etc., and drinking their blood reportedly consummating acts of sex-magic while animal blood was poured upon the fornicators.

The Solar Lodge of the O.T.O. was heavily opposed to scientology. In addition to anti-black rituals, they held anti-scientology rituals, mocking-up the enemy, so to speak.

Brayton was into collecting bikers and used telache or belladonna at the same time as Manson.

Aleister Crowley had been a noted user of drugs arcane and Brayton herself was known to use them all—like a wandering amphetamine-head on New York's Bowery who would pause and eat the pills contained in an old medicine chest that someone was throwing from a condemned building in the rain.

According to the depositions of her former followers, the Brayton gang used, for mind-zap reasons, marijuana, LSD, demerol, scopolomine, jimson weed, datura root, ether and belladonna. The weirder the better.

She had that great Manson trick of programming people while they were on LSD trips. She would get highly personal data from them under acid and then use it later, as a form of extortion.

The rumor was that Brayton was loan-sharking among dental students at USC. Certainly she was eager to cultivate them as good dope sources, especially for pain killers and ether.

Naturally there were a number of young hippie types attracted to Brayton's groups. Very young people today are sexually free as never before, with healthy sexual rhythms established early in life. Brayton interrupted these rhythms by forcing adepts in the early stages of cult training totally to forgo sex—a cruel act designed to confuse, frustrate and conquer the person for her purposes.

One member named George was having difficulty, sin of sins, in controlling his sexual drives. So Jean Brayton had George cut his wrists every time he felt sexual pleasure coming on. His arms became gouged with slashes.

One girl, whose husband Clifford finally turned state's-evidence against this spank-magic lodge, told the police that when she became pregnant, Jean Brayton was enraged. Brayton told the girl that she should condition herself to hate the child and upon birth the baby was to be turned over to the cult. The girl says she dutifully tried to hate her growing stomach, but could not, so left the creep cult during pregnancy.

One dentist associated with the Solar Lodge disappeared rather mysteriously. He had a practice in Palm Springs. One Monday morning he called in, saying he had suffered injury in a skiing accident. He has not been heard from since. Jerry Kay, the art director for the movie *Easy Rider*, was a member of Brayton's Solar Lodge.

Brayton had the great scam of owning houses which she rented to the cult creeps. Since 1963, Georgina and Richard Brayton have owned property at 1251 West Thirtieth Street in Los Angeles, a house—perhaps the only house in Los Angeles—where occult chicken sacrifices took place. This is the house Manson frequented.

They also own a house at 2627 South Menlo, the adytum for their Crowleyan magic group. This house is an old three-story mansion with light green siding and a dark green roof. Property also was owned at 1241½ West Thirtieth Street—a paradise pad for sex-magic chicken-snuffers.

They also acquired in 1966 a ranch off on a dirt road between Vidal and Blythe, California, about four miles from the Colorado River. Mrs. Brayton was the world's only up-front Baphomet-worshiping real estate speculator. One cynic, interviewed, said that it was in order to keep all her houses fully occupied with renters that Jean Brayton so zealously sought followers. They used the remote desert commune for initiation rites.

The Solar Lodge library and "temple" were on the third floor of 2627 South Menlo. The walls and ceilings of the third-floor temple were painted with magical and Egyptian murals by a cult member, in the manner of the paintings at Crowley's notorious Abbey of Thelema in Cefalu, which Mussolini stomped out of existence.

The Solar Lodge operated a bookstore directly across the street from the USC campus at 947 West Jefferson Boulevard—called The Eye of Horus Bookstore. It was a small bookstore, painted red and yellow, located in a building that has since been torn down. The bookstore was blessed with an amuletic eyeball of Horus painted on the outside.

The eye of Horus was used as a magic amulet by the Egyptians symbolizing the solar triumph of the hawk god Horus' eye. Horus got his eye bricked out by the evil god Seth in a heavy sky battle in the early stages of the universe. Horus' eye was saved and reconstituted through magic aka Magick.

There was another Eye of Horus Bookstore opened at 137 North Broadway in Blythe, California near their desert hideaway.

Before their arrest, Jean Brayton and her husband had applied for a liquor license to operate a magic bar-café complex in Vidal, California. They claimed to have an income of $3000 per month from a pension plus the rentals in the various cult houses in L.A.

The group also ran what seems to be the world's only known occult service station. One Richard Patterson, ardent follower of Jean Brayton, opened Richfield station Number 1087 in June of 1968 with a rock band and pom-pom dancers from USC. The station attendants tried to convert customers who drove up for a spark plug change or gas. The station was operated for a year until around June 1969 when Brayton freaked out and announced Helter Skelter was imminent.

As Brayton was preparing to marshal her cult forces to leave L.A. before Armageddon, a tragedy took place at the cult ranch in the desert. A young boy, Anthony Gibbons, age six, started a fire around June 10, 1969, which resulted in the main residence building being burned up and various animals fried. Brayton's group had been into stealing rare magic relics and valuable occult books over the years, particularly manuscripts of Aleister Crowley. Brayton even stole the so-called Golden Dawn robes once belonging to Crowley. Some of these rare books and manuscripts were burned up in the fire.

As punishment, Brayton locked the boy out of doors in a closed wooden box for fifty-six days in high desert temperatures.

Jean Brayton called a group meeting and announced that she

had punished six-year-old Anthony by holding a match underneath his hands. The boy refused to say that he was sorry that he had set the buildings on fire. Tsk tsk.

Jean put the boy into the box and even suggested that she might burn the box itself down while giving Anthony just enough chain to crawl away from the flames.

The six-year-old boy was held in a packing crate. His left ankle was chained to a metal plate fixed into the ground. There was a folded mattress in the corner for rest. For waste, there was a bucket full of excrement. The crate was closed over with a lid although there was a slight gap allowed to let in light and air.

No one was allowed to come near the boxed boy, much less to offer him any comfort. Temperatures in July 1969 were around 110 degrees at the desert cult-quarters.

There was another small child named Eric, this one only two years old. Mrs. Brayton felt that two-year-old Eric was acting uppity (in the manner of Anthony Gibbons) so she required that the baby sit in a yoga cross-leg position from sunup till sundown for several days.

While they waited for the race wars, they built an open-ended metal building as a temporary dormitory. On Saturday, July 26, the day Gary Hinman was being murdered, two horse buyers went to Brayton's desert residence to look at some horses. The two gentlemen spotted Anthony in the crate under the hot sun. They were horrified. They drove to a store in Blythe and called the police, who raided and arrested eleven of the cultoids, for felony child abuse.

The boy's father James Gibbons, separated from the mother, claimed to the police that he boarded the boy and his sister Tammy at the Vidal commune because he "liked what the group was doing"—as newspapers quoted him. He escaped arrest himself probably because he was a Los Angeles County probation officer associated with the Gonzales Work Camp in Malibu.

One grim anecdote tells how the cult had managed to instill its racism into the six-year-old Anthony Gibbons. After the arrests, the lad was sent to a foster home where he was cared for by a black lady. The boy requested a sword from her so that he might perform a magic ritual called "The Lessor Ritual of the Pentagram." The woman remained nearby as if to observe the ceremony but Anthony announced that "we don't let niggers watch."

One O.T.O. follower was later found buried near the desert commune in early August 1969. He seems to have died of an overdose of telache or jimson weed tea.

Following the issuance of warrants for her arrest, Brayton and select followers floated away to property she owns in Ensinada, Mexico.

Several followers who escaped her clutches came forward after her flight to testify against her. Eleven members of the commune were put on trial, including Beverly Gibbons, Anthony's mother, charged with felony child abuse. The trial was held in October–November 1969, resulting in convictions for all.

FBI fugitive warrants were issued against Brayton and various of her henchmen for refusing to stand trial. As of this writing, Jean Brayton and her closest followers are still on the lam as it were, but FBI agents are hot on her heels. And now back to Manson in April 1969.

Eleven

Donner Pass

While the family was still at the house on Gresham Street in early 1969, an old jail buddy of Manson began to hang around. His name was William Joseph Vansickle aka Bill Vance aka William R. Cole aka David Hamic (a name Vance borrowed from his nephew) aka Duane Schwarm. To the family he was Bill Vance and he became in the family structure sort of a Minister of Rip-off.

According to gossip, Vance was the former light-heavyweight boxing champion at Brushy Mountain Penitentiary. He was thirty-four years old, tall, with a broken nose and several teeth missing.

Vance seems to have taken residence in an apartment building on Gresham Street near the family. As the months passed, Vance came to lead a crack team of forgers and second-story men operating out of the Spahn Ranch.

Here is Paul Watkins of the family giving forth on Vance:

"When I first met Bill Vance, we were living in the Canoga house. We just came from the Barker Ranch for a while because it was getting cold up there in the desert; and Bill was a friend of Charlie.

"Bill started coming around and we turned him onto acid. He had some heavy trips with us. One night we just sat around and started eating. Every hour we'd eat a tab and get a little higher.

"And so Bill started staying around. Except that he had this thing about stealing. He just l-o-v-e-d to steal. Really, he had a demon in him that couldn't do nothin' but rob; even if he had all the things he wanted, he'd still have to go out and rob some."

Paul Watkins said that Bill Vance once owned something called the Topanga Stables in Topanga Canyon and that he had an interest in forming a dope-gobbling church so that psychedelics could be used legally as a religious sacrament.

Bill Vance was always coming on with a "money trip." At one point, he was going to set up Joe and Danny De Carlo with a motorcycle repair shop in Venice, California. Another great Vance scheme was the topless dancer caper.

Bob Beausoleil had met Mr. Jack Gerard, the head of the Gerard Theatrical Agency, a company specializing in supplying actors and actresses for porno movies and topless dancers for night clubs in the Los Angeles area. The agency was also a retail outlet for G-strings and dancing apparel. Beausoleil went to work for the Gerard Agency. Among his duties was delivering station wagons full of topless dancers to various clubs each night.

The Gerard Theatrical Agency was located up the hill from the Whiskey A Go-Go at 8949 Sunset Boulevard on the Sunset Strip. On March 23, 1969, Beausoleil signed a songwriting contract with the Gerard Agency. Beausoleil had a copy of the key to the front door of the Gerard Agency and was allowed to use the tape-recording equipment there to produce a demo tape of his songs.

When Beausoleil began talking about the Gerard Agency, Bill Vance became convinced, and Manson also became convinced, that it would be possible to send some of the girls from the ranch to the Gerard Agency to apply for jobs as topless dancers. Bill Vance agreed to act as the "agent" for the girls. He got all dressed up in a suit and a tie, and the girls old enough to have i.d. got dolled up in high heels and costumes thought befitting topless dancers. Charlie thought that each girl would make about $200 per week, and he figured that with ten girls working and turning the money over to the family, of course, that there'd be about $2000 a week coming in.

Part of the plan for escaping during Helter Skelter required the purchase of a very expensive gold rope that cost about three dollars a foot, and Charlie wanted a truck equipped with a winch and thousands of feet of this golden rope in order to dangle the family down into the Hopi hole during the end of the world. It was thought that ten topless skelterettes working full time would quickly pay for the world-end rope. Oo-ee-oo.

Joe of the Straight Satans took Vance and a gang of prospective nude dancers off to the Gerard Agency. He picked them up after the caper at Ben Blue's Coffee Shop on the Strip.

Sexy Sadie Glutz was so changed by lipstick and make-up that the people hardly recognized her. They set up an appointment with a lady at the Gerard Agency who interviewed the girls. Mr. Gerard himself then showed up, and because some of the girls had diminutive breasts Gerard evidently wanted to give silicone injections to them, in order to produce the ponderous, jiggly quality sought in topless dancers. No thanks.

During the spring of 1969, Bob Beausoleil was cultivating Dennis Wilson, Melcher and Gregg Jakobson, with hopes of furthering his own musical career. Jakobson went twice to the Gerard Agency to listen to Beausoleil's tapes.

In April, Beausoleil lived for about a week at Dennis Wilson's and Gregg Jakobson's house on North Beverly Glen. There Beausoleil met and later lived with a slender red-haired seventeen-year-old girl named Kitty Lutesinger.

Beausoleil and Kitty then lived for a couple of weeks at the Lutesinger Ranch owned by her parents on Devonshire Boulevard not far from Spahn Ranch. Kitty became pregnant and then in late May 1969 they moved to Laurel Canyon for a few weeks, then to the Spahn Ranch just in time to take part in hell breaking loose.

On February 12, 1969, the Polanskis entered into lease arrangement with the owner of the three and a half acre property

at 10050 Cielo Drive, Mr. Rudy Altobelli, the show biz manager whom Melcher and Wilson had tried to interest in the
Charlie Manson superstar project. Altobelli himself lived on the
property in a smaller "caretaker's" house located about 150
feet away from the main residence.

On February 15, they moved into the house. The rent for
the year's lease was $1200 a month, which seemed to be a
bit of a rip-off, especially since the house had only three bedrooms, although it was well lit by night and fully serviced by
landscapers and groundskeepers.

There was that elegant loneliness of the location, high in
Benedict Canyon, hidden in the wooded hillside. There was also
a swimming pool and that huge two-story living room with
that fabled living room loft edged with a white railing where
they found the black hoods and the black leather aprons.

The rent was made more palatable by the fact that, according
to dear friends, Paramount Pictures was picking up the tab.
Roman Polanski was going to put his offices in the apartment
above the garage.

On March 15, 1969, Polanski threw a catered housewarming
party at 10050 Cielo Drive. There was a brawl of sorts at the
party involving uninvited friends of Voityck Frykowski and
Abigail Folger, friends whom they met evidently through Cass
Elliott, the singer. Elliott lived near Folger and Frykowski's house
on Woodstock Road.

Someone named Pic Dawson stepped on Sharon's agent's foot
and jostling occurred. Humans named Tom Harrigan, Ben
Carruthers and Billy Doyle sided with Pic Dawson in the hassle.
Roman Polanski got angry and threw Dawson and friends out
of the party.

All through the following summer, however, the four mentioned above were frequent house guests at the Polanski residence,
while Mr. and Mrs. Polanski were working in Europe.

According to a story told by reporters in the hallways outside
the Manson trial, a story allegedly emanating from the producer
of *The Love Machine*, Nancy Sinatra was a guest at the party

and she grew incensed over the open dope-smoking. She requested that her escort take her away from the party forthwith. As they left, walking past a white wrought-iron settee on the elegant lawn, they noticed Warren Beatty and Jane Fonda and Roger Vadim sitting and talking together.

After Miss Sinatra and escort left the grounds and began to walk down the hill to their car, they encountered a group of long-haired hippies who asked them, "Where's the party?" They motioned back up the hill and to this day they have wondered if the hordes of Helter Skelter were pointed thus into the Cielo Drive estate.

The next day, March 16, Shahrokh Hatami, Sharon's photographer, and Sharon drove Roman to the airport, for a flight to Rio de Janeiro where Mia Farrow was given an award for her role in *Rosemary's Baby*.

After the Rio de Janeiro film festival, Roman Polanski was off to London to work on a movie script for United Artists called *Day of the Dolphins*—a spy tale involving dolphins who learn to speak. He was also slated to produce and direct the movie, probably through Cadre Productions, a company he co-owned with his good friend, Gene Gutowski.

Sharon was off to Rome where she made a film called *Twelve Plus One Chairs* with Vittorio Gassman. Additional scenes were filmed in London later on in the summer.

Even though they were to be gone for four months, the Polanskis decided not to put their belongings in storage but to keep their house open and get someone to stay there and care for the dogs, etc.

A young Englishman, Michael Sarne, the director of the motion pictures *Joanna* and *Myra Breckenridge*, was going to stay in the Polanski residence, but just prior to Roman Polanski's departure for Rio, he decided to rent a Malibu beachhouse instead.

Voityck Frykowski volunteered then to stay at the Polanski residence for the spring and summer. Polanski agreed that Voityck could move in, provided that Miss Folger stay there also.

The owner of the Polanski residence, Mr. Altobelli, planned to spend the summer in Europe. One day he picked up an eighteen-year-old hitchhiker from Lancaster, Ohio named William Garretson. Altobelli hired Garretson to serve as caretaker for the property while he was away in Europe. Garretson was given the "guest house" or caretaker's house on the property as his residence during employment. He was paid a whopping thirty-five dollars a week.

Garretson's duties included taking care of Terry Melcher's twenty-six cats, which Melcher evidently left behind for a while at the house. He also took care of Saperstein (Sharon's Yorkshire terrier) and, later, Abigail Folger's Dalmatian, plus Rudy Altobelli's hostile Weimaraner, Christopher, a dog that loved to bark and even to bite. Also on the care list was Altobelli's green singing finch. He was to keep an eye on the property, but not to fraternize, and he was to man the phone at the guest house.

On March 23, 1969, in the evening, Manson showed up at the front door of the Polanski residence at 10050 Cielo Drive.

Hatami answered the door. Shahrokh Hatami was occupied at the time, or so he testified, in filming Miss Tate as she was packing for her trip to Rome the following day. Hatami was making the film supposedly as part of a private-life TV documentary on movie actresses.

Why was the five-foot six-inch hairy-chested person with a woman tattooed on each arm named Charles Manson knocking at the front door of Sharon Tate's house?

Hatami testified at the trial that Manson wanted to know where "somebody" lived—referring to Terry Melcher. Hatami supposedly directed him to the caretaker's guest house on the other side of the pool, where Rudy Altobelli lived. While Manson was near the porch, Sharon Tate came to the door to ask who it was.

Rudy Altobelli also was packing to leave. He was going to fly to Rome the next day with Sharon Tate. Altobelli was taking a shower when Manson came to the screened porch.

Altobelli told the court later that his dogs, among their barks, bark two types of bark: people barks and animal barks—so he must have heard people-woofing.

He answered the door, clad in a towel, wet from shower.

Altobelli testified that the purpose of Manson's visit was to find out where Terry Melcher was living, even though Melcher had moved off of Cielo Drive almost four months previous.

Manson started to introduce himself according to Altobelli, but Mr. Altobelli said to him, "I know who you are, Charlie."

Altobelli supposedly told Manson that he did not know the whereabouts of the executive producer of the Doris Day Show, Terry Melcher.

Since Gregg Jakobson, a close friend of Melcher's, testified at Manson's trial that they were recording Manson while the family was still at the house on Gresham Street, it is hard to believe that Manson didn't know that Melcher had moved out to his mother's beachhouse. The family was living at the house on Gresham up till right around the time that Manson visited the Polanski residence. It is known that Manson made an appointment with Melcher for Melcher to visit the Gresham Street house and he didn't show up, miffing Manson.

The visit of Manson to Cielo Drive is still mysterious.

The next day on the plane to Rome, Altobelli and Sharon had a conversation about Manson.

On March 24, 1969, back in sleazo-ville, it was time for a little statutory rape. Two unknown male Caucasians, driving a shiny new convertible, managed to coax a seventeen-year-old girl from Reseda, California into the car as she walked along a Chatsworth street, about two miles from the Spahn Ranch. With the jail bait snared, they whizzed off to a sleazy ranch house west of Topanga Canyon Boulevard. Possibly they took the girl to the back house of the Spahn Ranch because the girl told the police that the house was a distance from the road. When she arrived, it was weirdness. The event is best described by the police report.

Victim states that this was the strangest place she had ever seen in her life; 20-25 people sitting, standing, lounging around in a living room; men, women, girls, boys and even little children; strobe lights were going off and on; things hanging from the walls, everything psychedelic; some were on the floor plunking on some types of musical instruments; and that they were all drinking out of a dirty looking jug and smoking something.

"Where am I?" asked the Reseda flower.

"This is where it is," replied an unknown female Caucasian.

Evidently the entrapped girl became hungry and some girl from the family offered her some corn flakes but, according to family custom, the lady offered the flakes first to a dog named Tom, then she could eat them—for the dogs always ate first, before the women, according to family table manners.

They introduced the young girl to Charlie. He took her out in private to explain the game to her and, according to the girl, raped her in an automobile and then pulled up his pants and went back into the house to sing to the assembly. Later the young girl had someone drive her to a liquor store in Chatsworth for some cigarettes and she ran away to her parents, who were loath to press charges, because of the publicity you know, and Manson got away with it.

Sometime following the film festival in Rio de Janeiro, Roman and Sharon took a short trip together to Jamaica where he lost his passport and had to go back to London. She returned to Rome. Later in the spring she traveled to London to be with her husband.

Mr. Polanski's career as writer and director and businessman was speeding along. As of April 1969, an original screenplay written by Polanski entitled *A Day at the Beach* had completed filming in Copenhagen by Cadre Productions. Adapted from a Dutch novel by Heer Heresma, the film was directed by a young Moroccan director, Simon Hesera.

And there was more.

When he went to Europe in early April of 1969, in addition to his United Artists project, Roman Polanski was working on two original screenplays evidently for Paramount Pictures.

One, a film of the life of Paganini, was to be written in collaboration with the author who wrote *L'Avventura*.

The other film, in collaboration with Ivan Moffat, was to be called *The Donner Pass*, a tale of pioneers turned temporary cannibals in the Squaw Valley disaster winter of 1851.

In an interview with Joseph Gelmis in early 1969, Polanski said, "The film is the story of people going from Illinois to California. At that time, there were only seven hundred Americans in California. So these travelers were going to this paradise and they were stranded in the snow in the Sierras in very early winter. Most of them died. The few that survived were accused afterwards of cannibalism."

"Cannibalism?" the interviewer asked, as if in surprise.

"Yes, yes, I know, I know. But it has nothing to do with any of my earlier pictures. What makes you think I am obsessed by the bizarre?"

On April 1, 1969, Voityck Frykowski and Abigail Folger moved into 10050 Cielo Drive.

Twelve

The Spahn Movie Ranch
April–May–June 1969

According to Danny De Carlo, it was red-haired eager Squeaky Fromme who persuaded George Spahn to allow the family to return to the Spahn Ranch en masse. The date of the return to the Spahn Ranch was sometime in the early days of April 1969.

Part of Charlie's master plan was to get George to sign the ranch over to Squeaky when he died. After all, George *was* eighty-two years old at the time, and Squeaky was assigned a permanent position in Spahn's saddle-filled house.

It was not outside the realm of possibility that Manson might have wound up owning a movie ranch. For, to this day, Spahn is eager to have the family ladies around him. And, according to numerous interviews with observers, he had no hesitance, say once a week or so, to get after it with girls sixty-five years younger than he.

Ruby Pearl, George Spahn's long-time associate, was still there, but somehow Manson seemed to overrun the ranch, as he had the previous summer. The family always had a fragile relationship with Spahn's family, but in spite of what any of the stunt men or his own family would whisper into Spahn's ear, Manson had the ace of love.

There always some hassle with Jim, George Spahn's son. Often he wanted to run the hippie freaks off the set. And, in turn, the girls were sorely hostile to him because he castrated the horses. Meanwhile Manson kept the house on Gresham in Canoga Park till May when they were evicted for nonpayment

of rent. There he maintained his own private stash of eight girls.
No other male was allowed in the house according to a next door
neighbor.

Manson seems even to have become involved in the fiscal
operations of the ranch. That spring, Spahn needed money to pay
his property taxes and Manson, according to De Carlo, helped
him with around $3000.

RuthAnn Morehouse aka Ouish was arrested and placed into
Juvenile Hall. She was released into the custody of George
Spahn, who served evidently as her foster parent. We shall have
to pause here for an oo-ee-oo.

Ouish had matured to the elderly age of fifteen. She began to
work behind the "register" in the office by the corral, collecting
money from horse renters. This is an example of Manson's
control of the scene.

When they first moved back to the Spahn Ranch they spent
a lot of effort to try to convert the Longhorn Saloon into a
"music hall" or a night club. Charlie persuaded George Spahn
that it was going to bring in the business. Later Manson told a
lawyer that he opened the saloon merely to give the girls something to do.

The girls remember the "music hall" caper as a magnet which
attracted the local youth from the San Fernando Valley area
in droves.

At the far right end of the saloon there was a stage with
guitar amplifiers and a sound system and drums, suitable for a
whole band. There was a rock-stocked juke box in the corner.
The ceiling was hung with white and orange parachutes. On the
left side was a long bar where they served free popcorn, chips,
soda, coffee and dope. On the floor were spread rugs and
mattresses for conjunction. These Spahn Ranch helter-skelter
teen-hops attracted a lot of heat from the cops, who came to visit
the ranch more and more frequently regarding young runaways.

The triumph of the Longhorn Saloon was a mural painted in
Dayglo and black-light colors, the fresco of Helter Skelter. In
the painting there was depicted a mountain and the desert and

Goler Wash. A personification, evidently the Angel of Helter Skelter, was depicted coming out of heaven, or the sky, to save. At the bottom of the mural were the words: "Helter Skelter, Goler Wash and Death Valley." Nearby on a table there was a jug with a notation: "Donations for Helter Skelter"—created by Ouish.

After several weeks the enterprise was snuffed by the police. George Spahn was handed a $1500 citation for operating a night club without a license. Adios Helter Skelter A Go-Go.

Manson had as many interests as a corporation executive. As the spring changed into summer of this year of murder, the pressures, most of which he himself created, mounted from every corner. There was no escape.

One source of pressure upon Manson was the Transcontinental Development Corporation, which avidly sought to purchase the Spahn Ranch in order to build a resort complex for German Americans. They began to purchase property around the Spahn Ranch and they were attempting to work on Spahn, himself of German ancestry, to sell out.

Spahn's family, of course, was eager to close the deal because of the profits to be reaped from the sale. Naturally the Transcontinental Development Corporation would immediately tear down such an asymmetrical eyesore as the Spahn Ranch and run off the hippie slime.

Things were pretty much the same at the Spahn Ranch as they had been the previous year, at least physically so.

In the hidden gullies and remote woody areas of the Spahn Ranch nudity was the order of dress. Only when on the front movie set itself, which was only about a hundred feet from the traffic on Santa Susanna Pass Road, was some body-covering required.

There were the same odorous toilets by George's house. There was a shower that broke down often. An auxiliary shower was the eight-foot waterfall down the creek behind the ranch.

Directly above the waterfall was a cave where occasionally some of the family slept and camped out.

There were a number of vans and old house trailers located in back of the movie set where people slept.

The whole ranch was heavily strewn with sleeping bags and lots of mattresses to aid instant gratification. There may have been a tendency to go to bed early because the longer at night people waited to crash the further away from the ranch they would have to roam to find a mattress.

The bikers, many attired in the grease-suffused leathers with Hitlerian medallions, some with l-o-v-e tattooed on one set of knuckles and h-a-t-e on the other, provided freedom-training for some of the girls who were afraid of them. Gypsy supposedly at first was extremely hesitant to have affairs with the Satans but grew to grok it.

"The motorcycle gangs would come out there and he would tell a girl, 'Take your clothes off,' and she would take her clothes off and he would just give the girl to any of the motorcycle guys there that wanted to screw her," remembered Sunshine Pierce.

As said before, Danny De Carlo of the Straight Satans set up residence in the Undertaker's Parlor, soon dubbed the gun room because of the small arsenal De Carlo owned. De Carlo was a reprobate and never did fit in with the scheme as Manson saw it.

What Manson did see was that De Carlo used to be president of his bike club and that, through De Carlo, they might be able to latch onto the Straight Satans and get them to be the family's brown shirts. But it never really worked out that way, because the theme of the Spahn Ranch was leisure. The family became masters at "hanging out"—that skill evinced outside drugstores in small towns everywhere.

The bikers would fit right in, drunk, carousing and taking their bikes apart at leisure. De Carlo and the bikers would cash in Coke bottles and buy wine and Manson would complain. De Carlo also grew a pot plant named Elmer up by the waterfall. Elmer was one of the least powerful pot plants ever grown, but has acquired a certain fame in that it was about the only gentle symbol at the ranch during that summer of death.

There were literally hundreds of ordinary L.A. people who visited the Spahn Ranch once in a while, just to hang out.

One "starlet" who had performed in a Grade B cheapo-cheapo movie filmed at the Spahn Ranch kept coming back every weekend.

At once, upon her arrival, somebody would haul her onto a mattress or into the bushes and slip her clothes off.

"Every time I come here I get raped," she complained.

A few of the bikers were offered bit parts in commercials and movie segs shot at the ranch. The relationship between the family and moviemakers, a hush-hush paranoid bribe-suffused area in the Manson saga, will be discussed later.

A gentleman who worked for a church in L.A. collected oodles of leftovers from the Van de Kamp's bakery in Los Angeles and used to drive up to the Spahn Ranch to give the family all sorts of pies and cakes and pastries. Sexy Sadie and Joe would take the extra pastries down to Venice or Santa Monica, to give them out to derelicts and hippies on the streets.

A word must be said about meat-fits. Sadie Mae Glutz was prone to meat-fits. The vegetarian diet at the Spahn Ranch was difficult to follow for some. Sadie occasionally would rush off to a restaurant somewhere and order a steak, the need was so great. Danny De Carlo and Joe, of the Straight Satans, also would go off once a week to Venice for a top sirloin meal.

There was one enormous difference at the Spahn Ranch compared to the previous year when the family first showed up. Murder replaced mind-games as the favorite conversational subject.

"They talked about killing all the time," recalled a young man who lived at the nearby Steele Ranch.

For a long time Charlie had been saying, "There is no good, there is no evil," but now he was saying things like "You can't kill kill," and "If you're willing to be killed, you should be willing to kill," and "It's the pigs turn to go up on the cross."

He began to talk about murder and carnage so openly that it was almost like a self-fulfilling prophecy.

Sometime that spring Manson acquired his "magic sword."

It was a homemade two-foot sword with a knuckle-guard that wounded a lot of people. A Straight Satan named George Knowl gave the magic sword to Charlie. Charlie, one day, just asked for it after he had paid a traffic ticket for Knowl down in Simi, California.

It became like Manson's ceremonial sword. As violence overwhelmed him, Manson would be seen jumping around on the ranch boardwalk slashing and jabbing the air with the sword.

During the filming of one of the family movies, Manson supposedly hacked someone's arm with it. God knows what flesh the sword cut.

It cut Gary Hinman's ear in two. It may have been carried into the LaBianca house. It was stuck into a metal "scabbard" on Manson's command dune buggy as he patrolled Devil Canyon.

After the murders the Straight Satans raided the ranch to get the sword. Perhaps they had heard hints about the deeds done with the weapon.

Manson made a deliberate decision to begin to kill. His series of raps, ever added to, like the repertoire of a night-club act, shifting and changing, pointed toward butchery.

Juan Flynn, the tall Panamanian ranch hand who'd worked for George since 1967 and who had been to Vietnam and had lived through horrible slaughter, counseled Charlie against starting to kill.

According to Paul Watkins, when Charlie began to talk about killing, Juan would say, "It's just like smoking cigarettes, Charlie; once you start, you just keep wanting to do it."

As the family got freakier and freakier, doors began to slam in their faces. They began to hate rich people, the piggies, they called them, of Brentwood and Bel Air and Benedict Canyon. One of Manson's favorite raps was built around a rural pig-slaughter. Those who have been unfortunate enough to have witnessed it will know how a pig is tied up and hung by its hind feet, de-skinned and then ripped open and innards removed. This is precisely what Manson preached for the so-called "pigs" of Brentwood. And this is probably the purpose for which Watson carried that forty-three-foot piece of rope into the Polanski residence. The origin of the so-called "list" of famous people to be killed may date from these early months of 1969 when violence overwhelmed the Spahn Ranch.

The family and the bikers began to race motorcycles and dune buggies around at night. Neighbors complained and Manson told one of them to shut up or he'd burn their houses down.

Spahn evidently complained to the police about the late night sound of the motors. It was scaring the horses and alarming the neighbors. A couple of sheriff's deputies came to investigate and to prepare a field investigation report. After they left, George told Manson that the police wanted him to run the family off the property. Manson went into one of his triggered rages. He screamed and yelled. He accused George of being an ingrate, of actually being able to see.

He supposedly flashed a knife in front of George Spahn's eyes to try to make him blink. He ordered a girl to strip in front of Spahn. No blink.

Then there was silence, and, depending on which family member is telling the tale, there was a grope-scene in the room in front of Spahn.

Manson then, according to legend, said, "I love you, George," and split.

In the spring or early in 1969, Patricia Krenwinkel bought ten or fifteen deer hides with some gift money that somebody, perhaps Sandy Good, obtained from daddy. From these skins, the girls attempted to make buckskin outfits for the men of the family. Snake and Ouish and Gypsy and the others started cutting and sewing the "buckskins," but they were creating apparel for mutants and could not even sew the seams straight, so that the project had to be removed from their hands. Manson evidently took the skins and hides to Brother Ely of the Process, aka Victor Wild, whose leather shop sewed the buckskin outfits for the men at his leather factory in Santa Barbara. Manson was wearing his "buckskins" when finally arrested in Death Valley on Aleister Crowley's birthday.

Because of the heavy war between the Hell's Angels and the Gypsy Jokers, Brother Ely had been forced to move his leather shop to Santa Barbara from San Jose. There, in Goleta, just north of Santa Barbara, he began to prosper.

He also was the chieftain of a clandestine occult group in Santa Barbara which police in Santa Barbara contend was a "chapter" of the Process Church of the Final Judgment. The police have a list of names of those associated with the Santa Barbara Process group. One of the members is alleged to be Danny De Carlo of the Spahn Ranch.

In the middle of April of 1969, a young Texan named Charles Pierce, aka Sunshine, was hanging out on the Sunset Strip when he met Ella Sinder aka Yeller and Sadie. Charles Pierce was a young man from Midland, Texas who had come to California in order to surf and hang out in the sun and just enjoy himself. Sadie and Ella persuaded Charles "Sunshine" Pierce to visit the Spahn Ranch, where Sunshine gave up everything—his money, his i.d. and his silver 1968 Plymouth Roadrunner, which Manson gladly received and used for a while, and then gave it away to Randy Starr.

Just before Neil Armstrong jumped down onto the moon in July, repossession agents from Texas took the Roadrunner back to the auto company. But while the family had it, they used it. The Roadrunner was really the only good, sturdy car at the Spahn Ranch at the time, so they used it a lot for various dope dealings.

"We was running dope down from San Francisco and Los Angeles, selling it on the street corners—" said Sunshine.

Manson had one famous incident with the new Roadrunner where he challenged a bunch of cops to a race.

About eleven o'clock one night, Charlie, T.J. the Terrible, Sadie and Ella went out in Sunshine Pierce's Plymouth Roadrunner to cop a few thrills. On Topanga Canyon Boulevard they challenged a cop to a race and sped off.

Danny De Carlo tells it like this: "Nobody outdrove Charlie. He, one night, got loaded on acid, and Ella, I think Sadie was there, . . . they went down to just antagonize the police . . . and he outran four cars. Finally, he pulled over and he just stopped, and they did not know what the hell to make of this guy, so they stopped 'way behind him and he jumped out of the car and he says: 'Come on, come on after me,' then jumped back into the car and took off again."

Ultimately the police caught them and they held Manson for several days but finally set him free.

Sunshine Pierce, as did all new recruits, received the usual Manson lecture series on Helter Skelter, The Hole, there is no good/no evil, everything belongs to everybody therefore let's steal, etc. Gradually as he gained trust, Pierce was allowed to partake in various criminal capers.

Sunshine Pierce said that one of Manson's dune-buggy fantasies was to kidnap schoolgirls after they got off their school bus in rural areas. They would scout out the area to see where the girls got off the bus and then snatch them up and take them to the desert hideout.

Guys like Sunshine Pierce and Joe and others left the Spahn Ranch partly because they found themselves slowly becoming one of those "program people" that Manson talked about. And who on earth really wants to become a zombie.

There were quite a few arrests for Grand Theft-Auto in April of 1969, charges however which were dropped. Leslie Van Houten aka Leslie Sankston and Stephanie Rowe aka Jane Doe 44 were among those arrested.

On April 23, 1969, Charles Watson, still dressed in a mod fashion, according to his mug shot taken at the time, was stopped by the Los Angeles police department on a charge of being drunk on drugs. Officer Escalente rolled Watson's fingerprints, a grim event for Watson, since it was the set of prints that the police would use to link him to his fingerprint on the Polanski front door.

On April 25, 1969, Bruce Davis, sent to London by Manson five months previous, left Process-land and passed through Heathrow Airport in London, bound for the United States. He left behind in England the former husband of Sandy Good aka Sandy Pugh, one Joel Pugh, who soon died.

Pugh, according to his wife, was the son of a doctor at the Mayo Clinic. His death in London was the first death connected with the family where there was writing in human blood upon the wall. He was found in a locked hotel room in London, wrists slashed. There was writing on the wall in his own blood according to a Los Angeles homicide officer. The coroner, through the testimony of a psychiatrist at the coroner's inquest, ruled that the wrist-slash and writing on the wall were part of a suicide. Scotland Yard still has the matter under investigation as a possible homicide.

According to Tex Watson, ever since early 1969 Manson had ranted and raved in his murder lectures about the Process. Weeks later some of the family, including Manson, began to wear black capes and black-dyed clothing just like the Process.

In early May, just before Mother's Day, Bruce Davis of Monroe, Louisiana arrived at the Spahn Ranch and threw himself avidly into the crime schemes. Davis developed a novel scheme, or thought he had done so, for getting free gas for the dune buggies. He wanted to drive up into the mountains to the edge of the desert to the location of the gas transmission lines. Then he wanted to tap the lines and put barrels there to collect a permanent supply of gasoline for Mission World Snuff. Sneers met this proposal from at least one biker, because it was either natural gas or raw petroleum—not gasoline. But Manson and Bruce Davis were convinced, so they tried it anyway, even hauling a few stolen fire-department water barrels up Devil Canyon for the purpose of collecting the gas.

In spite of preparations for the end of the world, or Helter Skelter, Charles Manson still found time to make attempts at becoming a superstar.

Beausoleil went to Frank Zappa, the brilliant composer and producer, and wanted Zappa to come to the ranch to hear the music. Beausoleil said that the family was building a tunnel to the Mojave Desert, or something. Zappa, to whom the freak-flocks always flock, did not have the time or desire to handle the "act," however.

Gypsy Share, the former child violin prodigy, arranged for Paul Rothschild, the producer of The Doors, to hear the family music, with no evident success. Gypsy had connections in the business, having once lived with the composer of the hit country and western song, "Don't Sell My Daddy No More Wine."

Gregg Jakobson and Dennis Wilson arranged for Charlie to record at a studio in Santa Monica, in Westwood, not far from the Mormon Temple. This studio was owned by a gentleman named George Wilder, whose attitude was "Where's the mon?" and was worried lest Charlie should burn him for the session money. Charlie got angry and walked out of the studio and left behind what Jakobson described as: "Two or three amplifiers, two electric guitars, an acoustic guitar and some other instruments." Manson managed to record about twelve songs or so, enough for an album. He spontaneously composed two new songs at the recording session. Some of the girls were there to provide choral backup, as was Bob Beausoleil. Dennis Wilson of the Beach Boys, Gregg Jakobson and Terry Melcher were on hand to grok the set.

It was at this recording session that Manson really freaked Melcher out with a little spontaneous guitar vamp. During a break, Charlie was strumming his guitar, scat-singing behind the strumming with apparently nonsense syllables—digh-tu-dai, deigh-du-doi, di-tew-deigh, etc.—and gradually the scat-song came clearer, until die-tew-dai, die-tu-day, die-today became die today die today die today.

In May or June of 1969, during an English tour, Dennis Wilson told an English rock magazine about Manson, in an interview. Wilson called him the Wizard and said that the Beach Boys' record label would probably release an album of Manson.

After Jakobson and Melcher and Wilson had recorded Manson, they talked several times out at Melcher's Malibu house about what to do with this enormous talent of the universe. Jakobson was pushing the potential of a documentary movie about Charlie and his gore groupies, but Melcher, the president of Arwin Productions and Daywin Music Publishing Company besides being the executive producer of the Doris Day Show, needed persuasion. Jakobson was eager for Melcher to serve as "producer and financer" of the flick.

It was the visual impact of the family that would "sell" them to the public, it was thought.

For instance, Jakobson was totally impressed by Charlie Manson's dancing ability. Says he: "When Charlie danced, everyone else left the floor. He was like fire, a raw explosion, a mechanical toy that suddenly went crazy." Now if they could just capture that on film. And then there was the whole visual "beauty" of the family as they lived and worked and loved and sang.

Several times Jakobson came to the ranch to take pictures of the family as it did its thing. The idea was to create a presentation on film, to impress potential backers.

There was conflict about the so-called direction the film would take.

It will be remembered that 1969 was the year of the movie *Easy Rider*—a nomadic flick with themes of violence, dope, communes, bikes, dope-dealing, honkies and hatred.

Manson had in mind a movie that could be given a title like "Easy Snuff." He wanted satanism. He wanted robbery and chase. He wanted the men of the family depicted in dune-buggy brigandry. He wanted good Armageddon footage with helter-skelter carnage. In other words he wanted to create an "honest" movie presenting the state of his current insanity and that of his followers.

It seems that Jakobson, Melcher, et al., were more interested in the gentler aspects of the family: the singing, the love, the tribal religiosity, etc. They seem to have wanted a here-come-the-hippies documentary with Lowell Thomas type narration.

On May 18, 1969, National Guard troops ripped up Peoples' Park in Berkeley.

Also, on May 18, 1969, Terry Melcher was persuaded to come

to the Spahn Movie Ranch for an audition of Charlie and his choir in their natural setting. Jakobson and Melcher picked up Bob Beausoleil and his girl friend Kitty Lutesinger where they were staying with her parents at the Lutesinger ranch, and they went to the Spahn Ranch for the "audition." Manson took Melcher on a dune-buggy ride. Melcher observed men putting a generator into the tractor truck. Manson told Melcher that the truck was being put together to transport dune buggies and motorcycles out of the city. Shortly thereafter Manson tried to drive the tractor truck loaded with dune buggies to Goler Wash but the truck broke down, thwarted they thought by the magic of the so-called scientologist gold miners.

The audition was held in a clearing in the woods in back of the ranch. The only way of getting to the audition was to Tarzan down the steep creek bank, holding onto a rope that was tied to a tree.

Everybody went down the stream. The girl choir walked in silence, equidistant apart—or so they seemed to Melcher. Charlie Manson sat on a rock as he sang and the girls gave up background percussion claps with their hands and hummed in harmony behind his singing, uttering "yeas" and "amens" as if aroused by revival fervor.

Melcher gave Manson fifty dollars, the contents of his pocket, as a gift to buy hay for the horses at the ranch. "I hope it wasn't construed as an advance on a recording," Melcher later testified at the Manson trial where he tried to assert he never ran around with the family.

People interviewed in the family claim that Melcher told Manson he'd have to sign some contracts—probably meaning film contracts plus songwriting agreements—with one of Melcher's music publishing companies. But Charlie was very much against signing contracts. Too plastic, man. He just wanted the money.

After the audition by the creek, they went back up to the front ranch and lo and behold, they ran into Randy Starr, who was in his pickup truck painted with the words "Randy Starr, Holly-

wood Stunt Man." Randy was drunk and belligerent and had a
gun strapped to his hip, and it seemed he was going to draw
the revolver. Charlie stepped in and slugged Randy in the stomach
and took the gun away.

Speaking of guns, no doubt there is heavy interest in knowing
a bit about the history of the 22-caliber revolver that Manson
et al. used in their murder activities in the summer of 1969. It
was sometime in the late spring that it showed up at the ranch.

The family acquired a 1952 Hostess Twinkie bread truck
registered to the Continental Bakery Company. It was in this
truck that Manson visited the Esalen Institute in Big Sur six
days before the murder of Abigail Folger and the others. Danny
De Carlo, former president of the Straight Satans, bought the
bread truck off of one Dave Lipsett, a friend of Manson.

De Carlo traded some stolen motorcycle parts, including an
engine, for the Twinkie truck. There has always been controversy
over the ownership of the bread truck. Manson has claimed that
the motorcycle engine and parts were actually stolen by his devices,
therefore the truck should have been his. But Charlie didn't
care; everything was everybody's.

One night Bill Vance was rip-roaring drunk and, in the manner
of extra y-chromosome drunks everywhere, he was belligerent
and was going to shoot up the ranch. Perhaps there was a dis-
honor-among-thieves squabble about rip-off booty. Other accounts
say that Vance was having hassles with Randy Starr, the stunt
man specializing in the neck drag.

Whatever the case, Manson entered the squabble and traded
De Carlo's bread truck for the gun that Vance was waving about.
De Carlo seemed to protest—my truck, my truck—but Manson
told him that Vance wanted to use if for a couple of months
then De Carlo could have it back. Okay.

The revolver that Vance turned over to Manson is a sixty-
dollar, three-pound item of western chauvinism, manufactured by
the U.S. Firearms Corporation. The description of the weapon in
the company catalogue is, for history, as follows: "This long barrel
beauty is reminiscent of the Wyatt Earp days when Ned Buntline presented the Marshall with a similar long barreled gun.

Shoots nine shots faster than 'fanning.' Crisp trigger action and button-swaging precision barrel rifling. Genuine walnut grips. Gold finish trigger guard."

This revolver killed Jay Sebring, shot Voityck Frykowski, shot a black dope dealer in the stomach, and God knows what else.

After Melcher visited, Manson kept asking Jakobson if Melcher was still interested in the project. Evidently there was a period wherein Melcher was to "make up his mind." Manson wanted Melcher's phone number, so Jakobson gave him Melcher's answering service number. Manson was really counting on Melcher to come through for him with the movie and the records.

On May 21, 1969, Manson called his parole officer and asked if he could leave immediately for a tour to Texas with the Beach Boys. He was going to earn $5000, or so he said. The parole officer said that he would have to furnish verification of employment dates. Manson waxed upset at this because he felt it would be an imposition to get the Beach Boys or their manager to supply a letter of verification of employment. A couple of days later, Manson called back and said that it was too late, the Beach Boys had already left. He told his parole officer that he had a song on the hit parade and that he had just recorded an album which was going to be released in about a month.

On Tuesday, May 26, 1969, Mayor Yorty, blatantly appealing to the okie-honk racism in Los Angeles, won re-election as Mayor of Los Angeles over black candidate Tom Bradley. Abigail Folger worked long and hard for the election of Mr. Bradley.

Only occasionally can the focus really be precise on actual details of a particular day in the life of the family, especially when they did not believe in time and months and days. It was all Now. One girl claimed, when arrested in Death Valley later in the year, that she didn't even know Nixon had been elected President.

June 3, 1969, however, can be scanned with some precision.

On June 3, 1969, Charlie tried to put out a contract on somebody's life.

On June 3, 1969, Terry Melcher and Gregg Jakobson again

visited the Spahn Ranch. They encountered two policemen who were on the set also, investigating Charlie's rape of the girl from Reseda in March. Melcher brought with him a gentleman named Mike Deasy, who possessed a van in which was a complete recording studio. Mr. Deasy had recorded several Indian tribes and was experienced in recording "tribes" in the field, so to speak. Melcher evidently was going to use Deasy perhaps to record the sound track for the documentary or to record an on-site live recording of Manson and the all-girl creepy-crawl chorus.

With Melcher was the beautiful "star" named Sharon or Shara who used to visit the Spahn Ranch wearing wigs. It was not Sharon Tate as Sunshine Pierce thought when he copped a visual on her. Sharon Tate was in London, six months pregnant and happily preparing to return to Los Angeles for the baby's birth.

Sunshine and Tex were changing the spark plugs in the green and white GMC tractor truck with which Charlie planned to haul the tarp-covered trailer to the desert. This was the tractor truck with the Olds engine. Manson had planned, but never accomplished, a false bottom on the trailer in which runaway girls could be hid on their way to the desert (or to a ritual). Hot and thirsty, Sunshine walked up to the front ranch into the kitchen and filled up a quart jar with water.

As he left the kitchen to return to the truck, he saw Melcher, the starlet, Gregg and Manson standing by the couch on the boardwalk. They were arguing and Charlie was cursing and yelling at them. Sunshine didn't think much of it, because Charlie was always chewing out somebody or other, threat-tripping the weak links in the family and chasing away undesirables, as is wont of a commander.

That morning, Charlie had gone down to "Hollywood" to discuss the film and record project and had come back with Terry Melcher and "this other guy that had come out there and taken pictures of us this one time"—as Pierce later told police. With dedicated intensity, Jakobson had taken many many photos of the nude commune of lovers, for the album cover. Now they were arguing.

Sunshine Pierce went back down to the GMC, the "jimmy" as it is known in trucker circles, and finished up the plug change. He then lay down under the trailer on a mattress and amused himself with Charlie's pet crow, Devil. About thirty minutes after Pierce had overheard the argument, Manson himself came to join him at the trailer. Pierce thought that, perhaps, Charlie was about to deliver himself of a lecture—as often he did to instruct his followers.

Charlie asked Sunshine how long he intended to stay at the ranch. Uh oh. Pierce was afraid that Manson was going to brick him off the ranch and not a dime had Pierce. His new silver Plymouth Roadrunner Charlie had long since given to Randy Starr. His i.d. too had disappeared. No car, no money, no i.d.—not a condition in which to be set adrift in America.

Sunshine replied that he planned to stay on two, three, maybe four weeks then hit the wind. Charlie asked him if he was interested in helping him pull off a job. After the caper, Pierce could then split. Charlie, according to Pierce, said he'd give him a three-wheeled motorcycle (with legal pink slip)—probably De Carlo's three-wheeler with the word LOVE written on the back with aluminum tubing—and some cash. No one would know about it but them—for that was a rule; you didn't discuss anything Charlie talked about with you, unless he said it was okay to speak.

Sunshine was interested because he thought, as he claimed, that the project proposed involved some sort of robbery. There had been action aplenty, of course, during the six weeks that Pierce had lived on the ranch: the antiques and paintings, the proposed armored car heist, the offed travelers' checks, the trading in dope. So Pierce thought that Charlie was going to cut him in on some plunder.

It was murder. Charlie revealed that he wanted Sunshine to help him kill someone, saying, in substance, according to Pierce: "Well, you know, if you ever want to get anything and you want it bad enough, you can't let anybody come between you when you are going to do something."

This was something new to the twenty-year-old lad from Midland, Texas, so he told Manson he'd have to think about it and would let him know soon.

"He said that he had one person in particular he wanted me to help him kill and he said that there might have to be some other people killed.

"He said he could probably round up maybe $5000 or more and give it to me if I helped him pull this job."

Later that evening, Pierce learned that the argument on the boardwalk was over the "direction" the film would take—already they'd shot pictures and made tapes for a presentation. The NBC officials, on the one hand, wanted a verité hippie-commune movie with a narrator. But Charlie hated hippies. Charlie wanted to make an honest movie presenting the family in an as-is situation, adding marauder elements, bikers, creepy-crawlie capers —in order to magnet in on potential followers and attract them.

And what about Pierce? Later on, after the arrests, he told the Richardson, Texas police the following: "I thought it over for a while. I figured, well, it's something I couldn't get away with and if I could get away with it, I don't know if I'd like going around knowing that I done it. So I told him no. And so, right after that, well then I called my mother in Midland and told her where I was."

The next day, June 4, the girls patched his pants for him, his mother wired him money, and Sunshine Pierce flew back to Texas.

On June 4, 1969, Charlie Manson was arrested as a result of a follow-up investigation on the rape in March of that girl from Reseda. But he got out the next day on bail of $125. Nothing ever happened with the charge and once again Charlie Manson got away with encroachment.

On June 6, Mike Deasy, the man with a recording studio in his van, visited the Spahn Ranch where he recorded Manson singing. Family gossip has it that Deasy took an acid trip with Manson, flipped and had a death-trip involving Manson that later required entrance into Jungian analysis.

Manson gave Deasy some four- and eight-track tapes of "the music" for his listening pleasure. Manson called him later and wanted him to bring his kids out to the ranch. No thanks.

In early June and once also in July at the Jack Frost Surplus Store in Santa Monica, Charlie Manson bought several hundred feet of white nylon three-ply rope, forty-three feet eight inches of which only sixty days later would be looped over the ceiling beam of the Polanski residence. The rope was fairly expensive but it was taken care of by running a phony credit card for it. Some of the rope was used around the ranch to tow vehicles. Charlie gave George Spahn part of the rope. The blind George felt the rope and admired it. Around 200 feet of the rope Charlie kept behind the bucket seat of his command dune buggy.

Danny De Carlo recalled one escape scheme Manson dreamed up for the rope: "He had a winch on the front of his dune bug, and the thing, what he wanted to do was, when the police were chasing him, see, he'd like take this winch and he'd throw the line out there and he'd winch himself up in a tree, and the police would just drive right on by. You wouldn't see the dune buggy sitting up in the tree up there."

Manson became more and more involved with blending violence into his transactions. He seemed to be eager to see which of his "program people" would kill.

After all, Manson said, "We are all one." Killing someone therefore is just like breaking off a piece of cooky. And did not the Manson adage say, "If you're willing to be killed you should be willing to kill?"

One of Manson's potential "program people" was the Vietnam veteran, the six-foot five-inch Panamanian ranch hand Juan Flynn. One day sometime in late May of 1969, according to Juan Flynn, Manson and Juan Flynn went to an ice cream parlor in Chatsworth and Manson talked a little bit about Juan's family, some of whom lived at the Porter Ranch, located in the north part of the valley, not far from the Spahn Ranch. Juan Flynn testified about it at the Manson trial: "So I wanted to see where they lived at, you know, and I was looking into it, you know.

"So I says, 'Why don't we look up this address and go down and see where my family lives.'" Manson agreed to drive him there. After they'd looked for the house and the street and they'd found it and parked, Manson asked if they had a little dog in there, and Flynn replied, "Yes, they have a little dog.

"And then he says, 'Well, why don't we go in there and tie them up and cut them to pieces,'" Flynn told the court in volume 103, page 11903 of the trial transcript.

Juan Flynn has claimed that on several occasions he and Charlie drove around Chatsworth, near the ranch, and Charlie tried to get Flynn to enter the houses, tie up the occupants, force-feed them LSD, kill the children in front of the parents, then kill the parents when they were going berserk.

There was another occasion when Manson wanted Juan to help him kill a black man.

Around June 13, 1969, Manson and Flynn drove in a dune buggy down the paved storm sewer of Brown's Canyon Wash, which twists down through Chatsworth and past the two-block section of Gresham Street, where the Manson family had once lived. Manson pointed to an apartment building near the former family house on Gresham Street, where some black dope dealer lived. And Manson asked Juan to help him kill him because the guy had been giving "his" girls dope and balling them.

Manson has denied, however, that there ever was any trouble with the black guy on Gresham.

Manson's snuff-offers to Sunshine Pierce and Juan Flynn pose a grim question: Was Manson, through his extensive fourteen-year connections with the California underworld, becoming a "hit man" who took murder contracts?

Charlie had trouble with his federal parole officer in June of 1969. He seems to have almost got his parole revoked because of his associations with three other federal parolees. Federal parolees are denied close contact with one another to prevent collusive criminal activities.

The three were dope dealers whom Manson gave access to the harem. One of the federal parolees visited the Spahn Ranch then returned to his home in Las Vegas where he mumbled something to his wife about living off the land and getting a dune buggy.

One wife of the parolees was upset because Manson tried to seduce her when he visited them in Las Vegas.

Another worry for Charlie, in this summer of pressures, was that he really hated to lose a follower, once the follower was enmeshed in the nets, so to speak.

Charlie was always talking about scientology in his various raps, and it should have been no surprise when some of his followers decided to investigate it. Around the middle of June, two of the family, a boy and girl, evidently left to pursue formal training with the Church of Scientology.

Vern Plumlee, who came to the Spahn Ranch in the middle of June, said this about the matter:

"They left right after I got there. They met some guy from scientology and the dude who was interested in scientology— he started talking to these two people and they left and Charlie'd been down on them ever since."

Charlie was miffed. It was not enough that sacred Goler Wash was being held by Crockett and crew but now his followers were defecting to scientology. Pressure, pressure, pressure.

Manson was a knife-freak. Everybody used to throw knives at the haystack. After all, the police could hear gunfire for miles in the desert but blades would be silent. And shrieks melt easily in the distant air.

He gave the girls lessons in knife throwing and later that year he actually got into lessons in throat slitting and skull boiling —evidently having in mind adorning the Barker Ranch with human skulls.

Machete chauvinism was one of Manson's ultimate devices, unless the stories are true that the family was into filming human sacrifices of young female Caucasian victims.

Charlie had an old sixteen-inch army surplus machete and he was the only one who could throw it. Charlie could throw it fifty feet, the family claims, and stick the target. He used to put girls up against the haystack and see how close he could throw the machete to them.

In his universe, women had no soul. They were to be slaves of Man.

The girls were required instantly to submit to the men Manson stated to be on the grope-list. Any time, anywhere. The girls supposedly were not allowed to ask for sex but had to wait, though they could smile alluringly if they wanted. Sounds like the Protestant ethic.

Manson is known to blame women for the institution of capital punishment, for jails and for practically all repression.

"We live in a woman's thought, this world is hers. But men were meant to be above, on top of women."

He hated women.

"I am a mechanical boy,
I am my mother's boy."

Went one of his songs.

Manson decreed that only the men could talk to the babies. The women, though they still cared for them, could only speak gibberish to the children. There was rebellion on this. Mary Brunner told Linda Kasabian that she didn't care what Charlie said, she was going to love and talk to Pooh Bear, her baby.

The women were not allowed to discipline the children in any way. After all, the child was the perfect state.

As noted, the women offered food to the dogs before they themselves ate. The children often were fed sour milk, according to Sunshine Pierce. Infant sexuality was encouraged. Susan Atkins told a cellmate later that she used to perform fellatio on infants.

More incredibly, the women in the family were not allowed to ask questions. The word "why?" was banned. Only a few knew exactly what the men were doing. The men had almost a separate life.

The girls were always saying, "He's not our leader. He falls down at our feet. But doesn't let us step on him." If they did, he'd punch them in the face.

When Charlie would beat any of the girls, they'd say, well, it was really because they wanted him to do it. Snake Lake, for instance, then fifteen, was to become a kind of punching bag for Charlie during his anger spasms. But she stayed on. The family claimed she wanted "attention," so she deliberately angered the Devil. The girls would fight among each other, but the rule was when a man told them what to do, they had to do it immediately. The girls would say, "I don't care or know about you, I've got my own love for me." They talked his raps, spoke his language, but over and over again, he told them that he was not really telling them what to do. As a matter of fact, that was the reason that Manson was amazed that he got indicted for murder. Because he claimed he never told anybody what to do. They'd walk around singing little ditties about themselves as "die, Leslie, do die," for that was the essence of the message, to die in the mind in order to live in The Hole.

But Charlie's greatest hold on the girls was fear. Threatening to cut off their breasts was one of his favorite snarls. He'd always manage to commit a few felonies in front of them and to get them involved in murders and the burial of bloody clothes and the wiping down of houses for criminal fingerprints and the forging of checks and the planning of robberies. They'd think they were equally implicated in events, even though they had merely witnessed them. He'd always blend them into this plexus of gore and grime and crime.

Early in the day Manson would "program" the girls—give them a list of things to do. They sewed a lot. Charlie always wore his corduroy vest—embroidered with those witchy whorls. Each girl wove a part of it, sometimes adding locks of human hair with bright threads depicting snakes, dragons, humans and animals in a mural of religious meaning that the family understood very well—it told stories and illustrated the concepts of Charlieism.

And people ask how on earth it happened.

All anybody has to do is open the nearest anthropology book and check out any number of weird religious cults throughout history that, among them, have believed every conceivable thing. Manson's scam was the old live-forever chosen-people hype.

It was all summed up by Country Sue:

"This group of people has come up from millions of years. It's like every one of them is just so familiar that each person is perfect. It's like, you can remember—after you took acid and stuff—you can sort of remember all the lives you've lived, all the people you've been and all the struggles and all the dying and coming back and over and over and over. But this is the last time. Like, the way I feel is like I've got exactly the body I wanted, you know for the last time. The perfect, the strongest one, the one that's going to make it through. And like, I'm willing to die for anyone, anyone who's me, 'cause it's like one soul. . . ."

Manson used to brag how he was a "man with a thousand faces." In a life-style where everything is a hype and a con, that is an assertion of virtue.

On the crime front in May and June of 1969 Manson was in full frenzy. Naturally there are many gaps in trying to depict criminal activities in the summer of '69.

Like any enterpreneur must, Charlie had to scheme constantly since only a certain percentage of the capers could come to fruition. He talked about a thousand capers. He wanted to rob an armored car. He wanted to break into a military reservation and steal weapons.

They had set up a whole network of crime, enabling them to fence anything or readily to get hold of any psychedelic substance they should require. They had a fence and a dope source in Santa Monica for sale of hot items. Manson had a strict rule that whenever he discussed with any of the family members any proposed illegal venture, the person was not allowed to discuss the criminal activity with any other person in the whole universe. Charlie sat at the top of a pyramidal structure of small criminal bricks.

Tex Watson had acquired extensive contacts in the Hollywood area when he was a co-owner of that wig shop on Santa Monica Boulevard. He was active in handling dope deals for Manson. He was completely under Manson's power.

Once someone with a full beard visited the ranch and Tex

admired the beard, saying: "Maybe someday Charlie will let us grow beards." And Tex wasn't just dealing nickel bags for Charlie. They were dealing big in acid, hash, pot and sometimes coke.

One L.A. dope dealer interviewed by this writer requested that if one ever ran into a certain family member, now under indictment for murder, one was to ask him for the $2000 he burnt him for in fake hash-bricks in 1969.

Vern Plumlee has told of the large amounts of cash the family sometimes obtained:

"There have been times when the family had $25,000, $40,000—gee, you know. At one time right before I came they had $30,000 and they went down and bought all kinds of sitars, guitars, drums, all kinds of things.

"Then they went out and they set 'em up in the back ranch house. Everybody dropped some acid, got loaded and started, you know, working out on the drums and everything. And at the end of the acid trip there wasn't an instrument that was playable."

It is known that Charlie was considering feeding four of the girls into a Hollywood prostitution syndicate. Manson probably kept up his ties in the pimp-hype from the 1950's when he claims he operated a whore scene out of the Roosevelt Hotel.

When stolen travelers' checks were brought in, various men would try their hand at forging the name. The one able to copy it was the one honored with cashing them.

In early summer 1969, members of the family stole an NBC-TV station wagon loaded up with film equipment. There was tens of thousands of dollars' worth of cameras, lenses and Nagra recording equipment aboard. The truck was dumped and the film equipment buried. Manson approached Gregg Jakobson to try to locate a purchaser but Jakobson refused to serve as a fence for it.

Most of the film equipment was given away. Torrid video-porn and perhaps brutality-films were shot with the NBC cameras. Manson took an NBC camera with him to Death Valley in September 1969.

With the sound-pack the family recorded their song sessions and other activities including the re-creation, in song form, of one of the murders.

Charlie hungered for male additions to the family and specialized in attracting youths with kleptomaniacal tendencies.

John Phillip Haught aka Christopher Zero aka Zero, and Scotty Davis were young boys from Ohio who got enmeshed in the webs of creepy-crawlie. Zero would die in the fall under suspicious circumstances. A young man named Lawrence Bailey aka Little Larry arrived from a chicken farm in Oklahoma and he joined up.

Zero, Scotty, Vern and Bill Vance formed a crack squad that plundered San Fernando Valley, stealing cars, robbing service stations and uttering forgeries. They even stole a bunch of checks from the back of George Spahn's checkbook and bounced them around the valley.

A human named Brother Bill was an antique dealer in Santa Monica who had helped the family in the past. The family was hard up for mon but Brother Bill refused to continue to give.

Bob Beausoleil aka Jasper Daniels took Bill out to breakfast one morning while Charlie et al., strangely enough happened along and looted Brother Bill's store of $70,000 worth of antiques and paintings which were taken to the Spahn Ranch. Bill came storming out to the ranch later claiming that Beausoleil had set him up. But once again, the family waltzed away free.

They buried items like ritual films or Voityck Frykowski's credit card. Less sensitive material they could hide by crawling beneath the wooden foundation timbers and sticking it on a rafter.

They were always burying things—food caches, the helter-skelter maps, guns, antiques, film. To this day, Manson's Spanish guitar lies buried in Death Valley, awaiting his escape. Shudder, shudder.

They set up a creepy-crawlie dune-buggy assembly plant in the trash dump behind the corral of the Spahn Ranch. They stole Porsches and Volkswagens and brought them to the Devil's Dune

Buggy Shop in back of the corral, and then the man would strip off the body and fenders, and cut everything up, and load the cuts onto a truck and cart it away. Then they'd make dune buggies out of the skeleton Porsches or Volkswagen frames. They would then sell the fresh fashioned dune buggies somewhere out on the desert, in exchange for dope and money. It was creepy-crawlie capitalism.

They ripped off an electric welding set and tools from a rental agency. They ran up an incredible electricity bill for George Spahn by day-and-night welding and drilling at the trash-dump buggy works.

Sunshine Pierce observed it: "He would go out and trade these dune buggies to these guys in the desert. . . . They were hippies, and he would trade these dune buggies to them for dope and money and things that they would steal from these little towns and stuff out on the desert."

They were forced to learn methods of quick auto theft. The family record for hot-wiring a vehicle was evidently held by Sadie aka Susan Atkins. It was rumored that she could hot-wire a vehicle in thirty seconds flat.

On June 24, 1969, thirteen-year-old Virginia Lynn Smith was found murdered in Cobal Canyon, Claremont, California. A person who spent time living at the Spahn Ranch had been dating her. Somebody from Florida has confessed to the slaying. However, considering that over twenty people have confessed to the evil Black Dahlia murder in L.A., anything is possible.

On June 27, 1969, twice-married twenty-year-old Linda Darleen Kasabian, a blond girl with a sixteen-month-old baby girl, Tanya, flew to Los Angeles from Milford, New Hampshire.

Since April 1969, she had been separated from her husband Bob and had been crashing with her mother in Milford. Prior to separation, she and Bob had been residing in communeland, Taos, New Mexico. In 1968, as was noted, they lived for a while in L.A., where once Linda had peyote fruit punch at the house next door to the residence of Leno LaBianca.

At her husband's invitation, she flew west for reconciliation.

Bob Kasabian and a human named Charles Melton aka Crazy Charlie invited Linda on a trip they were planning to South America, where they intended to buy a boat and sail the seas.

It is necessary to discuss at this point the hostilities Manson, particularly in June '69, had with a black drug dealer named Bernard Crowe. The hate scene culminated in Manson shooting Crowe in the lower abdomen and leaving him for dead.

Bernard Crowe, twenty-seven years old, five feet nine inches, 290 pounds, was a man bearing the nickname Lotsa Poppa. Numerous times he had run afoul of the laws regarding sale of drugs.

He lived in a house at 7008 Woodrow Wilson in the Hollywood Hills above Sunset Boulevard. The house was a famous crash pad in the area, with numerous complaints by neighbors regarding sun-deck sex and dope trafficking.

Manson seemed to have become entangled in hassles with a so-called "black dope syndicate" in Hollywood, the true facts of which are only partly known.

At the time there was definitely a group of black dope dealers in Hollywood, some of whom were arrested during the investigation of the murders at the Polanski residence.

There was plenty of gossip among those interviewed who lived in the group of houses near Crowe's place on Woodrow Wilson that Manson and his crew were hanging around Woodrow Wilson and Loyal Trail (a short road running right behind Crowe's place).

It seems clear that Manson and select associates used to hang around the Woodrow Wilson area both at Crowe's house and, according to several sources, at singer Cass Elliott's house. It may have been there that Manson met Abigail Folger and Voityck Frykowski and several Hollywood dope dealers.

"I've heard that Charlie went down to Mama Cass's place and like they were all sitting around jamming for hours and she'd bring out the food. Squeaky and Gypsy were down there. Everyone would jam and have fun and eat," related a former family associate named Melton.

Hearsay emanating from a tuba player for the Los Angeles Philharmonic Orchestra (who lived near Crowe) says that Manson spent time on Loyal Trail. A lady living right next door to Crowe claimed that the family bus had been parked there for a while. This would have had to have been late '68 when some sort of blue-colored Manson bus was roaming around the Hollywood and Bel Air hills.

One former family "member" interviewed said that in late 1968 some of the family used to visit "Bernie's house" somewhere in the Laurel Canyon-Woodrow Wilson area.

Snake once referred to Crowe as "the Negro member of the family."

The family also stole a red Toyota Land Cruiser for use in Helter Skelter which was owned by a person named Kemp who lived on Loyal Trail about a hundred feet from Crowe's house at 7008 Woodrow Wilson.

Gregg Jakobson has claimed he heard Manson say he was going to shoot Crowe days before the act was accomplished. It appears that Manson had actually been trailing Crowe, that he had Crowe staked out under surveillance, so to speak.

Sometime in the evening of June 30, 1969, Manson arranged for Tex Watson to burn Bernard Crowe. Watson never made a move without Manson's "programming." All the dope dealers in the family, except Manson have stated that it was totally Manson's idea to burn Crowe.

In March of 1969 Tex Watson met a beautiful girl named Rosina who lived at 6933 Franklin Avenue in Hollywood, right next to the Magic Castle. (The Magic Castle is reputed to be the home of the Count Dracula Society, a society of well-known filmmen and writers who groove behind old vampire movies.)

Tex spent a lot of time at the house on Franklin and occasionally Manson and some of the girls would also visit. A lovely member of the ill-fated Acapulco, Mexico production of the musical, *Hair*, was a roommate of Rosina.

Crowe's version, uttered under sworn oath, at the Manson trial, is that beautiful Rosina Kroner, Tex Watson and Crowe drove to an address in El Monte, California to cop dope. Crowe forked over $2400, allegedly to purchase marijuana. Tex left the automobile and entered the building, then left by the back entrance to return cackling to the Spahn Ranch.

Crowe and Rosina waited for a while, then returned to her apartment on Franklin Avenue. Crowe was enraged, vowing to maim the burners.

In a subsequent interview in a hospital after Crowe got shot in another altercation, this time in the foot—he keeps getting shot—Crowe claimed that it was actually a $20,000 deal and that the $2400 was merely a portion of it.

Thirteen

The Locusts
July 1969

About 2 A.M. on the morning of July 1, a phone call came in over the pay phone by the corral. T.J. answered the call. It was Rosina Kroner and she was hysterical. Bernard Crowe was at her house. He wanted his money and was threatening to kill her. She was calling from her apartment at 5933 Franklin Avenue in Hollywood. She wanted to talk to Charlie.

Charlie talked to her and then to Crowe. They had a heated conversation during which Crowe threatened to come over and shoot up the ranch. Charlie said, "Don't come over here. I am coming over there."

Tex and Bruce and T.J., Danny and Charlie were alone by the dusty corral. Charlie told them that Crowe threatened to do in everybody and he had to be stopped. He said, "I'm going to go over there. Does anybody want to go?" It is not recorded whether or not any hands were raised.

"Come on, let's go"—Charlie to T.J. the Terrible.

Charlie got into the car and put the revolver on the seat between them, the Buntline Special which later was to kill Jay Sebring. The automobile was wrangler Johnny Swartz's yellow/white '59 Ford—the same car which was to be driven to the murder of Gary Hinman, to the Polanski residence and to the LaBianca house.

It was a thirty-minute freeway ride from the Spahn Ranch to Miss Kroner's residence. Charlie got out of the car and walked up to the front door. T.J. picked up the gun from the front seat and followed Manson. He handed the revolver to Charlie, who stuck it in his belt.

Bernard Crowe wasn't there when they first arrived. Rosina answered the door. There were two men in the apartment, Dale Fimple and Bryn Lukashevsky, a friend of Dennis Wilson. They told Charlie that Crowe was enraged because of the burn. He wanted his money or else he was going to take vengeance on the girl and raid the ranch.

When he entered, Charlie placed the revolver on the table. In a few minutes Crowe re-entered the apartment and he and Charlie were talking calmly. Charlie told him to the effect that you can't take my friend's life, you must take my life. When Crowe said that no he didn't want to harm Charlie, just the people that had burned him, Charlie had him where he wanted him.

According to Dale Fimple, Charlie performed some sort of "ritualistic dance," and then got ready to leave. He picked up the gun. Rosina was sitting on the bed; T.J. and the other two men were at the door. Charlie was standing about eight feet from Bernard Crowe, gun in hand. Crowe stood up and said, "Are you going to shoot me?"—putting his hand to his abdomen, the evident trajectory of any possible bullet.

Charlie pulled the trigger—click. Nothing happened. Charlie, perhaps in an act of instant theater, laughed and said, "How could I kill you with an empty gun?" The trigger clicked again and then there was a shot—and Crowe fell down in a ball, clutching his stomach.

Charlie turned to one of the men and said that he liked his shirt and wanted it. It was a leather shirt; Charlie liked leather shirts. Quickly the guy gave it up, fearing a bullet. Charlie then walked over, kissed Bernard Crowe's feet and told him he loved him. Other versions say he kissed the feet of the guy who gave him the leather shirt. Then he split.

Manson thought Crowe was dead.

When they were driving back to the ranch, T.J. claimed that Manson told him he didn't like the way T.J. was looking at him because it made him question himself and he shouldn't question himself. Not Jesus. It was his first public gunfight, an act that triggered two months of violence, leaving around fifteen people dead.

Tex, Bruce and Danny were sitting on the boardwalk in front of the bunkhouse when they arrived. Charlie told about the shooting and T.J., freaked out by the apparent murder, walked back to the corral where he spent the night meditating with the horses. The next day he left the ranch.

An ambulance picked Crowe up at 4:15 A.M. and took him to the USC General Hospital Medical Center. He sent a telegram announcing impending surgery to his sister in Philadelphia, then was operated on by two surgeons. He evidently stayed in the hospital till June 17, after which he returned to 7008 Woodrow Wilson to recuperate.

The bullet lodged in Bernard Crowe's torso remains there to this day. In the spring of 1970, Bernard Crowe was incarcerated in the L.A. New County Jail where he ran into Manson again. If it is true that Charlie thought Crowe was dead, it must have been a weird surprise to see him in the jail. When the prosecutor learned that the bullet was still inside Crowe, he was very eager to secure possession of it since it would definitely link Manson with the murder weapon. They offered to send Crowe to the Mayo Clinic for a painless extraction of the lead but Crowe refused.

The next morning after Crowe was shot, things were panicky at the ranch. There were scared looks in the eyes of Tex, Charlie and Bruce Davis. Tex pulled out a wad of money—saying that it was $2500—and blew air into Danny De Carlo's face by fanning the mon.

T.J. was in grim shape. He announced that he didn't want anything to do with "snuffing people." And Charlie was, in the words of De Carlo, "chewing his ass off" about "getting on his case"—as they say in jails when a person butts into the affairs of another.

The story of the shooting of the black man spread throughout the family, but in mutated forms. Always it took the form of a so-called Panther meeting, not in its real context of a dope burn. The Crowe shooting is so garbled in its telling that there is a suspicion that there were several blacks shot and that only Crowe's shooting has surfaced.

One story, for instance, has it that there was a black guy chopped to death at a "meeting" attended by about ten people at a location near a college campus. This story emanated from a girl who supposedly overheard the family talking about it. Dan De Carlo said Manson said that the two witnesses called a couple of days later and told Manson they had dumped the body in a park.

In any case, Manson subsequently was to tell several versions of the shooting of Mr. Crowe, usually placing it in the context of a Black Panther meeting.

Manson seems to have considered any self-assertive black man a Black Panther. He certainly didn't know anything about the Panthers since in a jail interview he didn't know of Huey Newton, for instance. Manson was totally paranoid over reprisals from the "Black Dope Syndicate."

More specifically, the family was afraid that the black friends of Bernard Crowe would storm the ranch and kick faces. Each night armed foot patrols were set up to guard the grounds. Often men with guns would stand on the roof above the boardwalk at night awaiting the supposed Black Panthers. Little Larry slept on top of the haystack as a sentry.

One day, De Carlo discovered the Buntline special used to shoot Crowe sitting in its holster in the "gun room" on top of his radio. They wanted him to clean it, which he was hesitant to do because Dan was afraid it had been used to snuff the black guy.

In the first few days of July, Bob Beausoleil and his pregnant girl friend moved to the Spahn Ranch from their place in Laurel Canyon. Bob and Kitty moved into one of the "outlaw shacks," perhaps the one painted "Alice's Restaurant." Two humans named Little Joe and Fat Frank lived in nearby shacks, according to a dope dealer who dealt in the neighborhood.

At his second murder trial, Beausoleil testified that he returned to the Spahn Ranch because Gregg Jakobson had called him and said that the movie deal was on, that Terry Melcher wanted to do it. Jakobson, according to Beausoleil's testimony, wanted Beausoleil out at the ranch to help with the music for the sound track.

Just before he went back to live at the Spahn Ranch, Beausoleil second-storied the Gerard Agency to snatch up his contract and his demo tapes. He was seen by Gerard Agency employees slithering out of a second-story window. Shortly thereafter a videotape system was stolen from the Gerard Agency building which former Gerard executives suspect may have been ripped off by Beausoleil or Manson.

It is known that Manson approached his old friend and former manager of the Galaxy Club, stage hypnotist William Deanyer, with a videotape system to sell. Manson told him that the video system would help him in his hypnotism act.

On July 2, Tex Watson went to Butler's Buggy Shop on Topanga Canyon Boulevard to get a dune buggy customized for desert specifications. He wanted a forty-gallon gas tank installed so that the machine would have that 1000-mile raid diameter. The frame was to be fixed so that there was a sleeping area within it. He paid for it with $350 cash in advance.

On July 4, Gypsy aka Yippie aka Cathy Share and Manon Minette, saw fit to take herself to Topanga Lane near the beach in Topanga Canyon to visit Charlie Melton, a bearded friend who lived in a canvas-covered stake truck notable in that it had an automobile seat perched atop its cab. There Gypsy was to fall into a scheme which would add considerably to that helter-skelter contribution jar in the saloon.

Linda Kasabian, her husband Bob, Blackbeard Charles and Jim and Juli Otterstrom—all were living in the stake truck, preparing for that trip to South America. Charles Melton had inherited around $23,000 and some of that was going to pay for the trip. The rest he had been giving away, much to the delight of various Topanga residents.

Inside Melton's trailer, Gypsy picked up his guitar and began to sing "Cease To Exist." Gypsy began to tell Linda about the

Spahn Ranch and particularly about Charles Manson. She said that children were the most important thing at the ranch, that everything was communally owned, that everybody was going to live in the desert. She told her about The Hole, and the river of Gold which Linda had already heard about from Hopi legends. It sounded out of sight.

According to Linda, Gypsy told Linda that Charlie was above wants and desires—he was dead. That it wasn't Charlie any more. It was the Soul. They were all Charlie and Charlie was they. And the men. There were men there who were great lovers, lots of them, ready for love that was total. The others in the trailer were shining Gypsy on but Gypsy said that their ego wouldn't let them listen to the Truth.

Mrs. Kasabian, though reconciled with her husband for only seven days, was having trouble with him. It seems that already he and Charles Melton had cut her out of the trip to South America. Gypsy invited her to come to the Spahn Ranch.

Linda had been planning that day to go to the July 4 Love-In on Topanga Beach but she went to the Spahn Ranch instead, taking her sixteen-month-old Tanya with her. Everybody hugged her when she and Tanya arrived at the ranch. They took from her her identification and her carried belongings. All was love and peace.

And she was ready for it for she had grown up in the dope-trip love generation, roaming sweet from commune to commune since she was sixteen. Tanya was taken, of course, to join Pooh Bear. Linda was told that Tanya's ego must remain free from the programs of the mother, therefore she was not to speak to her with the English language.

Mrs. Kasabian soon became pregnant after intercourse with Beausoleil, Manson, Tex, Bruce, Danny, Karate Dave, Clem et al. It was Beausoleil, however, who claims to be the father of the child.

It is interesting to note that the family scarfed up all i.d.'s and credit cards to be held in one central place, usually with Squeaky, in George Spahn's house. When a new runaway appeared they would gather up the i.d. almost like a ritual. Linda Kasabian was no exception. Thus, when Charlie told her to drive to Sharon Tate's house, she had to obtain her driver's license from the central i.d. cache.

That night Linda Kasabian encountered her first mystic experience at the ranch. She and Tex Watson made love in a dark shed and it was, as she later testified, unlike anything she'd ever experienced. It was total, but eerie, as if she were being possessed by some force from without. Her hands were clenched at her side at the culmination of the sex and her arms were paralyzed.

Later she asked Gypsy about the meaning of such paralysis. Gypsy reportedly told her that such things occurred when you don't give in completely to a man; her ego was dying.

Tex, during the loving, learned about the inheritance money that Charlie Melton had in his truck. He was all ears. He kept up a steady chant of there is no good/there is no evil, and everything belongs to everybody. She accepted it and decided to rip off Charlie Melton.

Linda slept that first night on the mattress on the roof of the Longhorn Saloon. That was the last night that Charlie allowed anyone to sleep on the roof. "The Panthers could easily spot us and kill us," he said.

July 5 was a day of happiness for the family. In the morning Tanya, Linda, Gypsy and Mary Brunner went to Topanga Canyon to go to the beach. They ran into Charles Melton and Bob Kasabian behind the Topanga Shopping Center by the creek. They smoked some hell-weed and Bob and Charles went off to downtown L.A. to get their passports for their trip.

Linda and the girls drove to Melton's canvas truck-house to get her possessions. She dug up a buried Bull Durham pouch full of thirty pink acid tabs she had brought from the East.

She packed up her gear, including household utensils and the tape-handled knife that was later to kill Abigail Folger and the old Buck clasp knife that Sadie would lose in a stuffed chair at the Polanski residence. Then she went into Melton's duffle bag and removed a Velvet tobacco pouch containing fifty $100 bills which she took to Chatsworth to give the Wizard. $5000.

Charlie was working on his dune buggy with Snake and Brenda when Linda was brought to him to be introduced. To Linda, Manson looked magnificent dressed in his buckskins. Charlie asked her why she had come to them. Linda told him that her husband didn't want her any longer and that Gypsy said she'd be welcome here. Charlie received the money. He scanned Linda's legs—"He felt my legs; seemed to think they were okay," as she later testified with a smile. He was pleased.

He was told about the probability that Charles Melton and friends would be coming to the ranch to get back the money. Manson then decided to send Linda to the cave down the creek behind the ranch, to hide from the wrath of her husband.

For her efforts, Linda was rewarded with a grotto-grope. When on the night she stole the money, July 5, Manson came to the cave where Linda was staying, Manson and she got after it on the cave floor in the presence of Gypsy, Ouish and Brenda. Up to his old tricks, Manson told Linda that she was hung up on her father. She admitted that she had a stepfather she didn't dig.

All the next day, high up the hill by the cave, the young ladies scanned the dirt driveway of the Spahn Ranch below with binoculars. And, just as predicted, Mr. Melton, Bob Kasabian and Jim Otterstrom pulled into the drive in their stake-bed truck.

Charles Melton asked someone by the boardwalk to locate Gypsy and Linda. The person left and returned with Manson, who rewarded Melton with kill me/kill you routine.

According to Melton, Manson said, "Who are Linda and Gypsy? I can't even remember their names."

Melton replied, "They took $5000 from me."

Manson said, "What's money? Nothing is yours." Then Charlie took out his knife and handed it to Melton, urging him to kill Charlie with Charlie's own knife.

Mr. Melton refused the proferred knife. Manson said, "Then maybe I should kill you to show you that there's no such thing as death."

At this point, Melton and company were quick to drive away into the wind.

The person named Bryn Lukashevsky who witnessed the shooting of Bernard Crowe called Dennis Wilson several days later and told him about it. Gregg Jakobson heard the conversation and evidently told Melcher. Melcher was very upset about it and that may have been the cause of the final rupture in any and all plans to record or film Manson. And Manson was really counting on Melcher to come through.

One day Manson asked Jakobson if Terry had a green spyglass set up outside of his beachhouse in Malibu.

"Yes," Jakobson replied.

"Well, he doesn't now," chortled Charlie.

So it was Doris Day's telescope that the family used when scanning for Black Panther raids from the Santa Susanna hilltop.

Slowly, Manson began to become infuriated with Melcher. He was welching on his commitments. One day Manson sent Leslie and another girl to Malibu Canyon to see Melcher. Melcher wouldn't see them but talked to them through an intercom at the door. "They used to talk about kidnapping him," Miss Lutesinger remembered.

Kasabian leaped with full force into the ranch life-style. Tex Watson and Linda Kasabian became close companions, a fact which may hold the answer to many baffling aspects of the so-called Tate-LaBianca murders.

When Gypsy testified at the trial she spoke of Linda Kasabian's eagerness after stealing the $5000.

"She got a whole lot of attention for that. She just kept on bringing back presents."

Manson quickly accepted Kasabian, she claims, and began, she says, to give her trusted assignments. Manson told Linda about the good old days long gone when he had his bus full of girls traveling freely. Those were the days.

Manson would paraphrase a song by John Lennon:

> "Christ you know it ain't easy,
> You know how hard it can be,
> They're gonna crucify me."

This was absolute proof that Lennon was gonna take the cross upon himself. "They crucified me last time but now John Lennon is taking my place," Charlie chortled.

Charlie promoted himself as a miracle healer. Once he cut his arm and said to Kasabian something like, "Someday I'll be able to heal myself." Another time supposedly he sat down and talked with a dying horse, Zane Grey, and miraculously the horse recovered. Then there also was the miracle of the club foot. Someone, unknown as of this writing, came to the ranch who had an enlarged foot and limped. Charlie allegedly cured him over the days, gradually, by a series of commands.

Things remained crusted with a sense of normalcy though family life was rapidly becoming berserk. Every evening George, Ruby Pearl and one of the family, usually Squeaky or Ouish, would drive to the International House of Pancakes in Chatsworth to eat. On the way back they stopped to load the truck up with corn for the horses. Then Ruby would drive to her own house and aged George would sack out in his house by the movie set, attended by his teenage geriatrics squad.

The girls spent a lot of time cleaning tools and dune-buggy parts, organizing them and helping to build the buggies. Leslie, Katie, Little Patti and Brenda, for the most part, were occupied with the children.

But Charlie was really jumpy.

Once Snake dared to talk during one of his lectures at dinnertime and Charlie grew furious and told her never to speak when he's talking.

One day in July Charlie was late for chow so the family started to eat without him, a sin. He got really angry when he arrived and stormed out of the house. Tex, Bobby, Clem and Bruce followed him out, begging forgiveness. Soon they all came back and Charlie played the guitar and they held a songfest. All was happy again.

And his raps about imminent death from the blacks caused waves of paranoia—especially on acid trips. Charlie loved the fear emanating from the silent circle of paranoid young men and women in the Longhorn Saloon listening for the oncoming foot-steps of the marauder-killers.

On July 10, Charlie Manson took a wad of $100 bills into Butler's Dune Buggy Shop and purchased for $2400 four dune buggies for the battalion. His trusted assistants, Bill Vance, Danny De Carlo, Tex and Bobby, now would possess their own legally purchased iron horses of Helter Skelter—and the work began on them immediately to modify the dune buggie for the north desert campaign.

One day, around the 10th or 11th, a black man with a dog stopped on the road by the Spahn Ranch and checked it out. He then drove down and looked at the trash dump—where the dune-buggy assembly line was located. Tanya and Bear were playing by the "gun room" on the boardwalk. This triggered off the fear that perhaps the Panthers might sometime gun down the children, so it was decreed, and it came to pass, that all children were to be kept at a new camp by a waterfall in the hills about a mile north of the Spahn Ranch on the other side of Santa Susanna Pass Road. They set up a tent and a campfire to cook. All runaways, all children and some of the older girls were kept there.

It was possible to walk up the Spahn Ranch creek to the new camp. Charlie wanted to be able to drive the dune buggies all the way up it, which was difficult because of the rocks and boulders in the creek bed. He ordered the girls to remove the boulders. They did.

Linda was proud when she was named by M. to drive the girls back and forth on the creek bed from the waterfall to the ranch.

There was also a visit from two carloads of black men with cameras. Charlie hid in the hollowed-out haystack by the corral; the girls ran to hide in the trash-dump dune-buggy factory. The blacks, eight in number, took pictures and generally checked out the ranch, then split. Family paranoia dictated that this had to be an advance Black Panther snuff unit who were out to wipe the aware white world-savers. They found candy wrappers in the weeds across the road from the ranch—another sign that the Panthers were watching them.

On July 14, Danny De Carlo and Bruce Davis went to a store called Surplus Distributors on Van Nuys Boulevard in Van Nuys. There they purchased several weapons including a .45-caliber pistol and a nine-millimeter Radon pistol, under assumed names, a violation of federal law. Davis used the name Jack McMillan and De Carlo used Richard Allen Smith.

Davis later told the police that Crowe had said he was going to kill them, therefore they bought the weapons.

On July 15, Officer Breckenridge of the Los Angeles sheriff's office was hovering above the Spahn Ranch in a 'copter when he noticed "at least three" Volkswagen floor pans scattered about, indicating to him at least the possibility of car theft and car strip. The sheriff's office was beginning to gather data on the car-theft aspect of the ranch. In a month they would raid.

Late one night during the five days that the family camped at the waterfall, the girls were busy sewing an ocelot skin upon Charlie's dune buggy. Malibu Brenda had liberated various furs from her mother's closet. Her mother was to flip out when she was to see her furs, worth thousands of dollars, garlanded upon his buggy in the *Life* magazine cover story a few months later.

Just before dawn, Charlie sent Brenda from the ranch with scissors bearing a wonderful announcement: it was time for the sacred witchy Tonsure Rite. Charlie said that they were ready to cut their hair—for, at last, their egos were dead. It was special privilege time. Snake announced that she did not want her long red tresses shorn. She was told they'd hold her down and do it anyway so she submitted to it. Katie was spared the hair chop because her full witchy mane was to serve as the magic blanket when they were to find refuge in The Hole. Oo-ee-oo.

The next day the tonsured young ladies went to the ranch to reveal themselves to the Wizard. They had left one long lock uncut, each of them, hanging down. The girls, according to legend, each buried one of their cut hairs and each also burned a hair in the fire. They saved their hair, each wrapping and tying their own into a swatch which they gave to the Soul. Charlie was pleased. "It looks good." He then told four or five others to snuff their hair also.

Around July 15, 1969, Charlie decided to move everyone in the family about three miles up Devil Canyon to a secluded spot in the woods, off a fire road. There they remained for about a week until a motorcycle patrol of police rousted them off the set.

From the ranch, from the cave and from the Fern Ann Falls campsite, around twenty of Manson's followers thronged to a new location, a pleasant grassy croft with a birch tree bent over the edge of it, providing a natural tent pole. The girls set up a ten-man tent and placed a parachute over the dune-buggy factory as camouflage.

Unfortunately, fire trucks used a nearby road and there was a riding trail cut just up the hill from the camp, so that quickly the camp was spotted. Almost at once a police helicopter checked out the camp. Manson or somebody in the family seems to have threatened firemen patrolling the dry fire trails with menacing motions of their "Tommy guns"— as the family called their submachine guns.

They camouflaged with brush the short entrance driveway that led from the fire road to the camp. The girls strung a telephone wire a mile or so down the rocky Devil Canyon so that the field phones could be set up for guard outposts.

There was a twenty-four-hour guard set up at the mouth of the canyon on a hill that overlooked the Spahn Ranch itself. The purpose was to watch for the police and the "Panthers." If any should invade, the watch was to phone up to the camp with a warning. The watch was divided into three shifts.

Charlie decided to have the NBC motion-picture camera handy and to string up lights as if a movie were in preparation. That was to be part of the excuse to the police, should they raid and find long-hairs and young girls.

At one point Charlie told Linda and Vance to go hot-wire a large truck with a generator on the back and drive it to the camp. They drove a car to the location of the truck; she was to drive the car back, he the truck. The mission was aborted, however, when Vance couldn't get it started, and Kasabian became afraid. Charlie and Vance went back and started it up. They drove it up the steep canyon to the camp. Tex needed the generator so he could work on his dune buggy and finish it.

They used the generator for three to four days, after which Vance then took it back and parked it a block from the owner's house. Linda and an unknown visitor went to pick Bill up and drive him back to the ranch.

When everybody moved to the canyon, they left a skeleton geriatrics force back at the ranch to take care of George and to help cook for the ranch hands. Included in the group left at the ranch were Little Patti, Zezo, Squeaky and Ouish.

Charlie told the girls to hang "witchy things," usually made from beads, feathers and leather, from the trees so that, by touch, they might return to the campsite at night. The girls set up a camp kitchen. Staple sustenance was provided by a hundred-pound sack of brown rice. The girls were told to secure additional food from the wild, a difficulty in such dry unfertile country. Linda Kasabian located a hot sulfur spring which soothed with its mud the endemic family skin problems: sores and lesions.

People would swim in a large wooden water tower nearby. At night they would lie about on sheepskins and sleeping bags while Danny played drums and Bobby or Charlie would sing and play the guitar. And the creepy-crawlie chorale would raise itself in unison.

Devil Canyon is rather dry but heavy rains in the winter of 1968–69 had kept the creeks full of water even into the summer so there was water aplenty in which to bathe and to wash the dishes nearby but no one was to go there in the daytime or in large numbers.

On Sunday, July 20, 1969, some of the family listened to the Apollo II moon landing on Danny De Carlo's radio in the bunkhouse and gun room, located at the end of the Western movie set, by the corral.

Around July 20 a sixteen-year-old boy named Mark Walts was

found by the roadside in Topanga, gored to death as if struck by an automobile several times. His brother, according to Danny De Carlo, came storming out to the Spahn Ranch to confront Manson about the death since the young boy had been supposedly staying there. Several police officers visited the Spahn Ranch to investigate the death.

Sometime in this era, a young girl, referred to in police records as Jane Doe 44, was murdered and buried in a shallow grave near Castaic a few miles northeast of the Spahn Ranch on Whitaker fire road. Jane Doe 44 is thought to be Susan Scott aka Joan Junior aka Stephanie Rowe, the girl arrested with the witches of Mendocino in 1968. The girl, totally unidentifiable by the time she was found months later, wore a short, puffy-sleeved dress which several have identified as a dress they saw at the Spahn Ranch.

Around July 20, the day on which Mark Walts died in Topanga, Charlie went into one of his fits of anger. The only known reason was that Gypsy had sinned by rolling a conga drum down a hill.

Ella, Sadie, Mary and Ouish ran down to the ranch from the Devil Canyon camp upset and sweaty. Charlie was beating Gypsy. In fact, he was going nuts. Kicking her in the ribs, hitting her in the head, until she couldn't move. He had yelled at Mary, in substance: "Why don't you take Bear to your mother? That's what you want to do." Then he smashed his guitar, drums, saying something about how "nobody cares enough for the music." He even smashed the sound-pack for the stolen NBC camera.

The police found the outside container of the sound system by the Devil Canyon camp. After the recorder was smashed, the transistors from it were placed in Baggies and were hung around the canyon and ranch as those witchy nighttime trail markers.

Within two days after Manson went berserk, the police raided the Devil Canyon creep camp and everyone had to move back to the ranch. Fortunately for Manson, the artist John Friedman and his family, who had been living in the back ranch, moved out, hauling with them the out-of-service International Scout given to the family by Juanita, and Helter Skelter was able to move in.

Charlie made arrangements with George to rent the back ranch. He moved the trailer truck back there and for a while everyone, including the children, lived in the ranch building. Nouveau mattress-on-floor was the decor of the barren back ranch.

The police raided again, however, so Charlie had a few girls set up the tent in a thicket of woods down the creek across from the house. This is the residence referred to as "the wickiup" in the testimony of Barbara Hoyt, a family follower who was later fed an LSD-drenched hamburger in Honolulu to keep her from testifying. The children and all runaway girls were enjoined to sleep in the wickiup.

The dune-buggy works was set up again in the dump behind the bunkhouse. Security precautions were established by Manson. No one was to hang out at the front ranch, except those assigned tasks there by Satan.

When they moved into the back ranch, some of them reminisced about the good old days of 1968 when they had first lived there, how groovy it was with all those tapestries and pillows bought with Juanita's money. They also recounted the tale of the fire orgy of October '68 where no one got burnt even though they were hurled into the flames.

But it was tough going. It will be remembered that the Transcontinental Development Corporation was hot in pursuit of the various properties in the Spahn Ranch area for that German-American resort. Unfortunately for Manson, and another pressure upon him, was the fact that George Spahn's property line ran right through the middle of the back ranch building causing some problem regarding who actually owned it. Transcontinental had purchased a chunk of land adjacent to the back ranch and claimed the back ranch belonged to them. The officials of the Transcontinental Development Corporation were naturally eager to wipe the hippies out of the area so they began to pressure the family to leave the back ranch.

In honor of reacquiring the back ranch, Charlie decreed that there be an orgy, an event far-famed in the annals of Manson family lore, for it was to be the Initiation of Simi Valley Sherri.

Simi Valley Sherri was a fifteen-year-old local girl who tended horses at the ranch. Her last name is not mentioned here because she has since returned to high school.

The orgy was attended by about twenty people plus four "guests"—whose identity is unknown at this writing.

The event probably took place about July 22, 1969. Some people have claimed that it was filmed. Charlie positioned the fifteen-year-old girl in the center of the assembly then stripped her bare except for her bikini underpants. Everyone stared. Cameras whirred. She was less than willing. Charlie pushed her to the floor and began to touch her head to toe. He started to kiss her neck and her breasts. Simi Sherri bit Manson on the shoulder causing him to punch her in the face.

According to Linda Kasabian, a key participant in the orgy, Manson said, "Sherri, remember the time when I chased you down the creek with a brick in my hand and said if you didn't make love to me I was going to hit you over the head and rape you?"

She lay quiet and Manson ripped off her panties. He told Beausoleil to make love with her. This Beausoleil did.

Then Charlie flashed the signal to begin indiscriminate apertural-appendage caress and conjugation. "The whole scene was perversion like I've never seen before," declared Linda Kasabian. And was she active.

There was tri-love between Kasabian, Leslie and Tex Watson. Clem then lay with Linda. Snake Lake twined in love with the twenty-year-old Mrs. Kasabian. "Sometimes I looked up," Mrs. Kasabian testified at the trial when asked if she observed what was happening in other parts of the room.

Fourteen

Getting the Fear

One of Manson's summer 1969 raps was about how groovy fear was, is. "Getting the Fear," as he called it, was an exquisite physical experience. It's actually an old LSD phenomenon—conquering a period of intense fear. But Manson decided that the entire substance of expanded consciousness was fear—the "infinite plain of fear unto infinity."

He says the girls kept asking him what he meant about getting the fear. Manson would tell them, in substance, "Well, I go into Malibu and pick a rich house. I don't steal, I walk into the house and the fear hits you like waves. It's almost like walking on waves of fear."

He advocated going into wealthy homes where there were lights on. He taught that "the rich piggies" inside would be too scared themselves to do anything. He showed his followers how to shim open those pushover summer climate doors with a thin plastic card. He demonstrated how to cut open a screen with a knife.

"Do the unexpected," he said. "No sense makes sense. You won't get caught if you don't got thought in your head."

Forthwith all the trusted girls of the family began to jump in the waves of fear, crawling into houses and stealing jewelry and furs. They would wear dark clothing and open windows silently and crawl about in that Malibu living-room fear surf. Then they would leave, taking booty.

The actual term "creepy-crawl" began to be used in July of

1969 and was invented by the girls. "I didn't tell them to creepy-crawl. They just did it," Charles Manson said on June 24, 1970.

Sadie, it seems, was a creepy-crawler among creepy-crawlers. Dressed in a black cape and her newly purchased genuine Roebuck jeans, she would go scout for targets, peeking into windows. De Carlo says it like this: "And that's all they did. Spend all their time up in the rich district up there in Beverly Hills, and the Brentwood area. All around there where all the rich people hang out. And their theory was to make such a gruesome thing out of it, like he wanted to go as far as hanging 'em up by their feet and slice 'em."

It seems strange that all of a sudden they got into wearing black capes. The girls made Charlie one that reached to the floor. With a flourish Manson tried it on, remarking how no one for sure now would see him when he creepy-crawled. Mary Brunner had a black cape. Sadie had a cape. Squeaky, according to Danny De Carlo, used to dye clothing black in a pot in the Spahn Ranch kitchen.

Black capes, black clothes, getting the fear. Just like the Process.

Because guess what the Process was doing in the summer of 1969? They were preparing the "Fear" issue of the *Process* magazine, issue number 5, which has to be seen to be believed. The "Process Fear Issue" was published in the fall of 1969 after they returned from their proselytizing in America. The "Fear" issue is like a plane wreck. Page after page babbles about fear. There is a page devoted to quotes from members of the Hell's Angels motorcycle club, an article called "Satan Is Fear," a grim photo of all twenty-four Process Alasatian dogs lined up in a hostile row, and so on and so forth.

The centerfold, so to speak, of the magazine is a collage honoring the Lamb of Christ and the Goat of Satan. The gibberish of the centerfold ends: "The Lamb and the Goat must come together —pure Love descended from the pinnacle of Heaven, united with pure hatred raised from the depths of Hell."

On the back page of the "Fear" issue is a flaming pink skull on various sections of which are superimposed images of evil. As if

out of the skull's mouth there is a marching line of Nazis holding
a Nazi banner parading atop people burning in a fire. On the
lower right there is a depiction of the face of Hitler seen through
a warped fun-house mirror. In the left eyesocket of the pink skull
is a human, perhaps a Vietnamese monk, burning to death. Or it
may be one of those "meteorite hippies"—burning sacrificially like
a Druid. There is a snarling monkey above the skull nose, with
what appears to be a dead baby superimposed on the monkey's
ear. In the right skull eyesocket is a petrified or eroded upper
torso of a human.

At the top of the page the words: "Next issue: DEATH."

One of the things the Process was doing in the summer of
1969 was recruiting in the Los Angeles area, on the sly. They were
going around to various extant cults and seeking membership.
There is also indication that they had their own secret Process
commune out in the San Fernando Valley.

Tex Watson has said that Manson raved and ranted about the
Process in his lectures. Bruce Davis was involved with them in
England. The family knew about the Process group in Santa
Barbara. But when asked about the Process, most family mem-
bers merely dealt out that blank hostile stare they are famous
for.

Manson may have visited New York City during July of 1969,
using the name Chuck Summers—his "Hollywood name."

For instance, in July 1969, a man named Chuck Summers
bought a book in a scientology bookstore in New York.

Robert and Mary Anne DeGrimston-Moor, the founding couple
of the Process, are thought to have been in New York in July
1969. There are ominous rumors that Manson may have "hooked
up" with Robert DeGrimston, the co-founder of the Process
Church of Final Judgment.

When the Process returned to England from the U.S. in late
1969 they bore with them several converts from the Los Angeles
area. They claimed to a reporter for United Press International
to have "converted" over 200 to the Process in the United States.

When asked about the possibility that he knew DeGrimston,

Manson replied, "I am DeGrimston." He further explained that what he meant was that people who believe the same are the same person. Sure, sure.

Since the trials, Manson has been visited by Process members through the kind offices of his attorney. Manson has written an article for the so-called "Death Issue" of the *Process* magazine, issue number 6, which is forthcoming.

The Process symbol is a sort of inverted swastika. And why has Manson, since he has been found guilty of murder, carved an inverted swastika that looks remarkably like the Process symbol into his forehead?

There are subjects associated with the Manson case that are so soaked in evil that the mere knowing of them is like a nightmare.

All kinds of people, including Beausoleil, Manson, Vern Plumlee and others, admitted that people sometimes made motion pictures of family activities. The family made films in Topanga Canyon, Malibu Canyon, Death Valley, in Hollywood, at the Spahn Ranch.

Vern Plumlee said this about family filmmaking: "They made home movies; yeah—I watched the family make movies, you know, just crazy movies."

"What about subject matter?" he was asked.

"Well, just anything, you know, just anything that came up, like if a person was having a heck of an acid trip, they filmed that, you know. And like just goofy things."

Plumlee said that they had three super-8 film cameras with which they filmed.

He was asked about violent films. "Like dancing, you know. Like, they'd be dancing with knives, you know, and they'd pretend they were cutting each other up or something like that. I really didn't think that much of it—just another weird thing that they did." (Laughs.)

Another family associate independently described in an interview what seems to be the same pretend-to-hack type of film.

He was more exuberant about it than Plumlee was: "It's really a trippy flick—uh, it's maybe seven minutes long—but it's Charlie and everybody like running round in a circle . . . with knives—you know, the belt with the knife on it—and they're holding the knives, you know, flicking around and uh—for about three minutes this goes on and then they just start, you know, start charging everything and everything with the knives, you know, trees, to the house, and so on."

Plumlee told of several friends of the family who processed films for them. One was a person who lived on a dirt road in Granada Hills, east of the Spahn Ranch, who may have done film developing for the family. For a long time, the family films seemed merely to be sexual—with the added spice of a few famous faces and bodies. Ho hum.

Once this writer was in Los Angeles posing as a New York pornography dealer with Andy Warhol out-takes for sale. There was an opportunity at that time to purchase seven hours of assorted erotic films including Manson porn collected during the pre-trial investigations. But the price was $250,000. Then there was a note which was written to a reporter by a person named Chuck, a friend of Gary Hinman, claiming possession of films of "Malibu and San Francisco ax murders."

Later it turned out that a Los Angeles dope dealer allegedly sold a film depicting the ritual murder of a woman to a famous New York artist whose name will not be mentioned here.

Finally a person was interviewed who had been hanging around on the edges of the family for about two and a half years. He told a tale which, if true, and it seems to be, ushers in the ugly age of video-vampirism. He told about movies which the family would show at night, evidently in the woods behind or above the Spahn Ranch. It was sort of an outdoor light show with several movies shown at the same time.

"The family had things where they'd show flicks, you know, like light-show type things; they were running four or five different movies at once; you know, playing tapes at the ranch."

He said they played various tapes as a sound track. For movie screens they hung up white sheets. They rented four or five battery-operated eight-millimeter movie projectors down in Los Angeles for these grim events. The batteries supposedly ran the machines for a half hour or so. And the films shown seem to have been reels of family happenings, music, the already noted knife dance, lots of sex—but other films also.

According to a study called "The Blood Sacrifice Complex" by E. M. Loeb (printed in the *Memoirs* of the *American Anthropological Association*, Volume 30) there were human sacrifices performed in much of prehistoric America but somehow the California area was spared—spared evidently till recently.

The person who has been interviewed shall remain anonymous for obvious reasons.

After graduation from high school in the Midwest in 1968 this individual came to Haight-Ashbury where he met the family when they were crashing on Clayton Street. He possesses a lot of information about the Haight, the Haight-Ashbury Free Clinic, the Waller Street Devil House, etc. Manson, he says, invited him down to live in Los Angeles. He claims to have scrounged around with the family off and on since then.

There are a great number of reasons for believing that what he tells approximates the truth. The biggest is that, from ten or fifteen long interviews, it is apparent that his knowledge of the Manson family history is very detailed and accurate. He knows facts about the Process Church of Final Judgment that only someone close to it would know. In essence, he alleged that members of the Process and others were involved with members of an obscure bike club in a ritzy hilltop commune not far from the Spahn Ranch. He alleged that the family was involved with this group. That they went there to score dope. That they participated with them in out-of-door filmed beach ceremonies involving sacrifices. That some of the family were in the films. That screenings of the films were given secretly at the Spahn Ranch.

During a year of investigation, there were numerous rumors

and reports from people interviewed that there had been occult and magic ceremonies on various secluded beaches north and south of Los Angeles.

He alleged that the site of some of the filmed ceremonies was located on the beach by Highway 1 near a restaurant called Pete's Beef across the street from the County Line Mobil station. He also pointed out other locations.

There were three types of films that he seems to have witnessed: (1) family dancing and loving; (2) animal sacrifices; (3) human sacrifices.

The dates he gave for the making of the film varied. He claimed that some were made in 1969 and some, O Lord, in 1970 in the summertime.

In most of the films, he claimed that a lot of the participants were dressed in black and were wearing crosses, though some of them, however, wore white clothing. Some wore black hoods but others had no hoods on. In the dog-blood flick, the film allegedly began with everybody sitting around singing. Then it was all hideousness.

Here is his description of the dog-sacrifice movie:

"It was like a nighttime thing. It started out with the people, you know, everybody was sitting around—and they just, uh, one of the cats came, and uh, it was about eleven o'clock at night and uh, they started their trip, right—and uh, type thing. Just sitting around and a guy brought out a thing of blood and everybody took a hit. Then the guy was, you know, poured it over everybody. Then, like, this other cat came by and uh, and then this whole funny trip . . .

"They cut up a dog. Then they brought a girl in there—two girls. They took their clothes off and poured the blood off the dog on top of the girls. They just held the dog. And they took the girls and they put the blood—and the bodies—all over both of them. And everybody balled the two girls . . . it was a couple, two couples—they were being, uh—but I'm not, you know, this was a while ago. But I remember they were all taking hits of blood. It was really weird . . . I recognized maybe eight to ten people in that film. You know, people that I know, people that I've seen come to the ranch, you know, people that have, you know, for the weekend or so . . . They had two or three similar to that that I've seen of theirs."

He further fingered out two key Manson female followers as having taken part in the drinking of blood, one of them having sexual intercourse while blood was poured on her. All on film.

"I've only seen a few sacrifices," he said. "I've seen one with the dog. I seen, uh, one with the cat—that cat was the most gruesome."

Here is part of the interview dealing with the cat:

    Q. Where was it?
    A. It was outside. This was the one I was talking to you about, on the beach.
    Q. Where they had the cat?
    A. And the dog.
    Q. Same place?
    A. Yeah. I think they had their monthly things there. The out-of-doors freak-outs.
    Q. You know where on the beach that is? Malibu Beach?
    A. No. It's a private beach, uh, it's like just on the boundary line of Los Angeles County and Ventura. It's on Highway 1.
    Q. What's the name of the house?
    A. It's not a house. It's just a beach.
    Q. Who owns it?
    A. I don't know. Nobody. It's like a private beach I don't even know who owns it.
    Q. What day of the month (do they meet)?
    A. Wednesdays.
    Q. Full moon?
    A. Or full moon, whatever.
    Q. Every other Wednesday?
    A. Something like that, but, you know, I've seen three or four movies like that and the cat movie was the stupidest one I've seen; it was gruesome. They took firecrackers . . . what do you call it, M–80's, and lit it and

had the cat sit on it. Blew the cat to smithereens. It was just so gruesome. Sickening.

Q. What'd they do with the blood?

A. They just smeared it all over themselves and poured blood all over themselves, you know, they had maybe a pint of blood, they were, they'd pass around and everyone'd get a hit off of it. Those movies were really gruesome.

He gave considerable information about a short movie depicting a female victim dead on a beach. This film, he contended, was part of a larger movie.

He was asked initially if he was aware of such movies. His answer was:

A. I, I, I knew, I know, I only know about one snuff movie. I, uh, you know—

Q. Which snuff movie do you know about?

A. I just know like a young chick maybe about twenty-seven, short hair . . . yeah . . . and chopped her head off, that was . . .

Q. Whereabouts was that?

A. Probably uh, from the scenery somewhere around Highway 1, and the beach.

Q. Who'd they look like? Who was in the film besides the decapitated girl?

A. It didn't show anybody's face. It just had everybody on black creepy-crawlies with the black hood and uh—

Q. What do you mean black? Black hoods with eyeholes you mean?

A. (Nods) and uh—

Q. What else?

A. You know, long black type dress(es).

Q. Any crosses on?

A. No, it was all black and with these kind of straight type things to go over their faces with slits and they, uh, people were just dancing around it. Nobody ever said what it was. It was a short thing maybe five minutes.

Q. What'd the girl look like? What was the scenario?

A. What was the what?

Q. What was the scenario? Was she tied up. Did she look willing?

A. She was dead. She was just lying there.

Q. She was already dead?

A. Yeah. Legs spread, uh. She was nude but nobody was fucking her. They said her head was just chopped off and she was just laying there.

Q. That's when the movie started? They didn't show the actual sacrifice?

A. (*Shakes head no*) They showed people throwing blood all over, all around the circle.

Q. Did it look like anybody was the leader?

A. No, maybe it was a short. You know what I mean, don't you? It could have been just something, you know, shot, you know, that they didn't edit in one of the other movies. It was only five minutes long. It was just a small thing.

Q. Five minutes is thousands of frames. It sounds like one I know about. It was inside the footage that was shot this summer?

A. (*No answer*)

Q. What was the rest of the movie like?

A. I didn't see it. I just, you know—

Q. Red-haired?

A. Yeah.

Q. The head was just lying there?

A. Right next to the body.
   (*Gives a demonstration with his own head*)

Q. How many people were in the film with black clothes?

A. Five. They were circling around the body.

Q. Was there a campfire?

A. Campfire was about here (*points*) and you could see a few other people walking around, but you know.

Q. Were they in robes, all the other people too?

A. It could have been a continuation of something else, but I didn't . . . It was kind of an interesting flick. (! !)

Q. Was she lying on a rock?

A. No, she was just, you know, on a beach.

Q. On the sand?

A. Yeah. Just really weird.

Q. Did it look like a protected area?

A. Boy, you can't do stuff like that unless it's really protected.

Q. Do you think it's that area on the beach on Highway 1
where that restaurant is?

A. It doesn't look—I mean—there was so mu—you know—
you can usually tell that one place if you've seen it, but
you know it wasn't that place—it could have been somewhere else along Highway 1; they could have done that
and dug a little hole and dropped in the remains. You
can hide shit like that. This was a short one. Only five
minutes long. The only difference in the Apogee one and
the dog movie was that there was no crosses.

Q. In the dog movie they had the hoods on too?

A. Well, they didn't have them on all the time. Sometimes
they had them off.

Q. But sometimes they had the pointed cowls on?

A. But the thing is, you can tell who it was by the faces,
you know. It wasn't always the same.

Q. You don't think it was the same people then?

A. It probably—unless they didn't have crosses on. One time
they had crosses, another time they didn't.

Q. They wear gloves?

A. No.

Q. What kind of knives did they do their work with?

A. Bowie. Twelve-inch Bowie knives. It's the ones I've seen.
I saw Bowie knives and a hatchet. One of the persons
had a Bowie knife on this side and a hatchet on this side.

If this information is true, there is no girl, no woman, no bather
at the beach, no hitchhiker at the Freeway ramp who is safe in
southern California till these people are taken off the streets.

Section II

The Murders
July 25, 1969–August 15, 1969

Fifteen

The Death of Gary Hinman

Compared to the Spahn Ranch, the house on Cielo Drive was like a citadel of mental health.

Things were pretty casual at 10050 Cielo Drive while the owner Mr. Altobelli and the lessees, the Polanskis, were all in Europe during April, May, June and July 1969.

John Phillips, the songwriter, told a reporter that there were weirdos hanging out at 10050 Cielo Drive that summer of the type he had been studiously avoiding for years.

In April and May of 1969 Abigail Folger took an active part in the Tom Bradley mayoralty campaign. According to a co-worker, she worked at the Youth Headquarters on Wilshire Boulevard. She also worked for a few months as a volunteer helping children in Watts. During the mayoralty campaign, Abigail Folger became interested in a black group called the Street Racers who evidently served as security forces for the Bradley rallies and offices.

Sometime in June, after Mr. Bradley's defeat on May 26, Miss Folger and her mother visited New York City for a while. Abigail would travel frequently, almost commuting from Los Angeles to San Francisco.

In the spring and summer of 1969, Mr. Frykowski made lengthy daily entries into notebooks in order to work on his grasp of the English language. He was hoping to become a movie script writer.

In early June, Sharon Tate was seen at a party in London's

Mayfair section. After the party she was driven home in her new Rolls-Royce. "It was Roman's birthday present to me," she said. "We're taking it back to Hollywood to be with our seventeen cats, three dogs and the new baby. I can't wait to get back to start on the nursery."

Around July 7 or 8 Frykowski learned that Sharon was coming back around July 20. He and Miss Folger began to move clothing from Cielo Drive to their own home on Woodstock Road.

A Polish artist named Witold Kaczanowski aka Witold K. had been brought to the United States through the kindness of Roman Polanski. He naturally came to live in Los Angeles where he cultivated the Polanskis' circle of friends. He was staying, during the summer of murder, at the Woodstock Road home of Abigail Folger and Voityck Frykowski. He was a frequent house guest at 10050 Cielo Drive during the spring and summer of 1969. An actor friend of Voityck by name of Mark Fine also had been staying at the Woodstock address but moved out the second week in July, having stayed one week.

Early in July, several friends of Frykowski from Canada promised him samples of a new drug called Methlenedioxyl-amphetamine or MDA, a euphoric stimulant with overtones of aphrodisia that was coming into vogue. According to police reports, Frykowski was being set up to serve as a wholesaler of quantities of MDA manufactured in Toronto.

Both Mr. Frykowski and Miss Folger were enjoying MDA on the night they died.

In mid-July Frykowski's friends from Canada went to Ocho Rios, Jamaica allegedly to create some sort of movie about marijuana use there. This Jamaican movie project was a front for a large marijuana import operation involving private planes secretly winging the dope to the United States via Florida and Mexico. Investigation into the operation after the murders resulted in one of the biggest dope busts in Jamaican history.

They were making films on Cielo Drive. One day in July William Garretson, the caretaker, saw Voityck Frykowski taking pictures of a nude lady in the swimming pool. A cable TV repairman named Villela came to the Polanski residence and encountered some sort of a nude love set going on.

Around July 14 Voityck ran over Sharon's Yorkshire terrier, Saperstein. The dog had been named Saperstein after the doctor in *Rosemary's Baby* who prescribed weird herbal drinks during her satanic pregnancy. Voityck called London with the news. In London, Roman Polanski then purchased another Yorkshire terrier which was named Prudence.

Sometime in the middle of July, Brian Morris gave a catered party for 150 at the Polanski residence, seemingly to round up members for Bumbles, a new private club that was to serve the Polanski circle.

On Sunday, July 20, Abigail, Voityck, Jay Sebring, Lieutenant Colonel Tate and Sharon Tate watched the moon landing at 10050 Cielo Drive.

Mrs. Polanski asked Abigail Folger and Voityck Frykowski to stay at Cielo Drive until her husband was to arrive from London on August 12. He had remained behind finishing the script of *Day of the Dolphins* and also to receive an award for *Rosemary's Baby* at the Taormina Film Festival in Sicily.

In the days before her death, Sharon was seen in local department stores purchasing baby supplies. Her white Rolls-Royce was on the way home from London. Roman had employed an English governess who was to arrive in Los Angeles in the middle of August.

Sharon Tate was bubbling with happiness over the impending birth of the baby. She was exercising in preparation for the delivery. She bought books on child care and supplies for the nursery, which was being built in July in the north wing of the house.

Jay Sebring was a frequent house guest at the Polanski residence whenever he wasn't overseeing his far-flung business interests.

Jay Sebring served in the U.S. Navy during the Korean war. He was short, about five feet six, and slender, weighing maybe 125 pounds, and intense. Paul Newman, according to the San Francisco Chronicle, said that Sebring's method prevented him from losing his hair. Actor George Peppard allegedly spent $2500 to fly Sebring to a movie location to trim his locks. Frank Sinatra used to fly Sebring to Las Vegas to cut his hair. "He was a legendary name in hair styling," commented his friend Art Blum.

He was born with the surname Kummer, the son of a CPA in Detroit. In Hollywood, he changed his name, incredibly enough, to correspond to that of an automobile racetrack, Sebring.

Actors and singers and businessmen would play chess in Sebring's shop. When a particularly illustrious client would arrive, he would rush to cut his hair himself. By the time of his death, the fee for his personal haircut was fifty dollars. If his assistants performed the cut, the fee was about a third as much. Is it possible to imagine paying fifty dollars for a haircut?

The corporate offices for Sebring International were located above the hair shop at 725 North Fairfax in Hollywood.

In partnership with public relations executive Art Blum, Sebring opened another shop in the summer of 1969 in San Francisco at 629 Commercial Street. Shortly afterwards Sebring rented a houseboat in Sausalito, California, just north of San Francisco. Throughout the summer, he flew frequently north to check on his new enterprises. On several occasions he visited Colonel Tate and family at Fort Barry. Mr. and Mrs. Tate would stay at Sebring's houseboat in Sausalito when they came to San Francisco. One Saturday, either the last Saturday in July or the first Saturday in August, Sebring threw an afternoon publicity party at his hair shop in San Francisco attended by Paul Newman, Miss Folger and a throng of guests. In the days following, Mr. Sebring was in Los Angeles where he spent a great deal of time at the Polanski residence with Abigail Folger, Voityck Frykowski and Sharon Tate.

There was a so-called darker side to Sebring. The police, after his murder, found films at his house which revealed an interest in hoods, whips, studded cuffs and people chained submissively to fireplaces.

Every day for about a week Charlie instructed Mary, Bruce Davis,

Bobby and various others to use a bunch of the ripped-off credit cards to purchase a large supply of helter-skelter equipment. They bought hundreds of dollars' worth of sleeping bags, dune-buggy tools, lots of Buck clasp knives, mess kits, baby clothes.

Each girl wrote down her measurements. Charlie wanted each one to have a straight-looking dress and a dark creepy-crawlie outfit. Included in the clothing were ten or so sets of dark blue tee shirts and genuine Roebuck jeans.

A young man from Simi Valley named Hendrix came across a car wreck in San Bernadino where a man named Dries had died and his credit cards were strewn on the highway. Hendrix grabbed up the credit cards and took them to the Spahn Ranch.

Hendrix, a seventeen-year-old known to the family merely as Larry, was an example of the psychopathic youth attracted to the family. He was another gun freak, operating a gun business "on the street." He was also a teenage demolition expert, claiming that he once blew a hole in the side of a mountain. Once he was arrested and accused of blowing up a house.

Hendrix incurred Charlie's wrath by stealing a huge motorcycle using one of the family automobiles. Someone spotted him. He buried the bike in the sand and later claimed that as soon as he was released from the insane asylum, he was going to dig it up and it would be all his.

Late in July the family bought some bayonets and sharpened them at a shop on Devonshire. These were added to the arsenal in De Carlo's "gun room." The bayonets and swords, etc., were all kept in readiness in a slit between the door and the wall.

There was one caper discussed in July '69 involving the robbery of a gambling casino near Box Canyon. Manson and Linda Kasabian, according to Kasabian, actually drove up a steep dirt road to the casino to plot the caper. The plan was: he'd have one of the girls stand at a nearby stop sign and ask for a ride from anyone leaving the casino. Manson would follow behind him and make him pull over then seize the person's wallet. An alternative was to follow someone to his home and then get all his valuables.

A person named by the family "Karate Dave" spent several

weeks during July at the Spahn Ranch. He helped the group
with karate lessons—lessons which Tex Watson would use when
he was kicking bodies at the Polanski residence.

There was a car shortage in the family in late July. The '68
Plymouth Roadrunner had been repossessed. The sleazy dune
buggies could not be legally driven on the road. De Carlo's bread
truck had not reappeared as yet. About the only good automobile,
a yellow and white 1959 Ford with back seat removed to accommodate garbage crates, belonged to a ranch hand named Johnny
Swartz, who lived in one of the house trailers. It was the car
driven to the Polanski residence and to the La Bianca residence.

Manson seemed to have a number of private interpersonal
relationships, outside of his so-called family, where he was the
tormentor. There was one girl who worked at the Moonfire Inn in
Topanga on whom he pulled a terror scene. He threatened to
kidnap her baby and take it to the mountains. When a fireman
named Witt came to the ranch and told Manson to cut the weeds
for fire safety reasons, Charlie threatened to gouge out the
fireman's eyeballs. Manson threatened to kill Dennis Wilson's
son, Scotty, when Wilson refused to give him money. And then
there was Hinman.

Thirty-two-year-old Gary Hinman was near to getting his Ph.D.
in Sociology from UCLA. He had always helped out the Manson
family. People in Topanga Canyon would send people to crash
for a night at his house. For about a year he had been intensely
interested in Nichiren Shoshu Buddhism, a militant sect head-
quartered in Japan with Los Angeles headquarters located on the
Coast Highway at the Santa Monica Beach.

In Hinman's house were found considerable lists of names of
potential converts to Nichiren Shoshu Buddhism. Found in the
house were an abundance of gohonzas to give to new members.
A gohonza is a religious scroll used by the sect.

Hinman had a small setup at his house where he made quantities of synthetic mescaline. A young married couple who lived
with Gary right up to several days before his death were partners
with him in the manufacture of the mescaline. "We were making

mescaline. It was a really long long process but the advantage was that it was really cheap. You bought things and no one would ever connect the things you bought with what you were going to do. You could order zillions of them from the chemical supply houses and they'd never get hip not unless somebody really did some thinking. Gary had a degree in chemistry." His partner's wife has indicated that Hinman had developed a method of manufacture whereby two steps in the process were eliminated.

About four days before Gary Hinman was murdered, Eric, the mescaline partner, visited Hinman's house at 964 Old Topanga Canyon Road. When he entered the small hillside house he found Gary Hinman on the phone, arguing with Manson. He says: "When I came into the house they were arguing. Like, Gary was really into Nichiren Shoshu and the concept of leadership and the concept that people needed to be directed, which was something that Charlie was very opposed to, and so they were in a heated discussion about that and then it was like there was a response: it was pretty together and I talked to Gary afterwards to verify what Charlie said— He said, you know, like it's your last chance, Gary. And Gary responded to that: 'I'm sorry, Charlie. I'm not going to sell all my things and come and follow you.' Those were his exact words.

"And so Charlie said, in response to that, that he couldn't be responsible then for the karma that Gary was going to incur. He then reiterated that it was his last chance. And Gary said, 'I'll decide . . . I'll take care of my own karma.' "

Manson has claimed to jail visitors that Hinman had made drugs and that certain individuals had threatened Hinman as a result of the sale of bad dope. Hinman, he said, came to him seeking protection.

On Thursday, July 24, Manson sent Ella Bailey aka Ella Sinder, over to Gary Hinman's house to get the money and then to kill him. Miss Sinder had been a close friend of Hinman. Although she was a long-time Manson follower, she was not willing to snuff anybody for him. Bill Vance, who loved Ella, tried to intercede with Charlie but Charlie was furious. So Ella and Bill Vance left the ranch together and went to Texas. The family was enraged with this, muttering among themselves, how they were going to kill Bill and Ella if the two should dare to come back to the Spahn Ranch.

Everything was murder. One day around this time Cathy Gillies Myers went off by herself without checking out. When she returned Tex threatened her. "Don't you ever leave here without telling someone where you're going, next time I'll kill you, your life means nothing to me," he said, according to Linda Kasabian.

The next day, July 25, 1969, Kitty Lutesinger asked Beausoleil if she could leave. She was getting a little weary of living at the ranch, the constant hassles, the raids and the general atmosphere of impending doom. So Bobby said that he would ask Charlie if she could leave. He asked Charlie and Charlie said that under no circumstances could she leave the ranch.

Charlie and Kitty apparently never got along for Charlie would say that she looked too much like his mother, also a thin, short redhead. Manson came up to Kitty and accused her of trying to trick Bobby into leaving the family. He threatened to torture and to kill her. That afternoon Manson was seen pacing up and down the Spahn Ranch boardwalk, sword in hand, fencing with his shadow, jabbing the sword at bales of hay, angry.

Also that afternoon, Bobby and Charlie went for a ride in his dune buggy up Devil Canyon. They checked out an old abandoned mine whereupon, according to Beausoleil, Manson noted that it would be a good place to hide a body. Manson was armed. Indeed, he was armed: the magic sword was stuck in a metal tube on the steering column of the dune buggy; a pistol was in a holster on the bucket seat between Charlie's legs; and there was a knife strapped to his ankle.

Some say the long hair swatches shorn from the girls were tied together and were affixed to the dune-buggy roll bar. The canopy of ocelot fur decorated the back deck near the machine-gun mounts. Manson shifted in the bucket seat toward Beausoleil and asked if it were true that Bobby was thinking of splitting from the ranch. And when Bob said yes, Charlie according to Bob, said, "Maybe I ought to slit your motherfuckin' throat." Manson used his old con routine, saying that Bobby knew too much to be allowed to leave.

Abruptly, according to Bobby, Manson changed the subject to Hinman and asked Bobby if he would be willing to go over to Gary's house and try to get some money out of him.

Beausoleil, at his second murder trial, testified that the reasons for getting money from Hinman were to help the family move to the desert. "I was supposed to tell Gary about the idea of making the desert a place for a lot of people. Gary is the type of person who would be interested in something like that, making a place for people where they could express themselves in music."

Linda Kasabian remembered that around dusk she was standing in front of the ranch and Bobby and Charlie were in the bunkhouse talking. Sadie and Mary were outside the bunkhouse standing patiently, waiting for Bobby to come out so that they could go someplace. Sadie told Linda Kasabian that they were going to get some money and that she and Mary had been chosen to go in order to work out a personality conflict.

Manson has admitted several times that the entire Hinman affair was about some botched dope deal.

The story most circulated by family members was that Gary Hinman had an inheritance of $20,000 stashed away in his house, and they were out to get it.

One version of the grim tale says that Beausoleil, Sadie and Mary were driven to Hinman's house by Bruce Davis in Johnny Swartz's Ford, the same car they would drive to the murder of Sharon Tate and the others. Sadie and Mary evidently went in first to see if anybody was there. Sadie signaled out the window, apparently by lighting a cigarette, and Beausoleil went in.

But there are strange variations on this story. For instance, there is a black jazz composer, a close friend of Hinman, in Topanga Canyon who claims to have driven Manson and two girls to Hinman's house that night.

At the Spahn Ranch, while Beausoleil and Sadie and Mary were working Hinman over, the family ran the walkie-talkie system from the movie set a half mile or so to the back ranch. A girl would stand guard at the front ranch, prepared to call the back ranch in case of any invasion by the police or the blacks.

Hinman had been living with a young, red-haired girl named Diane right up to the end of his life. She and Gary were seen the day before the family began to torture him, smiling and waving as they drove through Topanga Canyon in Hinman's 1958 red and white Microbus with a red thunderbird emblazoned on the side. It is hoped that Diane, believed to have been a runaway from San Diego, was not subsequently killed by the family.

That afternoon Gary Hinman had gone down to Los Angeles to obtain a passport. In two weeks he intended to undertake a religious pilgrimage to Japan. He had taken with him Glen Krell, who owned a music school where Hinman taught piano, bagpipes, trombone and the drums. Hinman called Krell to ask if Krell would sit in as a witness for him in the obtaining of his passport. So about 2 P.M. they drove downtown to Los Angeles from Hinman's house at 964 Old Topanga Canyon Road, and returned to Krell's house about five o'clock in the afternoon. Hinman stayed there until about 7:10 when he said he was going to go to a meeting somewhere. That was the last time Hinman was seen on his feet.

Krell had wanted to borrow the Volkswagen Microbus for that weekend but Hinman said he couldn't because he was going to haul some rocks in for his driveway. But that Krell could use the Microbus the following weekend.

Beausoleil and Mary and Sadie talked to Hinman for a couple of hours but it was no use. Hinman told them, in substance, to get lost. Beausoleil had brought with him the nine-millimeter Radon pistol purchased by Bruce Davis in Van Nuys a couple of weeks previous. Beausoleil pulled the gun on Hinman and informed him that they weren't kidding. Beausoleil decided that he'd go check out the house and look for the money. So he handed the gun to Sadie and went into the other rooms. Then Beausoleil heard a scuffle and ran back into the living room. Hinman and Sadie were fighting, the gun discharged and a bullet hit the wall. Beausoleil grabbed the pistol and smashed Hinman a few times with it. Hinman's head was bleeding. They called up the Spahn Ranch and told Charlie it was no use because there'd already been a scuffle and gunfire and Hinman wouldn't do a thing for them. Shortly thereafter, close to midnight, Bruce Davis and Manson, waving his sword, arrived at the Hinman house. Charlie was angry. Right away he barked at Hinman that he wanted "to talk about that money." Hinman began to shout at him, telling him to get out and take his family with him and Manson raised up his sword and hacked Hinman's ear. It was an ugly five-inch wound, cutting deep into the jawbone area and angling up through the ear.

After this, Manson and Davis split, evidently in Hinman's Fiat. Before leaving, Manson told Hinman he'd better give up the money or else. Those left behind tied Hinman up and placed him on the rug on the living room floor next to his bookcase, where he lay wounded, cursing Manson and vowing vengeance. They decided they'd stay up all night and keep watch over him so that he should not escape. They pulled up a chair alongside the bleeding body. They gave him a drink of wine or beer, or something, and then Mary Brunner took some white dental floss and sewed up his gaping wound. Beausoleil and Mary thoroughly searched Hinman's house, turning it upside down, breaking open a cash box, looking here and there, and they couldn't find the money. Sadie went out to get some food and some bandages.

They made Hinman sign over his two cars—the Volkswagen Microbus and the souped-up Fiat—by signing the pink slips, dating them July 26, 1969. There is one report that they stole Hinman's bagpipe from the house and took it with them to the ranch after they killed him.

They waited all night with the wounded Hinman. On Saturday, July 26, two friends of Hinman, both also associates of the Manson family, tried to contact Gary Hinman while he was held victim by the family prior to his death. One, a boy named Jay, called Hinman's house on Saturday afternoon, July 26. The alleged purpose of his call was to try to get Gary to rent him the lower apartment in Hinman's house at 964 Old Topanga Canyon Road. A girl answered the phone, supposedly Sadie Glutz,

talking with an English accent. The English voice told Jay that
Gary was in Colorado where his parents had been involved in
an automobile accident. Maybe it was actually an English girl who
answered the phone. Another person from Santa Barbara named
Dave showed up in Hinman's house in person. A female Caucasian, none of the family according to Dave, answered the door
and wouldn't let him in.

Sometime late Saturday or early Sunday they called the Spahn
Ranch and, according to Danny De Carlo, Manson told them
to kill Hinman: "He knows too much."

It is known for certain that Hinman was threatening to expose
the family and their activities, perhaps to the police, and that the
family might have to break up. So it was decided that he would
have to die. There is another version that says the death was
a result of Hinman suddenly starting to scream.

Manson had said that they were all set to take Hinman out
to the ranch to let him heal his wounds but that Beausoleil
panicked, evidently when Hinman started screaming out the
window. Whatever the case, he was stabbed twice in the chest,
one of the stabbings cutting the pericardial sac causing Hinman
to bleed to death. Robert Beausoleil resides on Death Row, San
Quentin, convicted of the murder.

As he died, they put him on the floor of the living room near
his bookcase. Above him they fashioned a makeshift Buddhist
shrine for the Nichiren Shoshu faith. As Gary Hinman lay
dying, they gave him his prayer beads and he chanted "Nam
Myo Ho Renge Kyo—Nam Myo Ho Renge Kyo," the chant
of his faith, until he lapsed into unconsciousness.

Mary and Sadie removed the bloody bandages from Hinman's
thread-sewn face. They gathered all the bloody towels and
clothes and took them away to dispose of elsewhere. There was
somebody's black cape, bloodied—perhaps Mary's, perhaps
Manson's—that was carried out of Hinman's house and thrown
away also.

They covered Hinman up with a green bedspread. On the wall
in the corner of the room just above Hinman's head someone

scrawled, in Hinman's blood, "POLITICAL PIGGY." To the left of Political Piggy someone finger-painted in blood the paw of a cat, intended to be a panther. With a narrow brush someone painted the claws of the paw. They wanted the police to think that black militants committed the murder.

They wiped the house down for fingerprints and burnt some documents, evidently linking the family with Hinman, in the living-room fireplace. They locked all the doors and crawled out the side window. As they were leaving they began to hear Hinman making a lot of heavy rasping sounds so Beausoleil climbed in the rear window and went over to Hinman's body and started smothering him and Sadie came in and grabbed a pillow and put it over his face until he lay still. Mary pulled Hinman's wallet out and removed twenty dollars then thrust the wallet halfway into his back pocket.

Then they tripped down the steep, wooden staircase to the street where they hot-wired Hinman's VW van painted with the thunderbird.

According to Mary Brunner they were hungry after they left the house and drove over to the Topanga Kitchen at the shopping center where they had some cherry cake and coffee. They then drove back to the Spahn Ranch. When Hinman's Microbus arrived at the ranch some of the girls saw that there were some paints in the back so they used them to paint some pictures. Then right away Mary Brunner, Linda Kasabian and Kitty took Hinman's Fiat into Simi for a garbage run.

That night the family got together for a songfest and tape-recorded a re-creation of the murder of Gary Hinman in musical form. Each person played a role. Someone played the part of the dying Gary Hinman, who is supposed to have mumbled several times, "I wanted to live, I wanted to live." This taped recreation of the murder of Gary Hinman is among the tapes that Bill Vance, deep in hiding, has in his possession.

On July 27, the day Hinman was murdered, Jean Brayton's blood-drinking occult commune north of Blythe, California was raided by the police.

One Father Ryan of the Order of St. Augustine claimed that
Charles Manson, or Manson's simulacrum, a short hirsute hippie
with a new beard, on Sunday, July 27, 1969, approached the
back door of his parish house located about a half-mile from
the LaBianca residence. "I'm Jesus Christ," announced the short
fierce individual, according to Father Ryan. The Jesus-claimer
looked at the Father with a cold hard stare beneath heavy eye-
brows. He asked the Father why he was a priest and evinced an
intense dislike toward the priesthood. The Father claims he
shut the door in Manson's face. This incident has no doubt
provided the basis for many a sermon delivered by the good
Father on Sundays since.

Later that eventful day and night of July 27, around 1 A.M.
Charlie was lurking near the Spahn Ranch on Panther patrol.
He had concealed himself and his dune buggy in underbrush
near the turnoff from Topanga Canyon Boulevard onto Santa
Susanna Pass Road, awaiting the invasion of hostile forces.

A group of police cars from the California Highway Patrol
and from the Malibu sheriff's station, about five in number,
turned onto Santa Susanna Pass Road preparing another raid on
the Spahn Ranch about a mile and a half away. The police
gathered together near the turnoff to finalize their raid game-
plan because they came across Manson's hidden dune buggy.

Officer Sam Olmstead of the sheriff's department approached
Manson and asked him what he was doing. According to
Olmstead's testimony at the trial, Manson said that he was
watching for Black Panthers who were expected to attack the
Spahn Ranch.

According to Sheriff's Deputy George Grap, Manson said,
"We got into a hassle with a couple of those black mother-
fuckers and we put one of them in the hospital," after which
Manson told him that the blacks were going to wreak vengeance.
He said that the "Panthers" had been out to the ranch several
times scouting it out, riding horses.

Manson then pulled a great con routine on the assembled
officers. He told them that the people back at the ranch were

heavily armed and that, were the officers suddenly to raid, they might think them to be attacking hordes of Black Panthers and open fire. So Charlie obtained permission from the officers to proceed first to the Spahn Ranch and cool out the gun-toters. The police agreed to this. Charlie then leaped into his dune buggy, peeled out and raced back to the ranch, jumped from the buggy, raced into the Saloon, warned everybody, whereupon the youth pack fled to the four winds, leaving behind only their warm sleeping bags.

The five police cars were right behind Manson when he leaped and ran into the Saloon. The officers checked the buildings but no one was there.

Officers Grap and Olmstead ran what are called DMV's on the automobiles in the ranch driveway to see if any were stolen. One happened to be the red VW bus with the white thunder-bird on the side belonging to the recently deceased Gary Hinman. When they called in the license number and it came back as belonging to Hinman, one of the officers said: "Hey, I know Hinman; he must be out here visiting."

Charlie flipped part of his threat trip upon the officers by drawing their attention to the dark steep hills north of the Spahn Ranch. He told the officers that he had people scattered throughout the hills with guns trained upon the officers and that on Manson's command the police could be wiped out. He told police officer Olmstead that only dune buggies could reach his hidden troops, and to forget about reaching them with their patrol cars.

According to Deputy Grap, as he was filling out the standard Field Investigation Report (FIR), Manson approached him about joining up forces to wipe out the "Panthers." "You know, you cops ought to get smart and join up with us; those guys are out to kill you just like they are out to kill us. I know you hate them as much as we do, and if we join together we could solve this problem."

Horse wrangler Johnny Swartz was arrested during this raid for "false evidence of registration" for the '59 Ford.

On Monday afternoon, July 28, Bob Beausoleil went into the bunkhouse/gun room/office/undertaker's parlor where he joined Charlie, Danny and Sadie—who was sewing a knife case for Charlie. Mary Brunner came into the gun room in a huff, angered by rumors that Sadie had told Shorty Shea that "Charlie killed a black man and I don't know who else." According to Beausoleil and Snake Lake, Mary told Sadie that she was going to kill her unless she kept her mouth shut.

Charlie, taking up the theme, smashed Sadie's head against the wall, muttering something about Shorty "knowing too much." Unfortunately for Manson, there would be no wall in Sybil Brand Jail only three months later upon which he might bash the babbly head of Glutz as she confessed to Virginia Graham.

At 3:07 P.M. on July 30, somebody at the Polanski residence called the Esalen Institute at Big Sur, California. Charles Manson himself visited the Institute only three days later.

On Tuesday, July 30, Bob Beausoleil went back to the Hinman house to wipe down the house more thoroughly for fingerprints. The house was full of flies. Beausoleil neglected to remove a fingerprint from the kitchen door with twenty-six points of identification linking him to the house and to Death Row.

The same day that Bobby went to Gary's house to clean it up, his girl friend, the pregnant, attractive Kitty Lutesinger, ran away from the ranch. After Charlie threatened, according to Miss Kitty, to carve her up, accusing her of trying to lure Bobby away from the family.

Frank Retz, the agent for the Transcontinental Development Corporation, was on the property north and west of the Spahn Ranch at the very moment that Kitty made her move to escape. She went along the underbrush toward the back ranch in order to find a stretch of road away from the main ranch complex whereupon she might hitchhike out of the area safely.

Mr Retz had driven to the property with the then current owner, a Mrs. Kelly, in order to negotiate purchase of the land. Just minutes previously they had stormed in on the back ranch which, it will be remembered, was on the property line, and demanded that Manson and the others leave the premises. When Mr. Retz and Mrs. Kelly returned to his car they discovered that it had been robbed of Mrs. Kelly's pocketbook. Right at that time, Miss Lutesinger ran through the brush and asked for protection from Manson.

Retz drove Miss Lutesinger to a police station and she was transported by police officers to her parents' horse ranch. This sowed the seeds for the dissolution of Helter Skelter even before the murders were committed. For the police started visiting her home to get information about the Spahn Ranch, which they considered an illegal haven for runaways and an assembly plant for stolen dune buggies.

After returning home Miss Lutesinger was very afraid and kept all doors to her parents' house locked for several days because Charlie, she said, had told her he would kill her mother and sister if she left the ranch. She refused to answer the phone, even when Bobby called to say he was going to San Francisco.

Gary Hinman missed participating in a bagpipe parade in Santa Monica on the 27th and his friends began to worry. On Thursday, July 31, three of his close friends, fellow chanters and Nichiren Shoshu Buddhist adepts, came to his small brown-shingled house and walked up the steep ivy-sided steps to encounter the many flies of death swarming in and out of the open window on the second-floor front of the house. They called the police.

Late in the afternoon, a call came into the L.A. County Sheriff Homicide Office on the third floor of the Hall of Justice in aromatic downtown L.A. with details of a death in Topanga Canyon, a man badly decomposed, a hippie, so to speak; possibly a suicide. The sheriff's homicide officers handle all murders that occur in unincorporated areas of Los Angeles County and the two officers on duty that afternoon were Sergeant Paul Whiteley and Deputy Charles Guenther, two formidable gentlemen indeed.

They could have left the matter for the evening watch to handle, since their shift was almost over, but they decided to drive out to Topanga Canyon to check out the possible crime. After surveying the scene they felt it was murder, and from the state of the body, the murderer had at least a week's jump on them.

They sent out for a couple of six-packs of beer and some room freshener. The smell in the house was intolerable. For five days Officers Whiteley and Guenther spent almost all their waking hours inside the residence sifting through Hinman's personal effects, trying to locate the culprit. The earliest suspects were the couple who had been making mescaline with Hinman, but they were quickly cleared.

These two sheriff's office homicide detectives, Whiteley and Guenther, were the ones mainly responsible for bringing down the house of Manson, but it would take about ninety days—days replete with the screams of uncounted victims.

In fact, the $25,000 reward set up by Peter Sellers, Warren Beatty, Yul Brynner, John Phillips and friends perhaps should have gone to Officers Guenther and Whiteley instead of it going, as it seems to have gone, to Danny De Carlo and Shelley Nadell.

Sixteen

The Anvil into Tartaros

On August 1, the pages of the newspapers were crowded with outer space news—the first pictures of the moon, a report from Mariner 6 on climatic conditions on the surface of Mars, astronauts in motor parades across America.

Elvis Presley, with fifty gold records hanging on his wall, opened a four-week engagement at the International in Las Vegas. In San Francisco there were five homicides.

One day in early August, Linda Kasabian and pregnant Sandy Good went to Topanga beach to panhandle and to enjoy the ocean. They were picked up by a movie actor named Saladin Nader in an old white Jaguar. Mr. Nader had starred in a Lebanese movie called *Broken Wings*, about the youth of poet Kahlil Gibran. Sandy and Linda went with Saladin Nader to his apartment at 1101 Ocean Front in Santa Monica. Mr. Nader showed the girls pictures of himself in various movies. There, he and Linda got after it in the bedroom while Sandy took a nap.

Later he drove the girls to a shopping center in the San Fernando Valley. Early in the morning of August 10, Linda and Manson and Sadie and Clem would return to his house on Ocean Front to try to kill him.

Meanwhile, at the ranch, Charlie got rid of the nine-millimeter Radon pistol used at Gary Hinman's murder by trading it to that boy from Simi named Hendrix for a blue '55 Chevy four-door sedan.

Charlie gave one Mark Arneson Hinman's VW Microbus. Arneson also wanted Hinman's souped-up Fiat but Beausoleil needed it. The family wanted Mark for their membership rolls. Leslie Van Houten was working on Mark to join the family and she put him on the no-sex list to put the pressure on him.

On August 1, Charlie was talking about taking a trip up north to gather recruits. Beausoleil testified at his trial that he was called into a trailer where he had a conversation with Bruce Davis and Manson. According to Beausoleil, Charlie told Bruce he should be willing to do what "he" did at Gary's; he told Bruce that Terry Melcher should be ready for death; it was his karma.

Charlie had his ear-hacking sword at hand and told Bruce, according to Beausoleil, that he should be willing to go into the city and cut and slash until he had blood and guts up to here—motioning to his chin.

Around 6 P.M. that day, a resident at the Crest Haven Ranch on Fern Ann Falls Road up by the waterfall campsite saw some bikers prowling along the road and he heard automatic weapons' fire coming from the Devil Canyon and Ybermo Canyon area. After George Spahn went to dinner, it was always rifle practice time. The carbine was evidently Charlie's favorite weapon. He'd let all thirty rounds go in a burst of rapid-fire, standing in the surf of Fear.

In the evening, the girls cleaned up the Hostess Twinkies Continental Bakery truck, outfitting the bed in the back for the Wizard's important trip to Big Sur.

Danny De Carlo said that Charlie talked about being gone for about three months. Others say he talked about going north to recruit girls. Beausoleil has claimed that Manson left the Spahn Ranch for the trip about midnight.

The chronology of Manson's whereabouts during the days between August 1 and 8 is filled with gaps.

It is known from interviews that between 7 and 8 A.M. on Sunday, August 3, Manson purchased gasoline in a service station in Canoga Park, near the Spahn Ranch. He must quickly have sped north because his alibi for his whereabouts during a double homicide in San Jose on Sunday afternoon, August 3 is that he was visiting the Esalen Institute in Big Sur, enjoying the hot springs and steam baths.

On Sunday the 3, Randy Reno, a musician and occasional visitor to the Ranch, visited the family and they told him that Charlie was up in Devil's Hole. Beausoleil later testified at his April 1970 trial that after Charlie cut out, he felt that people were watching him, as if to prevent his leaving. Throughout the history of the family whenever Charlie took a bit of time off, that provided the opportunity for people to escape. Tex and Bruce Davis seemed to be keeping their eyes on him. Bobby waited. "I smiled a lot, tried to be myself. It seemed that they were trusting me so I left." He told the girls to clean up Hinman's customized Fiat station wagon which "was full of junk"—as he testified.

Why did Robert Beausoleil leave for San Francisco driving the car of the very man in whose murder he had participated?

So, around Tuesday, August 5, Robert Beausoleil drove Hinman's grill-less Fiat, witr Toyota motor and a radiator set at a 45-degree angle, toward San Francisco, unaware that Hinman's body had been discovered.

He passed through Santa Barbara and stopped at a restaurant where he was told by a policeman to take his Mexican sheath knife off. He put it in the car trunk. He continued driving north and sometime in the night the Fiat broke down on Highway 101 near San Luis Obispo.

At 10:50 A.M. a California Highway Patrol car stopped behind the parked car and, as it halted, Beausoleil raised up in the back from a sleeping bag. Beausoleil had no driver's license to show the officer but had identification for Jason Lee Daniels and a credit card plus a business card for the Lutesinger Ranch.

Officer Humphrey of the Highway Patrol called in Hinman's license number to the computer and he learned that the car was reported stolen from Los Angeles. He drew his revolver and arrested Beausoleil. When he arrived at the CHP station, there

was a Los Angeles sheriff's office "All Points Bulletin" that the
car be impounded and occupants held in regard to Hinman's
death.

As part of a prearranged scheme, Beausoleil said that he had
bought the car in the week previous from a black man. The
Fiat was locked up, to preserve fingerprints, and Jim's Tow
Service hauled it into custody in San Luis Obispo.

The same day around 8:30 P.M., homicide officers Paul
Whiteley and Charles Guenther and a fingerprint expert named
Jake Jordan arrived in San Luis Obispo to interrogate Beausoleil.
They brought with them the card bearing Beausoleil's thumbprint
lifted from the kitchen door jamb of Hinman's house. They had
the man.

Beausoleil remained pretty quiet during interrogation though
he finally admitted going to Hinman's house with two female
Caucasians. He claimed he did not reveal their names but only
that Hinman was injured, when they got there, and that they
came to his aid, sewed his face, etc., then left. He said that
Hinman rewarded them for suturing his face with dental floss
by signing over his automobile to them. Hinman, he said, told
them he got involved in some political hassle with blacks and
that one of them had knifed his face.

The next day, on August 7, Robert Beausoleil was brought
to Los Angeles and booked for homicide. As per California law,
he was allowed to call the Spahn Ranch. Linda Kasabian was
manning incoming calls that day and Beausoleil gave her the bad
news but said that everything was okay and that he was staying
quiet.

Beausoleil himself has said that Linda was upset and that she
asked what could be done to help him and a discussion was
held regarding possible plans of action. According to Beausoleil
the discussion involved copy-cat murders, or murders removing
those who might have known about the Hinman matter. Such
discussions of possible murder to get Beausoleil out may have
served to rev up the family for more snuffs, another example
of the self-fulfilling prophecy.

Sadie Glutz testified at the Tate-LaBianca trial that soon after Bobby called, Leslie, Sadie, Linda Kasabian, Katie and others had a homicide-klatch to discuss and to determine how to get Bobby, their brother, out of jail. According to the Glutz/Atkins testimony, one of the girls had seen a movie where copy-cat murders were committed over a period of time, enabling a killer to get out of jail.

They wanted to raise money for him to get a lawyer. The girls decided to hold a night of streetwalking to raise money for Beausoleil. They donned their finery and high heels, and painted their lips and hit the bricks.

Meanwhile, where was Manson during all this?

Manson seems to have left the Esalen Institute sometime late Sunday. Manson was then cruising around the Big Sur area in the 1952 Hostess Twinkie bread truck with two unknown male companions.

About 3 or 4 A.M. Monday morning, August 4, Manson met a pregnant seventeen-year-old girl named Stephanie who was entering the ladies' room at a service station. He scarfed her up.

This is her story:

"I was with this guy and we had gone to Nevada, saw his uncle and came back through San Francisco and down through Big Sur. He was weird; he wasn't my boy friend, I just went with him to keep him company. He did everything according to the rules and I was sick of it. So we stopped at this gas station late at night or early in the morning and this guy in a milk truck whistled at me when I went into the bathroom. When I came he went, 'Do you want a sweet roll?' I took one and he started talking to me and showing the flowers to me.

"Then he asked me if I wanted to come with them. He said, 'I'll take you back to San Diego, we will see Big Sur tomorrow as long as you come to my ranch.' I said okay and I was really freaked out and I went. Nobody forced me to, I just went."

During her time with Manson he became attracted to the lovely girl. She made Manson vow that he would not leave her side for two weeks, a vow that has long caused consternation and

disbelief among his female followers, who would not have
thought such a vow possible. He initiated her into a prolonged
session of LSD sex. According to her, Manson took her down
into a Big Sur canyon, stuffed a tab of dope into her mouth
and ordered her to swallow it. Then he said, according to the
girl, "Open your mouth and wiggle your tongue around."

"He wanted to make sure that I took it," she told an interviewer a few months later. "He sure did send me on a trip
that one day."

The two male companions who were with Manson when he
picked up Miss Stephanie outside the ladies' room, she testified,
were hitchhikers who left them shortly thereafter. The two new
lovers toured the Big Sur area for a couple of days then headed
south for the Spahn Ranch, arriving the afternoon of August 6,
1969.

Manson and Stephanie stayed part of the afternoon and
evening at the ranch then split toward San Diego where Manson,
as per the bargain, was to deliver Miss Stephanie back home.
They only got a few blocks when they parked and spent the
time of night in blissful repose in the back of the Twinkie truck.
The next morning they headed south to Jamul, California,
where Stephanie lived with her sister and brother-in-law, Mr. and
Mrs. Hartman.

At 4:15 P.M. near Oceanside, California, Manson and Stephanie were stopped by the California Highway Patrol. Manson
received a citation for not possessing a driver's license.

They drove on to Stephanie's sister's house. They had dinner
with the Hartmans and Charlie talked a lot, as usual. Charlie
was attired in gungy blue jeans and his witchy-whorled sequined
vest. He rapped for about two hours. It was a general sort of
Manson discussion. Slaughter, music, hypnotism and the Beatles.

Manson really weirdized the Hartmans, according to Mrs.
Hartman, by saying that soon "people were going to be slaugh-
tered and they would be lying on their lawns dead." Stephanie
was afraid her former boy friend was going to show up, so she
and Manson had to leave rather than stay for the night. Charlie
talked her into returning with him to Spahn land.

They drove in the Hostess Twinkies bread truck to somebody's lawn, a friend of Stephanie, and the lovers slept on the lawn, the night of August 7.

Miss Stephanie stayed with the family till October 1969 and is now operating her own dog grooming shop at the age of nineteen.

In the morning of August 8, Manson and Stephanie drove back north to the ranch, arriving about 1 P.M., with murder eleven hours away.

On Friday, August 1, 1969, a hair stylist named Carol Solomon and a girl named Linda, a Beverly Hills doctor's daughter now deceased through an overdose of doraden, attended a small party thrown by Voityck Frykowski at 10050 Cielo Drive. Sharon Tate and Abigail Folger were not there. Linda was Voityck's date and was known to have "hung out" at the home during the summer. Chicken and champagne were served at the pool. It was a quiet scene involving about ten people, some of whom spent time in the bedroom watching TV. The two girls, according to Miss Solomon, were invited over again for the following weekend.

During the weekend of August 1 and August 2, 1969, either Abigail Folger or Sharon Tate may have stopped in at the Esalen Institute in Big Sur for one of those famous Esalen weekends where people pay money for elitist mental health sessions.

It is known that the Esalen Institute is extremely uptight over the fact that Manson visited there that weekend. In fact, this writer received an oblique snuff-threat from someone representing Esalen interests.

According to the vice-president of Sebring International, Jay Sebring had visited the Polanski residence on Sunday, Tuesday and Thursday, during the week before the murders.

On August 4, 1969, Sharon rented a 1969 Chevrolet Camaro from Airways Rent-a-Car "to be leased from August 4, 1969 till August 8, 1969," as the contract reads. Her red Ferrari was in the garage being repaired, following an accident.

On August 4, Voityck's actor friend Mark Fine called Frykowski and reminded him that Frykowski had a meeting with a movie producer on the sixth regarding sale of a story. Frykowski told Fine that on August 6 he would have to pick up some friends at the airport coming in from Canada.

Sometime during that week, perhaps Tuesday or Wednesday, a dope dealer from Toronto named Billy Doyle was whipped and video-buggered at 10050 Cielo Drive. In the days before his death, Sebring had complained to a receptionist at his hair shop that someone had burned him for $2000 worth of cocaine and he wanted vengeance. Billy Doyle was involved in a large-scale dope-import operation involving private planes from Jamaica. There seem to have been many dope-burns, perhaps like the falling of a line of dominoes, during the days around the Tate-LaBianca murders.

Dennis Hopper, in a interview with the *Los Angeles Free Press*, said, about the video-bugger and the circumstances there:

"They had fallen into sadism and masochism and bestiality —and they recorded it all on videotape too. The L.A. police told me this. I know that three days before they were killed, twenty-five people were invited to that house to a mass whipping of a dealer from Sunset Strip who'd given them bad dope."

On Tuesday or Wednesday, August 5 or 6, there evidently was a party at 10050 Cielo Drive in honor of French director Roger Vadim, in celebration of Vadim's completion of a motion picture and his imminent return to Europe. An area of silence surrounds this event. Attempts to secure information about it have resulted in tense uneasiness from those alleged to have been on the set, so to speak.

Sharon, Voityck and Abigail on August 6, were at Michael Sarnes' house for dinner. Sharon was tired and got up to leave shortly after dessert. Her life revolved around the baby. She floated during the day in a rubber ring in her swimming pool—to take the weight off her stomach.

Mr. Frykowski seems to have acquired a new shipment of MDA two or three days prior to his death. Mrs. Chapman, the housekeeper at Cielo Drive, was off Wednesday and Thursday.

Sebring had some films developed at National General Film Lab on Wednesday, August 8, so the films may have been taken on Tuesday night.

Another of Voityck's dope-dealer friends from Canada showed up on August 6 and later claimed to reporters that Frykowski was in the fifth day of a "ten-day mescaline experiment." In fact, the Canadian claimed that both Jay Sebring and Mr. Frykowski were out to lunch on mescaline. The dope-hawker talked to Frykowski about an impending shipment of MDA. The same dealer showed up the next day about 4 P.M. and shared a bottle of wine with Frykowski. He met Sharon Tate that day, indicating that he was a recent friend of Frykowski, or from another circle of acquaintances.

Novelist Jerzy Kosinski and wife were supposed to come to Los Angeles on August 7 to visit at the Polanski residence and wait for Roman to return for his birthday and for the baby. Kosinski's luggage was lost on the way to New York from Europe so, instead of traveling immediately to Los Angeles, they waited in New York for the luggage. This probably saved his life, because he was not able to arrive in Los Angeles on the 7th or the 8th.

On Friday, August 8, 1969, the housekeeper, Winifred Chapman, arrived at the Polanski residence at 8 A.M.

Around 8:30 A.M. a Mr. Guerrero arrived to paint the nursery. He worked until mid-afternoon, completing the first coat. He was scheduled to return on Monday to complete the second coat of paint.

Before lunch, Winifred washed down the front Dutch door because the dogs had dirtied it. Pig and a fingerprint would dirty it later.

Mrs. Chapman testified that on Tuesday August 4, she washed the French doors in Sharon's bedroom where Friday midnight would find a murderer's fingerprint. Wednesday and Thursday were Mrs. Chapman's days off.

About 11 A.M. Roman Polanski called from London. Mrs. Chapman answered the phone. Then Sharon talked.

Sharon asked him if he wanted a birthday party when he returned. She was anxious for him to arrive soon so that he might attend a course for expectant fathers. Mrs. Polanski planned to have natural childbirth. She told her husband a little kitten had wandered onto the property and she was feeding it with an eyedropper.

In the afternoon, the gardeners and groundskeepers of the estate, Joe Vargas and Dave Martinez, arrived.

Joanna Pettit and Barbara Lewis, old friends of Sharon Tate, arrived about 12:30 for lunch. Abigail and Voityck showed up, after which Mrs. Chapman served a late lunch for Pettit, Lewis, Sharon, Abigail, Voityck and herself.

Joanna Pettit and Barbara Lewis departed at 3:30 P.M. Around 3:45 Dave Martinez, one of the gardeners, left the property. He asked Bill Garretson to be sure to water the grounds during the weekend.

Jay Sebring called at 3:45. A few minutes later Gibby Folger left in the red Firebird. Voityck left at 4 P.M. in Sharon's rented yellow Camaro. At 4:30 Miss Folger went to her usual daily appointment with her psychiatrist, Dr. Marvin Flicker.

Frykowski drove to Sebring's house on Easton Drive and picked up a Susan Peterson with whom Sebring had spent the previous night. With her, Frykowski drove to stick-artist Witold K.'s gallery-boutique at the Beverly Wilshire Hotel to get the keys to Voityck and Abigail's house on Woodstock Road where Witold K. was staying. Mr. K. did not have the keys to the house because they were left over at Mr. K.'s girl friend's house. Mr. Frykowski finally located the keys at the girl friend's house and then went with Miss Peterson to his Woodstock Road house. There they dallied, listening to records.

At 4:30 Joe Vargas, the gardener, signed for the arrival of Roman Polanski's two steamer trunks because he didn't want to awaken Sharon, who was napping in her room.

As it was extremely hot and dry, Sharon thought it would be uncomfortable in Mrs. Chapman's apartment so she asked Winifred if she wanted to stay over. No, thank you.

Around 4:45 Joe Vargas left the property, giving the house-keeper Mrs. Chapman a ride down to the bus stop. When they left, Sharon was alone in the house, asleep.

Sebring was seen on Easton Drive by a neighbor, whizzing past in his black Porsche, followed closely by another sports car, about 5:30 P.M.

Between 6:30 and 7 P.M., one Dennis Hearst delivered a lightweight bicycle to the residence. Abigail Folger had purchased it earlier in the afternoon. Jay Sebring answered the door, wine bottle in hand.

Sharon Tate had invited people over for the evening but later called them and said she was not feeling well.

Evidently Sharon was supposed to stay overnight with an old friend Sheilah Welles at Miss Welles' house. Sharon and Sheilah Welles were roommates for a year in Hollywood. Something caused her to change her mind.

Director Michael Sarne was considering going to Sharon's on Friday night. Also Dino Martin, Jr. and a host of others, including John Phillips. One popular folk singer, according to Leonard Lyons, claimed that he was supposed to go to the murder house that night to get a haircut from Jay Sebring.

If the number of people who claim to have been invited to 10050 Cielo Drive the night of August 8 had shown up, there wouldn't have been room for a murder.

According to a Mrs. McCaffrey, a receptionist at Sebring's hair shop, her boy friend Joel Rostau delivered cocaine and mescaline to the house on Cielo the night of the murders. She said that Frykowski and Sebring wanted more, but Rostau, unable to score, didn't return.

Frykowski called his friend Witold K. in the evening sometime and invited him over but Witold K. was busy laying down a rug in his new art gallery at 9406 Wilshire Boulevard.

The foursome Jay, Voityck, Abigail and Sharon had a late dinner at a Spanish restaurant, El Coyote, on Beverly Boulevard, about the same time as the coyote-worshiping Charles Manson was plotting his evil.

Miss Folger's mother called from San Francisco. Miss Folger was scheduled to fly the 10 A.M. United Airlines shuttle the next morning to Frisco in order to be with her mother for her birthday.

It was about midnight. They were in bed. Voityck was evidently asleep upon the flag-draped living room sofa. Abigail was reading a book in the northeast bedroom. Sharon Tate and Jay Sebring were talking in the southwest bedroom when the knife stabbed into the gray screen, scratching and slicing an entrance into the empty nursery at the far north end of the house.

In the early afternoon of August 8, 1969, Charles Manson arrived at the Spahn Ranch, bearing the pregnant runaway seventeen-year-old graduate of Anaheim High School, Stephanie. Charlie called Stephanie the "product of 2000 years of good breeding." He was proud of her. Charlie was quickly apprised of Robert Beausoleil's arrest. The whole trip up north had been a bummer for Charlie, who hated rejection. And now, with Beausoleil's arrest for murder, Manson's whole empire was threatened.

As soon as he got back, driving the 1952 Continental Bakery Hostess Twinkie truck, Charlie sent Mary Brunner and Sandy Good off to run a credit-card caper at the Sears store. Before they left they took Stephanie's credit cards and identification away from her, naturally, and filed them with the master credit-card horde in George Spahn's house.

Around 4 P.M., Mary Brunner and Sandy Pugh—for Sandy was using the name of her snuffed-out, former husband at the time—were completing purchases at the Sears store at 1030 Celis Street in San Fernando, California. They bought merchandise with a stolen credit card, recently ripped off from Vern Plumlee's brother-in-law in Bothwell, Washington. Mary Brunner forged the name Mary Vitasek on the credit card. The two young ladies left. If they had split right away, they probably would not have been arrested.

Instead of leaving they decided to make some more purchases at a different checkout counter and again presented the same stolen credit card. The cashier, an alert lady named Mrs. Ramirez, noted that the card was on the "warning sheet." Mrs. Ramirez became suspicious when she noticed that the pregnant Sandy kept looking over her shoulder all the time.

The store manager intervened and the girls fled. The Sears' store manager proceeded to follow the girls in his automobile, trying to get them to pull the bakery truck over to the side of the road. Sandy and Mary cut through a service station, trying to ditch the Sears officials. The chase led to the Chatsworth entrance to the San Diego Freeway, where the girls were stopped, evidently having some sort of accident. Sandy had managed to toss the credit cards out the window but the act was spotted by the pursuers.

Captured with the two young ladies were a creepy-crawl full house of various credit cards from Hancock Gasoline, J. C. Penney, Sears, Gulf, Texaco and Richfield, plus various forms of identification cards. Three of the cards belonged to John Dries, who had been killed in a traffic accident.

The police found the traffic citation given to Manson the day before in Oceanside, California. Mary and Sandy were charged with violations of Section 459 and 484e of the California Penal Code. Mary Brunner admitted that she, in fact, forged the credit card but Sandy Good proclaimed her innocence.

They were booked at the police station just as, thirty miles away, Abigail Folger was ending her appointment with her psychiatrist. Mary and Sandy Good were taken to the police station and then later that evening hauled into downtown Los Angeles where, at 10:21 P.M., they were booked into the Sybil Brand Institute Inmate Reception Center.

Meanwhile, back at the Spahn Ranch, murder was on the minds. Mary Brunner arrested. Sandy Good arrested. Bobby Beausoleil arrested. Charlie Manson rejected in Big Sur. It was a tragic time for California.

In the afternoon, someone went on a garbage run for the

evening meal. At the back ranch, they cooked dinner on the
Coleman four-burner camping stove. Everybody was excited that
Charlie was back. Charlie said that people up north were really
not together, they were just off on their own little trips and they
were not getting together. "Now is the time for Helter Skelter"
is what Charlie Manson said.

At the meal, Charlie issued instructions that all people under
eighteen were to sleep in the wickiup by the back ranch. After
dinner, the slave girls washed the dishes and Tex Watson and
Charlie plotted what to do about Beausoleil's arrest.

When Sadie and Mary were booked into Sybil Brand Jail at
10:21 they probably called up the ranch and told them the
grim news. Within an hour, the killers were on their way.

About an hour after dinner Charlie took Stephanie into a
trailer and left her there. "He told me he'd be back in a little
while," she testified at Manson's murder trial.

Manson didn't return till dawn.

Approximately an hour after the meal, Manson pulled Sadie
aside and told her to get a knife and a change of clothes. Sadie
immediately called the back ranch over the field telephone and
told Barbara Hoyt to gather three sets of dark clothing and
bring them to the front ranch.

Linda Kasabian had helped fix dinner, helped to clean up,
had walked to the front ranch and was standing by the Rock
City Café when Charlie came up and pulled her off to the end
of the boardwalk and told her to get a knife, a change of
clothing and her driver's license. With Mary Brunner arrested,
Kasabian seemed to be the only person at the ranch with a valid
driver's license, and one of the few who could be trusted with
such a heavy mission as murder. Linda Kasabian walked across
the dusty driveway from the Spahn Ranch movie set and went
into George Spahn's saddle-lined house to look for her creepy-
crawlie accouterments. There she rummaged through a box and
found a blue denim mini-skirt made from chopped-off blue jeans
and a lavender knitted top. She asked Squeaky, who ofttimes
served as the family quartermaster, where her driver's license was.

Squeaky told her to look in some chests of drawers. Not there. In a box on the mantel of the fireplace. Not there. Then she went into the Saloon to look for her knife. Couldn't find one. She was looking for the Buck knife she had brought with her to the ranch. She walked down the boardwalk, east, went into the Rock City Café kitchen, saw little Larry Jones there and got her kitchen knife from him, a knife with a flawed handle that required it to be wrapped with dark electrical tape. Sadie was using Linda's old Buck clasp knife.

Patricia Krenwinkel was already asleep, coming down off an acid trip, when she was awakened and told to get a knife and a change of clothes. She really didn't want to get up but she did, summoned by the Devil.

Someone must have called in advance to the Polanski residence to see who was going to be there or at least that there was no party going on. Vern Plumlee, for instance, has claimed that they thought Sharon Tate was not going to be there.

In the hot August evening, people were sitting and chatting on the boulders and rocks and chairs that were situated in front of the Spahn Ranch, unaware of what was going on. In the presence of Manson, Brenda came up and handed Linda her driver's license. All was prepared.

The automobile, an old yellow and white 1959 Ford with another car's license plate on it, was parked and ready in the space between the end of the Rock City Café and George Spahn's house. George Spahn was not at home. It was his custom to dine about this hour at the International House of Pancakes in Chatsworth. Or perhaps he was visiting his relatives, following his meal.

Linda Kasabian got into the car, in the right front passenger seat. Sadie and Katie were in the back of the car. Also in the back of the car were a pair of red-handled bolt cutters and a long, coiled, three-quarter-inch nylon rope. Tex got into the car and the car backed away and then headed out down the dirt driveway toward the exit to the west, by the corral. About halfway down the drive, Manson stopped them. He came over and stuck his head into the window on Linda's side and said, according to Linda, "Leave a sign. You girls know what to do. Something witchy." Then Manson stood alone, watching the car drive off.

The car belonged to Johnny Swartz, a horse wrangler at the Spahn Ranch. He was sitting in his trailer near George Spahn's house when he recognized the sound of his engine and walked to the window of his trailer just in time to see the taillights of his automobile fade away down the road.

Tex told Linda that the gun was in the glove compartment. Three knives were on the front right floor of the automobile. Tex told her to bundle up the knives and gun, and then to throw them out the window if the police attempted to pick them up. This Linda did, bundling them with her very own shirt. Linda Kasabian testified that she believed she was merely going on a second-story caper in Beverly Hills. A second-story caper with forty-three feet of rope and gun, change of clothing and three sharp knives.

After the 1959 Ford, license plate GYY435, had pulled away toward its desolate goal, Barbara Hoyt came trundling to the front ranch from the back ranch, bearing the three sets of dark clothing that Susan Atkins had ordered over the field phone. Charlie was angry at her and snapped, "What are you doing here?" Because it was a rule that all those who didn't have a reason, particularly soul-less females, were to stay in back out of sight and not appear in the public part of the ranch. Miss Hoyt told him what Sadie had asked her to do and Manson said that they had already left.

In the speeding car, the girls seemed to be barefoot. Sadie had on blue denim genuine Roebucks and a baggy blue tee-shirt. Linda was barefoot and in her lavender top and dark blue denim skirt. Tex wore moccasins, jeans and a black velour turtle-neck sweater. Katie wore a black tee-shirt and jeans.

In the car, Tex said that they were going to Terry Melcher's former place, but that Melcher no longer lived there. He described the setup of the house, including the rooms inside, and evidently noted that there was a smaller guest house on the property, and to make sure that the guest house was creepy-crawled also.

According to Sadie, Tex said that they were going to kill whoever was in the house and then get all their money.

They drove there straightaway, leaving around eleven o'clock in the evening. They evidently drove along the Ventura Freeway, San Diego Freeway, grabbed a left on Mulholland to Benedict Canyon Boulevard, and then drove up the Valley side of the Canyon, up and over the mountains, such as it is, and down the hill to Cielo Drive, where they grabbed a right and proceeded to the house on the hill.

Seventeen

Death on Cielo Drive

Bill Garretson, the caretaker of the guest cottage at the Polanski residence, got sick Thursday night, August 7, on four cans of beer, a dexedrine and two marijuana cigarettes, so he stayed home all day Friday until the evening.

It was the windup of Mr. Garretson's employment at the Polanski estate. The owner, Rudy Altobelli, who had been in Europe all summer, was due to return. In addition to the thirty-five dollars a week that he was earning, Altobelli promised to buy the young Garretson an airplane ticket back to his home town, Lancaster, Ohio.

It was Garretson's habit to go to bed late and get up early in the afternoon and go check on his mail. By arrangement, Garretson took care of Sharon's Yorkshire terrier and Abigail's Dalmatian. The guest house sat at an angle to the main house, up against a steep hill. Between the two houses lay the swimming pool. Four entrances and numerous windows make the guest house a pushover to creepy-crawl. There is a back door, a door to the dog's room, a door to the back yard and front door.

Unknown people came around 8:30 in the evening who took Garretson down the Canyon to the Sunset Strip. Garretson went to Turner's Drugstore, got a TV dinner and a Coke and a pack of cigarettes, and then walked up, then down, the Strip. Boredom. He then hitchhiked back to Benedict Canyon Drive from Sunset, then hitched up Benedict to Cielo Drive. He walked up Cielo then up the hill to the back house. It was around ten o'clock. He watched a movie on TV, then he put the TV dinner in the oven. While his dinner cooked, the American boy ate potato chips and drank Coca-Cola. Around 11:45 P.M., Steve Parent arrived unannounced, with an AM/FM clock radio to sell, or one like it. They talked. Parent evidently asked Garretson who the two pretty young ladies were who were inside the main house.

Garretson thought that Voityck Frykowski was Roman Polanski's younger brother, so Garretson explained that Mrs. Folger was the "younger Polanski's" girl friend and the other one was Polanski's wife, to which Parent replied, "You mean Polanski has a girl friend and a wife?" And Garretson said, "No, the younger Polanski has a girl friend and the other one was the older Polanski's wife." Finally, Parent got it straight.

Steve Parent placed a phone call around 11:45 or 11:55 or so to a man named Jerrold Friedman on Romaine Street in Hollywood and Parent told him something to the effect that he was at the home of a movie star, "somebody big." Friedman asked him if there was a party going on, and Parent said there was not. Parent was going to help Friedman build a stereo, so they made a date for Parent to come to Friedman's house in about forty minutes, which would help put Parent at Friedman's house at 12:30 A.M. Garretson gave Parent a can of Budweiser beer. They listened to the stereo, which was located next to the couch in the living room of the guest house.

As Garretson walked Parent to the door, Christopher, the Weimaraner, began barking and Steve asked, "What's the matter with Christopher?" Garretson said, "Oh, I don't know. He usually barks." According to Altobelli's testimony at the trial, Christopher gave forth two types of barks, a generalized bark and something called a people bark when anyone approached the house. Probably Garretson was not able to distinguish between the two types of barks. The Weimaraner was not known for its gentleness. In fact, at one time, it had even bitten Rudy Altobelli.

Around 12:15 A.M. Garretson said good-by to the young man
from El Monte, Steve Parent. The dog was yipping and barking.
Garretson contended that he only walked Parent to the door.
He never heard any shots or any shrieks or any screams during
the ensuing butchering on the lawn, less than 150 feet from the
house. He claimed that he spent the night writing letters to
a friend of his named Darryl Kistler and listening to the record
player, which was turned up to medium volume. At one point
in the middle of the night, the Weimaraner began to bark and
Garretson looked up from the couch in the living room and
noticed that the bar-shaped door handle had been turned down
by something or somebody. He leaped up and walked to the
bathroom and looked out the window to see if anybody had
tried to force the door. From the bathroom window it was possible
to see out onto the screened porch where the front door to the
guest house was located. Garretson also noted that something
or some force had cut loose the screen to one of the windows
in another part of the house near the kitchen.

When the polygraph interrogation officer, Lieutenant Burdick,
ran a polygraph examination on Garretson on Sunday, August 10,
Garretson admitted that perhaps he may have gone out to the
back yard at some point during the night.

Patricia Krenwinkel has contended that they creepy-crawled
the back house and found no one there. So perhaps Garretson,
hearing the shrieks and the bullets and the screams, ran out
back to hide then crept back into the house in the early dawn,
fearing either for his own life or that he would be charged for
the crimes.

At 12:15, Garretson saw Parent to the door of the cottage.
Before he left, Parent reached over and unplugged his unsold
Sony AM/FM clock radio, taking it with him. When the police
found it the next morning on the front seat of the Ambassador,
the clock was frozen at 12:15.

Steve Parent walked off the screened porch, past the redwood picnic table, past the small swimming pool set against the steep hillside; he walked down the east path, on the walkway by the white split rail fence, then down the paved driveway. He got into his car. Sebring's Porsche, Abigail's yellow Firebird and also the Camaro which Sharon had rented while the red Ferrari was being repaired were parked there.

He backed his car out of the driveway so quickly that he broke the split rail fence that borders the parking lot. The paint from the fence was found on the underside of his car the next morning by Officer McGann. He may have seen the killers in the house or coming out the drive or cutting the communication wires. Or he may have heard the splat of the telephone cables as Watson cut them. He turned on his car lights. He drove down the parking lot. The parking area narrows at a point a few feet in front of the electric gate. At this narrowing point, on the left side, is the housing box for the electronic button which activates the main gate. Parent never got as far as this button; he never pushed it. Death punched his face.

The white and yellow, back-seatless, 1959 Ford four-door sedan pulled up the paved, winding, cliffside driveway to the top, facing the rattan fence. The car turned around at the gate. The lights were off. Coyotenoia was. They parked the car facing down-hill on the right side, away from the main gate, next to the tele-phone pole that juts up above a cliff-like hill that falls down to the north. Eighteen feet up were the telephone communications lines.

Tex asked for the red-handled bolt cutters from the back seat. They were given to him, and the six-foot two-inch, 190-pound, former All-District halfback for the Farmersville, Texas high school football team shimmied up the pole and cut two wires— one a telephone wire which did not fall and one an old communi-cations line from the days when Mark Lindsay and Terry Mel-cher first rented the property in 1966. Splat. The communications line fell to the ground, but it draped over the right side of the iron-framed, wire, electric gate.

Tex Watson slid back down, jumped, hit the road, got into

the car on the driver's side and coasted down the hill, lights off. At the bottom of the driveway, he grabbed a right and parked on Cielo Drive, to avoid suspicion. They all got out of the car— Linda Kasabian, Tex Watson, Sadie Glutz and Katie Krenwinkel. All was chop.

The entrance to 10050 Cielo Drive is located at the northwestern edge of the property, consisting of a wrought iron fence and a gate. The gate is six feet high, twelve feet wide and located in the center portion of the fence. On either side of the iron gate, rattan facing has been placed. On the left of the gate, a cliff falls away. On the right is a steep hillside going up at about a fifty- or sixty-degree angle.

The gate is electronically controlled from both the inside and outside. Affixed to the telephone pole that Tex had just shimmied up was the electronic button. The electronic button was housed in a metal box on a three and a half-foot metal stalk pipe. There was a locking device on the button, to be operated by key, but it was never used. Someone would push the button and the gate would swing inward, allowing them to enter, with the gate automatically closing behind them.

Tex wasn't sure just what sort of line he had cut that had splatted across the electric-eye gate. In any case, it had fallen in a north-south direction, but right over the gate, and they were afraid it was some sort of utility cable, charged with electricity. Fear of electrocution caused the young murderers to hesitate to enter via the front gate. They had nothing to fear, since the wire hadn't been used since the Polanskis moved into the estate. At one time the wire had been connected to two speakers, which were used for communications between the house and the front gate.

So they trudged up the hill, carrying their changes of clothes, their weapons and their rope. They arrived at the gate, where they located an area about ten to fifteen feet up the steep embankment on the right where, by cover of bushes, they were able to climb over the fence. Sadie ripped her shirt on the barbed wire. Tsk, tsk. Then, after they had crossed the fence, as they were creeping down the embankment toward the driveway, lights appeared, a car, moving down the driveway-parking lot. Tex said, "Lie down and be still." All lay down. Tex leaped forward, having evidently deposited the coils of rope from his left shoulder but holding his revolver in his right hand, his knife God knows where—probably in his left hand or in a scabbard.

Evidently Parent spotted them coming in and he said "Hey, what are you doing here?" Watson seems to have believed, luckily for Garretson, that Parent was the caretaker. Parent must have just been slowing down to touch the exit button when Tex ran up in front of the white, 1966 Nash Ambassador two-door sedan and yelled, "Stop! Halt!" It must have been around 12:20 A.M. Through the open driver's window, Tex jammed his formidable weapon up against Parent's head. It was a weapon right out of the spirit of the American West: a .22-caliber, nine-shot, walnut-handled, blue steel, long-barreled, Ned Buntlined to Wyatt Earp, longhorn, fifteen-inch revolver, loaded with .22 long rifle bullets. Parent said: "Please don't hurt me. I won't say anything."

Bang, bang, bang, bang.

Mrs. Seymour Kott, living just over the lip of the hill, on the other side of the driveway, about a football field distance away, heard, just as she was about to go to bed around 12:30, four shots fired in quick succession. Bang. Parent was shot in the upper chest. Bang. Once in the back of the left forearm, exiting on the other side. Shot in the left cheek—exit wound through the mouth. Shot in the lower chest. Somehow, Parent's Lucerne wristwatch got torn off—perhaps Tex was jabbing him with a knife as he was shooting him. It was found in the back seat with a severed watch-band. There was a defensive wound in Parent's left arm—a deep wound between his ring and little fingers that severed the tendons.

The young man, Steven Parent of El Monte, California, was attired in a red, white and blue plaid shirt, blue denim pants, black shoes and white socks. His body slumped slightly into the direction of the passenger's seat when he was shot, part of his weight against the armrest that separated the bucket seats, his head leaning back and out to the right, into the separation. Blood was spattered on the dashboard, blood and bone chips, bullet fragments on the rubber floormat and the right front door from Detroit.

Tex reached into the car, shut off the lights and the engine, put the gear selector in neutral, pushed the car back a few feet, turning the automobile a quarter circle to the southeast, out of the way. Then he put the gear in second forward and ran back to the crouching girls by the fence. Tex picked up the rope coils, put them on his shoulder and said, "Come on."

They had stashed their clothing on the estate side of the fence, in the bushes, as per Charlie's helter-skelter instructions.

On Watson's left shoulder were about seven coils of the white, three-quarter-inch, three-ply nylon line—seven or eight coils, a total of forty-three feet eight inches. And why was this Texan carrying a rope? Part of the game-plan, which later was abandoned in their haste, was to tie the victims up to the beams and draw and quarter them. They walked past the Porsche, the Firebird, beneath the trees that hover over the edge of the front lawn, and up the walkway, where they paused to scout the house. Tex ordered Linda Kasabian to go around the back of the house to check for any open windows or doors. Linda walked around between the north edge of the house and the three-car garage and checked the back porch door, looked into the kitchen windows and the back door into the living room, but there was nothing open. On her way back, evidently she spotted the bouquet of flowers on the table in the dining room, or so she testified a year later. She came around front and found Tex standing at the fresh-painted window of the unfurnished nursery room on the far north end of the house, next to the garage. He was cutting the lower part of the screen, slitting it with his bayonet.

Tex told Linda to go down by the fence and keep a lookout for people coming. She complied, walking downhill to the gate end of the parking lot, by the fence, and she knelt down on one knee, waiting. She could see Steve Parent, the young boy, slumped over his bucket seat. Sadie and Katie walked up the elliptical sidewalk which curves from a north/south direction to an east/

west direction, where it hooks into the covered flagstone front porch. Never say why. Cease to exist. You can't kill kill.

Tex crawled in through the window once he had slashed the screen and pulled it off the frame. There was the smell of fresh paint in the nursery being prepared for the late August arrival of the baby. The first coat of paint had been finished that very afternoon. Tex entered the kitchen walking south, through the dining room, into the entrance hall then opened the front door and let the two girls in. They grabbed a left out of the entrance hall into the large, white-walled, cream-carpeted living room. Bordering the west side of the living room was a loft carpeted and furnished with chairs and a telephone, reached by a redwood ladder, located adjacent to the left side of the large stone fireplace on the west wall of the living room. In the southeast corner of the living room, facing out into the room at a triangular position, was a baby grand piano with a metronome on the left side. On the music holder of the piano stood two compositions. One on the left side: a song called "Straight Shooter" by John Phillips of the Mamas and the Papas, a song off their first album. The song on the other side of the music stand was "Pomp and Circumstance" by Edward Elgar.

The grounds were lit up all around the house. The bug light on the north edge of the two-story garage was on. Several lights out on the front lawn were on. The poolside light was on. The two front porch lights were on.

The stereo inside the front hall closet beneath the shelves of film and videotapes was blaring, which may have prevented the four shots that killed Steven Parent from being heard.

In the center of the east wall was a large desk, jutting out into the living room. On the desk was a candelabra, flowers, various scripts and papers and a white pushbutton phone.

On the high-backed chair next to the desk was Jay Sebring's blue leather jacket, with his wallet, containing four twenty-dollar bills, and a tube of white powder. Nearby was Jay's briefcase, containing hair dryer, mirror, electric clippers and address book, some sort of pilot's map and miscellaneous barbering tools.

Dark wood stereo speaker cabinets were positioned on the east wall. The area of the living room which was to serve as the tableau for the murders was a sort of enclosed section near the large stone fireplace on the west center wall, in front of which was a large zebra-skin rug. Piles of books and movie scripts lined the hearth, as well as several throw pillows. Facing the fireplace, a few feet from the zebra skin, was a large, three-cushioned, beige velvet sofa.

To the immediate left of the couch was an end table, to the east. Two comfortable, cream-colored, stuffed easy chairs were set at angles on each side of the beige divan, forming sort of a closed area, facing the fireplace. Near the chair on the right was a brown, wide-reed, woven basket for holding magazines and a floor lamp.

Above the couch and parallel to it, running the entire length of the living room, east to west, was an apparently solid, four-inch by twelve-inch beam, painted white, over which the satanist Texan was soon to throw the nylon rope.

Draped over the back cushions of the beige divan was a large American flag, turned upside down. This was, in spite of the mutterings of the police officials a few hours later, about the only powerful symbolic element in the decor of the room. The flag, about five by three feet in size, had only been in the house about two weeks, according to the testimony of the maid, Mrs. Chapman.

On the north end of the living room was a bar, serving liquor. Also on the north end of the living room, near the hallway door, were Roman Polanski's two large, shiny blue steamer trunks which had just been delivered that afternoon, while Sharon was taking a nap. They stood stacked one on top of another, just inside the door.

Voityck Frykowski lay on the couch, in front of the fireplace, dozing off, zonked under the pleasant influence of the moderate psychedelic, MDA. Past the desk and toward the back of the couch crept the death-minded butcher. Evidently Watson walked around, standing on the zebra skin, his back to the fireplace, and leveled the Wyatt Earp revolver at Voityck's head. He motioned with his knife hand for Katie and Sadie to line up behind the couch, prepared to enact their helter-skelter exactitude. Voityck woke up, stretched and asked, "What time it is?"

"Don't move or you're dead."

"Who are you?"

"I'm the Devil. I'm here to do the Devil's business. Give me all your money," said Tex Watson, tall and hairy, knife in one hand, gun in the other. Voityck must have seen the two girls at this point, standing silently by the flag. The one, Katie, with her long, brown, magic hair that would be the blanket for the chop clan when they went into The Hole. The other, Sadie, with her dark brown hair now shorn closely, except for one long strand which hung over her left shoulder in witchiness. This Southern boy would later, in Death Valley, tell sixteen-year-old Snake Lake, "It was fun," to tear down the Polanski residence.

Elegant Abigail Folger was lying alone on the antique bed in her bedroom in the extreme southeast corner of the house, clad in a full-length, white nightgown, reading, wearing her reading glasses, slightly stoned on the euphoric MDA. Most of her and Voityck's personal belongings had been taken back to their house on Woodstock Road. But she and Voityck were remaining with Sharon until Roman Polanski should return from London. Her Nikon camera was visible on the chest of drawers. Inside the small bedstand nearby was the box containing capsules of MDA and a Baggie full of cannabis, for spiritual comfort.

In the living room, Voityck Frykowski kept asking the creepy crawlers who they were, what they wanted, over and over. "My money is in the wallet, on the desk," he said.

Sadie went over to the desk to look for it and announced that she couldn't find it. Later, Sadie would claim to her jailhouse snitch, Virginia Graham, that she put a palm print on the desk when she was looking for the wallet, but her witchy force field prevented it from being identifiable. She said, "My spirit is so strong that obviously it didn't show up, 'cause if it had, they would have had me by now."

Tex told Sadie to go get a towel in the bathroom with which to tie up Frykowski. Sadie went looking for the bathroom. She took a towel back to the couch by the fireplace and tied Voityck's hands behind his back with a loose knot. Frykowski was then made to lie back down on his back, trapping his hands behind him. Tex then told her to scout the house for other people. Sadie evidently climbed up the redwood ladder to look in the loft. And then she walked to the south, toward the hallway off which were the two main bedrooms of the house. In the one on the left, Abigail Folger lay reading alone. She looked up, she saw Sadie and Abigail waved! Waved and smiled and Sadie smiled back and walked away. Hi, death.

Sadie turned, crossed the hallway, walking west and glanced into the bedroom of Sharon Polanski. Sharon, her stomach tanned and full of child, was lying in bed, propped up on pillows, her blonde hair down over her shoulders. She was wearing matching blue-yellow, floral-patterned bra and panties. For jewelry, she had on her wedding ring and gold earpins. The lime green and orange sheets were pulled down. It was about 12:25 A.M. On the edge of the bed where the beautiful Sharon Tate lay sat Jay Sebring, clothed in a blue shirt, black high-top boots and white pants with black vertical stripes. On his wrist was an opulent Cartier watch. They were talking. They did not see Sadie.

On each side of the bed were semicircular, marble-topped tables. The one on the right held a princess phone and an oval-framed wedding portrait of the Polanskis. On the right marble table sat a bottle of Heineken's beer, Jay Sebring's favorite drink.

There was a white, louvered, double French door leading out to the swimming pool on the south wall of Sharon Tate's bedroom. The windows looking out onto the pool area were shuttered also with white, louvered blinds. It was out this door just minutes later that Abigail Folger would run for her life and Katie Krenwinkel would leave her Death Row fingerprint.

There was a large closet in Sharon's bedroom. Also a bathroom and a dressing room. On the east wall of the bedroom was a tall armoire with drawers near the bottom. One of the drawers was full of photos of Miss Tate. On top of this wardrobe was a new white bassinet for the baby, wrapped in clear plastic; and, to the right, an ornate hookah. To the left of the armoire was a television set and a Sony videotape viewer.

Sadie returned to Watson in the living room and told him that there were people in the bedrooms. Tex was angry. Where was the money? He told Sadie to go into the bedrooms and bring them out into the living room. Sadie unfolded her Buck clasp knife and walked into Abigail Folger's bedroom waving her weapon: "Go out into the living room. Don't ask any questions." She did the same thing on the other side of the hall in Sharon's bedroom.

Sadie waved her knife at Jay and Sharon and they all walked out into the living room confused and angry. Jay Sebring said, "What's going on?"

"Sit down!" Sebring refused to sit.

A crisis occurred for Katie at this point. She had no knife! So she walked outside and went down past Steve Parent's Ambassador to the gate to get Linda Kasabian's knife with the taped irregular handle. Katie told her, "Listen for sounds," then walked back up the hill to the house.

The tendency of Sebring—cool, experienced businessman—and Frykowski—survivor of Hitler—must have been not to panic or to fight—at first. But when Tex told everybody to lie down on the floor on their stomachs atop some pillows near the fireplace, Sebring would not stand for that and said: "Let her sit down, can't you see she's pregnant?" Then Sebring lunged for the gun and Tex waxed murderous and shot Jay in the armpit. Jay fell and Tex drop-kicked him in the bridge of the nose. Abigail Folger screamed.

The bullet entered Sebring's left axilla, penetrating downward through the left fifth rib, through the left lung and exited out the left side of his mid-back. The bullet was found by the coroner several inches from the exit wound, trapped between skin and shirt.

Christopher, the Weimaraner, left the back patio porch of the guest house, barking and excited. The dog evidently trotted into the front door of the main house about this time. Sadie told

Virginia Graham that a "hunting dog" came around. Sadie even thought that somehow the dog got hold of her knife: "We looked all over for it. . . . I really think the dog got it."

The sight of Jay Sebring lying on his side gave the former cotton picker, Charles Watson, instant credibility. "All right, where's the money?"

Abigail said that her money was in her purse on the couch in the bedroom. Sadie stuck her knife up to Miss Folger's back and marched her into the bedroom where Abigail opened up her black canvas shoulder bag and took out seventy-two or seventy-three dollars for the satanist. Sadie refused Gibby's offer of her credit cards and they walked back into the living room. Five souls, seventy-two dollars.

Tex then tied them around and around their necks with the nylon rope and threw the end of it over the white ceiling beam and told Sadie to choke the rope so that Abigail and Sharon had to stand up or else strangle. Jay's unconscious body acted as a dead weight on the other end of the rope which was knotted around his neck. A large hematoma was swelling on his left eye.

Tex was worried lest Voityck Frykowski should get loose so he told Sadie to retie his hands with a bigger towel. She went into the bedroom and got a larger towel, a beige forty-six-inch Martex bath towel, and tied his hands behind him more securely, then she pushed him back down onto the couch, standing guard over him.

Tex told Katie as he was wrapping the rope around their necks to turn out all the lights in the house. This she did, according to Susan Atkins. The next morning the only lights the police found on in the house were the hall light leading into the back bedrooms and the desk lamp on the east side of the living room.

Katie assumed choke duties on the end of the rope. One of the ladies asked, "What are you going to do to us?"

Charles, the smug muscular boy from Copeville, had them trapped in his own phoneless hamburger universe. "You are all going to die." And again he told them that he was the Devil. Immediately the moans and shrieks and beggings rose up from the trussed victims. They struggled to get free.

Tex ordered Sadie to kill Voityck Frykowski. Voityck lay quaking up and down, desperately trying to loosen the knot behind his back. Sadie raised her knife and, by her account, hesitated. Voityck wrenched his hands free and reached up from the couch and grabbed hold of her hair and pulled her down, grabbing her knife arm. He hit her on the top of the head and they fell against the end table to the left of the sofa and rolled onto the stuffed chair.

Sadie got her arm free and stabbed blindly, one, two, three, four times, parallel down the front of his left leg. He turned toward the front hall as if to flee. She managed to stab him once in the back but the knife hit bone. Then she stabbed him deeply in the right back lung. The skin surface widths of the wounds were three quarter inch, the same as the width of her Buck knife. In the scuffle she lost her knife somehow, the knife the little terror-addict thought the dog had carried away. The police found the knife lodged blade up between the cushion and the back of the overstuffed chair, seven feet from the north wall and four feet from the west wall. Knifeless, she clung to his back and yelled.

Still, Voityck staggered onward. Tex ran up, wrestled Frykowski around and shot him below the left axilla, the bullet lodging in his middle back. He shot him also through the front right thigh. Still he walked on. He shot again—the gun misfiring. (The gun had a history of misfiring, as when Manson shot Bernard Crowe on July 1). Tex began to club his face and scalp with the gun, holding it by the barrel. Voityck's blood type was found on the intact left gun grip and on the inside of the cocked hammer of the gun. The right walnut grip broke into three pieces, two pieces falling in the front hall, the remaining tiny piece skittering out onto the front porch.

What was William Garretson doing during the screams and the shots? According to his testimony he was sitting in his living room, just fifty yards away, listening to The Doors and a Mama Cass album. And two freeways distant, on the northwest edge of the San Fernando Valley, Charles Manson was waiting by the dusty driveway in front of the Longhorn Saloon for the return of his patrol.

When Tex ran up to the hall door to get Voityck, Sharon and Jay and Abigail struggled to get free from the knots on their necks. Katie was holding the rope where it trailed down on the other side of the beam. Abigail broke loose and headed for the back bedroom, where the door to the swimming pool led to freedom.

Krenwinkel dropped the rope and gave chase. Abigail, taller and stronger, fought for her life. Meanwhile, Tex spotted the struggling Sebring and ran up. Stab stab stab stab, four times Watson hacked him in the left back, into the lung. The wounds were one and a half inches wide on the surface, penetrating deeply. Tex's knife was sharpened, of course, along its normal cutting edge but the top edge had been sharpened also, for about an inch. The coroner was able to declare this long before the arrests by noting that vital organs were pierced by a double-edged instrument while the skin surface wound indicated that the upper knife edge was thick. Tex kicked his face, then turned, his attention caught by the yells from Katie, his black velour turtleneck beginning to get bloody, his eyes shiny. He ran up to Abigail, who was wounded only defensively at this point, in the hands and arms. Abigail surrendered. "I give up. Take me." He did, slicing her neck and smashing her head with the gun butt. He stabbed her in various parts of her chest and abdomen. She clutched a gaping tear in her lower right stomach. She fell.

Watson glanced up when he heard Voityck screaming near the front lawn. He ran to the front porch to see him rise up from the bush into which he had fallen and stagger across the grass toward the southeast, yelling. Sadie Satan told her cellmate, Shelley Nadell, about it. "He got to the lawn and was standing there hollering, 'Help! Help!' and nobody even heard him." An unlikely story. The police undertook noise tests at the Polanski residence and you can hear yells all over Benedict Canyon, not to mention a guest house with open windows. Did you hear those screams? Shut up and go back to sleep.

Deep in flower-power knelt the young mother Linda Kasabian by the dark fence. When she heard the screams, she claims she looked over at the dead Steve Parent and it dawned on her on a sudden that the occupants of the house were being killed. Then just like a tadpole wriggling toward a light source, she raced toward the shriekers, "to try to stop it"—as she later testified. She ran up the walkway, onto the grass. "I ran over to the hedge" —probably the almost s-shaped hedge to the immediate north of the front porch.

"Waited a minute—then I saw Frykowski staggering out the door—drenched in blood—I looked in his eyes—he looked in mine—I saw the image of Christ in him, I cried and I prayed with all my heart."

In her testimony at the trial she mentioned two mental events that occurred as their eyes met: her silent prayer, "Oh, God, I am so sorry. Please make it stop"; and also that in the midst of the terrible glance she began to feel Charles Manson no longer to be Jesus Christ the Son of God. He was a Devil.

Tall Voityck stood up against the square wooden support post on the northeast corner of the porch and he tried to step from the flagstone onto the sidewalk, holding onto the post. His balance failed; he spun around the post and fell head first into the dirt.

Sadie ran out of the house upset that she had lost her knife. Linda testified that she tried to tell Sadie to make it stop, that she heard voices. Sadie said, "It's too late." They talked and somehow as the witches chatted Voityck got to his feet and began to scream into the smog, down the Canyon. Someone had to hear.

It must be noted that where Linda claims to have trotted back into the parking lot after watching Frykowski fall into the bushes, Patricia Krenwinkel has said that Mrs. Kasabian entered the house as she was struggling with Abigail Folger. Katie/Patricia called for her to help. Then, according to Krenwinkel, Linda gave her a stare, turned on her heels and walked out the door.

Tex was out the front door in a red-dog chop blitz and rode Frykowski to the ground, stabbing in the unprotected left side of his body. Frykowski suffered sixteen defensive wounds in his left lower arm trying to ward off the Evil. Fifty-one wounds Tex dealt to the spleen, abdomen, left lung, right back, heart, chest, hands. And still the man who twenty-five years before survived the Nazi atrocities in Poland crawled on, till he crumpled.

Inside the house Abigail somehow got to her feet and careened toward the French doors to the pool, leaving a trail of blood, as Katie, who was standing guard over Sharon and Jay, chased after her, chopping. Gibby clawed at the shuttered door smearing blood, to open it up. Katie put herself on Death Row when she tried to prevent the door from being opened, leaving the print of her left little finger with twelve points of identification just above the knob on the right French door.

Abigail Folger got out of the house dripping upon the side-walk leading to the pool. She ran left, splattering the green garden hose in the grass. She almost reached the split rail fence, past the pole light near the tall fir tree. Collapse. The white-gowned heiress who believed in integration, the tall expert equestrienne, butchered by the racist harem girl from the Pit.

Linda could see it as she looked through the porch over the shrubs. Linda turned and ran down the hill, past Sebring's Porsche, past Parent, through the narrows, sprinted left, up the bank, crossed over the fence, and ran down the hill to the '59 Ford and lay down in some bushes, panting.

As Linda ran away, all the killers were out of the house, leaving Sharon, as yet untouched, and Jay Sebring, dead, inside. Mrs. Polanski, unguarded, started toward the front door just as Katie Krenwinkel re-entered the back door by the pool and walked into the living room.

Sharon was alive, crying for the life of her child. She must have gotten to her feet and Sadie got her in a headlock. Tex told her it looked like Sharon wanted to sit down. "So I took her over and sat her down on the couch."

"All I want to do is have my baby."

Sadie was worried that Sharon might get hysterical so she talked with her to calm her down, about how she had no mercy for her. Words, getting her attention. After all, Sadie didn't want the woman she was about to kill to get hysterical, did she?

They killed Sharon last. About a month after the murders,

Barbara, the girl who was late with the clothes, overheard Sadie tell Ouish at the Meyer's Ranch in Death Valley National Monument that Sharon Tate was the last to die because she "had to watch the others die." That was a favorite Manson fantasy. To kill someone in front of an observer.

Sharon sat on the couch quietly. They waited a few minutes. It is not known what was done during that time. Finally it came. Sadie told Virginia Graham that she held Sharon's arms back behind her. She told Snake in Death Valley that she held her legs. What a flimsy memory. She held Sharon's arms and Sharon turned her head around and looked back at Sadie, beseeching her, "Please don't kill me, please don't kill me. I don't want to die." She was crying.

"Please, I'm going to have a baby."

Sadie, ever crude, replied, according to Graham, "Look, bitch! I don't care if you're going to have a baby. You'd better be ready. You're going to die. . . ." Sadie to Graham: "Then we killed her a few minutes later."

In a final plea, Sharon begged Sadie to take the baby, the perfect unborn Richard Paul Polanski. It was impossible. Sadie could chop, but she couldn't do that.

Tex told Sadie to kill.

No. Tex, I can't kill her, you do it. Katie? No, Tex, you do it, but she was willing enough to hold her legs. Tex, ever eager, was the one. He stabbed her several times in the left breast through the brassiere. Screams. Stabs. Aorta. Death.

Then they all stabbed her, sixteen times, with both knives. To Sadie it was thrilling: "It felt so good, the first time I stabbed her."

Then the little acidassin vampire licked blood from her own fingers.

But it wasn't adventuresome enough for her. "We were going to mutilate them but we didn't have a chance to." To both cellmates, Sadie confided that part of the game plan included gouging out their eyeballs and smearing them against the walls.

All of a sudden, Tex said: "Get out." The girls left and then Tex came out and proceeded to go berserk in a final dutiful circuit to check out death. He ran in a counter-clockwise direction. He ran over to Abigail: chop chop chop. He ran over to the lifeless Frykowski who actually lay clutching the grass in his hand, with his left arm still perpendicular to the ground in death, where he crumpled. Tex used some of his football training on him. Then the hell-creep ran inside to arrange the tableau.

While Tex was inside the house, Sadie and Katie walked around whisper-yelling for Linda. They couldn't find her. Tex came out of the house, saw the girls, and told Sadie to go in the house and write something on the door. Something witchy, Charlie had said. Tex left on the front Dutch door a Death Row fingerprint.

Tex and Katie walked down the walkway and Sadie went in the front door. Sadie walked into the haunted room. Evidently Tex had looped the nylon rope twice around Sharon's neck. There was a double loop around Sebring's neck with an overhand knot formed by the second loop. The rope led from one end, which was under Jay's body, around his neck twice over to Sharon, who was lying in front of the couch beneath the flag, around her neck twice, then back along the couch and over the ceiling beam, the rope just touching the floor on the other side.

Sharon seemed to Sadie more cut up than before, probably from Tex. Then Sadie got a towel. Sadie next went over to Sharon Tate and put her head on her stomach to listen, kneeling on the floor by the velvet couch. Sadie picked Sharon up slightly off the floor and sat with Sharon's head in her lap and embraced her. Finally Sadie went over to the yellow towel used to tie Voityck's hands and came back, obtained some blood from Sharon's breast, walked the front hall and knelt down to print PIG in blood type O–M. She turned, walked back into the living room, threw the towel toward the hearth and split. She left the door wide open and also she left, as she moved east off the porch, her two bare-foot prints in blood.

One hundred and two stab wounds riddled the bodies. Thirty minutes, one stab every twenty-seconds, and Sharon's black kitten walked mewing among the bodies.

When Sadie reached the electric gate she found them waiting for her. Tex forgot electrocution and touched the button, leaving a smear. The blood was Sebring's. The gate opened. They scooped up their spare clothes and trotted down the hill huffing. Murder is hard work. The gate closed.

Meanwhile, by the Ford, Linda lay down for about five minutes in the brush. Then the floweroid, who today is a free woman, stood up, entered the automobile and started the engine. Was she going to split? The others arrived with their knives and clothes in hands. "They looked like zombies," she later wrote; the dead-eyed, dead-alive.

Tex, baleful with murder, yelled at her. He stopped the engine and pushed her over into the passenger side. Then he chewed out Sadie for losing the Buck knife. He started the car and crept off, turning right onto Benedict Canyon Drive. Then he turned the lights on. Up Benedict Canyon Drive drove the creepy-crawlie four, fresh from battle, changing their clothes as the car drove up the hill. Linda steered for Tex as he slimed out of his wet black velour and jeans. They talked excitedly. It was hot.

Linda took all the clothes and made them into a ball—the black velour turtleneck, black jeans, genuine Roebuck jeans, blue jeans, bloody white tee-shirt which was probably used as a weapons-cleaner hand towel, black tee-shirt and blue tee-shirts. A Death Row hair, belonging to Susan Atkins, clung to the bundle. Also clinging to the bundle when the Special Investigation Division officers got hold of the clothes on December 16, 1969, were many long fourteen-inch blond hairs belonging to an unknown female. Since the car was about the only working vehicle at the Spahn Ranch, some girl or other, one who had not undergone the family tonsure rite, probably had brushed her hair in the car and left some runaway strands which were picked up from the floor by the wet clothing.

Tex told Linda Kasabian to wipe the prints off the gun and the two knives. He pulled off to the right of Benedict Canyon and stopped. Linda threw the bundle down the ravine on the right. It bounced down intact, lodging within eyesight of the road, against a bush.

She was told to throw out the knives. She did—first one, which went down a hillside, then the other, which bounced on the curb

as the car moved away. Evidently Tex had turned around before
the tossing of the knives because Linda testified that the car was
heading downhill. He announced that next they had to find a place
to wash up. He pulled off Benedict left onto Portola Drive, just
a block north of the street where Jay Sebring lived.

A couple of hundred yards from the turnoff they spotted a
garden hose hooked up to the home of Rudy and Myra Weber.
They turned the car around and parked the car toward the canyon
road so they could get away easily. They walked to the house.
It was twenty feet from the street.

Rudolph Weber was asleep but the sound of running water
woke him up. He thought it was a leak in his plumbing so he
grabbed a flashlight and walked down to his basement, opened his
garage door and went in to check out the pipes. No water was
leaking so he figured everything was all right. Then he heard
voices, from the street. Goddamn kids. He went over and flashed
the light on them. "Just what do you think you're doing?" They
looked like teenagers.

Tall Tex dialed his mind to smiling psychopath and said, "Hi—
we're just getting a drink of water and we're sorry to have disturbed you." Rudolph walked over and turned off the water,
whereafter the girls started walking down to the car.

"Is that your car?"

"No, it's not. We're walking."

Weber followed the young folk and by this time Myra was
awake and by his side, announcing that her husband was a member of the Sheriff's Reserve. Tex opened the door for the girls
and Weber was offended by the disarray inside. Tex got in and
flooded the engine. Weber made as if he were trying to remove
the keys from the car, reaching in while Tex was trying to start it.
Finally the engine caught and Tex peeled out, wrenching Mr.
Weber's clutching hand. As the car sped away, he memorized the
number and later wrote it down, GYY 435.

Tex didn't turn on his lights until he reached the San Fernando
Valley, where they stopped for two dollars' gas. Tex went to the
john to wash, as did Sadie and Katie. Sadie noticed when coming

back to the car that there was some blood on it. She hoped the attendant didn't see it. Tex told Linda to drive. On the way Tex evidently threw the Longhorn revolver out the right window down a ravine at a location about one and a half miles from the slaughter zone. It is strange, however, that none of the murderers seems to have mentioned throwing the revolver away. Perhaps Manson threw it away later.

During the remainder of the drive, the foursome seemed to relax, becoming even jovial. The weapons, the blood, the clothes, they were gone, weren't they? They were Helter Skelter's finest butchers. And they began to chit-chat.

To start it off, poor Tex had hurt his foot and it was killing him. Sadie's hair was hurting terribly where Frykowski had pulled it. Katie babbled on about how the knife handle hurt her hand each time she stabbed. All agreed that the knives were inadequate. Next time they would need heavier equipment. Sadie complained about the toughness of Voityck's legs when she strained to stab them. They had quite a time describing the moans of the murdered, how Sharon kept calling out to God and Abigail kept crying out to her mother.

"How come you're back so early?" Charlie asked when they arrived at the Spahn Ranch. Charlie was waiting in the driveway, sitting by the Saloon. It was 2 A.M.

Sadie told Charlie that she had seen blood on the Ford. He told her to go to the kitchen and get a sponge and water and wash it down. Linda and Katie were to check the interior for spots. They found none, so Manson told them to go into the bunkhouse while Sadie washed the outside of the car. Charlie then took Tex aside to debrief him.

Clem and Brenda were in the bunkhouse when Katie and Linda arrived. They were totally exhausted. Pretty soon Tex and Charlie came into the bunkhouse for a general discussion of the evening. Tex told Charlie that everything had been messy; bodies were lying around, but all were dead. Charlie was happy.

Tex made several laugh when he revealed that he had said to people in the house, "I'm the Devil, I'm here to do the Devil's business, where's your money?" Ha ha. Manson then polled the hackers to see if any felt remorse for what they had done. Katie: "No." Sadie: "No." Linda: "No."

There is some indication that someone removed a credit card belonging to Voityck Frykowski from the murder site. One witness claims that the credit card was brought out on later occasions as a relic to be passed from hand to hand during family gatherings.

People were sleepy. Kasabian went to the back ranch to sleep. Sadie made love with a human—she thinks it might have been Clem—then sacked out. Katie and Tex slept in the Saloon, according to Kasabian. It was over. But not quite.

There is considerable discrepancy between the scene of the murders, as left by Susan Atkins, Patricia Krenwinkel, Tex Watson and Linda Kasabian, and the one found by the police the next morning. Neither Susan Atkins nor evidently any of the others tucked any face towel over the head of Jay Sebring, yet the police found a towel over his head.

There was not enough slack in part of the rope extending from Sharon Tate to Jay Sebring for her to have been standing and moving around, yet she moved around the room the killers say. So the rope perhaps was affixed some time after her death. The murderers, including Susan Atkins, do not mention fixing the rope, although the effusive Atkins gave long detailed accounts to anybody who would listen about every aspect of the crimes. Nor did Susan Atkins talk about the brown framed glasses found by the bloody steamer trunks. These glasses were found face down with the frames open and jutting up perpendicular to the floor. They had belonged to a person with severe eyesight problems.

There were two large pools of blood on the front porch, one to the left of the door mat, type O–M, Sharon Tate's, and the other on the north edge of the porch, type O–Mn, Jay Sebring's. All the females involved, Linda, Katie and Sadie, have claimed that at no time were Sharon Tate or Jay Sebring ever near the front porch. How did the blood get there?

Steve Parent's, Frykowski's and Folger's blood types were all B–Mn, so that none of the blood on the porch could have been theirs. A police report describing the homicide scene said, regarding the blood of Sharon Tate on the front porch, that: "From the amount of blood there it would appear that she remained there for at least minutes prior to movement."

The police also thought that Mrs. Polanski's body may have been moved from one location to another, because of its condition. There were various spatters of Sharon Tate's blood in the front hall and on the door sill, but never, while the killers were at the estate, was she in the hall.

There were two steamer trunks in the living room by the hall door which were knocked away during the night. The killers didn't do it. The right end of the top trunk was resting on the left end of the bottom trunk, and the left side of the top trunk had tipped to the floor. There was a stain of blood, apparently from the same dripping, extending from the left side of the upper trunk to the top of the bottom trunk. It is Sebring's blood, yet the killers claim he was shot and stabbed and killed in one spot and never moved.

Manson stated one time that he had gone to the Polanski residence after the murders. "I went back to see what my children did," he is alleged to have said. Later, Manson denied that he had gone to the house. Whether he did or not, the crime scene was disturbed by someone during the night before the police arrived.

One of the Manson game plans involved hanging "rich piggies" up on their porches and slicing them. Perhaps he or someone went to the house and the bodies of Sebring and Tate were carried out onto the porch to do just that, but there was nothing adequate to string the rope over, or through, to support the weight of the bodies. Then they may have decided, through panic, to recreate the original scene and accordingly carried the bodies back inside, leaving spatters of blood behind. Manson also told someone he had purchased the brown eye glasses in a pawn shop and placed them by the steamer trunk to cause confusion.

What is more likely to have occurred is that Manson, master of disguises, or one of his henchmen was wearing the glasses and was carrying Sebring out to the porch, or back in from the porch, and because it is difficult to see out of the glasses, made for an extremely myopic person, bumped into the steamer trunks. The top trunk, its end tipping off, almost fell onto the floor. Blood dripped from the dead body onto the end of the top trunk and the top of the bottom trunk. During the bumping of the trunk, the glasses fell off, hit the floor and were abandoned.

Then the bodies were carried back to their original places by the sofa and armchair, the white nylon rope was looped around their necks and the end proceeding from Mrs. Polanski's neck was thrown back over the white ceiling beam with the rope-end just touching the floor on the other side. Someone then took that beige towel and hooded it over the head of Jay Sebring, tucking the towel ends under the rope-loops. There is no way of knowing what else could have occurred.

Danny De Carlo has related to the police about a night around August 8, 9 or 10, 1969, when Tex, Charlie and Clem left one night and returned the next morning. They asked De Carlo if he wanted to go along but he said no thanks. When they returned in the morning, De Carlo spotted Clem meandering in the dirtway by George Spahn's house. When De Carlo walked up to Clem and asked, "What'd you do last night?" De Carlo looked back over his shoulder and spotted Charlie behind him, smiling. Clem then placed his hand on De Carlo and said, according to De Carlo, "We got five piggies." Then Clem turned heel and walked away grinning.

Stephanie, Manson's new-found love, testified that Manson woke her around dawn the morning after the murders and took her in to Devil Canyon, probably the waterfall campsite, where she stayed about a week.

It was over. Over for five sparks of the universe, butchered by some new form of programmed zombi-spore.

Eighteen

Fear Swept the Poolsides

There were a number of screams and shots reported in Benedict Canyon during the night. Various people in various locations near the Polanski residence heard them between 2 and 4 A.M. Most of the screams were after the murders were committed. Nothing much, just ordinary Friday-night screams.

Between 4:30 and 5 A.M., Steven B. Shannon delivered the morning *Los Angeles Times* to the Polanski front gate and noticed that there was a wire down, draped across the fence. At 7:30 A.M., Mr. Seymour Kott, the temporary resident at 10070 Cielo Drive, walked out of his house to get his paper and noticed the wire down and saw the yellow bug light on the Polanski garage, shining in the distance.

Mrs. Winifred Chapman, the Polanski housekeeper, a well-spoken lady who had been working for them for just over a year, took a city bus to Santa Monica and Canyon Drive at the southern end of Benedict Canyon, arriving about 8 A.M. She was late and was considering calling a cab for the remainder of the trip to the Polanski residence when she saw a friend of hers, a man named Jerry, who took her up Benedict Canyon and Cielo Drive to the front gate of the estate. It was 8:30 A.M.

Mrs. Chapman pushed the button of the electronic gate, noted that the wire was down, picked up the *Los Angeles Times* and walked up the drive. She reached the garage, snapped off the yellow bug light, then walked past the front of the three-car garage, turned right, out of view of the bodies, walked along the extreme north edge of the house to the back, turned left and went into the house through a service entrance door.

She reached up on the rafter above the door and obtained a key from its usual place, unlocked the door, put the key back, walked into the service area, right, into the kitchen where she switched off the back patio light and put her purse down. She picked up the phone. It was dead.

She went into the dining room, walking south, to wake someone up to tell them there was no phone service. She saw the bouquet of flowers that Linda had seen the night before, resting on a small stand in the dining room.

When she reached the front hall, she saw a towel, she saw the steamer trunks, saw blood, saw a door open, saw out over the front porch, over the bloody doormat, saw Frykowski. Panic.

She ran back out of the house as she had come in, picking up her purse on the way. She ran screaming down the hillside parking lot, pushed the bloody exit button at the narrowing of the driveway, the gate opened up and she fled. She rang the doorbell of the house immediately down the driveway from the front gate. No answer. She ran down the hill to the Asim residence, where she encountered fifteen-year-old Jim Asim, a member of Law Enforcement Troop 800 of the Boy Scouts of America.

"There's bodies and blood all over the place! Call the police!" Mrs. Chapman was distraught to the degree that the young Boy Scout called up the police emergency number to seek assistance himself. Three times he called and finally a patrol car arrived, then another and another and another, sirens keening.

At 9:14 A.M., Officer J. J. De Rosa, operating West Los Angeles unit 8L5, and Officer W. T. Whisenhunt, operating West L.A. unit 8L68, were given a call by the Central Dispatch: "Code 2, possible homicide, 10050 Cielo Drive."

Officer De Rosa arrived first, encountering the young man Jim Asim and the hysterical housekeeper Mrs. Chapman. She told him of the blood and the body and she showed the officer how to operate the electronic gate.

De Rosa, rifle in hand, walked onto the property and encountered Steve Parent slumped in the Ambassador. The motor was off, lights off. As officer De Rosa was checking out Parent's automobile, Officer Whisenhunt arrived, having "received a call to back up a fellow officer investigating a possible homicide" as he later testified.

They radioed for an ambulance and verified death. Whereupon they walked up into the property again, into the chaos of stilled souls. They noted Parent, then walked toward the garage, rifles ready to fire. They went up into the second story of the garage, where Roman Polanski was to set up his office, by the steps on the side, and checked it out. Nothing.

They walked past Sebring's black Porsche and the Firebird and the Camaro in the garage, and into the front yard, across the lawn where they encountered Voityck Frykowski, wearing colored bell-bottomed pants and a purple shirt, and buckled, brown, high-top shoes. They saw Miss Folger a few yards to the south, white gown red.

Officer Burbridge of Unit 8V5 was the next officer to arrive, joining the two policemen in the investigation. The three policemen could see the great amount of blood on the front porch and, of course, the open front door. They paused. Who could know what sort of maniac might lurk within the house? With De Rosa covering, Whisenhunt and Burbridge went around to the back of the house to check out possible entrances, but the door was locked. Whisenhunt and Burbridge decided to enter the open nursery room window on the far right of the house, the very window that Tex Watson had crawled upon. The window screen, with a slit, was resting against the house.

A few seconds later, Officer De Rosa observed his fellow patrolmen within the house, so he made to join them, walking over the flagstone porch into the hallway, avoiding the blood. He saw the ugly PIG scrawled in ugliness. And he walked into the ugly ghostly desolation of Manson's tableau. They noted the bodies and the rope and quickly searched the house, the bedrooms, the loft. Later, Officer De Rosa was unable to recall seeing the two red barefoot prints on the porch.

Their job was to protect the scene and to make note of the original physical circumstances of the area, leaving it undisturbed.

The officers completed search of the house and were evidently checking out the rest of the estate, the pool area, and were proceeding toward the guest house when they heard dogs barking. Then they heard a male voice within the guest house yelling at the dogs to quiet down. Five dead bodies and someone yelling at a dog.

Bill Garretson heard the dogs barking as the cops approached and yelled: "Quiet down!" and started to get up from the couch in the living room where he had been sleeping since shortly after dawn, or so he testified. He was a short, tanned boy with slightly long brown hair, age nineteen, barefoot, shirtless, and wearing pin-striped pants. He looked out the window onto the front porch and what he saw was an officer pointing a rifle at him. The officer told him to freeze. Christopher, the Weimaraner, was barking furiously. Garretson saw another officer leveling a rifle at him from the redwood picnic table on the porch. It was time for fear.

The first cop, Officer De Rosa, kicked the front door in and the Weimaraner rushed forward and chomped the officer's leg. They threw Garretson on the porch floor, ripping his pants knee, and handcuffed his hands behind his back. Garretson kept asking them, "What's the matter? What's the matter?"

"You want to know what's the matter? Well, we'll show you what's the matter."

They marched the handcuffed Garretson across the lawn to Abigail Folger, who lay upon her back in her nightgown. He thought the body was that of the maid, so destroyed was it. They marched him over to Voityck Frykowski. He looked away from the unidentifiable victim. Then they took him to the Ambassador, where he couldn't identify the person inside.

Thinking that the first body was the maid, Garretson was taken aback encountering Mrs. Chapman alive, in the custody of an Officer Gingras, when he reached the front gate. When he asked whose body it had been, he was told in error that it was Mrs. Polanski's.

The police had captured the person who had probably been the last human to have seen the victims alive and the first person to have seen them dead. It was a classic investigation, requiring only that a lot of pressure be forthwith applied until he or she confessed and the case would be solved.

Mrs. Chapman and William Garretson were driven to the police station by Officers De Rosa and Whisenhunt while Officer Burbridge remained behind to protect the location. Mrs. Chapman evinced hysteria and was taken to the UCLA Medical Center for sedation and then was escorted by Officer Richard Gingras to West Los Angeles police headquarters for questioning. Bill Garretson was led daze-eyed into the lockup and sometime later an officer walked up and said, "There's the guy that killed those people."

Fear swept the poolsides of Los Angeles on the hot August morning as the news of the murders seeped through the network of phones.

Media sources, who monitor police radio broadcasts, were quick to note that something had happened on Cielo Drive. Reporters heard something about fires in Benedict Canyon with five people killed and that Sebring was a victim so one of them called Jay Sebring's house and spoke to an employee of Sebring, who had stayed over to paint or to repair the house. After the reporter called, the employee called John Madden, the vice-president of Sebring International, who called Sharon's parents in San Francisco. Mrs. Tate called Cielo Drive. Even though the phone lines were severed, the telephone appeared to ring, giving the appearance that no one was home. This was not startling. Sharon was supposed to be staying at a girl friend's house.

All at once six squad cars sped up to the gate. Then more arrived.

Sergeant Klorman, the first uniformed supervisor, arrived with Officer Gingras, who took Mrs. Chapman to the station house.

Aerial photos taken a few minutes after the police arrived, show the front gate of the estate aswarm with reporters, none of whom was allowed through the electric gate onto the property.

The reporters badgered the policemen as they entered and left the front gate. Security was tight but Sergeant Klorman, the first uniformed supervisor on the set, saw fit to announce to reporters about the condition of the beds: "All of the beds, including those in the guest house, appear to have been used. . . . It looked like a battlefield up there."

And thereafter the police entering and leaving began to give out bits of information on the crimes. One officer said about the murder scene that "It looked ritualistic." Those three words set the tone for early reportage of the events. The *Los Angeles Times* hit the stands that afternoon with a page-one story about "Ritual Murders."

The police gave out so much information that they were depleting the possible supply of "poly keys"—polygraph interrogation keys—which are key bits of information about the murders that only the killers could know, so that on a lie detector test the possible killer could be asked questions about these facts. If the facts were printed or broadcast, they would be spoiled for such a purpose.

One officer told the press that the victims were attired in "hippie type clothes." Another saw fit to announce that one of the victim's pants were down. Another that it looked like a "typical fag murder." There is no knowing what led reporters to print or officers to say that Sebring was wearing a black hood over his head. There is a great difference between a light-colored bloody towel and a black hood.

The police swarmed upon the residence, upon the roof, upon the grounds, scraping, dusting, making notes. It seemed like half the Los Angeles police department showed up at Cielo Drive that day. Over forty officers, including the chief of the Beverly Hills police department, plus ambulance drivers and four members of the coroner's staff, visited the property.

Police photographers took hundreds of photos of everything in the house and grounds. One of the jobs was to find out as much as possible about the victims immediately—with emphasis on enemies and people with motives. There were literally thousands of things to do immediately. First, they looked in purses and wallets to learn the identity of the deceased.

Around 10 A.M. the police called Sharon's mother in San Francisco. They were terse. They obtained from her the name of William Tennant, her business agent. The police then seem to have located Mr. Tennant at his tennis club. He traveled immediately to 10050 Cielo Drive, arriving about noon, still attired in his tennis clothing.

He identified Mrs. Polanski, Miss Folger, Mr. Sebring and Mr. Frykowski, and left the premises at once, sobbing and holding back his stomach, refusing to talk to the congeries of reporters at the gate. A female TV gossip asked him if it was "really Sharon."

"Oh, don't be an ass," was the anguished reply.

When Mr. Tennant called abroad, it was early evening in London, and Roman Polanski was at the apartment of Victor Lownes, managing director of the London Playboy Club. At first Mr. Polanski thought it was a joke and hung up. The phone rang again and it was true. The rest is grief and tears. "She was such a good person," Mr. Polanski said over and over during the early shock.

Before 10 A.M. a team of West Los Angeles detectives arrived to take charge of the investigation. For the history, they were Lieutenant R. C. Madlock, commander; Lieutenant J. J. Gregoire, Sergeant F. Gravante and Sergeant T. L. Rogers. In addition, there were numerous West L.A. patrol officers on the property.

Officer Rivera covered the bodies with sheets. They went into the guest house to look for weapons, for Garretson at that time was a prime suspect. They checked immediately for signs of robbery and ransacking. There were no drawers open. Sebring still wore his $1500 watch. They went up on the rooftop to trace where the downed telephone and communications wires led. The glasses were found, face down, ear frames open and sticking up, just east of the blood-spotted steamer trunks.

They took for inspection Mr. Polanski's engraved .45-caliber revolver, which had been given to him by the cast of *Rosemary's Baby*. They took into evidence all knives to check for blood.

When Mr. Raymond Kilgrow of the phone company arrived between 10 and 11 A.M., newspaper and media reporters were already flocking at the outside rattan fence. Forthwith, Mr. Kilgrow discovered four lead-in wires fallen down, severed a few inches from the attachment at the top of the pole. He repaired two telephone wires and left two down pending police investigation. The police wanted to know what sort of device had severed the wires, so the phone man examined the wire to see what might have clipped it.

Later, Sergeant Varney found a rivet setter in the driveway and a pair of pliers and shears in the guest house. These were received as possible evidence. The officer cut a piece of the telephone cable to test these instruments on it to see if the cut marks were the same. They weren't. A foot and a half length of wire was cut off containing on one end the actual marks of the instrument used by the killer or killers to sever the wire. This was taken into evidence.

A call went out for the Special Investigation Division (S.I.D.) of L.A.P.D. to send in blood analysts. Sergeant Granado arrived at 10 A.M. and began to take blood samples from forty-three locations all over the house and grounds. In effect, the officer created a blood-map of the murder house which was useful in determining how the crimes were committed. They removed the flag from the couch since it was spattered. They located three pieces of broken pistol grip from the Wyatt Earp revolver.

Everything was weird. There was that bloody flag. There were those blood-barefoot prints on the sidewalk to the driveway. There were bloody pink ribbons hanging on the front door. There was a blood soaked purple scarf found by Frykowski. These were removed.

Some police officer or other tracked blood on the front porch, leaving three red footprints. This created problems later when the police were trying to recreate the undisturbed crime scene. They had to find out what sort of soles officers had on their shoes in order to determine that the bloody shoe prints were in fact made by a policeman at the scene.

What seems to remain a part of the mystery is an evident bloody boot-heel print on the flagstone front porch that was not made by the police. Whose is it? Probably not Watson's or Manson's since they seem to have been wearing moccasins.

Sometime around noon the investigation of the murders was reassigned from the West Los Angeles division of L.A.P.D. to the robbery-homicide division of L.A.P.D. Inspector McCaulay appointed Lieutenant R. J. Helder, supervisor of investigation, robbery-homicide division of L.A.P.D. to take charge. Lieutenant Helder sub-assigned responsibility for the investigation to Sergeant Michael J. McGann, and Sergeant J. Buckles, Sergeant E. Henderson, Sergeant D. Varney and Sergeant Danny Galindo. These homicide investigators finally arrived between 1:30 and 3:30 P.M.

Officer Jerome Boen and Officer Girt, fingerprint specialists, arrived at the Polanski residence about 12:30 P.M. and immediately began dusting for prints. The ridges of the fingers, palms and soles ooze with oil and fluid, constantly. An impression of the ridge patterns is made wherever surface contact is made. On hard, smooth surfaces the ridge impression or print can be removed.

First the officer powdered the surface with a gray powder. The powder was then brushed away with powder sticking to the ridges of the fingerprint or footprint. The print is then sprayed with iodine and transferred to a card with a special tape. Photographs are made of the precise location of the print.

The fingerprint officers were joined that afternoon at 5:30 P.M. by Officer Dorman and civilian fingerprint expert, Wendell Clements. Another method of detection was used on those prints where dusting didn't detect the "moisture ridges" sufficiently because of the faintness of the ridges. They sprayed on an iodine chemical mixture and within twenty-four to forty-eight hours the print appeared.

There were fifty fingerprints found at the Polanski residence. Twenty-two were eliminated, three were "unmakable" and twenty-five remain unidentified. Of this twenty-five, quite a few were located on the freshly painted window sill of the nursery window, indicating that they were left there either the afternoon or the evening of the murders.

The Chief Medical Examiner of Los Angeles County, Dr. Thomas Noguchi, took charge of the bodies. Noguchi ordered the bodies not to be disturbed till he and three assistants should arrive at the scene. The nylon rope connecting Sebring and Tate was ordered severed by Coroner Noguchi. Later the police cut sections of the rope to trace source, manufacturer and possible purchasers. It was all grim.

A deputy coroner took liver temperatures of the victims, as an aid in determining the time of death. Hands were wrapped with bags to save possible hairs and skin from the struggle with the killers. The ambulance crew brought wheeled stretchers and removed the victims, leaving behind pink death slips.

As he ran the query-gauntlet at the front gate of the estate, Dr. Noguchi told reporters he would announce autopsy reports about noon on Sunday, August 10.

Officers quickly went to Sebring's home to look for evidence. Several friends of Sebring rushed over to Sebring's house on Easton Drive to clean it out of contraband, evidently ahead of the police.

Sergeant Varney gathered up all the cutlery in both the caretaker's house and the main house. He also visited the Folger-Frykowski house at 2774 Woodstock and confiscated ten address and notebooks, some or all of which were written in Polish. Also taken into possession were various personal papers of the decedents and a box of "miscellaneous photographs and negatives" as it was listed in item number 65 in the police property report. This is a notorious photo collection containing erotic photographs of some of Hollywood's most prestigious people.

Later the police backed a van up to the Polanski house and carted a truckload of stuff down to S.I.D. headquarters for examination. A few days later they evidently brought most of it back and placed it in the same order to try to recreate the original undisturbed crime scene.

Someone picked the glasses up from the floor and put them on the table in the foyer. They were given to Mrs. Polanski's father, who held them for two weeks trying to locate the owner, who would have been a prime suspect.

The caretaker, William Garretson, was "questioned by investigators" at West Los Angeles jail at 4 P.M. He was advised of his rights and agreed to speak without counsel. "He gave stuporous and non-responsive answers to pertinent questions," a police source said. Shortly after the 4 P.M. interview, he retained the services of Los Angeles attorney, Barry Tarlow. Garretson was then transported to Parker Center, the downtown L.A. police headquarters, where he was interviewed again, this time in the presence of Mr. Tarlow. It was fruitless. It was agreed that Garretson would submit to a polygraph examination (lie detector test) on Sunday, August 10, with Mr. Tarlow present.

Police instituted a day-and-night guard on the house that lasted almost two weeks. The Animal Regulation Department removed the dogs and the kitten.

The police conducted a dope search. They found a Baggie half full of twenty-six grams of marijuana in the living room in a cabinet against the west wall. They found thirty grams of hashish in a box in the nightstand in Frykowski and Folger's room, plus ten MDA capsules. They found cocaine and marijuana in Sebring's Porsche and that vial of coke in his coat pocket.

Steve Parent's body remained unidentified for quite a while, lost in the rush. A reporter at the electric gate could see the license plate on Parent's Ambassador so he ran a make on it and got Parent's home address. A priest friend of Parent went down to identify the body. Steven Parent's father and mother evidently learned of his death over television. Already the murders were becoming the Tate Murders.

And so it went. Some policemen would not sleep for three or four days, so forceful was the investigation.

There were thousands of things to do. There were grief-whelmed relatives and friends. There was fear as never before. Thousands of rumors poured out of mouths. Acquaintances of the victims, some of them with enemies also, seemed to ask themselves, "Am I next?" What maniac was slouching through the smog with a grudge?

Nineteen

The Second Night

Sadie woke up in the morning and went into the trailer to watch the news. Immediately she encountered bulletins of the murders. She was excited. She hurried out to summon Katie, Clem and Tex so that they too might get a few thrillies from the tube. Tex seemed satisfied when the identity of the victims was revealed and commented: "The Soul really picked a good one this time."

Everything was normal at the Spahn Ranch for a Saturday. There were the usual weekenders on the scene to ride the horses. Ouish or one of the girls was in the corral-side office receiving the money from the riders. There was a garbage run down the hill into Simi. Some girls took care of George. Others got a load of corn for the horses. People worked on the dune buggies, preparing for the desert. Groins were clinked. But, in spite of the usual work, things seem to have been pretty tight-lipped. A young runaway named Maureen overheard Charlie chewing out various key people over the sloppiness of the murders.

It was generally known that it had been necessary to discorporate a few bodies into The Hole. Only a few knew who had done it and where. Everyone was acting calmly. Tex was his normal smiling self.

In the late afternoon, Sadie entered Johnny Swartz's trailer and demanded to watch the six o'clock news on Channel 2. She left immediately after the report on the homicides was over, commenting, "We're going to get all those pigs"—evidently referring to the KNX–TV broadcaster. Juan Flynn, Barbara Hoyt, Katie, Linda and Tex were also in the trailer. The killers laughed during some of the broadcast, seeming to enjoy the report. Miss Hoyt later testified that she received enough information in the trailer to solve the case, had she been a snitch.

There was a garbage gobble about sundown. Everybody sang together and smoked some dope, after which there was a clean-up in the kitchen. Kasabian said Gypsy had driven back from the waterfall and was talking about taking more girls there. She gave Linda Kasabian some Zu-Zus—Manson's term for candy—which Linda put in her pocket to eat after the long hard night ahead. Linda was going to go with Gypsy to the fall until Charlie came to the boardwalk and called her and Leslie and Katie outside.

He told Linda to get her license and a change of clothing. Linda has claimed she tried a beg-off with her eyes: "I looked at him—his eyes—my mind told him I didn't want to go—afraid to say it." It didn't work.

Charlie told the girls to meet him in Danny De Carlo's bunk-house gun room. Stuck in a slit in the wall by the door were four bayonets and the Straight Satans' club sword. De Carlo was not in his room while Charlie briefed his disciples. But later that night when he returned to the room he noticed that the weapons were missing from their slit.

There they were: Tex, Sadie, Clem, Katie, Leslie, Linda and the Wizard. Charlie said they were going out again. He seemed upset because of the messy caper of the night before. Tonight he would lead them himself, to show them how it should be done. Vern Plumlee, eager to be cut in on the caper, came up and asked Charlie if they needed any help but the car was too crowded.

Tex complained about the quality of the weapons used the night before. They decided to use sturdy bayonets and the Satans' sword. Once again they would use the yellow and white '59 Ford. Charlie drove with Linda and Clem in the front seat. Leslie sat on Tex's lap in the back with Katie and Sadie.

They started out of the driveway then stopped. Charlie called for Bruce Davis. Several minutes later Bruce came out of the woods where he had been sleeping. Charlie got out of the car and talked for a while with Bruce and Bruce gave him some money for gasoline. Although all concerned have been extremely hesitant to talk about the second night, it is known that everybody was on acid. Charlie drove away down Santa Susanna Pass Road to Topanga Canyon Boulevard, turned right, drove to Devonshire, turned left on Devonshire. They stopped for gas on Devonshire, after which Linda Kasabian drove. They turned onto the San Diego Freeway and drove to the Ventura Freeway. They drove off the Ventura Freeway at the Fair Oaks turnoff in Pasadena. Throughout the drive Manson kept up a steady reassuring stream of conversation.

The trip to the LaBianca house was hesitant and tortuous. Charlie announced that the mission was to be split into two units of three. Up and down the streets of Pasadena drove the '59 Ford looking for a quiet reserved suitable location. They stopped at a house and Charlie got out. He told Linda to drive around the block and when she returned, Charlie was waiting. He got in and told them to wait and look.

In a driveway a few doors away a rotund gentleman and a lady got out of a parked car. Charlie said, drive on. They were informed that Charlie had seen pictures of children through the windows. Later, perhaps, they might have to harm children, but now they were to be left safe. Still in Pasadena, they cruised into an area of hills and larger houses. Charlie decided to drive. He drove to a hilltop and contemplated the possibility of crawling a two-story house there. He decided against it because of the nearness of neighboring houses. Someone might hear it.

On drove Snuff. Soon they passed a church and Charlie turned off onto the paved parking lot of the fane. God, you could just picture the headlines. But there was no one there. It was locked. Charlie got back into the car.

He drove to the Pasadena Freeway, proceeding westerly; hooked onto another freeway, winding up on Sunset Boulevard whereupon he allowed Linda to drive. She drove west, turning onto a dirt road near Will Rogers Park, not far from Dennis Wilson's house of the good old days. Manson decided to game a bit, directing Linda through a series of turns and maneuvers that left her confused.

She drove up a steep hill to a closed gate in front of an estate of some sort. She went into a series of left and right turns, arriving at a house. Charlie told her to return by the same route she had come. He was pressuring her. Finally he showed her how to get back to Sunset Boulevard.

They traveled east on Sunset Boulevard where it twists through Brentwood Park when lo, Manson spotted a small white sports car driven by a young man, headed the same direction. Manson told Linda, "At the red light pull up beside it." Charlie was going to strike.

Charlie started to get out of the car. Was Satan to write upon the white metal? Luckily for the young man, the light changed and the car got away.

From this point onward the Wizard seemed to know exactly where to go. Straightway he directed Linda to Silverlake. She drove down Sunset Boulevard, past Sunset Strip, past the several miles of garish hoardings advertising the latest rock and roll recordings, through the foothills of hype.

They arrived at the Los Feliz district just south of Griffith Park, pulling up in front of the home of Leno and Rosemary LaBianca on the other side of the street from their driveway. Both Sadie and Linda recognized the house right next door to the LaBiancas' residence. Linda recalled at the trial that she had been served a peyote fruit punch there the summer of the Chicago riots, when Harold True had lived in the house.

Linda said, according to her testimony, "Charlie, I've been here before. You're not going to 'do' that house, are you?"

Manson, according to Linda, then said, "No, the house next door."

Charlie got out of the car, grabbed a weapon and sneaked up the steep driveway, twin thong-nooses slapping his breast. While in the car, Linda lit up a Pall Mall King Size and passed it around, awaiting the return of the Soul.

On August 5, Mr. and Mrs. Leno LaBianca had gone to the

home of Leno's mother, Corina LaBianca, where they picked up
their speedboat which they kept stored in her garage. They drove
it north to Lake Isabella where their son, Frank Struthers, age
sixteen, was visiting family friends. They left the boat there for
Frank to use and returned to Los Angeles.

On Saturday, August 9, the LaBiancas returned to Lake
Isabella accompanied by Rosemary's attractive twenty-one-year-
old daughter, Susan Struthers. Their purpose was to visit the
Saffie family where Frank was staying, to pick him up and to
haul the boat back to Los Angeles. They spent the day on the lake,
had dinner and prepared to leave. Frank Struthers was asked by
his young friend, Jim Saffie, to stay on till Sunday. Accordingly,
Susan Struthers and the LaBiancas left the Saffie residence at
Lake Isabella around 9 P.M., leaving Frank there. They were driving a green 1968 Thunderbird, hauling the ski boat.

They drove immediately to Los Angeles. At 1 A.M. they dropped
Susan off at her apartment in the 4600 block of Greenwood Place,
not far from their own home. Shortly after 1 A.M., John Fokianos,
who operated a newsstand at the corner of Hillhurst and Franklin
Avenue, near the LaBianca house, observed their green Thunderbird pulling a boat-trailer, headed east on Franklin. It turned
into the Standard station, made a U-turn and pulled up adjacent to
Mr. Fokianos' newsstand.

The LaBiancas remained in the car. Leno bought a Sunday
Herald-Examiner and the Sunday *National Daily Reporter,* a
horse-betting publication. Rosemary LaBianca expressed concern
about the murder of Sharon Tate and the others so Mr. Fokianos
gave her a front-section filler from the Sunday *Los Angeles Times*
with its "ritualistic murders" page-one story.

They talked for several minutes about the murders, shocked at
the gruesome details. "She seemed quite emotional about it,"
Fokianos later was to tell reporters. Leaving the newsstand, Mr.
and Mrs. LaBianca then drove to their home, parking the car on
Waverly Drive just west of the house, with the boat still hitched to
the back.

The white one-story house at 3301 Waverly Drive was in a

quiet upper middle-class neighborhood near Griffith Park. The house, once owned, according to United Press International, by cartoonist Walt Disney, had been owned for a number of years by Leno's mother. Leno had lived in the house before, for a while, but moved out in 1959 when he married Rosemary. In 1968 Leno and Rosemary purchased the home from his mother, Mrs. Corina LaBianca. They moved to the location in November of that year. Rosemary's son of a previous marriage, Frank Struthers, Jr., also lived in the newly purchased house.

To the west of the LaBianca residence was the former estate of Troy Donahue, movie giant. To the north was an unoccupied hillside. To the east at 3267 Waverly Drive was the large house once rented by acquaintances of Charles Manson during the period September 1967 to September 1968. The three renting the house were Harold True, Ernest Baltzell and Allen Swerdloff. It was at Harold True's house the summer before that some of the family had undertaken a group LSD journey.

Leno LaBianca was the chief stockholder of the State Whole-sale Grocery Company which operated the Gateway food market chain, businesses begun by his late father and later managed by Leno prosperously. Mr. LaBianca had extensive property interests in California and Nevada. He owned an enterprise called Arnel Stables and possessed nine thoroughbred race horses, including Kildare Lady, a horse of some prominence. He formerly was a member of the board of directors of the ill-fated Hollywood National Bank. He left $100,000 in various life insurance policies.

He was an avid coin collector, owning at times, $10,000 to $20,-000 worth of rare coins. At the time of his death, Mr. LaBianca had $400 worth of uncirculated nickels in the trunk of his Thunderbird. At the time of his death, he was negotiating the purchase of a ranch in Vista, California for $127,000. Whereas his financial affairs were amazingly intricate, one thing remains apparent: he was rich. Leno liked to gamble, visiting the race track often. He did it in style, often betting as much as $500 in a single day. For some reason the LaBianca telephone was tapped. This is known because a telephone repairman was called to the home the day before the murders due to some trouble on the line. The repairman discovered the tap. It is thought that the phone was monitored because Mr. LaBianca may occasionally have used the services of a famous bookmaker known as The Phantom who lived just down the street.

Mr. LaBianca was only forty-four years old.

Rosemary LaBianca was thirty-eight years old. She was co-owner of a successful dress and gift shop, Boutique Carriage, located at 2625 North Figueroa within the Gateway shopping center which her husband owned. She herself was a successful businesswoman, speculating in stocks and commodities. She left her children an estate valued at $2,600,000.

To ward off theft, they removed the water skis from the boat and carried them to the back entrance of the house and set them on the fender of Mrs. LaBianca's '55 Thunderbird, which they had left parked by the garage. When they entered the house Mrs. LaBianca placed her purse on the liquor cabinet in the dining room. She went to the bedroom, turned down the covers and prepared to go to bed. Both put on sleeping attire.

A few minutes later Leno was sitting in his pajamas in the south side of the living room, checking out the *Herald-Examiner* sports section and the racing form, drinking a can of apple beer. The rest of the newspaper and his reading glasses rested on the table in front of the L-shaped sectional sofa on which he was sitting.

He was creepy-crawled. He looked up and saw a short hairy male Caucasian wearing a black turtleneck sweater, levis, moccasins and waving a cutlass. Charlie told Leno, "Be calm, sit down and be quiet." He located Mrs. LaBianca in the bedroom. He told them to stand up and tied them up, back to back, using two forty-two-inch leather thongs from around his neck. The knot was a double square knot. He told them that everything was okay and they weren't going to get hurt. He sat them down on the divan, and then he walked over to the liquor cabinet, removed Mrs. LaBianca's wallet from her purse, and walked out the front door, leaving it unlocked.

Linda Kasabian was just finishing her Pall Mall cigarette when

Charlie walked down the driveway to the car and looked in. He'd been inside the house about five minutes.

Sadie claimed later that when Charlie looked at her, she begged off of the mission with her eyes and that Charlie could scan her mind and know that she didn't want to do it. Linda too contended in her various statements that she confronted Charlie with silent vibes so that he would refuse to nod her into the murder crew.

Charlie called Tex, Leslie and Katie out of the car and gave them a few final instructions. They could hear only parts of the briefing in the car. He said there were two people in the house and that he had tied them up. He told them that the people were calm and not to instill fear in them. Then kill them. Then they were to hitchhike back to the ranch. Katie was to go to the waterfall.

Charlie opened the door and Linda slid over into the passenger side and Charlie got in, handing her Rosemary's billfold. He started the engine and drove the Ford away, bearing the second half of the two-part squad.

They walked into the house bearing their changes of clothes. Once inside the front foyer and entering the living room, they saw the terrified couple. They went to the kitchen to choose the weapons. From a drawer they obtained a white-handled ten-inch bi-tined carving fork, belonging to a set, and an eight-inch serrated wood-handled knife. They pulled down the kitchen shades to avoid detection. Everything was calm. Nothing was said about the Devil.

The girls, Katie and Leslie, untied Rosemary LaBianca and took her to the bedroom where they placed her face down on the bed. She was attired in a shorty nightgown over which she wore a robe. They removed the pillowcase from one of the pillows and fitted it over her head. Then they pulled out the plug and tied her neck with the cord of a heavy bed lamp which was attached also to another bed lamp, knotting it near the end. Everything was going to be okay, they told her.

Tex pushed Leno back upon the couch and ripped open his pajama tops, exposing the large full stomach of the businessman.

Homicide Sergeant Galindo was to find a ripped-off button lodged in a buttonhole of the pajamas the next night. Tex began stabbing him and Leno struggled and screamed and shrieked, his hands behind him. He fell against the table, knocking the apple beer and newspaper all over the floor. Blood covered the cushions.

Tex had him down on his back and slashed him four times in the throat leaving the serrated knife buried deep within. He stabbed him four times in the abdomen into the colon, all fatal wounds. He bled to death, helped by the throw pillow with which Tex smothered his face to stop the screams.

When Mr. LaBianca began to shriek, Mrs. LaBianca began to struggle. She fell to the floor pulling the neck-cord taut and the lamp toppled. Over and over again she kept screaming, "What are you doing to my husband!"

Later, when everybody had returned to the Spahn Ranch, Sadie was quick to debrief Katie about what had gone on inside the LaBianca house. Katie told her about the screams: "That's what she'll carry into infinity." Sadie agreed.

Leslie held her, Katie stabbed. She crawled approximately two feet, the lamp cord on her neck, dragging the heavy lamp. Her spine was severed and she was paralyzed, lying on her face, parallel to the bed and the dresser.

Tex left the dying Mr. LaBianca in the living room and raced to the aid of the girls. Forty-one times they wounded her, mostly in the back; three were in the area of her chest. There were three linear abrasions on her back, made with a dull instrument, perhaps the electrical plug. All wounds were made with the same knife.

They pulled her nightgown and her robe over her shoulders and over her head, exposing her back and her buttocks. Leslie was not participating.

Tex wanted Leslie to stab. So did Katie. Leslie was very hesitant but they kept suggesting it. She made a stab to the buttocks. Then she kept stabbing, sixteen times. Later the nineteen-year-old girl from Cedar Falls, Iowa would write poems about it.

They were dead. It was time to leave the world a few signs. Tex took the bayonet or perhaps the metal prongs of the electrical plug and made a series of scratches near the navel proceeding toward the chest of Leno LaBianca which, from a distance, looked like a row of overlapping X's. Up close the bayonet cuneiform scratching turned into the word WAR.

Not to be outdone, Katie took the carving fork and stabbed both bodies with it. Seven double punctures she punched here and there into the abdomen of Mr. LaBianca, till she left it embedded in his flesh near the navel to the bifurcation of the tines. Katie said she was fascinated by the fork. She reached over to it as it stood out from his stomach and she gave it a twang and it vibrated.

Knife in the throat, fork in the stomach, acts insanely inspired by the song "Piggies": "You can see them out for dinner with their piggie wives, clutching forks and knives to eat their bacon."

They took the white electrical cord attached to a massive floor lamp near the couch and tied it around his neck, knotting it. They put the small throw pillow over his face. Then they fitted a pillowcase from the main bedroom over both his head and the pillow. They left him on his back, the WAR and the fork exposed.

Then they wrote on the walls. They removed a long narrow tapestry on the north wall facing the front door and placed it on the floor. There, in Mr. LaBianca's blood, they scrawled for all to see as they entered: DEATH TO PIGS. Later, when Sadie debriefed her, Katie told how she had seen pictures of the children in the house. Katie said that she figured that the kids would probably be coming over for dinner Sunday and they'd find the dead bodies.

Six feet eight inches up on the south wall of the living room, directly to the left of the front door, they printed the word RISE, above a painting. They folded a piece of paper to use as the blood brush. It was found, bloody and frayed on one end, in the dining room.

In the kitchen on the double doors of the refrigerator Katie began to scrawl. She meant to write HELTER SKELTER but committed some sort of psychological slip by writing HEALTER SKELTER instead.

Leslie wiped the house down for prints, taking her time, wiping all the surfaces they had touched and more, leaving no family prints for the police. Then they took a shower together in the rear bathroom and changed their clothing.

They went to the kitchen. Boy, were they hungry. But first the girls fed the dogs. They patted the three dogs who had watched silently throughout the massacre and who had licked the gory hands of the killers. Then the humans ate, locating some food in the icebox. They left a watermelon rind in the kitchen sink then they found some chocolate milk which they drank and carried with them as they left by the east door, leaving it ajar. Clutching their bloody clothes, down the hill, drinking the milk.

None of the expensive camera equipment, diamond rings, rifles, shotguns, valuable coins were disturbed. Leslie Van Houten seems to have taken a sack containing about twenty-five dollars' worth of rare domestic and foreign coins. These she sorted out at the ranch.

They threw the clothing away into a garbage can a few blocks away. They walked to the Golden State Freeway, found an entrance and began to hitchhike, securing a ride all the way from Griffith Park to Santa Susanna Pass Road, near the ranch. The driver was familiar with the Spahn Ranch, even going so far as to ask them if that was where they were going. Oh no, they said. This person's identity, although known by some, was never determined by the police.

Meanwhile, the second triad of killers had driven away in the yellow and white Ford. After Manson handed her the wallet, Linda Kasabian checked out the credit cards and saw the i.d.— Rosemary with some Italian surname.

They drove quite a distance on the Golden State Freeway out into the valley to Sylmar where they pulled off onto Encinatus Boulevard. They drove into a Standard station where Linda Kasabian walked into the ladies' room to dispose of Mrs. LaBianca's billfold. She placed it inside the water closet above the flushing mechanism where it remained for four months, although it is company policy at all Standard service stations to change the bluing agent in restroom water closets once a day.

When Linda returned, Charlie was displeased that she had placed the wallet in so obscure a location as inside the water closet. They drove then to a beach south of Venice, near some oil tanks, where they parked the car on a hilltop. They all got out, Manson with Linda, Sadie with Clem. Then the young mothers walked hand in hand down the beach with Clem and Charlie.

According to Kasabian, Manson asked her on the beach if there wasn't some "pig" nearby that she and Sandy had met. According to Manson, on the other hand, Linda aka Yana the Witch announced that she wanted to waste some "fat pig" in Venice, so he agreed to drive her there but she didn't have a weapon.

The person in question was the actor, Saladin Nader, whom Linda and Sandy Good had met a few days previous on Topanga Beach. It was he who had played a role in a movie about the youth of poet Kahlil Gibran. Nader's apartment was located on the fifth floor of 1101 Ocean Front Street, near the Beach House Market, in Venice.

The four drove there from that beach south of Venice. After they arrived Linda agreed to show Manson Nader's apartment. She said that she took Charlie to the floor below Nader's and pointed to another door, evidently seeking to save Nader. They then walked back downstairs.

Clem, or one of them, went to a biker's house and borrowed a gun.

"If anything goes wrong, just hang it up," Charlie said.

Manson said for Kasabian to knock on the door while Sadie and Clem waited down the hall. When she was able to get into the pad then all should pounce and kill. Charlie gave her a pocket knife and showed her how to slit a throat.

Then Exterminans got into the '59 Ford and evidently drove back to the Spahn Ranch.

Mrs. Kasabian, two months pregnant, having already decided to save Mr. Nader, instead led Clem and Sadie to an apartment on the floor below Nader's apartment. There she seems also to have deliberately spared the occupant. She knocked on the door. Someone opened it a little ways. Mrs. Kasabian then excused herself, saying she had the wrong apartment and the mission was voided.

They walked along the beach. Sadie went into the ladies' room on the beach near a pier. Clem seems to have buried the revolver in a sand pile or by a pier. They hitchhiked north along the Pacific Coast Highway. Someone gave them a ride to the mouth of Topanga Canyon.

Then they stopped to visit a house next to a business known as the Malibu Feed Bin. They went in, sat around in the living room for a while, smoked a joint, then Sadie, Linda and Clem went back to the street to hitch to the ranch. A second ride picked the three up and took them up and over Topanga Canyon and down into the valley.

A third car drove them up Topanga Canyon Boulevard through Chatsworth and let Linda and Clem off at Santa Susanna Pass Road. During the third ride, Sadie and Clem sang snatches of George Harrison's song, "Piggies."

Sadie went further up the highway to the road leading the back way to the waterfall campsite where she and Katie talked about the details of the second night of terror.

Section III

Manson Captured
August 16–December 1, 1969

Twenty

The Search

The investigation facing the police was extremely complex and, for the most part, a labyrinth of blind alleys and tedium. Everything at the Polanski residence, even the wastebaskets, had to be sifted for data. Address books, personal papers, house and grounds, everything, sifted for enemies. Police combed the brushy hillsides of Benedict Canyon looking for the murder weapons. Others began to search for the type of revolver to fit the bloody bits of walnut pistol grip found in the residence. 10050 Cielo Drive was kept under continuous police guard for about two weeks.

On Sunday morning, August 10, the Los Angeles County Medical Examiner, Dr. Thomas Noguchi, supervised the autopsies of the victims, he himself conducting the examination of Sharon Tate. Several homicide investigators were on hand during the autopsies. Included was one of the sheriff's office detectives investigating the Gary Hinman murder. This detective approached the officers handling the Polanski murders and told them about the similarities between the two sets of murders: writing in blood, wounds inflicted by knives, etc. The officers of the Tate investigation considered the similarities insignificant, however, since there was already a suspect arrested for the Hinman murder when the Sebring-Parent-Folger murders were committed.

Press accounts of autopsy findings took care to note that the baby was perfectly formed, evidently to curb possible speculation pertaining to one of Polanski's movies. The wildest assertions appeared in national publications about the physical state of the decedents, based on inaccurate information supposedly leaked from an employee of the coroner's office. All around the world there were articles and broadcasts speculating about the circumstances of the crimes and lives of the deceased. In Los Angeles, reporters thronged at police headquarters for data.

Since everything any officer said was being printed, they had to be careful. On Sunday, Lieutenant Robert Helder, the head of the investigation, told a news conference that efforts to locate the killer or killers were centered on acquaintances of the short, slim caretaker William Garretson. Sergeant Buckles explained later that homicide detectives were "not entirely satisfied" with Garretson's answers to their questions. In the afternoon Garretson was given an hour-long lie detector test, in the presence of his attorney, Barry Tarlow.

Lieutenant A. H. Burdick of the scientific investigation division, L.A.P.D., administered the polygraph examination at 4:25 P.M., August 10, at the Parker Center police headquarters. Investigators had found Garretson "stuporous and vague" as if he were under the influence of some kind of narcotic. During his polygraph interrogation he still seemed confused and unable to remember things.

Garretson was extremely vague about what had gone on at the Polanski residence the evening of the murders. The polygraph examination revealed that someone seems to have arrived at the residence immediately prior to Garretson's trek down to the Sunset Strip where he bought food. Here's what he said: "And so I stayed home all day Friday, August 8, and I cleaned up the house a little bit and did the dishes and everything, and they came around 8:30, 9 o'clock, somewhere around there. And I went to get something to eat, and I went down on the Strip; I had something down there, and I could see her light all the way down from Cielo—not Cielo, but Benedict Canyon, all the way down to the Strip."

Who are the "they" who arrived about 8:30? The victims returning from dinner at the El Coyote restaurant? Or guests?

Garretson was even more vague about what he was doing during the murders. At the trial he testified that he spent the time writing letters to a friend named Darryl and listening to The Doors and a Mama Cass album. During the polygraph examination he admitted he may have gone out in back of his house. The back yard of the guest house is out of view of the main house and grounds so perhaps he hid there. In spite of inconsistencies, his answers regarding his innocence were shown on the polygraph to be truthful, so Garretson was eliminated as a suspect. The matter of William Garretson is far from cleared up however. There remains the possibility that he was hypnotized, drugged and left at the murder site as a fall guy.

Steve Brandt, former press agent for Miss Tate and a gossip columnist for *Photoplay* magazine, arrived on Sunday, August 10, from New York where he had been working on assignment. He was questioned repeatedly by police investigators and supplied "voluminous information," according to reports at the time, about Sharon Tate and her circle of friends and about dope and Frykowski's ten-day mescaline experiment. Mr. Brandt had been a legal witness when Mr. and Mrs. Polanski were married in London in 1968.

Friends of the deceased began to fly to Los Angeles and some were interrogated and given polygraph examinations. Rudy Altobelli arrived from Europe Sunday evening. Since the residence was sealed off, he went to a hotel. He was interviewed by the police. They asked him about the party in March where Roman Polanski threw a person out. Early speculation held that the PIG on the front door was actually PIC, the nickname of one of the men thrown from the party. They also asked him questions about the relationship between Mr. and Mrs. Polanski. Mr. Altobelli was asked at the trial when he, Altobelli, first thought that Manson might be responsible for the murders. Altobelli replied that he thought of Manson as a suspect on the plane trip back to the United States just after the murders. He did not volunteer the information to the police, he said, because he was not asked about it.

Later on Sunday evening, August 10, Roman Polanski arrived at Los Angeles International Airport and was silent coming through customs when the reporters crowded about with lights and microphones. His friend and associate, Gene Gutowski, read a short statement to the press that spoke against sensationalistic printed rumors of rituals, marital rifts and so on that had filled the front pages and airways of Europe and America. Roman Polanski at once went into seclusion in an apartment located within the Paramount Studios complex.

Late Sunday night police found Polanski's 1967 red Ferrari, license number VAM 559, in a body repair shop where it had been taken for maintenance—thus removing the possibility that it may have been used as a getaway car by a robber-killer. Around this time, artist Witold K., speaking nervously in Polish, called a friend in New York from a phone booth in Los Angeles. He claimed that he knew who the killers were and that he was afraid.

Friends in New York then called a *New York Times* reporter in Los Angeles and related the development. The reporter thereupon called the Los Angeles police.

Since Witold K. expressed fear for his life, the police promised him twenty-four-hour protection if he would talk. Then his friends called Witold K. back at the phone booth where he was waiting and he agreed to the guard. Three police cars picked up Witold K. and took him to the apartment at Paramount Studios where Roman Polanski was in seclusion.

Witold K. told police that Frykowski was offered an exclusive dealership to sell the drug MDA, evidently in the Los Angeles area. Subsequent friction developed, he claimed, and one of the suppliers threatened Frykowski's life. Witold K. claimed not to know the names of the possible killers but to know them by face only. And that they were Canadian. One close friend claims that Witold K. went around, escorted by police, to the many prestigious addresses in Frykowski's notebooks to try to locate the killer—always leaving behind his business card. Witold K. claimed that the identity of the killers was contained perhaps in these notes and diaries but he seems to have said that "it would take two weeks" for him to decipher the killers' identity from Frykowski's notebooks.

Like many new arrivals from a foreign country, Mr. Frykowski made voluminous notes and took many phone numbers and addresses. He also kept a diary, written in Polish.

Witold K.'s painting career was enhanced by his revelation. One newspaper account showed a picture of Witold K. posing with several of his paintings on the Polanski front lawn. A friend has claimed that Witold K. even sold a couple of his paintings to two policemen investigating the case.

This is typical of the hundreds of leads followed vigorously by the police that led to blind walls of cool, silent traffickers in dope. And nothing is more secret than the big-league dope trade.

Around 8:30 P.M., August 10, the sixteen-year-old son of Rosemary LaBianca by a previous marriage, Frank Struthers, was driven home from his vacation at Lake Isabella and was dropped off in front of 3301 Waverly Drive. He saw the family car, the '68 Thunderbird, parked on the street with boat attached. He walked up the driveway past the kitchen windows, noticed that the window shades were drawn, evidently an unusual condition. He walked up the driveway to the garage to the back door and knocked. No answer. The door was locked. He saw the water skis on the fender of the other family car, also a Thunderbird, parked by the garage. He knocked on the den window. No answer. He walked down to a Charburger stand and phoned. No answer. He made another phone call to try to locate his sister, Susan Struthers. In a while, Susan Struthers called back and her brother told her of his apprehension.

About 10:30 P.M. his sister Susan and her fiancé, Joe Dorgan, arrived at 3301 Cielo Drive where they met sixteen-year-old Frank Struthers, Jr. They obtained the house keys from the ignition switch of Mrs. LaBianca's Thunderbird. The three walked into the house through the back door. Susan stayed in the kitchen while Frank Struthers, Jr., and Joe Dorgan walked through the dining room into the living room and saw Mr. LaBianca "in a crouched position" on the floor. They knew something was wrong. The two about-faced and fled. Dorgan picked up the phone in the kitchen as if to call, then dropped it. They ran into the yard yelling for help and a neighbor called the police. About 10:45 P.M. police cars began shrieking to the scene.

In short order the property was aswarm with reporters and homicide investigators. The *Los Angeles Times* made it a page-one story with the caption "2 Ritual Slayings Follow Killing of 5," as if linking it to the murders of Friday night. Police released practically all the major details of the LaBianca murders to the media. The newspapers made mention of the knife and fork in Mr. LaBianca and the word "war." They told of the white "hood"—the pillowcase over his head. What evidently was not released to the media were the bloody words "Healter Skelter" written on the icebox doors. But they did release the fact that there were blood words on the icebox doors. The *Los Angeles Times* story, for instance, mistakenly related that "the words 'Death to Pigs' had been smeared on the doors of the refrigerator, apparently by the heel of a slayer's hand . . ."

Manson's good friend, Gregg Jakobson, was questioned right after the murders by the police because of his association with Rudy Altobelli. Had the words Healter Skelter on the icebox been released to the media by the police, Jakobson, who was one of scores of people who knew what the words meant, certainly would have told the police about the Manson family. Then Manson and crew probably would have been arrested immediately and further murders would have been prevented. It is possible, however, that the police, alarmed by the untoward discussion of the so-called Tate murders by the police at the Polanski residence, may have wanted to make certain that a number of polygraph interrogation keys remained this time. Therefore they may have withheld Healter Skelter as well as the bloody word "rise" in the living room.

On August 11, in the afternoon, authorities released the caretaker, William Eston Garretson, having held him for two days. He walked out of custody with his attorney, Barry Tarlow, into a barrage of cameras.

On August 11, police "backed away" from linking the Cielo Drive and Waverly Drive murders. "There is a similarity," remarked Sergeant Bryce Houchin of L.A.P.D., "but whether it's the same suspect or a copy cat, we just don't know." The difference in life styles, the different circles of friends, the lack of any apparent connection, were important factors in the decision to split up the investigation of the two sets of murders. By Tuesday, August 12, 1969, detectives officially ruled out any link between the Tate and LaBianca crimes.

The LaBianca investigation team was headed by Captain Paul LePage and detectives from robbery-homicide including Sergeant Phil Sartuche, Sergeant Manuel Gutierrez and Sergeant Frank Patchett, all of whom played considerable parts in bringing down the house of Manson. The LaBianca investigation centered on business dealings and gambling activities of Leno LaBianca. It was discovered that there was about $200,000 missing from Gateway Markets, one of Mr. LaBianca's business enterprises. Mr. LaBianca was a rare coin collector with collections worth thousands of dollars. A rare coin collection, believed to be Mr. LaBianca's, was found in a house on Waverly Drive a couple of blocks from the LaBianca residence. This house was owned by a notorious bookmaker known as The Phantom aka Edward Pierce and had been abandoned by him a week after the LaBianca murders.

Close associates of Mr. LaBianca denied the possibility that the Mafia had contracted his death. If it had, they said, they would have heard about it. Police made an activity chart by date divided into half-hour increments showing the activities of Leno and Rosemary LaBianca between August 4 and August 10, 1969. They gave lie detector tests to most major acquaintances of the decedents.

There were twenty-five prints found in the LaBianca house. Nineteen were eliminated, six remain unidentified. 41,634 suspects were checked against the print on the liquor cabinet where Mrs. LaBianca's wallet was stolen by Manson.

The LaBianca investigation team arranged so-called "M.O.

runs" with the CII (State Bureau of Criminal Indentification and Investigation) computer, in Sacramento at the California Department of Justice. The CII crime computer has a huge amount of information stored regarding crime and criminals. An M.O. run collects all crimes with the same methods of perpetration. A police agency can, as in this case, get a list of every murder where the killer tied up the victim, or wrote on the wall, in order to obtain the identities of potential suspects.

One of the problems facing the police in the Polanski residence murders was the overwhelming number of suspects. The decedents lives were fraught with relationships that could have spawned violent grudges. The police investigation can be examined in three major areas of concern: 1) dope traffic 2) fame-porn and 3) the occult—areas about which there is a veil of secrecy extremely difficult to penetrate.

The murders provided impetus for a great number of narcotics arrests. Some individuals, however, were promised immunity from dope prosecution if they would provide information about the deceased and possible culprits. Three L.A. homicide detectives went to Vancouver to help the Royal Canadian Mounted Police to organize a dragnet for the Canadian dope dealers that Witold K. and others had fingered out. The dope dealers were believed headed toward Edmonton, Alberta or already holed up in the Western Canadian woods.

U.S. Treasury agents investigated aspects of drug traffic to see if there was a pattern of interstate trafficking. In the days following the murders there were large-scale cocaine arrests around the country which have been linked to the reverberations resulting from the murder investigation. Police traveled around the country administering polygraph examinations. They even went to England to interrogate suspects.

Lieutenant Colonel Paul Tate, Sharon Tate's father, resigned from the service two weeks prior to his scheduled retirement after a twenty-year career. He proceeded to work ceaselessly in pursuit of the killers, concentrating on drug motives. He grew a beard and infiltrated dope lairs. "I guess I've seen just about everything in

hippie communes while checking out drug angles," he commented
in an interview after Manson's arrest.

Mr. Peter Folger, Abigail Folger's father, according to numerous
people interviewed, initiated an intense investigation into the matter, as did Roman Polanski who was assisted by several famous
Los Angeles private investigators. "Polanski worked on it himself. But Polanski didn't realize it was hippies. He was working in
his own area," reported one of his investigators. Polanski was protected constantly by two armed bodyguards. In fact, at least ten
private investigators in Los Angeles were used extensively throughout the investigation of the case, both by private parties and the
district attorney.

In the mater of the movies, police found a bunch of films and
videotapes during the follow-up investigations. Some were found
in the Polanski residence in the main bedroom closet. One particular videotape was found in a room off the living room loft and
was booked as item #36 in the police property report. Other
films were taken into possession in Jamaica and in Annan-
dale, Virginia. Part of the films involved an elite underground film group in Hollywood that swapped torrid films of each
other.

During Manson's trial, his lawyers were approached by a
representative of a rising movie actress who had left a roll of
undeveloped 35 MM film containing pictures of herself getting
after it at the Polanski residence on the day of the murders. The
representative asked Manson if the family had removed the film
from the house that night since she had been unable to find out
what happened to it, and she felt that if the film were publicized
her career would be adios'd.

The police found evidence that some of the residents at 10050
Cielo Drive were into collecting humans from Sunset Strip and
from various clubs in the area for casual partying at the estate.
It was thought for a while that perhaps the murders were the
result of a "freak-out" from one of these pick-ups.

Meanwhile, as the police investigation progressed, all forms of
wild speculation was passed from mouth to mouth regarding the

crimes. There was speculation from close friends of Frykowski that it had been done by the Polish secret police who took a plane from Los Angeles to Rome right after the crimes, in reprisal for Polanski's defection from Poland. There was every form of speculation regarding mutilation and ritual.

There was a flame of violence in Los Angeles in early August 1969 where from Friday the eighth to Tuesday the twelfth, twenty-nine people were murdered. Ken's Sporting Goods Shop in Beverly Hills sold 200 guns in two days following the murders. The Bel Air Patrol, a private security force serving the exclusive Bel Air area hired something like thirty extra men. People slept within hands reach of the electronic panic buttons which could summon the Bel Air patrol. Bodyguards were in great demand. Individuals placed their own homes under 24 hour surveillance by teams of private detectives. People packed guns at the funerals of the deceased.

The spirit of Moloch prevailed. Quickly, the movies in which Sharon Tate had performed, were re-issued. *Valley of the Dolls* went into twelve theatres in the Los Angeles area, with Mrs. Polanski receiving top billing. Also showing up was *The Fearless Vampire Killers*, starring Sharon and Roman Polanski. Distributors hit the screen again with a movie made in 1966, called *Mondo Hollywood*, a section of which was devoted to Jay Sebring as hair styler of the stars. Also playing a part in *Mondo Hollywood* was Bobby Beausoleil who portrayed Cupid addressing his bow, in a brief section. The role in the flick was the origin of Beausoleil's nickname, Cupid.

Around August 15, 1969, two lawyer friends of Jay Sebring, Harry Weiss and Peter Knecht, hired Dutch psychic Peter Hurkos to scan the murder scene in order to try to pick up vibrations regarding the identity of the killers. On Sunday August 17, Peter Hurkos, accompanied by an assistant, Roman Polanski, a writer named Tommy Thompson, and a photographer named Julian Wasser went to the death house at 10050 Cielo Drive to enable Hurkos to perform a death-scan. Mr. Hurkos crouched down in the blood-stained living room, picking up the vibes while Roman

Polanski gave Mr. Thompson a running narrative about the crime scene. The photographer took Polaroid snapshots and some color photos of the event. The entire event was written up for a photo spread in *Life* magazine several weeks later. Mr. Wasser gave Hurkos some of the Polaroid test snaps which somehow wound up published in the *Hollywood Citizen-News*. It was John Phillips, the songwriter, who talked Roman Polanski into allowing Hurkos into the house.

After his void-scan, Mr. Hurkos announced that "three men killed Sharon Tate and her four friends—and I know who they are. I have identified the killers to the police and told them that these three men must be stopped soon. Otherwise, they will kill again."

It was felt that possibly the Canadian dope dealers involved in that Jamaican grass-trafficking were also involved in a Jamaican voodoo group that was somehow connected with the crimes. According to a reporter named Min Yee, he and John Phillips went to a voodoo astrologer who informed them that midnight August 8-9 was a fitting time for a voodoo sacrifice. There was also indication that one of the voodoo adepts had threatened Voityck Frykowski a few days prior to his death.

On Tuesday, August 19, Roman Polanski held a press conference at the Beverly Wilshire Hotel in Los Angeles where he announced that he was leaving town. He decried the scandal-oriented news accounts of the murder house: "A lot of newsmen who for a selfish reason write unbearable for me horrible things about my wife. All of you know how beautiful she was and very often I read and heard statements that she was one of most, if not the most beautiful woman of the world but only a few of you know how good she was. She was vulnerable." He decried public speculation about orgies and dope, acknowledging the occasional smoking, as in almost every house in Hollywood, of cannabis. He denied that his wife used drugs and that there had been any marital rift, saying: "I can tell you that in the last few months as much as the last few years I spent with her were the only time of true happiness in my life . . ."

Shortly thereafter, Mr. Polanski and John Phillips flew to Jamaica to continue investigation into drugs and voodoo, according to Mr. Yee. At the end of the month a Los Angeles Police Department polygraph expert also went to Jamaica where he spent about a week investigating.

On September 2, 1969, Rona Barrett asserted on KTTV, a Metromedia station serving Los Angeles, that Roman Polanski had received $50,000 from Life Magazine for the photos and story from the murder house. The charge was hotly denied by Polanski and his attorneys. Mr. Rudy Altobelli became incensed over the alleged $50,000 and later sued Roman Polanski and the estate of Sharon Tate for around $668,000 dollars, charging "trespassory conduct" regarding Abigail Folger and Voityck Frykowski in that the house had been rented for one family residency. He also sued for damages, depreciation to property, emotional distress and back rent.

On September 3, 1969, Peter Sellers, Warren Beatty, Yul Brynner and others announced the establishment of a reward of $25,000 for the arrest and conviction of the murderers. "We handed the money over to Roman Polanski and his lawyers in the hope that that would bring the killers to justice," Sellers commented in an interview.

In Los Angeles, after the initial release of information about the crimes, there was a tight lid kept on information about the police investigation. Los Angeles Police Department sent only a three line homicide report to the State Bureau of Criminal Identification and Investigation (CII)—barely complying with the law that requires information about crimes to be collected with the CII. After a month of investigation the chief causes of the crimes under consideration were a residential robbery, a drug grudge, or a "freak-out" of some sort.

A dope burn, whether large or small, tends to trigger off violence. When a burn involves thousands of dollars, deaths or death-threats often occur. Manson had said several times that, if the true story were known about the Tate-LaBianca murders, there would be a "big stink" of a scandal. He has said that he has chosen silence because of the age-old code of criminal behavior that makes telling the names of people involved in a crime equal to the crime itself. Manson has, naturally, also said that the Polanski murders were the idea of his followers. "I don't care. I have one law I live by and I learned it when I was a kid in reform school, it's don't snitch and I have never snitched, and I told them that anything they do for their brothers and sisters is good, if they do it with a good thought," Manson testified on page 18,123 of his trial. A dope burn, however, remains as the motive.

One former family associate stated that he was told by Gypsy that the burn involved "63 keys [kilos] of grass, something like fifty dollars' worth of smack and some speed." One of Manson's closest friends outside the family told this writer on 12–1–70 that an $11,000 LSD burn was involved and that involved also was a "real millionaire" friend of Manson whose car Manson wrecked around the time of the murders. Vern Plumlee also claimed that the motive involved LSD. Plumlee, certainly a trusted family member during the time of the murders, worked closely with Bill Vance in committing various robberies and forgeries during those days of murder. Plumlee, in a taped interview, said that Bill Vance told him that the Tate and LaBianca murders were both committed as a result of an acid burn. This is what Plumlee said about Vance's explanation of the motive: "You see, I worked with him for quite a while, you know, burglaries and things like that. . . . And during the time I was doing it I was, you know, we got to be pretty able to talk with each other.

"I heard things about something to the effect the LaBiancas were supposed to have sold to 'the Tates,' the Tates were supposed to have sold to the family, and some people got uptight about it, 'cause it was a burn. . . . Like, I was told by him, he says, '. . . don't worry about it though because they'll never find out who did it.' So I just let it slide."

On another occasion Plumlee told a reporter that the family went there to get Frykowski and anyone else present. According to Plumlee, the family had received information that Sharon Tate was not going to be at Cielo Drive.

Even while the Manson murder trials were underway, in the fall of 1970, several private investigators, working for the district attorney, were looking into the possibility that the murders were contracted. It was believed that a wealthy individual in Kansas City, Missouri contracted the crimes because of a grudge against Polanski. They checked banks in Kansas City, Kansas to see if money had been deposited for Manson, Watson or Susan Atkins, Bill Vance and three others. They also checked possible bank deposits in a coastal town of Texas, perhaps Corpus Christi, to no avail.

A reporter covering the Tate-LaBianca trial got hold of Tex Watson's address book and found the phone number of a former Polanski residence in it. A private investigator who worked on the case for the family of one of the decedents for months after the murders told this writer that the motive for the crimes was that "they knew too much about what was going on."

Sadie Glutz aka Susan Atkins said the impetus for the murders was twofold: to get Beausoleil off and because Linda Kasabian was burned on a purchase of MDA. On Volume 180, page 23,049 of the trial transcript she testified that Linda Kasabian came to her and complained about being burned at the Polanski residence: "You remember the thousand dollars I had? I told her yeah—and she said, 'Well, I went up to some people in Beverly Hills for some MDA'—some new kind of drug . . . MDA. Oh anyway, she went up there to buy something and they burnt her for the bread."

Robert Beausoleil has claimed that Tex Watson and Linda were operating together during those weeks prior to the murders and that the key lies there. There remains the possibility that Manson wanted to raise a large amount of money in an attempt to pay off someone for the purpose of freeing Beausoleil. Danny De Carlo said this: "Mary and Bobby got busted. It was all—the main objective was to get money to get them out of jail so they could all get in the wind which was to the desert. Mary's bail was $500 and they were going to get out—they needed some fantastic amount of money to get Bobby out. Hell, I didn't understand. There was no bail on him." So perhaps the family went into a flurry of quick dope deals or took a snuff-contract to raise large amounts of fast cash.

De Carlo, after his testimony at the Tate-LaBianca trial, told a CBS–TV reporter that the true motive has not been told, but he would not elaborate. Since then, De Carlo has abandoned his gun shop in Medford, Oregon and has gone underground.

Considerable information will possibly come out of the forthcoming trial of Tex Watson where he is expected to tell all. Watson's IQ has dropped thirty points from the use of telache so he may have a memory problem. His tapes, reportedly containing the whole story of the Tate-LaBianca murders, have been sealed up in Texas where he was held for about eight months, fighting extradition, and not even the L.A. district attorney has been able to secure them.

Twenty-one

Berserk!
The Spahn Ranch
August 10-31, 1969

Around 7 A.M., Leslie, alone, came to the back ranch. Little Patti, Cathy Meyers, Barbara Hoyt and Snake were there asleep. Into the stone fireplace she dropped a short length of rope, a credit card, a fancy leather purse and a woman's blouse. It burnt with an awful smell. She had a plastic sack of change which she counted out. Then she slept.

Around 7:15 A.M. three or four men came to the back ranch, evidently to rout out the sleepers. Leslie covered herself over with covers and said to Snake, according to Snake, "Don't let that man see me or let him in because he gave me a ride from Griffith Park." One or two of the men entered the sleazy ranch house and one of the men questioned the girls, "Where did you get these field phones?" The man said that the girls had a lousy bunch of men on the ranch. They stayed about three minutes, then split. They cut the clandestine lines tapping the electricity before they left in a pink-colored automobile. Intruders gone, Miss Van Houten came out from under the sheets.

People were completely jittery at the Spahn Ranch in the week between August 10 and August 17 when Charlie began moving stuff to the desert. The removal into the Inyo County area was interrupted by the Great Raid of August 16, but finally, by the first week of September, Manson and his armed chumps were safely in the desert.

On August 10, Sunday, Sergeant William Gleason of the Los

Angeles sheriff's office visited Kitty Lutesinger at her parent's ranch where she had fled following Manson's kill-threats. Sergeant Gleason was compiling a file of disturbing information about the Spahn Ranch preparing for a huge police raid to come the following week. He had become aware of Miss Lutesinger when she had run away from the Spahn Ranch on July 30 and Frank Retz had driven her to the police station. During the conversation she asked him if it had been the "Panthers" who had committed the so-called Tate murders. He replied that it didn't appear that any blacks were involved. "I had been programmed to believe it was the Panthers who did it," Kitty recalled.

About August 11, Ruby Pearl hired a new ranch hand named David Hannon, a twenty-one-year-old blond boy from Venice, California, who was befriended by Manson. Hannon began to talk with Manson occasionally. Manson told him about the "Black Panther" he had shot. Hannon knew a lot about California desert areas and Charlie was eager to talk about the subject. Manson talked as usual about raiding and plundering small desert towns. Once they walked through the desert together and Hannon killed a rattlesnake. This enraged Manson and he told Hannon he was going to chop his head off.

Hannon, being a newcomer, was actually unaware of the large number of girls living in the area. He only saw two or three, the others of course being hidden in the various hillside camps.

Hannon told Manson about a twenty-six acre ranch owned by his mother in the desert near Olancha, a few miles from Goler Wash. On this property were two ranch houses. The property was located on a remote rural road and Manson was eager to move his family there.

On August 11, Linda Kasabian, on orders of the Wizard, put on her high heels and dress, tease-combed her hair and borrowed David Hannon's '61 Volvo and drove to downtown L.A. to the Hall of Justice court building to see if Mary Brunner had a court hearing. She was supposed to see Bob Beausoleil also but she did not have proper identification. Linda was unable to locate Mary Brunner so the mission was a total failure.

The next day Manson sent her in again to the Hall of Justice. There was a hearing and Sandy Good was set free but Mary was held on a forgery charge under $850 bail. However, Linda never showed up. Having again borrowed the white Volvo and acquiring a credit card from Bruce Davis, the family comptroller, she picked up two hitchhikers she had met the day before and proceeded forthwith to drive to New Mexico. A couple of days later near Albuquerque, she was forced to abandon the automobile when a service station attendant wouldn't honor her credit card for repairs.

David Hannon was sorely unhappy a few days later when Linda sent a letter to the ranch notifying him that she was sorry but his car was parked at a service station outside Albuquerque, should he care to come pick it up.

Mrs. Kasabian's baby, Tanya, was left behind at the waterfall nursery because she felt that those guarding the children might get suspicious if she demanded to take Tanya to the court building with her.

One thing that remains a mystery is why Manson let Mary Brunner remain in jail. Her bail was only around $850, a sum that easily could have been raised by sending a trusted zombi on a bank robbery or perhaps a dope burn or something. Since the credit card that Mary had forged belonged to, or had been stolen from, Vern Plumlee's brother-in-law, the girls were thinking of driving up to see him to try to talk him out of pressing charges, they would pay him back, etc. But Manson, for reasons unknown, let Mary Brunner remain in jail until her release on probation late in September.

Charlie drove around looking for money. On two occasions around the days of the murders he and Stephanie drove to Beverly Glen Drive to try to obtain some money from Dennis Wilson but were unsuccessful. As they were leaving Wilson's house one of the times, Wilson told Manson, according to Stephanie, that the police had questioned him about a guy who was shot in the stomach, evidently referring to Bernard Crowe.

The second time Manson visited Wilson to beg for some money, a human named Richie Martin was there and overheard Manson threaten to kill Wilson's son Scottie, a child by a former marriage. Wilson was visited by his son Scottie on weekends, so this would indicate that it was the weekend of the murders since Manson would be in jail during both of the following two weekends.

Manson visited Gregg Jakobson's house around the time of the murders also, but Jakobson's wife was alone in the house and refused Manson's request to use the shower. Manson looked like a wild man and snarled that if she wasn't Gregg's wife he'd seriously injure her.

Mary Brunner called an old family friend, Melba Kronkite, from jail to ask for bail money but Melba was not able to help her. The following night, probably August 12, Manson appeared at 1 A.M. banging loudly on her door. When she answered, Manson demanded money for Mary's bail. When she refused, Manson left in what the lady later described as a "big black car which he was driving"—and he was angry. The black car that Manson was seen driving belonged, according to a close friend of Manson, to a rich friend of Manson—"a real millionaire" as the friend described him.

Around Tuesday, August 12, Manson threatened to slice up Juan Flynn. Flynn had been working outside feeding corn to the horses. He then went into the Rock City Café to prepare some food. He then sat down at the table to eat. Several girls were in the café kitchen. Others were sitting and chatting outside on the boulders and chairs on the porch. In the door walked Manson, flashing a signal to the girls in the kitchen to leave, a flicking, brushing motion of his right hand on his left shoulder. They left the room.

Manson, five-foot-six, grabbed the six-foot-five Juan by the hair as he sat in the chair and passed a knife close to his throat. "You son of a bitch, I am going to kill you." he said to Juan. "Don't you know I am the one that is doing all the killings?" Manson said, according to Flynn's testimony.

Manson wanted Flynn to come to the desert to live in The Hole. Charlie proffered his knife to Flynn and bade Flynn to begin killing him but Flynn demurred. According to Flynn, Manson bragged about taking thirty-five lives in two days. Manson evidently offered tall Juan the opportunity to be his actual personal zombi. He wanted Juan to wear a ring in his nose and serve as slave. Manson was always terrorizing Flynn, according to Flynn, and once Manson took a few shots at Juan with a pistol as Juan and a girl friend were walking down the creek.

After knowing Manson only about seventy-two hours, David Hannon, the new ranch hand, offered the family the use of his mother's ranch in the desert near Olancha, California. The ranch was located on the edge of the Panamint Valley, just an hour or so from sacred Goler Wash. It was ideal for the family. The opportunity to move everybody in the family away from the L.A. area couldn't be passed up. Things were simply too hot for the family on the coast of California.

On August 14, Tex and Juan Flynn and Hannon loaded up the bread truck with dune-buggie supplies and, towing a dune buggy affixed to the Twinkie truck with some of the famous white nylon rope, headed for Olancha. They unloaded the skelter gear and drove back to the Spahn Ranch. Tex remained behind at Hannon's ranch in Olancha.

When they arrived back at the ranch in the early morning hours of August 15, Manson asked them to return immediately with more dune-buggy equipment and parts. Hannon and Flynn refused but did help load up the truck. Bruce Davis drove the truck back to Olancha, accompanied by the melancholic sixteen-year-old Snake Lake, who remained in Olancha with Tex.

The architect of the August 16 Spahn Ranch raid, Sergeant Bill Gleason, was an expert on motorcycle gangs for the Malibu station of the L.A. sheriff's office. For a couple of months he had been gathering data about Manson. He knew about Manson's threats to various firemen. He knew about Manson's alleged shooting of that "Blank Panther." He knew about the weapons and machine guns at the ranch and about the incident in the spring where Manson raped that girl from Reseda. He knew about the dune-buggy manufacturing line at the ranch and that the famliy, so to speak, was girding for a war with the blacks. He had learned from Kitty Lutesinger about the hideous death-threats with which Manson terrorized his followers. From the officers involved, Sergeant Gleason learned about the July 27 mini-raid where Manson announced that he had hidden guns trained on the policemen. A decision was made to mount a large nighttime land-air operation against Manson involving helicopters, horses, patrol cars, submachine guns and 102 law enforcement officers.

On August 12, 1960, Sergeant Gleason along with "Malibu detective personnel" met at the Van Nuys district attorney's office to discuss the proposed raid with deputy D.A. Robert Schirn. They reviewed the facts, then Mr. Schirn issued search warrant number 2029, dated August 13, 1969, and it was signed by Malibu Justice Court Judge John Merrick. The search warrant was good only for the day indicated upon it but the raid did not take place on the thirteenth. The fearsome Special Enforcement Bureau of the sheriff's office (S.E.B.) whose purpose is "saturation patrol of high crime areas"—in the words of an officer interviewed—was picked to raid the Spahn Movie Ranch.

Several days prior to the August 16 raid a couple of family friends came to the ranch in a blue Camaro to warn Manson about the impending arrest. Among them was the daughter of a law enforcement officer and she supposedly had inside information but Charlie scoffed at the data.

On Friday night, August 15, the Straight Satans came to the ranch in several cars, to get Danny De Carlo back and to collect the club sword and for other reasons unknown. They threatened to kill Manson and burn the ranch. The Satans wanted Danny to leave that night but he talked them out of it. "So they gave me until five o'clock the next day to get my ass back to Venice; they said they would burn the place down"—as he testified at the trial on September 18, 1970, volume 92, page 10, 842.

After the sword was taken back to Venice, it was broken up, perhaps deliberately, by the Satans. They may have been fearful that the sword was linked to too many grim deeds. After it became known that Manson's group was responsible for murders, the sword pieces were taken into custody by the police.

There was a great possibility of a gang fight. Clem leaped up on the haystack with a weapon and was going to shoot but Manson was able to turn the violent affair into a party which lasted far into the night. Charlie decreed an emergency flood of female bodies from the surrounding hills. According to Kitty, Charlie came up to the waterfall and told all the girls to come down to the ranch. David Hannon was amazed at the number of girls that appeared from the hills to make love with the bikers.

Violence was quelled and most of the Satans left. De Carlo got so drunk that a couple of girls had to carry him into his bed in the bunkhouse-gun room. Sleep was. The front driveway was littered with Olympia beer cans, an uncommon scene at the Spahn Ranch where only dog blood, pot and acid passed the lips.

The night the Straight Satans raided the ranch Kitty Lute-singer called the Spahn Ranch and asked for someone to pick her up. She had called the ranch several times to talk to Beau-soleil. She did not know that he had been arrested for murder. Finally she talked over the phone to Manson, who said that Beausoleil had been arrested but that it was nothing, he would be out soon and why didn't she return to the ranch to wait for him. The seventeen year-old girl, pregnant by Beausoleil, was having problems with her parents, one of whom wanted her to get an abortion. There was quarreling and she decided to split.

About midnight Sadie, Gypsy, and a male Caucasian named Junior, came to Northridge in Swartz's car to pick up Kitty. Right there, in the driveway of her father's horse ranch, Sadie cut Kitty's hair off, leaving the single witchy tail adangle. They told her to burn one hair, bury one hair and turn the rest over to the Soul.

She arrived just in time to party with the Straight Satans, to catch a couple of hours sleep, then to get arrested in the dawn raid of the sheriff.

On August 16, while the family and the bikers were reveling, there was a 2 A.M. briefing at the Malibu sheriff's station given by the nominal head of the operation, one Inspector Graham.

Then they darted forth, with a warrant seventy-two hours out of date: 102 policemen in twenty-five squad cars, aided by various support vehicles and aided, according to the family, by a canteen truck supplying coffee. They arrived near the ranch at 4 A.M. in silence.

Large numbers of Special Enforcement Bureau personnel (S.E.B.) started hiking into the ranch from the hills of the south side, some toting their M-15's purchased through the National Rifle Association and some even creeping along with bayonets fixed to their rifles. They surrounded the ranch from the west, east and south, an encircling maneuver, according to Deputy Gillory, that had its origins in techniques used to surround suspected Viet Cong villages.

According to an officer who was in the raid, there were orders not to fire the weapons. Some of the officers had large patches with the word SHERIFF sewn on the back of their uniform.

The raid was filmed by the authorities, who wanted to use the raid footage in a training film. Evidently the land-air operation against the Spahn Ranch was the first of its kind and would serve as a model for future encircling raids against alleged hippie communes. Some of the officers appear definitely to be out of uniform in the photos of the raid, wearing an admixture of Marine Corps fatigues and regulation sheriff's-office clothing. During the raid they posed for the cameras in front of their commune arrestees, their automatic rifles held high.

Everything was still when just before dawn the officers kicked down the various doors to the main Ranch Western set, the three trailers, the "lean-to," the parachute room, George Spahn's home. They hauled the suspects out of the buildings and placed them sitting in a circle in the driveway in front of the movie set. Gypsy, Kitty, Barbara Hoyt, Krenwinkel, Little Larry, Sandy Good and Vern Plumlee were arrested in the Saloon.

Manson and Stephanie were asleep in the Rock City Café when the police began kicking. Flash—Charlie was out the back door and under the porch, crawling into the dirt beneath the building.

They arrested Larry Craven and David Hannon sleeping on a

mattress at the north end of the green house trailer. They were
taken outside to the cong circle. In a ditch, some distance from
the ranch, the police found a stripped, stolen and abandoned
1969 Volkswagen providing a legal basis for the arrest of the
group.

Out of the back door and off the porch of the Saloon leaped
one Herb Townsend, Simi Valley Sherri and beautiful Ouish—
they ran down to the creek where they were arrested. John
Friedman, the twelve-year-old boy whose parents had moved out
of the back ranch, was found sleeping on the roof, was hauled
down and herded into the circle. Clem was arrested at the beginning of the raid, trying to glide unnoticed off the front porch.

In the trailer next to an old abandoned 1930 Dodge were
the nurses: Leslie Van Houten, Kathy Gillies and Little Patti.
They were "sleeping nude" attired in panties upon a mattress,
arms and legs dangling upon the floor. With them was the infant,
Dennis De Carlo. They were covered with a sleeping bag.

Next to the trailer was a small wooden hut/trailer—the "Gypsy
Trailer"—in which were sleeping Sadie, a young runaway named
Laura and Malibu Brenda. They were sleeping with Zezo Ze-ce
Zadfrak, Pooh Bear aka Valentine Michael Manson and little
Tanya Kasabian. The three children, in the language of the raid
arrest report, were "detained as non-delinquent, and Mr. Pickens
of Probation Intake Control authorized taking them to foster
homes."

The ranch was rotten with filth and refuse. The police found
a dish of "fecal matter" in one of the iceboxes in the trailer.

At 6:15 A.M., George Spahn sat quietly, his cowboy hat on
head, his hands folded in his lap, facing the root beer clock on
the opposite wall above a poster for the movie *Roman Scandals*.
Near him, two stuffed chairs were pulled together with a blanket
and pillow on them as if the slim Squeaky were sleeping there,
before the raid. Two officers posed in George's house with a
display of booty: a revolver, a rifle and a violin case containing
a "tommy" gun. They ripped down the curtains in the front
window, evidently to get more light for the photos.

Two bikes were parked outside the bunkhouse, one with a

flame job painted on the gas tank, and both with high "sissy bars" on the back end, sticking up. The bikes belonged to Robert Rinehard, a bearded balding Straight Satan, and De Carlo.

In the undertaker/bunkhouse De Carlo lay collapsed upon the floor where two girls had carried him drunk. With him was Rinehard, wearing his thong-laced sleeveless club jacket with the picture of the devil on the back. Deputy Gillory and Deputy Neureither crashed in; De Carlo went for his .45 automatic and Neureither stomped him in the bridge of the nose. The two deputies quickly subdued the suspects, using clear plastic disposable handcuffs. Deputy Neureither guarded while Gillory searched the bunkhouse.

They really cleaned up in the bunkhouse, seizing a motorcycle engine, De Carlo's radio, a Polaroid camera, binoculars, the .45, a .30-caliber Winchester carbine, a radio/stereo tape player, a soldering iron, a Spartan bullet crimper, a rifle stock, various ammunition and other important items. Click click went the police cameras. There is a photo, among the file of police shots, of the top of De Carlo's radio, in the room where ten murders were schemed, upon which lay a dusty paperback copy of Hunter Davies' "authorized biography" of the Beatles.

They removed the two bikers from the bunkhouse. They threw De Carlo, nose abraded, down into the dust. Rinehard sat nearby on a truck bed for a while, then they ripped apart his Straight Satan one percent jacket with the devil's head. The two policemen spread it out over the hood of a car and posed for photos with their automatic rifles raised erect, one of the deputies bearing a field radio over his shoulder, a monitor in his ear and an antenna on his Marine Corps cap. The police took into custody the Straight Satan cutaway jacket, to hang as a memento upon the wall of the East Los Angeles sheriff's station.

The trailer truck with the electric generator, some dune buggies and Johnny Swartz's '59 Ford with the license plate GYY 435 were found in the alley between the movie set and the barn. In Swartz's car truck the fuzz found an assortment of weaponry: a 30–06 rifle, an Enfield rifle, a .20-gauge shotgun, a pellet gun, a Winchester 67A, a large box of ammunition and powder and a gun cleaning box. Deputy Earl Loobey asked Swartz about the guns in the trunk and Swartz replied: "They brought them up last night and were supposed to get rid of them today."

All vehicles—the '59 Ford, Randy Starr's '54 Ford truck, the two bikes, the '62 Ford, the four dune buggies—were towed to Howard Sommers Garage in Canoga Park by Howard Sommers Towing Company. The '59 Ford—the Crowe, Hinman, Tate and LaBianca murder automobile—was to remain in Sommers Garage until 12-2-69 when Officer Granado of S.I.D. checked it for bloodstains.

It seemed surreal. Everybody was arrested and placed in the circle. Two helicopters whirred overhead, creasing the hair below when dipping near. One of the dogs was running around wearing a brassiere placed on it by someone in the family.

But where was Manson?

"Where's Jesus?" The officers began to look about for Satan. At last, they crouched down in the early air and beamed lights into the space beneath the floor of the Saloon among the foundation timbers.

Deputy Dunlop spotted Charlie lying face down thirty or so feet from the back porch. They told Manson he'd better haul himself out. So he did, and when he reached the edge of the porch, Dunlop pulled him the rest of the way out by the hair. As Charlie stood up, a folder of credit cards fell out of his shirt pocket, belonging to a Dr. Weiland of Hayvenhurst Avenue. They dragged him down the alley in front of the barn. They handcuffed his hands behind him and carried him, arms bent up like a plow tiller, to the circle. He was barefoot, wearing buckskin trousers and a light-colored dusty shirt. They dumped him next to De Carlo.

Everybody was charged with auto theft.

Manson was also charged with burglary, probably because of the credit cards that fell out during his arrest. De Carlo was charged with assault with a deadly weapon: Section 245 Penal Code, because he went for his .45 as they kicked in the gun room.

Out of the twenty-five arrested, seventeen used pseudonyms.

Squeaky, as usual, began to cry. She asked if anyone might stay to cook George Spahn breakfast. Simi Sherri pleaded: who's gonna take care of the horses? The police were concerned about the dirt ratio so they made the group take showers, after which, according to the family, they were sprayed with DDT. That night they slept on blankets at the sheriff's sub-station in Malibu then were transported to the county jail in elegant downtown L.A.

The hippie car theft and runaway ring was smashed. What the sheriff's office unfortunately did not know is that they were arresting murderers, murderers that would be set free again about seventy-two hours after their arrest.

The day after the raid on the Spahn Ranch, either Sergeant Whiteley or Deputy Guenther, the officers in charge of the Hinman investigation, called the number listed on the Lutesinger ranch card found in Beausoleil's jeans when he was arrested. Beausoleil evidently told them that Kitty Lutesinger was his girl friend so the officers called to find out where she was. They wanted to talk with her about Beausoleil.

The officers at this time knew nothing about the Spahn Ranch or Manson or Beausoleil's connection with the family. Kitty was not home for she had run away the night before. In fact, unknown to the officers, Kitty was sitting at that moment in jail. Mrs. Lutesinger told the officer that she hadn't reported Kitty as a runaway because she'd "been through that before." She was told that her daughter was being sought on a murder investigation warrant.

Mrs. Lutesinger filed runaway papers on her pregnant daughter. Officers Guenther and Whiteley made arrangements with the police station near Kitty's home to be notified should the girl show up. This arrangement sowed the seeds of Manson's downfall.

Bruce Davis returned to the Spahn Ranch from Olancha after

he had delivered a load of dune-buggy parts and family equipment and was shocked to find everyone arrested. Tex and Snake
Lake stayed behind at David Hannon's ranch in Olancha. On
Monday, August 18, Snake was arrested for sunbathing nude in
the rocks near Hannon's ranch. While they were at the ranch
near Olancha, Tex went into town and returned with a paper
that accused "Mau Mau devil worshipers" of the murders. Tex
laughed and told Snake, according to Snake, that he killed
Sharon Tate: "I killed her. Charlie asked me to. It was fun."
Tex told Snake to keep quiet about it and that he didn't want
to discuss it further.

Also on Monday, August 18, the evidence for consideration of
a complaint against the twenty-five arrested in the Spahn raid for
violation of sections 487.3, 245 and 12200 of the California
Penal Code was rejected as not sufficient. Also, the search warrant under which the arrests were made had not been valid.
Manson, Van Houten, Krenwinkel, Clem and the others were
set free. All the children, Zezo, Pooh Bear, Dennis De Carlo and
Tanya Kasabian, were sent to foster homes. A few days later
Sadie kidnapped Zezo back from the foster home.

Johnny Swartz called Shorty Shea from the Los Angeles County
jail and asked him to come and help pick them up. Vern Plumlee
came instead, driving Shorty's car. Shorty was murdered a few
days later.

When they got out of jail, the ranch was in a shambles: doors
kicked in; dune buggies, tools and credit cards removed by the
Law. The police wiped out the gun room armaments. All De
Carlo had remaining, for instance, were his boots.

Manson was only out of jail for three days before he was
arrested again.

On Friday afternoon, August 22, Charlie and Stephanie were
alone together in an outlaw shack near the back ranch, getting
after it. During the love, Sadie quietly entered the shack and
placed a wrapped crimp-ended reefer in Charlie's blue denim
shirt, then crept away from the Devil and his partner. Afterwards,
Manson was sitting, shirt off, and the abundant Stephanie sat

also, shirt off, and two sheriff's deputies raided the outlaw shack and arrested them.

Miss Stephanie was asked a year after the incident why they were arrested. Her answer:

"Because we didn't have any clothes on and because we were trespassing and because they found some dope. I don't know who brought the dope in there. I think Sadie may have done it. She may have thought it would be groovy to give it to us. I remember seeing her out of the corner of my eye and I thought she just walked in and out then all of a sudden they saw it there and I didn't even know it was there."

The police loaded the couple into the back of the patrol car and drove along the dirt path that led to the front ranch. Passing the Western set, Manson yelled out the window, "Call the station house." Manson called the Spahn Ranch from jail and issued a command that whoever put the "j" in his shirt pocket should haul themselves down to the Malibu sheriff's station and cop out to the deed. According to Manson, the deputies were disgusted that he should make some follower take the guilt upon herself. Gypsy was going to volunteer to go to the station house and say it was her grass but it was unnecessary.

The police sent the joint to the laboratory for chemical analysis and, truth stranger than fiction, the results came back that it was not dope. Manson says that the girls were growing what they believed to be grass but evidently it was some sort of fool's dope or perhaps male plants, or maybe a few leaves from De Carlo's weak pot plant, Elmer. Anyway, it was not cannabis. And there apparently was no law preventing Stephanie from resting bare-breasted in the privacy of an outlaw shack, and since she denied any fornication, the sheriff could not charge Manson with anything. Once again, Manson was set free.

As for seventeen-year-old, pregnant Stephanie, she was sent by the court to her parents' house in Anaheim and placed on probation. She spent about two weeks at home then she dialed DI 1–9026 and asked to be taken back within the family. Clem and Gypsy drove to pick her up on September 5. "In spite of

Charlie, I loved everyone so much," Stephanie deposed, when asked why she decided to return to the ranch.

Manson approached the Butler Dune Buggy Shop to get duplicate sales slips for the four buggies purchased there and seized by the sheriff's office during the raid a week previous. Mr. Butler refused so they couldn't get them back from the police. The buggies removed from the ranch were later sold to the LeMans Salvage Yard for junk. Manson's fur-covered command dune buggy later wound up as a special attraction at a car show in Pomona, California. It really didn't matter because the family quickly stole replacements. They also stole a red '69 Ford that was used a lot in transporting people to the mouth of Goler Wash.

Vance, Vern and Zero used the red '69 Ford to rob a few gas stations in the San Fernando Valley. Vance would conceal a revolver in a briefcase, engage the station attendant in chitchat, draw the weapon and rob the till.

Sometime during this era they robbed the Deer Vale Road home of singer Jack Jones, the husband of Jill St. John. Armed with a sawed-off shotgun, they entered boldly at 2 A.M., even though the lights were on in the house. No sense makes sense, Manson decreed. They stacked everything they wanted from the house by a window. They went down to get the car but by the time they got back the police were there so they kept right on going.

Vance managed to steal one thing, however—Jack Jones' own white Stetson cowboy hat which Vance wore to the Barker Ranch in Death Valley.

In late August, Bill Vance and Vern took a trip up north to Portland, Oregon. They brought back a young girl named Diane Von Ahn and one Ed Bailey to add to the family. After a couple of days spent at the Spahn Ranch, Vern, Ed Bailey, Diane Von A. and Bill Vance moved into a rented house off Victory Boulevard in Burbank. There they continued rip-off forays until they joined Manson in Death Valley.

Manson was released from his marijuana charge around August 26, 1969. That night the family killed the rotund stunt-

man, forty-year-old Donald Jerome "Shorty" Shea. "While he
was in jail, Shorty was doing a lot of nasty talking about Charlie,"
recalled Kitty Lutesinger a year later. Charlie believed that it
was Shorty who set up the raid on the outlaw shack where he
and Stephanie were arrested.

Shorty and Johnny Swartz were working together to try to get
the family thrown off the ranch. Manson threatened Johnny
Swartz around this time, saying, according to Swartz, "I could
kill you any time. I can come into your sleeping quarters any
time." Swartz left the ranch thereafter in fear. De Carlo claimed
that Shorty was going to work for the German-American resort
builders as watch guard of the back ranch property. Manson has
said that he got down on his knees and begged Shorty to stop
stirring up dissension against the presence of the family, but that
Shorty was relentless, so he had to be killed.

Some family members liked the outgoing Shorty Shea. Shorty
wanted to become a movie star so he had at least three friends
who allowed him to use their phones as answering services in the
event a producer or director should want to call Shea about a
movie job. Every day the stuntman would call these friends to
inquire if any filmmaker had called. These daily phone calls
ceased to exist August 27, 1969.

Another "sin" of Shea in the crazed eyes of the family was
that he had married a black dancer whom evidently Shorty had
met in Las Vegas. The family was upset because his wife's black
friends started coming around. He was working with John Swartz
to get the family run off the ranch. But the murder was really
triggered because Shorty knew something about the Tate-La-
Bianca killings.

The murder of Donald Jerome "Shorty" Shea is probably the
most sickening of their crimes, if the stories circulated by dis-
affected members are to be believed. They tortured him and,
during the torture, tampered with his mental state, as if they were
conducting experiments. The entire family was involved in the
offing of Mr. Shea. Some killed, some buried, some burned, some
packed his gear. "By that time, we all had our job to do," Leslie

Van Houten remarked, discussing her assigned task of burning Shorty's clothes. As she began to burn them, a ranch hand wandered nearby, so she had to abort the mission, cover them up with brush and burn them later.

They buried him during the night down the creek by the railroad tunnel back of the ranch, in a crude, temporary, brushtopped grave.

Full moon for August 1969 occurred at 10 A.M. on the 27th, which is just about the time several girls reburied Shorty in broad daylight. His body, chopped into sections, was emplaced somewhere down the road toward Simi, probably in Box Canyon.

They packed up the belongings of Mr. Shea and loaded them into the trunk of his automobile, which had been parked at the Spahn Ranch. Bruce Davis left a fingerprint on one of Shorty's trunks, a grievous mistake for Mr. Davis. Gypsy aka Cathy Share later admitted to the police that she helped drive Shorty's automobile to be abandoned in Canoga Park. A bloody shoe belonging to Mr. Shea was taken into custody of the Los Angeles County sheriff but his body, or head, was never recovered.

Only three people—Steve Grogan aka Clem, Bruce Davis and Manson—are under indictment for the murder as of this writing.

Bruce Davis owed De Carlo money so he gave De Carlo the pawn tickets on Shorty Shea's matched brass-handled pistols. De Carlo evidently bought the weapons out of hock. They were seen around the Spahn Ranch for a while. Later he sold the pistols to a Culver City gun shop for $75, using the alias Richard Smith.

Whereas there was almost a complete silence about the Hinman-Tate-LaBianca murders within the family, the Shea murder was discussed from zombi to zombi. Charlie used to joke about it at campfires. When asked by Ruby Pearl and wrangler Johnny Swartz about the whereabouts of Shorty, Manson told them: "He's gone to San Francisco. I told him about a job there."

At the end of August, Charlie sent Sadie, Katie and Leslie to the Fountain of the World in Box Canyon to seek permission to live there. Charlie had a scheme to slowly encroach upon the

Fountain and ultimately take it over. "Sadie blew it," remembered Kate, "by calling a lady at the Fountain a pig." The sister in charge ordered them off the property and as the cropped-headed killers split, they were reported by the sister to have sung a song by George Harrison called "Piggies."

On September 1, an eleven-year-old boy, Steven Weiss of Long View Valley Road, located in Sherman Oaks, was out in his hillside back yard repairing a lawn sprinkler when he located the .22-caliber Longhorn murder weapon in the brush.

About fifty feet up above Long View Valley Road and running parallel to it is Beverly Glen Boulevard, off the side of which the grimy revolver was flung, down into the brush in back of the Weiss residence.

The young boy, Steve Weiss, forthwith turned the pistol over to an officer of the Van Nuys division of the Los Angeles police department. The boy was careful not to touch the revolver to protect fingerprints. The police smudged it up and filed it away, the chambers of the weapon containing seven spent shells and two live bullets. Not till December would the police, after young Weiss reminded them, remember about the revolver found on Labor Day.

Twenty-two

Rommel
The Barker Ranch
September 1969

In early September, Manson moved his troops to Death Valley. Over a period of several weeks they stole a bunch of dune buggies, about seven in number. They tried to steal a red Toyota from Dennis Kemp on Loyal Trail just a few feet down the road from where Bernard Crowe was living at 7008 Woodrow Wilson Drive. Kemp was able to drive the robbers away. A few days later, however, on September 1 they followed Kemp's Toyota to Ventura Boulevard and while Kemp was in a house in a card game, the coyotes stole the red, four-wheel-drive Toyota and drove it to the desert.

The same batch of happy people—Barbara, Ouish, Kitty, Sherri, Snake and Charlie—drove to the mouth of the Wash, then charged up the dynamited waterfalls seven miles to the Barker Ranch. Charlie drove back and forth in the various rented and stolen cars, personally escorting his family to the desert paradise. There ultimately were thirty or forty humans living there. Charlie left Squeaky and Katie Krenwinkel behind at the Spahn Ranch to take care of George.

Manson and Tex Watson drove in early September to see Ballarat Bob in Trona, a small town adorned with a plant owned by American Chemical and Potash Corporation. The town is encrusted with a mist of potash and a sulfurous smell hangs in the air. Ballarat Bob told them it was okay with him to stay at the Barker Ranch. He asked Manson to round up his burros for him and take care of them for him because he wanted to go prospecting later.

Sometime in September Manson also visited Mrs. Arlene Barker, the owner of the Barker Ranch, at her home in Sunland. Mrs. Barker flew up on weekends in her own plane to a ranch called the Indian Reservation located just north of Ballarat. Manson asked Mrs. Barker if he could stay a few days and she gave her permission.

In Los Angeles, on September the 4, Linda Kasabian hit town from New Mexico to try to get her kid back from the foster home where it had been placed following the August 16 raid at the Spahn Ranch. She came on timid and anxious when talking to Mr. Kroeger, the officer conducting a dependency investigation for the Department of Public Social Services for the county of Los Angeles. Linda said she had no idea how terrible the living conditions were at the Spahn Ranch and that she had left her daughter Tanya with Mary Brunner and had gone to Arizona to meet her husband.

She said to Mr. Kroeger, "I planned to return in about a week to pick up Tanya to return to New Mexico, and when I called the Spahn Ranch, they told me that Tanya had been placed in custody. I called Sergeant Jones at the Malibu sheriff's station and he advised me to see you." Linda told the officer that she planned to establish a permanent home for Tanya at the Church of Macrobiotics located at a ranch near Taos, New Mexico. She was given custody of Tanya after the interrogation. The young mother took her daughter to New Mexico, then to Miami and finally back home to her own mother's place in Milford, New Hampshire where she remained till she was arrested for murder on December 1, 1969.

On September 4, Robert Beausoleil had a hearing in Malibu justice court where it was decided that he stand trial for murder on November 12, 1969.

And on September 4, Stephanie called from her parents' place and asked the family to help her run away. Clem and Squeaky drove to pick up Stephanie in Anaheim and brought her to the ranch. It had been two weeks since she had been arrested with Charlie at the back ranch and placed on probation. They stayed four or five hours at the ranch and near dawn they took off for the desert in a green 1969 Ford, just rented by Brenda with a stolen credit card.

When Stephanie arrived at the Barker-Meyers Ranch area, Charlie gave her a knife. Charlie gave everyone instructions in throat-slitting. There was talk of decorating the Barker Ranch with skulls. Manson talked about boiling the skulls in large kettles to de-meat them. "We were all sitting around and he asked if we could do it. He asked if it came down to it could we do it and everyone said, 'Oh yeah' and I said, 'Oh yeah,' " Miss Stephanie remembered ten months later when she was interviewed just prior to a class at her dog grooming school. She said, "When I said, 'How? I don't really know how,' he used me as a live demonstration—how you cut from here to there" indicating throat gash—"Then he said, 'You have to know how to hide everything so no one will find it.' We were down in some canyon somewhere."

A few days later Stephanie had a conversation with Manson about going back to her sister's house in San Diego. The *farouche* young lady was standing holding a rifle in her arms. "I guess I looked homesick so Charlie asked me if I wanted to go home." She said that it was true that she was homesick. Manson then told her, according to her testimony at the trial, that he'd give her one more chance to go home.

Then he had one of his anger spasms. "Then he took the rifle and hit me in the head a couple of times and told me to forget about going home."

Months later she was asked by interviewers why she tolerated a person punching her in the face with a rifle butt. She replied, "I never wanted him to hit me but I wanted to be made to see in a different way. And the only way Charlie knew how to make me see in a different way was to do that."

One of the barriers preventing total takeover of Goler Wash was the so-called scientologist gold-miner Paul Crockett, who had snared away two of the family—Brooks Posten and Paul Watkins. Mr. Crockett and his new-found disciples were living in a tarpaper-roofed cabin located at the Barker Ranch itself.

Manson told Brooks Posten that he still belonged to Manson and that he was released from none of his agreements. Manson tried the time-worn "Kill you—kill me" routine with Brooks, handing him his knife saying, "Brooks, kill me." And when Brooks refused, Charlie seized the knife and said, "Then I can kill you."

Manson had a remaining grudge against the sheriff's deputy from Shoshone, who had led the raid against the Barker Ranch in February 1969 after several of the family had given his step-daughter some marijuana. Posten claimed that Charlie said that if Posten loved Charlie then Posten would walk to Shoshone and kill the deputy. "That was if I loved him," Posten said.

Then Juan Flynn began to consort with the so-called scien-tologist gold-miner Paul Crockett and the two ex-family members, Posten and Watkins, to the point where he began living with them in their tarpaper shack surrounded by bins of gold ore samples. Another follower was snared away by Crockett. Crockett even began to bad-mouth Manson to some of the girls, an ineffable sin in the eyes of Manson.

One night at midnight, Crockett, Posten, Watkins, Juan and a German shepherd were asleep in the cabin. The dog began to bark so that Paul, Little Paul and Brooks went outside to check it out. They didn't find anything unusual so they went back to sleep. Later on, the dog began to growl so Juan stood up and looked out the window. In the moonlight he saw Clem and Manson creep-walking toward the cabin. Flynn claimed that Manson had a knife and that the fringes on Manson's buckskins were going swish, swish. Naked, armed with a shotgun, Flynn left the cabin to confront Satan and Satan's latah. But nothing came of it. Charlie and he just had a conversation and walked away.

Many times Charlie put his knife up to the throat of the six-foot five-inch Juan Flynn demanding that he give in and accept the will of the so-called Wizard.

Charlie and the gang, using a stolen Master Charge card, began to buy all sorts of supplies for the end of the world—tools, toolboxes, cases of oil, twenty sleeping bags, lots of knives, food, camouflage parachutes. Over and over he claimed to Crockett and the other miners that all the items brought to the desert were legally acquired. Such a claim was credible because of the several times Charlie had been able to get large sums of money from rich young ladies in search of truth.

He had two large spools of telephone wire which he had brought in to set up desert communication. They stayed away from the Barker Ranch mainly because of the presence of Watkins, Posten and Crockett in the little cabin. But they would visit all the time, roaring in and roaring by. On a couple of nights, the family did build a bonfire and smoke dope. Charlie lifted up his guitar to lead the singing outside the Barker Ranch. In the middle of the night, Charlie would roar into the ranch bragging about all the people he had killed, according to Paul Watkins, and "sending out pictures" of slaughter. According to Watkins and Posten, Manson laughed about how he had made some girls bury Shorty Shea and how he had shot a "Panther." But there was no mention of Tate-LaBianca-Hinman.

Manson talked about General Rommel and desert campaigning. He was going to be the Desert Fox of Devil Hole at the head of a flying V of dune buggies racing across the desert for plunder. Manson spray-painted his stolen dune buggy and then, while the paint was wet, threw dirt on the paint to create a brown camouflage effect.

They talked a lot about taking over the Death Valley town of Shoshone and also Trona. Manson felt a bit of hostility toward all the desert people, wanting to ping them one by one. Manson talked about terrorizing the police. He talked about killing approaching policemen, removing their bodies from their clothes, then leaving the uniforms and shoes and hats neatly arranged on the desert ground, as if the bodies had somehow just disappeared from their uniforms.

Everybody, even when nude, wore a hunting knife strapped to the leg or waist. The family was so completely into gore that everybody was armed, not so much in fear of the police perhaps, but in apprehension of possible spontaneous slashing from fellow family members. Charlie liked to comment on those whom he considered the weak links in the family. The girls must have been desperate not to be thought of as a weak link. For weak links could find themselves on the receiving end of a satanic ritual. Accordingly, the behavior in the desert was brutal and freakish. For instance, one witness reports Gypsy as being absolutely fearless with regard to handling live rattlesnakes: "She'd just pick it up and hold it and stare at it. . . . It was really far out." No, thank you.

And there were deaths, according to Sadie, Vern Plumlee and others. There are supposed to be two boys and a girl buried about eight feet deep behind the Barker Ranch. They filmed some of their despicable activities also. Several witnesses have described what might be termed the Barker Ranch chop-stab dance, where they danced in a circle, then pretended to go into slash-frenzies—attacking trees, rocks and one another with their knives. God knows what else they shot with their stolen NBC camera.

Torture seemed to comprise the substance of most of the conversation about Manson in the final few days before his capture. He became feral beyond description, mean beyond description. In the wilderness the man of a thousand masks could slip them all off and could assume his cherished role of exterminator. "He got wild when he was out there. I don't know, he was just beating on Snake all the time—or everybody," Kitty Lutesinger remembered a year later. She was asked about the threats and she replied, "Oh, the usual stuff, like 'We'll hang you from the trees and cut out your tongue,' or 'We'll tie you up to a tree and put honey on you and let the ants crawl all over you.' "

At first the family set up camp at the Meyers Ranch, a lush, foliage-covered forty acres of patented land, purchased by Kathy Meyers' grandparents from a legendary local miner named Seldom Seen Slim for a side of bacon. They also occupied several cabins at the Lotus Mine—owned by Warner Brothers, according to Ballarat Bob—located about a mile down from Sourdough Springs in Goler Wash. They moved from cabin to cabin on orders of

the Wizard, spending some time at the Newman cabin, another
small dwelling a couple of miles further down Goler Wash toward
the dry waterfalls.

At the Meyers Ranch, they filled up the swimming pool and
fixed some of the watering devices for the wild fruit trees and
foliage which made it like an oasis in the high desert.

Once Snake got caught wearing a murdered man's work shirt:
"One time I was up at the foot of the Lotus Mine. I was wearing
a man's blue shirt and Charlie said, 'Where'd you get that shirt?
You've got Shorty's shirt on.'

"I was on acid when he said it."

It was all pain. One night, Kitty committed the pardonless
transgression of falling asleep during a fireside rap of Charlie's
and he punched her in the face, knocking her into the ashes.

One day Kitty and Sadie were sitting by the Meyers Ranch
swimming pool. Kitty was already five months pregnant and unhappy. Nobody talked about Bobby Beausoleil. Kitty tried to
strike up a conversation with Sadie about Bobby but Sadie wouldn't
look her in the eye. Charlie had told Kitty several times that
Bobby was in jail but that it was a minor charge and he implied
that Bobby would be back soon.

Kitty was determined to find out about it.

"What's he in for?" asked Kitty.

"Oh, nothing, just some little thing," replied Sadie. But Sadie
looked sneaky about it, Kitty thought.

"He's in for murder, isn't he?"

"Yes."

"Is it serious?" asked Kitty.

"Whatever serious is," Sadie replied. Sadie then burst into
laughter.

There is a story from Death Valley '69, passed from mouth
to mouth, which, if true, relates the first known belladonna truck
hijacking. Several people have told how the girls sometimes wore
pouches of crushed telache leaves or belladonna with which
they could disable people by slipping it into food or water.
Leslie, Sadie and perhaps Little Patti were hitchhiking somewhere

between Shoshone and Las Vegas when along came a refrigerator truck bound for Vegas bearing a load of fruits and vegetables. Naturally, the driver picked up the pretty young hippies.

Sadie supposedly began a pattern of very positive hints that she was willing to ball the driver. The driver was ready right then and there. But Sadie said something like, "Come on, come on. I know a place."

So she directed him on Route 178 into Death Valley. They turned left just past Ashford Mills on Furnace Creek Road and drove into the desolation. The trucker was anxious to stop immediately and create conjoinment but Sadie said, "No, no, we have to drive further." They passed the road sign that read, "Warning: Road not patrolled daily," and Sadie said, "No, no, drive on." So they drove forward up into the foothills of the Panamint Mountains. Finally they stopped. Sadie said something like, "Before we make love, I have to make you some coffee." Instead of coffee, she made the muddy, brown, bitter telache tea from her little Baggie of flip-out. Allegedly the truck driver passed out from the telache.

Meanwhile, one of the other girls ran to get a brush-covered dune buggy and while the driver was out cold, they broke open the truck hatch, loaded up the produce onto the buggy, took the dune buggy away to the ranch and then drove the driver to an obscure location and abandoned him there.

And so it went with The Hole in the Universe Gang. For about two and a half weeks the family swarmed all over Goler Wash and the southwest part of the Death Valley National Monument. Then Manson flipped out and attracted the attention of the Park Rangers and the California Highway Patrol so the family had to go into hiding. But that's why they went to the desert, to hide. Now it was like hiding within the hideaway.

Twenty-three

The Burning of the Michigan Loader

On Sunday, September 14, a computer engineer named Gary Tufts, who was a temporary family associate, plus Gypsy, Bruce Davis and Tex Watson drove the red '69 Ford, stolen by Vern and Vance, to the Death Valley area from the Spahn Ranch. They parked the Ford at the slim mouth to the Goler Wash waterfalls and Tex walked up the Wash and returned with the red four-wheel drive Toyota stolen from Van Nuys, California on September 1, 1969, police DR #69–068 #306.

Following Tex back down Goler Wash was Manson driving his mud-painted camouflaged command dune buggy. Fair-voiced Gypsy jumped in with Charlie and the computer engineer Tufts rode with Bruce and Tex in the Toyota back to the Meyers Ranch where they spent that night and much of the next day, Monday, September 15.

Around this time Manson humiliated Barbara Hoyt and Simi Valley Sherri. Simi Valley Sherri was commanded to perform an act of fellatio with Juan Flynn. She refused and for this defiance, Manson beat her up. Next, he ordered Sherri's close friend, Barbara Hoyt, the girl who later was fed the LSD hamburger in Honolulu, to perform the act and, in fear, she complied.

The two girls decided to sneak out after this grim scene and some of the others, like Gypsy and Ouish, expressed desire among themselves to split also, but only the two actually dared to leave, walking down the entire length of Goler Wash to the Wingate

Road along the salt lake to the Ballarat General Store, barefoot: twenty-eight miles of sharp rocks. The sneak-trudge occupied the greater part of the dark night and near dawn they crawled exhausted into a car near the store and slept.

Manson was furious when he found out they had cut out. He roared down the gulch the next morning prepared to kill them. He found them eating breakfast in Mrs. Manwell's Ballarat General Store. He stood outside the door and flashed the girls inside one of his silent signals, evidently, according to Mrs. Manwell, some sort of rolling eye-whirl as indication that he wanted them to come outside for a chitchat or chit-chop.

The girls told Manson that they were leaving, and just like a wind that changes its direction and therefore changes its name, Manson calmed down, commenting that well they couldn't leave without money, so he gave them twenty dollars. And away he roared in his iron horse of the hairy locusts. Mrs. Manwell took the two young ladies across the salt lake and down south into Trona where they bought some tennis shoes and caught a bus toward Los Angeles. Later Manson sent Clem down to Los Angeles to find them.

A few days previous, Manson had met on a road somewhere a friendly resident who possessed detailed knowledge of caves, camps, shacks and hot mineral springs in the vast Death Valley-Panamint area. This was a twenty-four-year-old bearded gentleman named Larry Gill, who was evidently living in a cabin off Furnace Creek Wash Road near Ryan, an old borax ghost town, on the Death Valley side of the Panamints. At least this was where he was living a few months later, according to an Inyo County sheriff's deputy.

Mr. Gill, trusting the hirsute group because they were driving a new Ford, agreed to show Manson the hard-to-find springs and camps. So, on Monday afternoon, September 15, Manson led a group of vehicles out of Goler Wash onto the Panamint Valley floor where they set up temporary camp for the night. Perhaps he feared that the cut-out of Simi Valley Sherri and Miss Hoyt would prove that it was easy for any of the girls to leave the area, so he wanted to find a more remote locale for the family. Or perhaps it was dune-buggy imperialism. In his raps, Charlie talked about stashing dune buggies every ten or fifteen miles all over the desert, with hordes of food, ammunition and gasoline buried near them. Because he had in mind raiding little towns like Shoshone and Trona in some dune-buggy Rommel scene, he naturally wanted to be aware of any potential hideouts and raid outposts.

It is known that he hid some 300 gallons of gasoline near Greater View Spring in the Striped Butte Valley, in an old airplane wing tank. Also there were several other tanks of gasoline that were buried in the desert, not to mention the barrels that the owner of the Ballarat Store saw the miner Mr. Paul Crockett haul down Goler Wash as his own following the October arrests of the family.

Manson, Gypsy, Ouish and an unknown female Caucasian drove away in the red Ford on Monday night, while the others remained at the camp at the mouth of Goler Wash. They went up north through Emigrant Pass up around Devil's Cornfield and down into Death Valley south to Ryan to Larry Gill's cabin to see him about the promised scouting maneuvers.

The next morning, Manson and the girls brought Mr. Gill back to the Panamint camp. And then from the camp a caravan of vehicles headed north to the Hunter Mountain-Race Track area of the Death Valley Monument and on into the Saline Valley to check out certain mineral springs. The red Toyota, the green '69 Ford, hyped from Hertz, the red '69 Ford and a dusty-blue flecked dune buggy stolen from the La Paz Buggy Builders on September 11 formed the caravan.

Gill showed them some camping spots and cabins near Jackass Springs southwest of Hunter Mountain. The red and green Fords were not able to drive into the Saline Valley because of the nearly impassable condition of the road so they were stashed on Hunter Mountain in the forest. There are two roads leading into Saline Valley from the southern end and the M. brigade drove in via the southernmost route over the high twisting pass and down into the desolate salty valley to the northwest.

The Saline Valley is where two travelers had burnt up in the friable air of around 140 degrees Fahrenheit in July of 1969. But the hot baths known as Palm Hot Springs were especially interesting to Manson in his continuing search for the entrance to chocolate-land.

Late that night, the group ran into a high government official named Boyd Taylor who was evidently camping out with his wife in the Saline Valley. The U.S. Commissioner for the Eastern District of California, Mr. Taylor was later to testify on December 3, in Inyo County court auto theft proceedings against Manson, that he saw Manson "in the middle of September" driving the stolen blue flecked dune duggy at 2 A.M. Also he would bring charges, in his official capacity as U.S. Commissioner, against Bruce Davis because of the gun used to pistol-whip Gary Hinman that was bought by Davis under an assumed name, in violation of U.S. law.

After encountering the campers, the family drove back over the pass to Hunter Mountain and spent the night. Larry Gill evidently drove or was driven back to his cabin because there was never any testimony linking him to the burning of the Michigan skip-loader.

The next morning, Wednesday, September 17, the red Toyota and one or two dune buggies, evidently including the camouflaged command dune buggy, bore the family back into the Saline Valley to the hot springs where once more they encountered the campers. According to Kitty, Charlie talked to them and shortly thereafter they pulled away in their camper.

Kitty Lutesinger and Diane Lake say that the following citizens spent two days exploring and having fun in the Saline Valley: Kitty, Diane, Scotty Davis, Tex, Clem, Ouish, Manson and Gypsy. One incident was related by Miss Lutesinger. When they encountered one of the hot springs, Manson commanded Clem and Ouish Morehouse to jump in and see if they could swim to the bottom, but the water was too hot. Nevertheless, Clem jumped in feet first but was unsuccessful. They then tried to tie a string on a rock and sink it down but the spring-cleft went off at an angle. Charlie mentioned something about getting skin-diving equipment and going down to see if the springs led to The Hole.

Late Thursday night or early Friday morning, September 18–19, Manson led his troop out of the Saline Valley over the bumpy wilderness trail up the mountain pass, the single headlight on his dune buggy his only guide. At the very top of the pass which would have led him down to the Hunter Mountain campsite, he stopped. Right in front of him were two large wide holes in the dirt-way, evidently scooped out by some nearby earth-moving equipment.

According to Kitty, Manson thought the authorities had deliberately dug the holes in his path so that he would crash his dune buggy into them! Manson commanded her and Gypsy to fill up the large but shallow gouge-outs with rocks and dirt. As they did this, according to Snake Lake, Scotty, Tex, Manson and Clem removed some gasoline tanks and a grease gun from the $30,000 Clark Michigan skip-loader, the evil machine of the Beast that tried to wipe out Jesus' dune buggy. Then they let out the fuel oil, poured some gasoline on the wires and the engine, then poofed it.

Then the family raced away and the rest of the night was spent in a roaring dune-buggy frenzy. They arrived at the cabin in the forest area near Hunter Mountain and proceeded to get the '69 green Ford stuck in the wilderness. Finally they rammed it into a tree. They stripped what they could off it and then abandoned it, speeding away in the red Toyota, leaving telltale Toyota tracks in the dusty trails for many miles. "It was a wild night," as Miss Lutesinger remembered eight months later.

The burning of the Michigan loader enraged the rangers at the Death Valley National Monument, which owned it. Relentlessly the Park Rangers, the California Highway Patrol and, to a lesser degree, agents of the Fish and Game Commission would begin to track down this un-cool group of murderers.

If they hadn't roamed the Death Valley area as marauders, the

Mansonists could have lived in that wilderness for years without any trouble. As one of the policemen said after the raid, "You could hide the Empire State Building out there and no one could find it."

It would take three weeks for the Rangers and the Highway Patrol to catch Manson.

Twenty-four

The Capture of Manson
September 20–October 12, 1969

Death Valley law officers began to enter the Manson nightmare. The Toyota tracks from the burnt Michigan loader led south, so Park Rangers and the Highway Patrol officers responsible for the area began to work south down into the Panamint Valley, asking questions to try to locate suspects owning a four-wheel-drive Toyota.

On September 20 Officer Manning of the C.H.P. found the smashed green '69 Ford that had been abandoned near Hunter Mountain. Miners in the area advised the officer that they had observed a group of "hippie-type people." Near the wrecked Ford they found Toyota tire tracks which were the same as those found near the burnt-out Michigan loader.

On September 22, some of the girls took the stolen red Toyota into Hall Canyon which is a beautiful canyon about fifteen miles north of Ballarat, climbing over 10,000 feet into the Panamint Mountains. The girls were exploring waterfalls and old mineworks, wandering from rock to rock, when Park Ranger Powell and California Highway Patrol Officer Pursell drove into Hall Canyon and encountered the group of "four female and one male suspects"—as the police report read. The license plate on the red Toyota did not belong to it but belonged to Bob Beausoleil's old '42 Dodge power wagon which was registered in the name of Beausoleil's wife Gail. The officers did not have radio equipment to run the plate through the computer. When they reached the

Highway Patrol Station and learned that the plate was illegal, they then had suspects.

California Highway Patrol owns an IBM system called the Automatic Statewide Auto Theft Inquiry System which in great part was responsible for bringing down the house of Manson. This auto theft system feeds out data regarding stolen vehicles to 200 police agencies including eight California Highway Patrol offices. It was data from this system that revealed stolen dune buggies.

On September 24, Park Ranger Powell and an Inyo County sheriff's officer named Dennis Cox returned to Hall Canyon to seek out the suspect hippies they had encountered two days previous. They were informed by miners there in the canyon that the red Toyota and suspects had split about four hours after the cops had left.

Park Rangers and other officers began to visit the Ballarat General Store, the only store for about forty miles. Various family members had made purchases there both in 1968 and in late summer '69 so the officers started obtaining data about the Mansonoids. They learned from the owner of the store about the two barefoot girls who had walked twenty-four miles to escape Goler Wash. More importantly, from the view of spotter planes, they learned that a large light green bus belonging to the group was parked at the Barker Ranch where they lived.

Sometime around mid-September Sandy Good-Pugh gave birth to a baby boy named Ivan aka Elf at a hospital in Los Angeles. Why the Wizard allowed Sandy to deliver her baby in an institution is not known. Quickly thereafter, Sandy took Ivan to Death Valley. Danny De Carlo also went to the desert but has claimed that he only spent about three days there before returning to Los Angeles.

On September 23, 1969, Mary Brunner was set free from jail on probation for that Sears credit card forgery. Her child, Valentine Michael Manson, had been taken by its grandmother to Wisconsin. Mary herself evidently did not journey to Death Valley but visited for a few days at the Spahn Ranch after which she went home to Wisconsin.

In the days following the burning of the loader, Manson continued his terror operations against the gold miner Paul Crockett and the trio of former family members that were living with him. Charlie sent girls in once to try to steal their shotguns. Other times he waved his hunting knife at their throats.

During their final days, the family spent a great deal of time in the area of Willow Springs and Mengel Pass and Anvil Springs which is on the Death Valley side of Mengel Pass in the Striped Butte Valley. About a half mile from Willow Springs is a valley where there's a cabin also owned by Arlene Barker. Charlie set up his dune-buggy repair shop at Willow Springs. It was far easier to truck automotive parts to Willow Springs from Shoshone than it was trying to negotiate the waterfalls of Goler Wash from the Panamint Valley.

There was once a road over Mengel Pass from the Striped Butte Valley down to Goler Wash during the gold rush in the early part of the twentieth century but it had long ago washed away. Mengel Pass was named after a prospector named Carl Mengel who lived from 1868 to 1944. He was a famous local prospector and operated a mine near his cabin. He filed for water rights on Anvil Springs oozing out of an abutment below his cabin on the west ridge of the Butte Valley. When he died, his ashes were buried on the pass top beneath a steel-banded conical pile of rocks, with a large cherry-shaped rock on top. Inside this rock pile with his ashes was buried Mr. Mengel's wooden leg. Near Carl Mengel's old cabin, Manson and crew hid 300 gallons of helter-skelter gasoline in an old airplane wing tank.

On September 29, 1969, Park Ranger Richard Powell and Highway Patrol Officer James Pursell paid a visit to the Barker Ranch. The officers approached the ranch from the northeast over Mengel Pass. They checked out the two dwellings at the Barker Ranch where they encountered what they termed "two females uncommunicative"—evidently two family members who were rifling through Crockett's cabin. The girls said that the person who lived at the ranch had gone to Ballarat and would be coming up Goler Wash.

That morning Juan Flynn and Paul Watkins had gone away to get supplies and make arrangements to go to another place to live until the Manson problem was solved.

Charlie had hauled to the mouth of Goler Wash a batch of tires, tubes, batteries and equipment for servicing his dune-buggy assault squad. Crockett agreed to haul the supplies to the ranch and drove down the waterfalls in Beausoleil's old orange truck to pick them up. As he was driving back up the sheer creek bed, he ran into California Patrol Officer Pursell and Park Ranger Powell. And as Crockett later recounted it, "They wanted to know what it was that I was doing and what I had in the truck and what was going on."

The police officers asked Crockett and Posten to tell them about the family. Crockett agreed to talk but the battery in the truck was low so he couldn't kill the engine. Therefore, the officers followed Crockett back to the Barker Ranch for a discussion. Crockett filled them in on Manson's schemes of becoming a Devil Hole Rommel and so forth.

Crockett did not reveal much to the cops because of fear that Manson was perhaps listening. "He can sneak into Shoshone and sit six feet from you in back of a window and hear everything that is going on and the next time he sees you he tells you the whole conversation and he starts laughing at you and tells you how stupid you are. . . . I didn't know whether he was ten miles away, a hundred miles away, or six feet."

Posten, who was riding with Crockett in the orange pile wagon, told them that the entire family had been arrested on August 16 in Chatsworth for grand theft auto. This information enabled the Inyo County authorities to coordinate their investigation with the Los Angeles sheriff's office.

After the officers left Crockett's cabin, they were scouting around the area in their four-wheel-drive vehicle when they encountered a nude group of hippies, seven in all—scampering away in a draw near the Meyers Ranch. They also found a red Toyota which did not have a license plate on it but they noted down the vehicle inspection number and were able to run it through the computer when they got back to discover that it was Dennis Kemp's Toyota stolen during that card game on September 1. They also found a dune buggy which they later learned was stolen in Santa Ana. Both of them were concealed by tarps and sleeping bags and clothing.

While the police were chasing the suspects, Manson came running up to the canyon, ran into Crockett's cabin and grabbed Crockett's double-barreled shotgun and sped up over the hill, evidently taking a position on the ridge between the Meyers and the Barker Ranches. Brooks Posten said that he heard Manson fire the shotgun three times. Manson claimed later that he dodged around behind the rocks, shouting, trying to unnerve the police.

That night into the Barker Ranch compound roared Rommel and his teenage vampires in their attack vehicles. They had an engineless dune buggy set up in the front yard. Tex and some female Caucasian called Linda, probably Little Patti and Manson asked Crockett to help them haul in a motor for the buggy which they had stashed in the canyon behind the ranch. Crockett helped them lift the motor onto a wheelbarrow and they carted it down to the dune-buggy frame. They put the motor into the dune buggy by lantern light and then drove away, giving forth the family coyote yips and shooting off pistols.

Around 10 P.M. on September 29, after the officers returned from Goler Wash, the policemen had a strategy meeting. Homer Leach, Chief Ranger for the Death Valley National Monument, contacted Sergeant Hailey of the Lone Pine Resident Post of the California Highway Patrol and informed him about the situation in Goler Wash. Accordingly, four representatives of the Inyo County sheriff's office, four National Park Rangers and six California Highway cops drove back in to the Barker Ranch area in four-wheel vehicles to snare the hippie car thieves.

At dawn, Ranger Powell and Officer Pursell came to Paul Crockett's cabin and asked Crockett and Posten if anyone had come into the campsite during the night. Crockett told the officers about the dune-buggy motor-mounting and that the family had ridden away into the night, possibly proceeding over Mengel Pass.

Then many of the officers converged on Crockett's cabin for a chitchat. Crockett gave them some more information but they were suspicious of him. They suggested to Crockett that he haul himself out of the area there but Crockett claimed that he felt that he was still of use to Charlie so that Charlie wouldn't kill him yet. Therefore he thought he'd stay on at the ranch. The cops told him to drive out in the old orange pile wagon if Charlie came back but Crockett felt that Charlie's forces would be guarding both exits on the Barker Ranch, the exit west through the mouth of Goler Wash and the exit northeast over Mengel Pass. Therefore he and Brooks would have to walk out by night.

On September 30, spotter planes buzzed overhead to locate the hippie deployments. But the family covered themselves with tarps or froze in their tracks and evidently were not seen.

That day the police raiding party drove over Mengel Pass where they located two vehicles near Willow Springs: a gold-flaked 1962 Volkswagen dune buggy stolen in the San Fernando Valley and a yellow 1967 Volkswagen dune buggy stolen in Culver City. They also located all the automotive supplies that were being hauled in the day before by Posten and Crockett. They removed the wiring and the distributor caps and rotors from the dune buggies to prevent their use.

That night, Crockett and his helpers were sitting on the front porch of the Barker Ranch when they heard a noise. They went to get their two shotguns out of the cabin. That night someone creepy-crawled the cabin, the dog growled, the door was open and Crockett claimed that Charlie had a half dozen girls chasing around to grab the guns.

It was right about that time, after it became really obvious that the police were after him, that Manson banned all daytime activity. By day everybody was to remain hidden in the wilderness. They were to freeze if there were any spotter planes or cover themselves with camouflage parachutes and remain completely out of the way. Food became scarce. No one was allowed to use the Meyers Ranch swimming pool for baths.

After splitting from Death Valley, Simi Valley Sherri spent time with Danny De Carlo in Venice prior to his arrest. De Carlo got the bread truck out of the impound garage around October 1. It had been there since Sandy and Mary had been arrested the day of the Polanski residence murders.

Bruce Davis and Clem were dispatched to Los Angeles to look for Sherri and Barbara—perhaps to kill them. De Carlo caught Clem going through the glove compartment of the bread truck somewhere in Venice. Clem brought back to Death Valley a sixteen-year-old boy named Rocky whose mother was an official at the Fountain of the World sect near the Spahn Ranch. Rocky was infatuated with Katie aka Patricia Krenwinkel, talking with her for hours about motorcycles and horses.

Around October 1, Vance, Vern, Zero and Diane came to the Goler Wash camp, bringing with them an advance copy of the new Beatles album, *Abbey Road,* which was played on a battery-operated machine. Late on Wednesday night, October 1, Crockett and Posten were asleep hugging their shotguns. Around 2 A.M. Charlie and Tex drove up and gave them some tobacco.

Earlier that night, at the other end of the Panamint Valley, one Filipo Tenerelli, a biker from Culver City, California, was shot near Bishop, California. It was first listed as a suicide. However, three days later his car, a Volkswagen, blood smeared on the inside and on the outside, was found 400 feet down a cliff near Crowley Peak which is on the road between Ballarat General Store and Olancha. It is quite a distance between Bishop where the body was discovered and Crowley Peak where his car was found.

On Thursday, October 2, there was a hostile confrontation between Manson and Paul Crockett. Manson went into a snuff-spasm when Crockett told him that the police had accused him of abetting and aiding a fugitive from the law, namely Manson. "He told me just before I parted and walked out that I should be more afraid of him than the law," Crockett said. Crockett and Posten, in order to save their lives, packed up a few cans of food and walked out over Mengel Pass, down the Striped Butte Valley to the trailer camp near the Warm Springs talc mines, where they found safety.

The next morning, October 3, early in the morning, Crockett and Posten had a nice long discussion with the police, which was taped. Crockett offered the suggestion that the best way to get Manson was either to pick the family off one by one or to mount a large raid against them. They also told the police that Manson had seized Crockett's shotguns and that all the girls were armed with knives and that the girls were all like zombies trained for instant obedience.

On the night of October 2, 1969, Charles Tex Watson seized the '42 Dodge power wagon, drove down Goler Wash, bumping into the night, to the mouth of the Wash and he crossed the semi-dry salt lake evidently seeking a shortcut to the Trona Road. He slowed down or stopped in the middle of the lake and became mired in the salty mush. Watson was fleeing.

He spent the night sleeping by the side of the road. The next morning, a man named Mr. Holliday, a pipefitter, from Rialto, California, picked up Watson. Watson told him that the Forestry Department was after the commune he was living in so Holliday drove Watson to the heliport in San Bernardino and then to the San Bernardino railroad station where he dropped Watson off. Watson said he was going back to Texas where his parents owned a chain of supermarkets. When he returned to the commune he was going to bring a truckload of groceries because that was what the commune needed most. Watson returned to Copeville where he seems to have maintained a routine existence, dating a doctor's daughter, till the end of November when he was picked up by his cousin, the sheriff of Collins County, Texas, for murder.

With Crockett and crew ousted from the set, Manson began to use the Barker Ranch as headquarters but only at night. Everybody, by this time, was on hand, including Sadie and Katie. By night and by day the police tried to catch them.

Once a day, after dark, the girls would prepare a large meal for everybody in the Barker Ranch kitchen and everybody would skulk in and get a little chow. Sometimes in the middle of the night they'd have to walk for supplies from the Barker Ranch eighteen miles over Mengel Pass to Willow Springs and back.

"We walked to Willow Springs and back in one night. We had to because of the police. Of course, we were helped by some good sunshine," said one of the girls a year later. "We were carrying dune buggies down the hills when the police were chasing us," she said.

They began to leave false campfires to lead the police away from their real campsites.

Some of the girls spent the light of day at a campsite about a mile and a half east-northeast from the Meyers Ranch where they carried sleeping bags and bottles of water. Other girls were required by day to hang out in the hot rocks near Mengel Pass. They "hid out all over the hills, hiding in parachutes," according to Kitty. By night, after supper, they were honored with the task of building the so-called bunkers.

Manson issued an order that all of the girls were to stop smoking cigarettes. Subsequently, he asked for a show of hands as to who exactly had obeyed his order, and was chagrined to find that there were some who had ceased to obey. So he commanded that those who refused to stop smoking cigarettes dig several bunkers by night which were to serve as hidden shelters. Evidently, against the police and against the winter air.

They built a bunker on a hill south of the Barker Ranch which they roofed over with metal and on top of the metal they placed sand and stones. Inside the bunker was a huge Playboy mattress on which bounced the bodies of Helter Skelter. They had a telephone set up. They ran field wires leading from this bunker up to a rectangular rock command post about 300 feet up the hillside so that from this bunker by telescope a spotter could look about a mile and a half down Goler Wash.

There was a set of bunkers to the north in a draw between the Meyers and Barker Ranch, one a rock-lined hillside bunker, and down in the gulch near a spring was another bunker built with debris and old window frames.

According to Diane Lake, just before the police finally netted the family, Charlie sent Cathy and Zero down to Los Angeles in order to kill her grandmother, enabling Cathy to inherit the

Meyers Ranch. This would have legitimatized Manson's position in the area. This grim caper was aborted evidently when the automobile they were driving broke down.

On October 8, Manson and Bill Vance left the Barker Ranch area and traveled to Los Angeles together. There's not much known about the reasons for this little trip but it had to be important because Manson had been sticking close by his followers.

As usual, the golden opportunity to escape the family occurred whenever Charlie took a trip away. This was no exception.

Life was grim for the pregnant girls, Kitty and Stephanie: little food, no showers, living by night, hiding by day, fearful, threatened by a maniac, confused. Kitty recalled it: "Now when I start thinking about it I remember how bad it really was. How he just talked about it so much that you just . . . you know . . . about snuffing people and torturing them, and all kinds of different orgies. You get so you just can't listen to it any more. It really was pretty bad."

So, on Thursday night, October 9, Kitty and Stephanie sneaked away a couple of hours after sunset. Clem had been assigned bed-check duty and discovered the girls missing. He yelled immediately for everybody to roust out and capture the runaways. Manson had issued proclamations that if they found anybody escaping, they were to beat them up, or worse.

Night held the young girls in safety as they wandered up the Wash to Mengel Pass and on to the Willow Springs area. They had gone in the opposite direction that Barbara Hoyt and Simi Sherri had taken when they escaped in September. Clem and Rocky went to sleep down the Wash in the middle of the creek bed armed with a sawed-off shotgun, prepared the next morning to go out looking for the young ladies.

On October 9, 1969, the same night that Stephanie and Kitty skulked away from the camp, the police set up their final net to catch the car thieves. There had evidently been careful surveillance of the area by the police who determined that the ranch was being used until daylight. Patricia Krenwinkel had been assigned the job of seeing that everybody got out of the Barker Ranch and out of sight before dawn. It was getting cold in the high desert with winter approaching, and on this morning it was very cold and the family hung around the Barker Ranch area too long and were caught.

By cover of darkness the police approached the Barker Ranch from two directions: from the mouth of Goler Wash and from the Striped Butte Valley over Mengel Pass and down the long seven and a half miles to the ranch. The California Highway Patrol supplied radio equipment for these two advancing parties so that when they got close enough they could communicate with each other and exchange information.

Up Goler Wash came the following officers: Brad Hailey, E. B. Anderson, A. B. George, J. B. Journigan of the California Highway Patrol. Also in this crew was Ranger Powell. The party was directed by Lieutenant Hurlbut of the California Highway Patrol.

The other party parked their four-wheel drive vehicles at the summit of Mengel Pass and walked down through the wilderness on foot. The Mengel Pass party was comprised of James Pursell and Officer O'Neill of the California Highway Patrol and others, including a warden of the Federal Fish and Game Commission by the name of Vern Burandt. There were numerous Inyo County officials, including the Inyo County D.A. and assistant D.A., on this important mission. The idea was to converge on the Barker Ranch at dawn.

Just before dawn the two advancing teams of police officers achieved contact via walky-talky. The team of officers coming in from the west, from the Panamint Valley up Goler Wash, encountered, sleeping in suspicious tandem on the creek bed between blankets, Clem and Rocky. Near Clem's head was Clem's sixteen-inch sawed-off shotgun and twenty rounds of ammunition.

Officers Journigan et al. awakened them and put them under arrest for having a sawed-off shotgun and for arson and for grand theft auto. The officers parked their four-wheel-drive vehicles evidently in a small draw to the west of the Barker Ranch. Officer O'Neill took a position high on the south slope across from the

Barker Ranch up above the bunker. It is not known if the police were really aware of this disguised bunker. However, shortly after dawn, Sadie, wearing a red hat, emerged from the hidden bunker to relieve herself. She was evidently spotted by the cops. The cops, according to the girls, let loose a friendly shotgun blast on top of the metal hidden bunker roof causing the girls to come out.

Arrested at the south hill dugout were Leslie Van Houten using the name Louvella Alexandria, Sadie, using the name Donna Kay Powell, Gypsy, using the name Manon Minette, and Brenda, using the name Cydette Perell. Inside the ranch house, the cops arrested Marnie K. Reeves aka Patricia Krenwinkel. They arrested Robert Ivan Lane aka Soup Spoon. They arrested Linda Baldwin aka Little Patti. Some of the girls were nude. Official note was made of it on the arrest report:

"When the initial group of female prisoners were arrested, several of the females disrobed. Several of them urinated on the ground in the presence of the officers. They also undressed and changed clothes in the presence of the officers."

Proceeding north in the small draw between the Meyers and Barker Ranches, the police raided the "spike camp,"—as they called it, where they arrested Sandy Good, who was carrying Sadie's baby Zezo, Ouish, using the name Rachel S. Morse and carrying Sandy Good's one-month-old baby Ivan, and Mary Ann Schwarm aka Diane Von Ahn. The babies were burnt raw from the sun and one of them had a large cut on his face.

These three girls had in their possession a Miramar mail bag which contained the magic swatches of hair which had been cut off during the tonsure rites of the preceding July. Also in the mail bag was a stolen .22-caliber single-shot Ruger pistol and a ring of keys, one of which fitted the stolen red Toyota.

All day long the police stayed in the area checking it out. Finally, around dusk, a group of ten women, three men and two babies were chained together and transported down Goler Wash. Followed by police vehicles, they walked down the steep waterfall area to the mouth, the chains clanging in the night.

They were all transported to Independence, California by Sergeant Hailey and Warden Burandt, to be booked for arson and theft and receiving stolen property.

As officers searched the area they found the stolen Toyota at the dry wash camp a mile and a half northeast of the Meyers Ranch. The Toyota was out of gas and covered over with sage brush. The same Toyota was used to escort Clem and Rocky and Soup Spoon down Goler Wash on the way to jail.

Officers continued to search the area, and in addition to the dune buggy at the bottom of the canyon and the stolen Toyota, they rediscovered the two vehicles that were dewired on September 30. They called the Don Lutz Tow Service of Olancha, California, 130 miles away, and requested the company to haul the stolen vehicles out. What a towing charge.

Then they proceeded to search north along Mengel Pass and found the mud-painted command dune buggy down a cliff with punctured tires and seemingly abandoned although it was covered and camouflaged with brush. The police took color photographs of the vehicles and the arrests.

It was nighttime before the rest of the officers drove over Mengel Pass, their mission accomplished. As they drove toward Death Valley, through the Striped Butte Valley near Anvil Springs, Kitty Lutesinger and Stephanie Schram stepped out of the brush and flagged down the officers. They told the officers they had run away from the family and were afraid for their lives.

Clem Grogan called up the Spahn Ranch from the Inyo County jail in Independence, California and asked to "speak to the Devil." Clem told Charlie about the arrests. Manson for reasons unknown seems to have left for Death Valley about a day later.

Early in the morning of October 11, Stephanie and Kitty were allowed to call their parents, collect. When Kitty called her mother at the Lutesinger Ranch, her mother asked her if she knew that Officers Guenther and Whiteley were looking for her in regard to the murder of Gary Hinman. She did not know. Kitty wanted her parents to come and pick her up but her mother said that she would just have to turn her over to homicide officers anyway, so they couldn't pick her up.

Kitty's mother spoke to Officer Dave Steuber, an energetic auto theft officer for the California Highway Patrol, and told Officer Steuber the details concerning her daughter's connection with Robert Beausoleil. Afterward, Officer Steuber contacted the L.A. County sheriff's office, homicide division, and evidently spoke to Deputy Guenther. Officer Steuber supplied Deputy Guenther with considerable data regarding Charles Manson's activities on Death Valley and the August raid on the Spahn Ranch. This is evidently the first time that Deputy Guenther had learned of the connection between Beausoleil and the Spahn Ranch.

Officers Whiteley and Guenther spent a day researching the Spahn Ranch, Manson, the August 16 raid and various other activities involving the family there. They obtained pictures of the people arrested at the August 16 raid from the Los Angeles County sheriff's office, auto theft division, and on October 12 they proceeded to drive up to Inyo County to secure possession of Kitty Lutesinger. It was the beginning of the solution of the Tate–LaBianca homicides.

The same day, perhaps on the same road, that Guenther and Whiteley were driving to Death Valley, Charles Manson also was on the way there. October 12, 1969, was Aleister Crowley's birthday, a fit day for the arrest of killers.

Why was Manson returning to Death Valley?

He probably realized the amount of fear he could generate to keep everybody in line was greater if he were near his followers. Also, Manson knew that Bruce Davis and others were in Las Vegas getting supplies so he wanted to avert their arrest when they returned.

What did he have to fear? Manson had been arrested that year alone on March 30, June 3, August 16, August 23, for a variety of charges and had walked away free. He had shot, killed, plundered according to his own schedule and gotten away with it. Why not now?

There are indications that Manson was about to undertake his wildest scheme of all, a series of assassinations of prominent Los Angeles citizens against whom he held grudges. The dune-buggy locusts would raid from The Hole, destroy, then return. Perhaps he liked the media attention given to the Tate murders. After all, he had been trying for fame as a recording artist for several years. Now he could be Charlie the Knife.

Central to a discussion of plans to kill famous people is the "list," about which a heavy area of silence has been created. The "list" was found in Death Valley and it marked out those to die.

In one report it contained thirty-four names of stars and businessmen to be killed. This "list" of family enemies included supposedly those who had helped out in the past but had ceased to aid. It is a common phenomenon for cults to have a hate list or enemy list. At least two groups operating in lower California, besides the Mansonoids, have, or had, enemy lists.

High Inyo County officials visited Miss Lutesinger down in L.A. following the Barker Ranch raids and told her they had in their possession a written list of people to be killed, and she was on the end of the list.

Taken into evidence by the Los Angeles police department from family material seized by the police in Inyo County was a mysterious pack, perhaps Manson's, which may have confirmed visual aids for the preparation of the "list."

The "army type pack," as the police report read, contained, among other things, sixty-four movie and TV star magazines, one canvas money bag marked "Federal Reserve Bank of Dallas" and one paperback book *Stranger in a Strange Land* by Robert A. Heinlein.

Manson may have returned to his original game borrowed from *Stranger in a Strange Land*, where the novel's Valentine Michael Smith took to murdering or "discorporating" his enemies. There was one occult shopkeeper on Santa Monica Boulevard who reported selling Manson a copy of *Stranger in a Strange Land* around this time. The movie magazines may have been brought in to help stir up hatred.

Quite a few of the family members escaped arrest on the October 10 raid. Among them were Diane Lake and Claudia Smith aka Sherry Andrews. Both of these girls hid under a canvas not far from the front ranch gate of the Barker Ranch when the raid occurred. So they were around when Charlie got back. Others had fled and were lurking in various parts of Goler Wash, never to be caught. The police seized the last of the stolen NBC film equipment, a camera loaded with unexposed film. Bill Vance is supposed to have disappeared later with some of the Death Valley footage.

Late in the afternoon of October 12, Charlie walked up to the Goler Wash, stashed his pack near the Lotus Mine, then proceeded to the Barker Ranch, guitar in hand, ready for chow. He was in the company of three other male Caucasians. Bruce Davis, in a stake truck that Clem had rented, came back from Las Vegas and got the stake truck stuck in the sandy wash between Mengel Pass and the Barker Ranch and abandoned it.

California Highway Patrol Officer Pursell and Park Ranger Powell and another Ranger went back in to the Barker Ranch area on Sunday, October 12, to look for more dune buggies and check out the various family campsites for contraband. A passing motorist told them that a stake truck was abandoned in the Wash so the officers checked it out. Pursell and the two Park Rangers located the Chevrolet truck still loaded down with drums of gasoline and supplies. They decided that un-caught hippies, perhaps even Manson himself, had re-entered the Barker Ranch area.

So Pursell radioed out on the C.H.P. radio equipment and talked to other officers. It was decided that then was the time to noose Satan. About five o'clock in the afternoon police entered the area and took up clandestine positions near the Barker Ranch. They waited. Meanwhile other officers were summoned who were on the way up Goler Wash from Ballarat.

From a position on a ridge up above the Barker swimming pool north of the ranch Officer Pursell and Ranger Powell observed Manson and a couple of other people walk up the gulch and into the house. Manson was carrying a guitar case. Ranger Curran worked his way around to the front of the ranch so that he could meet the officers who were coming up the Goler Wash from Ballarat. They began to hear giggling and laughter and conversation from the house so they knew there were quite a number of people in there.

The Chief Ranger for the Death Valley National Park, Homer

Leach, Deputy Don Ward of the Inyo County sheriff's office, and
Al Schneider of the sheriff's office arrived just after dark. Then they
radioed Officer Pursell, who walked down the hill in the back,
slinked along the back side of the cabin just to the left of the
Barker Ranch and walked in under the ivy-trellised side porch,
kicked open the side door and said, "Stick 'em up." He slid along
the wall to the left using it as a cover in case any of them should
care to attack him and he told them to put their hands on top of
their heads. In slow-motion defiance, the killers complied.

"I ordered the subjects out backwards one at a time where
Deputy Ward took charge of them," Pursell recounted later.
Once again, as in the Spahn Ranch raid of August 16, the ques-
tion had to be asked, "Where was Jesus?"

It was about six-thirty in the evening. Seven dirty hippies had
been hauled out and handcuffed. The quick desert darkness was
imminent. Officer Pursell carried the single candle which had lit
the supper around the four-room cabin. He paused at the small
blue bathroom with a poured concrete bathtub and a small blue
lavatory. Beneath the lavatory was a little cabinet out of which,
as the officer placed the candle's flame near, protruded hair. Then
he saw wiggling fingers and he said, "All right, come on out, but
slowly." And before he could ask, the small human uncoiling
from the tiny cabinet said, "Hi. I'm Charlie Manson."

After the police arrested Manson, Pursell went back into the
house and ran into Bill Vance standing in the bedroom. After
being handcuffed Vance had somehow gotten away and was
hiding in the house.

The girls arrested were Beth Tracy aka Collie Sinclair, Diane
Bluestein aka Snake Lake, Sherry Andrews aka Claudia Leigh
Smith. All suspects were marched down to the draw and when
they got to police vehicles they were escorted in the vans to the
head of the waterfalls whereupon they walked down to the
Panamint Valley.

They put them in units of three and began to march them down
to the draw toward the vehicles which were parked in the Barker
Ranch dump area. Men arrested were Manson, John Philip

Haught aka Christopher Jesus aka Zero, Kenneth R. Brown aka Scott Bell Davis who was a partner of Zero from Ohio, David Lee Hamic aka William Rex Cole aka Bill Vance, Vern Edward Thompson aka Vern Plumlee, Lawrence L. Bailey aka Little Larry, and Bruce Davis.

As the chop-fallen killers were walking down the wash from the Barker Ranch, Manson tried an escape caper. He told the officers that he had left his pack very near there and he requested the officers to help him find it. The officers looked and they couldn't find it so Manson asked them to open his handcuffs and let him look around in the darkness for his pack. Then he might have escaped. The pack, probably the one containing those movie magazines, subsequently was found by one of the officers and "booked with the rest of the property."

The officers noted that several times during the walk Manson said something and his followers replied with "Amen, Amen"— as if in gospel response. Also, a mere hostile glance from Manson was enough to cause the giggling of the suspects to lapse into silence. Manson told the officers that the blacks were going to take over the country and that the blacks would wipe out the police.

Just as the car thieves arrived at the mouth of the wash, followed by the bouncing headlights of the four-wheel-drive police vehicles, Country Sue and Cathy Meyers were arriving at the Goler Wash in a black Oldsmobile full of $500 worth of groceries. The two girls also were arrested. The food was taken in custody also to save Inyo County taxpayers money by supplementing the jail diet of the prisoners.

Twenty-five

The Breaking of the Case
October–November 1969

Mark Arneson, the human to whom Manson had sold Gary Hinman's Microbus, sold it in turn for $350 to another human named Louis Puhek. In Puhek's possession, the bus still looked the same with the thunderbird printed on the side. It even had the same license plate PGE 388. Someone, however, had put a new engine in the vehicle. There was an all-points bulletin out for the stolen Microbus. Sometime around October 5 or 6 police in Venice, California stopped Puhek and ran the license number, discovering that the vehicle was to be impounded regarding the murder of its owner. Police in Venice questioned Puhek and it was learned that one of the possible owners of the vehicle had been Danny De Carlo of the Straight Satans, who then became a possible suspect in the murder.

Around October 7, Sergeant Whiteley asked Sergeants Gleason, Elliott and Sims of the sheriff's office about Danny De Carlo and if they had a present address on him. They also wanted general information on the Straight Satans regarding possible connections with Hinman. The officers promised to check out De Carlo and get back to Sergeant Whiteley with the data later.

When Sergeant Whiteley and Deputy Guenther learned about Kitty Lutesinger they temporarily forgot about Danny De Carlo however. October 12 they drove to Inyo County and brought the girl back to the San Dimas sheriff's station where she was interrogated.

The words "gas chamber," when uttered by police officers, had a magical way of causing some family members to wax loquacious. At first the officers suggested to Kitty that she was one of the girls that had accompanied Beausoleil to Gary Hinman's house. She replied that the girls were "Sadie and Mary" but certainly not she, and that they had "screwed up" at the Hinman's residence, having been sent there by Manson merely to acquire money.

Another factor that caused mouths to open was that Manson evidently uttered a few threats over the phone directed against weak links, either when Clem called him down at the ranch or when Manson called out after he was arrested. She was worried about her life and that of her parents.

The next morning at 9 A.M., October 13, the officers flew from the Ontario, California airport to Independence to talk to Susan Atkins aka Sadie Glutz. They arrived about noon. They brought with them photos of the family. The Inyo County jail was so crowded with car thieves that interrogation was difficult so Officers Whiteley and Guenther took Sadie to Lone Pine substation of the Inyo County sheriff's department for a chat.

During the officers' skillful interrogation, Atkins admitted participation in the Hinman murder and shortly thereafter even did some talking about Shorty Shea. But she refused to tape-record it. They talked for about twenty-five minutes. Then the officers flew with Miss Atkins back to Ontario. They drove her to the San Dimas sheriff's station and booked her for suspicion of murder. The next day they drove back to Inyo County.

On October 13, Kitty was interviewed by the Los Angeles sheriff's office regarding auto thefts. Sergeants Gleason and Sims interrogated her for four hours. She told about the Michigan loader arson, about various dune-buggy thefts, about stolen credit cards, about the crashing of the '69 Ford from Hertz and about the Hinman case. Kitty was held for several days in Juvenile Hall then released in the custody of her parents.

Sadie Glutz was arrested under the name Donna Powell but the police had been able quickly to determine who she was. The identity of the "Mary" who had been at Gary Hinman's house remained a problem. Patricia Krenwinkel had been arrested as Marnie Kay Reeves, and had a prior arrest under the name of Mary Scott. Therefore she was taken down to Los Angeles on October 14 as a possible murder suspect.

Kitty had revealed that "Mary" was a slim redhead, because Officers Whiteley and Guenther also took red-haired Squeaky Fromme aka Lynette Alice Fromme aka Elizabeth Elaine Williamson with them. On the ride down to Los Angeles, Squeaky, according to legend, told the officers that Charlie had the girls perform fellatio with dogs as part of his mental-death program.

Krenwinkel quickly told the police that it was Mary Brunner not she who had gone to Hinman's house. Krenwinkel, Sadie and Squeaky were held in the Los Angeles sheriff's facility in Lancaster.

The team of investigators working on the LaBianca murders had requested from the Los Angeles sheriff's office information regarding any murders carried out in styles similar to the Waverly Drive homicides. The LaBianca team had rigorously pursued its investigation.

They had connected the bloody "Helter Skelter" and "Rise" with the Beatles album, catalogue number SWBO 101. Also they had correctly interpreted the knife and fork in Mr. LaBianca: "The words in the song 'Piggies' make reference to a knife and fork in the bacon"—as a police report read.

By the time of the LaBianca team's second homicide investigation progress report, dated October 15, 1969, Manson and crew were prime suspects in the LaBianca murders although Manson had not yet been interrogated. Manson's association with the Satan Slaves was noted. Several Satan Slaves had been suspects previously in the LaBianca matter.

The murders were similar, the police noted. Blood writing on the wall, knives as the weapons, both crimes involved the placing of a pillow over the victim's face. And one suspect in the Hinman murder, Susan Atkins, had been free the night of the LaBianca crimes, unlike Beausoleil, who was in jail. Because of all this information about Manson supplied by Officers Whiteley and Guenther, the LaBianca team began to concentrate on the family.

Plans were made by the LaBianca investigators, as of October 15, to compile a list of everybody who had lived at the Spahn Ranch and to obtain a handwriting sample and fingerprints of each. Sometime evidently in mid-October Manson submitted to a polygraph examination but terminated it in the middle. He must have known that the noose was set around his operations and several deaths may have resulted to create silence and fear.

Sadie and Katie were asked to write Helter Skelter to see if either had written it on the LaBianca refrigerator.

On October 15, fourteen of the Mansonoids were arraigned in Inyo County Superior Court on twenty felony charges. The bail totaled out at $263,500. Ten were set free with charges dropped.

On October 15, Danny De Carlo, a Straight Satan named Al Springer and six others were arrested in Venice for receiving stolen property and possession of marijuana. De Carlo's charge stemmed from a hot engine he traded to acquire his bread truck. De Carlo was released on bail. His troubles were mounting. De Carlo had a child custody hearing on September 12 to try to gain possession of his son Dennis, seized during the August 16 raid at the Spahn Ranch and placed in a foster home. At the hearing De Carlo was arrested on a federal charge of purchasing a pistol under a fictitious name. De Carlo also had a five-year conviction for smuggling marijuana in from Mexico which he was then appealing. Danny's many troubles with the law forced him a few days later to finger out the family as the killers of Sharon Tate and others.

Meanwhile, up in Independence, California, where the so-called family was being held, the brave girls would raise their dresses in the exercise yard. Manson would utter coyote yips and his disciples would yip in return. Once during their stay in jail there they asked for peanut butter and honey for a purification rite, whatever that meant. It was all happiness.

On October 16, Inyo County sheriff's deputies plus Los Angeles sheriff homicide and auto theft teams, and CHP officers scoured the Barker Ranch area for incriminating data. There they located some more dune buggies and, according to the police report, numerous food and equipment caches and, perhaps most important, a grease gun and cartridge that witness Lutesinger had earlier described to the investigating officer in San Dimas as being stolen from the National Park Service loader prior to its being found by the hippie group. The cached vehicles were covered with sage brush, willow branches and camouflaged parachutes.

On Thursday, October 16, Susan Atkins aka Sadie was arraigned in Malibu Justice Court for murder. A preliminary hearing was set then for November 12.

In the afternoon of October 17 the sheriff's office in Lancaster called Patricia Krenwinkel's father. Mr. Krenwinkel drove to pick her up. Katie stayed with her father for five days and then on October 23, 1969, she flew to her mother in Mobile, Alabama via National Airlines.

Also on October 17, assistant Los Angeles Police Chief Robert Houghton told a press conference that the initial part of the Tate investigation was over and that now the police would backtrack over the entire case and compare notes. More than 400 police interviews had been conducted to that date.

At the end of forty days' intensive investigation, the chief possible motives for the Cielo Drive homicides were considered to be a drug burn or a drug freak-out.

October 20.

Officers Whiteley and Guenther were impressed that Miss Lutesinger told them that she had overheard Susan Atkins talking about stabbing a man in the legs as the man was pulling Susan's hair. The man was someone other than Gary Hinman, and since Susan Atkins had been free the night of the so-called Tate murders, they felt that she might have something to do with it.

Whiteley and Guenther informed the Tate team about Manson. The Tate detectives waited until October 31, eleven days after they were informed, to interview the young lady.

October 21.

At the Inyo County Courthouse in Independence, California preliminary trials were held for Leslie Sankston aka Leslie Van Houten, Nancy Pitman aka Brenda McCann, Manon Minette aka

Gypsy and Robert Ivan Lane aka Scotty. The theft charges were dismissed but all four defendants were held to answer to charges of violating section 182 of the California Penal Code.

October 22.

Charles Manson "aka Jesus Christ"—as noted on the arrest report—Manon Minette (Gypsy), Diane Bluestein aka Snake Lake and Rachel S. Morse aka Ouish were held to answer for violations of Section 449a of the California Penal Code, referring to the burn-job on that Michigan loader.

October 23.

Sandy Collins Pugh-Good and Mary Schwarm aka Diane Von Ahn and Ouish were held to answer in the Inyo County Court at a preliminary trial on the charge of receiving stolen property (the Ruger pistol that was inside the Miramar mail bag with the witch-swatches of hair, when the three young ladies were arrested in the gulch back of the Meyers Ranch).

Zero, Bill Vance, Little Larry, Vern Plumlee, Sherry Andrews aka Claudia Smith, Beth Tracy aka Diane Von Ahn, Sue Bartell and Cathy Gillies were all released with charges dropped.

Quite a few of the freed family then went to Los Angeles where they stayed in Venice at the residence of one Mark Ross located at 28 Club House Drive, just off the ocean. It was there that Zero would die.

October 25.

At the Sybil Brand Jail for Women, in Los Angeles, news broadcasts were available to the inmates, and Sadie was stimulated to babble more than once by news bulletins about the investigation into the Tate murders. Around October 24 and 25, the airways were filled with announcements of a hot new clue in the homicides —the possibility that the murders were committed by a nearsighted bullet-headed freak with deformed ears. A newspaper had printed the story of the pair of glasses found near Mr. Polanski's blue steamer trunks, lying open with the ear bars sticking straight up, as if the murderer had been wearing them and they had fallen off. Local radio stations flashed broadcasts derived from newspaper accounts of the glasses. The police had taken the glasses to a Hollywood optometrist who opined that the glasses, because of certain bendings in them, belonged to someone one of whose ears was lower than the other, and who was very very myopic and who had a rounder head than most humans. So, when the broadcasts occurred about the glasses, Sadie talked about it with a fellow inmate nicknamed Casper aka Roseanne Walker, a young chunky brown-haired lady in jail for various offenses relating to a passion for taking downers.

Casper was that sort that you find in many jails, a business-woman selling cigarettes and candy to fellow inmates on the sly. She would have people hold her merchandise and her excess profits for her, since it was against prison regulations to have more than a certain fixed amount of money or cigarettes. Accord-ing to Casper, Sadie became friendly with her because of her pleasant open disposition and because literally Sadie had not a dime, and Casper had lots of candy and cigarettes she was willing to share.

Sadie and Casper had a debate whether or not the person owning the glasses was connected with the murders. Sadie said that just because glasses were found it didn't mean they were the murder-er's, for, indeed, they might have been planted there "to spread confusion." In fact, Sadie, according to Casper, thought it funny that someone innocent might be arrested and accused because of those glasses. Sadie's comment, after some of the broadcasts about the homicides, was, "That ain't the way it went down."

It was Casper, the friendly cigarette saleslady, to whom Sadie told the frightful story that Sharon Tate had asked Sadie to cut out the baby and save it, but that Sadie claimed she lacked the nerve. She could only kill.

October 31.

Halloween. Detectives from the Cielo Drive homicide investiga-tion finally interrogated Kitty Lutesinger. A believable informer can do wonders for a murder investigation. This is what Miss Lutesinger did, pointing the Tate investigation toward a set of dreamland criminals: a death-crazed band of so-called hippies.

Also on Halloween '69, Steve Brandt, personal friend and former press agent for Sharon Tate, and also a columnist for

Photoplay, a witness for the Polanski wedding in London in 1968
—and, of course, also that excellent early information source for
the police—called up Eddie Fisher, reached Mr. Fisher's secretary
and announced that he had taken enough downers to kill himself
at his apartment on 1260 N. Kings Road. As he regained consciousness sometime later, in County-USC Hospital, his dimmed
eyes focussed in on two Tate detectives who asked him forthwith
if his attempted suicide had anything to do with the homicides.
"They wanted to know if what I'd done had been connected with
the case," Brandt told reporters.

November 1.

Detectives checked in with Sam Barrett, Manson's federal
parole officer, in order to obtain all the data available about
him. Around November 1, one Virginia Graham, one Ronni
Howard aka Shelley Nadell, and Sadie Glutz-Atkins were moved
to an open fifty-person sleeping area called dormitory 8000, a
so-called working dormitory whose residents every day worked
in various parts of the jail.

Virginia Graham was very concerned that she was going to be
returned to Corona State Prison for Women on a parole violation. She had done time there in 1966 and was on parole when
she was picked up on October 20. Virginia had many aliases she
had used over the years, including Virginias Browne, Lopez,
Ciocco and Benedict. She entered the jail, spent four days in the
infirmary, then a week in another cell block before she was transferred into the bunk-bedded dormitory 8000.

Sadie was brought into dormitory 8000 about a day or so
after Virginia, according to Virginia's testimony at the trial. Sadie
was assigned a top bunk bed in the back of the dorm. Virginia
was assigned lower bed number 3, in the front. Ronni Howard,
who was an old friend of Virginia Graham for about ten years,
was also brought into dormitory 8000, incarcerated since August
27 for a charge that she forged a prescription for drugs. After a
few days in dormitory 8000, Sadie would move to a sleeping
position right next to Ronni Howard, so that literally they were
within inches of one another.

The inmates made fun of the young Sadie Glutz saying, when she would come by, "Oh, here comes Sadie Glutz." Sadie was singular among the others because of her weird name and because she would sing and dance torrid go-go steps to the piped-in music and she would bend over and contort during physical exercises, without underwear. The others would kid her, and for this, they claim, Ronni and Virginia befriended her, feeling sorry for the hot-blooded girl.

Mrs. Graham has said: "She was singing and dancing all the time. In fact, it didn't seem to fit a place like that, that type of happiness."

November 2.

Anonymous phone calls were made to the *Los Angeles Times*, *The New York Times*, KNXT–TV, etc., informing the media of the connection between the Hinman case and the LaBianca-Tate cases. And, in the Sybil Brand Institute, Virginia Graham helped her new-found friend Sadie Glutz get a job as a prison runner, a job that Virginia herself had been assigned a day or so before. Runners carried messages all over the prison for the authorities. They also delivered the yellow visitor slips to the various inmates whenever visitors came to the jail, so that the job seemed to be a happy one.

"I did speak with somebody about it," Miss Graham replied when she was asked if she helped Sadie get a runner job.

So Sadie and Virginia began working side by side. Much of their time was spent sitting on little stools near what is called "control" waiting for messages to be needed to be delivered. They would take turns delivering them. The hours of their employment were from 7:30 A.M. till 3:30 P.M.

Naturally, at some point they discussed the charges for which they were incarcerated.

November 4.

Danny De Carlo, Al Springer and the others arrested in Venice were held over for trial on November 18 on charges of possession of marijuana, receiving stolen property and theft of automotive parts. Springer evidently remained in jail while De Carlo was out on bail.

In the afternoon, Sadie and Virginia were sitting on their stools near "control," awaiting message chores, when Miss Graham asked Sadie, "What are *you* here for"? as if in mild reproach that such a tender small girl as Sadie should be in jail.

"First degree murder."

"Oh, you are, huh."

Sadie told Virginia a little bit about her charges. She was very upset about Bobby Beausoleil, because she felt that he had mentioned her name to the police. She told Virginia Graham that the police had shown up with a deal for her, if she would testify against Beausoleil, but Sadie had a plan to act crazy, and it wouldn't be necessary to do anything at all. Each day would find Sadie telling Virginia more and more.

November 5.

Christopher Zero died in Venice of a gunshot wound in his head. It happened at 28 Club House Drive while the owner of the house, Mark Ross, was away attending an acting class. A witness to the grim deed said that Cathy Gillies Vance, Claudia (Sherry Andrews), Bruce and others were sitting in the living room when Zero died.

Zero and Little Patti were in a bedroom and, according to the witness, Little Patti was sleeping on the bed. Country Sue was preparing Zero a cup of tea in the kitchen. She heard laughter from the room, then a sharp splitting sound, as if a firecracker had gone off.

Little Patti came stumbling out of the room, saying, "Just like in the movies, just like in the movies."

"Then," Sue said, "Bruce went in and picked up the gun on the bed," an act that caused Sue to yell at him. A fingerprint belonging to Davis was found by police on the finger guard of the weapon.

Sue held Zero as he lay dying. "I held him till he died. I felt his pulse. Which was real fast and fluttery." Then the pulse began to slow down, "and, uh, his face got all purple." Then he died. Little Patti, long since in hiding, called the police, using the name Linda Baldwin.

After the police arrived and entered the bedroom where Zero

lay, evidently inside a sleeping bag, Sue walked around on the
outside of the house to the bedroom window and looked in
and she claimed that his eyes were then closed, his face had
whitened and he had a slight smile on his face.

Vern Plumlee was told by a female family member about the
shooting. "She said, he wanted to know what it was like, you
know, to die. And he had been laughing and everything like that,
on an acid trip."

Vern didn't believe it though. "Acid doesn't make you want
to kill yourself," he commented.

Later Plumlee claimed that family sources revealed the killer's
true identity to him, telling him that Zero may have been one of
those who "knew too much." The family told the police that
Zero had been playing Russian Roulette so the death was ruled
a suicide. It must be noted that Mr. Zero, if he in fact killed himself, tampered considerably with the odds of the game because
there was only one empty chamber in the loaded revolver.

A day or so after the demise of Zero aka John Philip Haught,
Country Sue visited Susan Atkins at Sybil Brand Institute where
Sue told Sadie how Zero had rouletted himself. She'd held his
hand, wasn't that groovy, while he died and that he had "climaxed
all over himself."

Ronni Howard was working in visitor receiving at the Sybil
Brand Jail, so Sadie introduced Sue Bartell to Ronni before Sadie
visited with Sue. When Sue told her about the roulette, Sadie,
enthusiastic as ever about gore and death, rushed out to tell Ronni
about it, in gruesome detail.

November 6.

At 1:30 P.M. Lieutenant A. H. Burdick of the scientific investigation division of the Los Angeles police department, the
gentleman who ninety days previous had administered a lie detector test to William Garretson, was in Independence, California,
interviewing Leslie Van Houten. He claimed, in a report to
Sergeant Patchett of the Los Angeles police department robbery-
homicide division that Miss Van Houten indicated to him that there
were "some 'things' that caused her to believe that someone from

her group was involved in the Tate homicide but denied knowledge of the LaBianca homicide. At this time she declined to indicate what she meant and stated that she wanted to think about it overnight, and that she was perplexed and didn't know what to do." The next day, Miss Van Houten had gained her composure and refused to speak any more about the matter.

The friendly runners, Sadie and Virginia Graham, ran messages all day till 3:30 P.M., then they went to dinner, returning to the 8000 dormitory about 4:35 P.M. Virginia was all set to go take a shower when Sadie came over to Virginia's bed and asked if she could sit and talk for a minute. Virginia said okay. They talked. Somehow the subject centered at first on LSD, which the thirty-nine-year-old Virginia had taken for the first time on October 1, a few days before her arrest. Sadie had taken hundreds of trips, so it was something in common to talk about.

Then Sadie began to talk about the Hinman matter, confessing freely to participating in it. Miss Graham reproached Sadie for her loose talk.

"I told her that I didn't care particularly what she had done, but I didn't think it was advisable for her to talk so much," Virginia remembered later. Graham told Sadie she had heard of cases where people in jail were victims of entrapment after confessing to crimes to cellmates who later snitched.

Sadie replied that she wasn't worried because looking in Virginia's eyes, she just knew she could trust Virginia. April Fool.

Sadie then began to talk about Death Valley and the people arrested up there and the Underground City for the chosen. And she began to talk about Manson. Then Sadie became visibly excited and began to talk quickly. What triggered it off? Evidently a general discussion of crime and murder.

"We were talking about crime and, you know, various murders, and all that," remembered Miss Graham.

And Sadie said, in the course of the conversation, according to Graham, "Well, you know, there's a case right now. They are so far off the track they don't even know what's happening."

There was a pause.

"What are you talking about?"

"That one on Benedict Canyon."

"Benedict Canyon?"

"Benedict Canyon, yes!"

"You don't mean Sharon Tate?"

"Yeah," Sadie said. Then she grew excited even more and the baleful words of chop-mania were spewn out. "You're looking at the one that did it."

Several times Sadie raised her voice and Graham had to tell her to lower it. Out came the horror, the deathly details, the scenarios. And Miss Graham began to ask questions to determine if Sadie was really telling the truth, querying Sadie about the rope, what the victims were wearing, etc., in order to trip her up. But the story seemed to hold, except that Sadie claimed to have left a palm print on the living room desk and to have lost her knife in the fray, events unmentioned in the media. (And any palm print would already certainly have led to Sadie's arrest.)

For just over an hour they talked. At 6 P.M. there was a jail prisoner count so it had to stop, but not before Miss Graham's mind was filled with an unforgettable mixture of shocking data. Right away, Miss Graham rushed over to her ten-year friend Ronni Howard and told her what Sadie had related. They weren't totally convinced but they planned to try to find out more from Sadie.

"We'll ask her certain questions that only a person would know who had been in on it," Miss Howard said to Miss Young. "Try and ask her what color the bedroom was, or what the people had on or anything."

Because Sadie had moved into the bed right next to Ronni, Ronni was able to begin to talk to Sadie, by night, in privacy. Since the prison matrons counted the sleeping inmates each half hour, it was possible by means of a system of lookouts to visit each other intimately for half-hour periods in between head counts.

November 8.

Virginia Graham didn't want to rouse Sadie's suspicions, so she waited to bring up the subject of murder. One day, she told

Sadie, approximately two to three days after the bedside conversation, this: "Hey, you know . . ." revealing to Sadie that she and her former husband years before, around 1962, had been to the residence at 10050 Cielo Drive to see about renting it. "Is it still done in gold and white?" Taking a shot in the dark, because she had never actually seen the interior.

"Uh huh," Sadie replied.

On November 8 or 9, Sadie came to Virginia's bed with a movie fan magazine in her hand. The magazine was opened to a picture of Elizabeth Taylor and Richard Burton. Sadie seemed jolly as she disclosed to Virginia a list of future victims, including Richard Burton, whose groin was to be trimmed of appendage, Elizabeth Taylor, Frank Sinatra, Tom Jones, who was singing over the jail radio at that moment and Steve McQueen—although Sadie said that she hated to have to do in Tom Jones because he turned her on. She also expressed enmity for Frank Sinatra, Jr. The most hideous of deaths Sadie plotted for those on her list.

November 12.

Both Susan Atkins and Bob Beausoleil had hearings at the Santa Monica Superior Court, on the Hinman matter, but before different judges. Sadie appeared before Judge John Merrick, in a hearing to determine if she should be held for a trial. Her lawyer was court appointed, a Mr. Gerald M. Condon.

Deputy Guenther of the Los Angeles sheriff's office homicide division, testified about information obtained from her on October 13 at the Lone Pine sheriff's station house. Officer Guenther also testified that Sadie told him that she held Mr. Hinman while Beausoleil stabbed him. Deputy Guenther told of interviewing Kitty Lutesinger, who evidently had overheard a phone conversation wherein Susan Atkins had talked about killing Hinman, "indicating that Bobby and Susie had screwed up, that they had to kill Hinman." Sadie was angry, to be sure, at Kitty when she heard this.

Judge Merrick found that there was sufficient cause that Miss Atkins be brought to trial and, accordingly, he set a trial date of November 26, 1969.

Sadie came back to Sybil Brand Institute an upset woman.

Evidently, she had made notes which she showed to Ronni Howard. Gosh, how could Deputy Guenther testify that she held a 200-pound man's arms, little old she, while Beausoleil stabbed him? What she told Graham and Nadell was that she stabbed Hinman, not Bobby.

It so happened that on November 12, Virginia Graham had a parole hearing and it was decided to send her back to Corona State Prison for Women. Just before she left (after Sadie had returned from her own court appearance) Ronni and Virginia had a short conference about what to do about Sadie's confession.

Ronni said that she had been talking every night to Sadie, commenting, "Boy is she weird."

Ronni aka Shelley aka Veronica felt that she could ask Sadie the question which would determine if Sadie was telling the truth. Ronni knew what it was like to stab someone, since she had once stabbed her former husband. So Ronni decided to ask Sadie what it was like, physically, to stab someone.

Ronni evidently agreed with Virginia that the key might be to start out by talking about LSD trips, since that seemed to get Sadie going. As Virginia Graham left to go to Corona, she told Ronni that if she found out more, she could then go to her parole agent.

Ronni replied that, since she worked down in receiving, there were always lots of homicide detectives coming to the jail, and she'd just tell one of them. Whereupon, Virginia said that, if Ronni decided to tell anybody in authority about the matter, Virginia could be reached at Corona State Prison.

The hour for lights-out in dorm 8000 at Sybil Brand Institute is 9:30 P.M., and that very night, after taps, Sadie and Ronni Howard were talking face to face. "Oh, how I got her to tell me about it; I told you we were talking about an acid trip. You know, because not too many of the girls take acid in there and I guess I was one that she could talk to," is how Miss Howard described her method of getting Sadie to talk.

Ronni had taken twelve acid trips. Sadie told her that there was nothing that could shock her, nothing that she hadn't done.

Then, upon the subtle prodding of Miss Howard, the subject somehow shifted to butchery and Miss Atkins began to tell all. Ronni scoffed enough and asked enough questions to force Sadie to reveal all the details, whispering in the dark dormitory.

Each night, from November 12 through November 15 or 16, Shelley Nadell aka Ronni Howard would lie down with Sadie Glutz in the darkness collecting data. Sadie really upset Ronni, however, when she told Ronni that the deaths were going to continue and that they were going to occur at random!

Venice detectives interviewed biker Al Springer in the L.A. County jail. Springer had not been able to raise bail. The police were interviewing anybody who had any connection with the family in the hope of finding someone with information who would talk. They hit pay dirt this time, a rare occurrence because of the veil of fear that kept the family quiet. Springer told them about a conversation that Danny De Carlo had allegedly heard from somebody after the Tate murders, something like "we got five piggies."

The Venice detectives located De Carlo living with his mother, who was caring for Dan's two-year-old son Dennis. Hesitant to talk, De Carlo had so many charges against him that pressure forced him to loosen his tongue.

Then the LaBianca detectives interviewed both Springer and De Carlo on November 12, and the road to victory was entered at last.

November 14.

Testimony was heard against Robert Beausoleil, following jury selection which took most of the preceding day. Because the case had not yet become such a media trip for the district attorney, it was agreed, with trial Judge John Shea concurring, that the death penalty was not being sought. Testimony was heard from twelve prosecution witnesses and one defense witness so that the trial was scheduled to conclude after two days of testimony, with the closing arguments of defense attorney Leon Salter and prosecuting attorney Ross to be had on Tuesday morning, November 18.

The case against Beausoleil, at that time, was circumstantial and fairly weak, until the very day that the trial would probably have ended, when the prosecution learned about De Carlo and the confession that Beausoleil allegedly had made to him.

It is this writer's opinion that the two ladies, Graham-Ciocco and Nadell-Young entered into a pact between them to milk a confession out of Susan Atkins, possibly in pursuit of a reward offered privately by a concerned individual.

Around November 14, Virginia Graham claims to have decided to talk about Susan Atkins' confession. She filled out a "blue slip" or request to speak with a staff member and sent it to the psychologist at Corona State Prison, Dr. Vera Dreiser, with the note:

"Dr. Dreiser, it is very important that I speak with you."

Dr. Dreiser sent a "blue slip" back indicating that Miss Graham was to talk with Dr. Owens, Dreiser's administrator. Finally about twelve days later she told her counselor, Miss Mary Ann Domn, about the Manson family.

November 16.

Police called Gregg Jakobson to make an appointment to see them about Manson. The next day, several officers including Lieutenant Helder, the head of the Tate investigation, and Sergeants Patchett and Gutierrez of the LaBianca investigation came to Jakobson's house on Beverly Glen for a long interview. A key incentive for Jakobson to talk, as in the case of De Carlo and Lutesinger, was that Manson was in jail and off the streets, therefore seemingly unable to harm. They asked Jakobson to relate everything he knew about Manson's group.

At 3:30 P.M. on November 16, an unidentified body of a girl was found in the Hollywood hills off Mulholland Drive near Skyline Drive. This girl, referred to by the police as Jane Doe number 59, had been dead for about a day. Again the crime had been committed with savagery.

November 17.

Ronni Howard aka Shelley Joyce Nadell aka Veronica Hughes aka Veronica Williams aka Connie Johnson aka Connie Schampeau aka Sharon Warren aka Marjie Carter aka Jean Marie Conley had an appearance in Santa Monica Superior Court before Judge Brandt regarding her false prescription charge.

California law allows a defendant a phone call for each separate court appearance, so Ronni called the Hollywood division of the Los Angeles police department, because she believed that the Hollywood division was handling the Tate investigation. She told them about Sadie's confession.

After Miss Howard returned to Sybil Brand Jail from court, L.A.P.D. Special Investigators Brown and Mossman came to Sybil Brand and talked to Ronni in a private room for about an hour and a half. She supplied them with most of the information that Sadie had given her, except she left out some of the names involved.

What made it totally believable to the police was that Sadie had told Ronni of things only the killer could have known, such as the Buck knife that Sadie said she lost in the house.

There are some interesting aspects to Ronni Howard aka Shelley Nadell snitching to the police. Nadell testified at the trial that she told certain details to Officers Brown and Mossman but that she never repeated these details later.

On Monday, November 17, the same day Ronni Howard aka Shelley Nadell was telling the police about Susan Atkins, other officers at L.A. police headquarters were taping a long interview with Danny De Carlo of the Straight Satans. De Carlo came in voluntarily.

The interview ranged over every aspect of the family and De Carlo's memory was very exact. He told them about the white nylon rope found at the Polanski residence. He talked about the Hinman murder, the Shea murder, the death of the sixteen-year-old boy in Topanga and numerous other crimes.

When interrogating officers suggested that De Carlo, since he was seen sporting one of Shorty Shea's matched .45's after his death, may have been involved in the murder, De Carlo replied, "I got no balls to put anyone's lights out."

De Carlo was uptight about reprisals from Manson and Bruce

Davis. The family girls now set up headquarters in Venice where they had been spotted by the Straight Satans. The police assured him that Manson was going to remain in jail. But Davis was a free man.

De Carlo was interested in obtaining some part of the $25,000 reward in order to put his boy Dennis through military school. The police agreed not to turn De Carlo over to federal authorities on the gun violation nor to turn him in on a charge filed in Van Nuys.

Late in the afternoon Sergeant Manuel Gutierrez called Deputy Guenther of the Hinman investigation and told him of De Carlo's statements bragging about Hinman's death. He gave Guenther De Carlo's home address.

November 18.

In the afternoon Dan De Carlo had a hearing in Santa Monica Superior Court regarding his theft bust in Venice on October 15. He agreed to testify against Robert Beausoleil in exchange for the Venice charges being dropped. Accordingly, De Carlo waited by the phone all morning for a phone call summoning him down to court to testify.

Both prosecution and defense now rested in Robert Beausoleil's trial and both sides were set to discuss jury instructions with the judge, when the prosecution became aware of De Carlo. Around 10:30 A.M., the deputy district attorney, Mr. Ross, requested a continuance till 2 P.M. He told the court that there was an "individual" with information relative to the case.

That morning Sergeant Whiteley and Deputy Guenther were handling a kidnapping case on trial at the Hall of Justice in downtown L.A. At the noon break the officers sped out to Santa Monica Superior Court where they apprised the prosecution of De Carlo's evidence against Beausoleil. Thereafter the policemen returned to downtown L.A. to continue their testimony in the kidnapping case.

At 2 P.M. the D.A. requested a week's continuance till Monday, November 24. The motion was granted over the strenuous objections of Beausoleil's attorney, Mr. Leon Salter. After all, both sides had rested and now there was to be more evidence given against Beausoleil.

Evidently only one lieutenant and five detectives were still assigned to the Polanski residence case. Right away, after Ronni Howard aka Shelley Nadell snitched, the full investigation involving two lieutenants and sixteen men was reactivated. With the evidence supplied by Nadell, De Carlo, Kitty, Jakobson and others, it was all over.

On November 18, 1969, at 2 P.M., District Attorney Evelle Younger assigned Deputy D.A. Vincent T. Bugliosi and Deputy D.A. Aaron Stovitz to handle the case. These two energetic gentlemen proceeded to coordinate the gathering of conclusive evidence against the murderers.

November 19.

Deputy D.A. Vincent Bugliosi, Sergeant Calkins, Deputy Guenther, Sergeant Whiteley and other officers went to the Spahn Ranch to gather data. They were looking for .22-caliber shell casings and also for knives. They had not located yet the Buntline Special turned over by Steve Weiss on Labor Day and stored by the police. The officers obtained George Spahn's consent to search the ranch. Sergeant Lee, of the special investigation division of the L.A. police department, found twenty-two .22-caliber shell casings around 100 yards south of the Western set and also a quarter of a mile up the canyon toward Hialeah Springs. White panels were placed on the gulley where the .22-caliber casings were found so that a plane overhead could take aerial photos.

Deputy D.A. Aaron Stovitz, possessing a search warrant for the green and white bus, traveled to the Barker Ranch to acquire data, leading a team of L.A. police officers.

Various law enforcement officials in the Inyo County area, notably Sergeant Dave Steuber of the California Highway Patrol, prepared detailed reports regarding the Mansonoids. Officer Steuber produced, on November 20, a skillful document entitled: SUMMARY OF THE ARRESTS AND THE CRIMES COMMITTED IN THE DEATH VALLEY AREA OF INYO COUNTY BY A GROUP OF HIPPIES KNOWN AS "THE

FAMILY" UNDER THE LEADERSHIP OF CHARLES
MILES MANSON.

November 21.

Sergeant Phil Sartuche of L.A.P.D., robbery-homicide, who
had been a part of the resourceful LaBianca team of detectives,
collected from Inyo County courthouse a large quantity of boots,
moccasins, shoes and clothing seized at the Barker Ranch. Officials had not yet located the bloody attire used by the murderers
and possibly wanted to match the boots and shoes with the new
heel print on the Polanski sidewalk. All items were turned over
to Sergeant Granado for analysis at the L.A.P.D. crime lab.

Also taken into custody by Sergeant Sartuche was that "army
style pack" containing the sixty-four movie star magazines, the
copy of *Stranger in a Strange Land*, the Federal Reserve money
bag, etc.

On the evening of November 21, 1969, two scientology students,
one of them a girl friend of Bruce Davis, were murdered near a
scientology commune called Thetan Manor located at 1032 South
Bonnie Brae. The victims, particularly the girl, were unspeakably
slashed.

Doreen Gaul, twenty-one—a scientology "clear"—from Al-
bany, New York, and James Sharp, fifteen, of Crystal City, Missouri, were living in the Westlake area near L.A. scientology
headquarters in separate residences. Miss Gaul lived at Thetan
Manor, an old three-story Victorian house then filled mainly with
students of scientology. Several humans connected with a voodoo
group lived there also, according to an official of the Church of
Scientology who investigated the murders.

They were last seen alive at 7:30 P.M. hitchhiking in front
of Vons Market. Their desecrated bodies were found four hours
later at 11:30 P.M. dumped in a nearby alleyway lined with pastel-
color garages lettered with strange and ornate teen-gang spray-
paint writing called placa.

November 23.

Sergeants Patchett and McGann of L.A.P.D. in the evening
interviewed Shelley Nadell at the Sybil Brand Institute. The next
day, Nadell was removed from the dormitory where she slept

alongside Susan Atkins. Nadell could not continue to stay in the same dormitory lest it appear to the court that she had attempted to entrap Miss Atkins into a confession.

November 24.

The trial of Robert Beausoleil for the murder of Gary Hinman ended with Danny De Carlo being allowed to testify. With De Carlo's added testimony, the Beausoleil jury went into deliberation and after considerable debate was unable to come to a decision. The jury remained locked 8 to 4 for conviction so a mistrial was declared. This was unfortunate for Beausoleil, for in the retrial of April 1970, the district attorney decided to seek the death penalty and ultimately secured it.

The night of November 24, a newscaster for Channel 11 in Los Angeles announced, after a tip to one of his sound men from a detective, that a "Break was coming soon in the Sharon Tate murder case." The press entered the investigation of Manson several weeks before the December 1 arrests. Reporters checked facts with the police and the police, in turn, learned details from the newsmen. An official of Los Angeles radio station KFWB reported that his staff uncovered a link between the Hinman case and the Tate case in the middle of October 1969.

One radio station picked up on the family after it noticed that an unusual number of L.A. sheriff's deputies were filling out travel sheets for Independence, California where the killers were incarcerated.

By November 19, the *Los Angeles Times* had a general knowledge of the Manson family and had a page-one story already written a week before Police Chief Davis announced the breaking of the case to a press conference.

TV camera and light crews who roam L.A. tragedy sites began to get informed, "in strictest confidence," that the case had been solved. Helicopters bearing TV camera crews showing up in Goler Wash. CBS considered venturing to the Barker Ranch via dune buggy but heard that the family was armed and that they employed walky-talky warning devices. A helicopter was used instead.

Pressure mounted for the solution to be publicly aired. On the other hand, the press refrained from announcing details because of the possibility of further murders or suicides or that crucial evidence would be destroyed.

Some police officers have expressed privately that, had the arrests been held off for a while, "we could have got them all." One key homicide investigator stated that the murder of Jane Doe 59 probably would have been solved had the arrests been delayed. But the police knew about Zero's death, and about possible connections with murders in Bishop, Ukiah, Topanga, etc., so there was great concern to get such maniacs immediately off the streets.

November 25.

Sergeant Gutierrez of L.A.P.D. Robbery-Homicide visited the Spahn Ranch. There he talked to Juan Flynn, who showed Gutierrez a cabinet door in his trailer bearing "various writings." Flynn allowed the door itself to be removed from the cabinet and brought into custody. The writing on the door was as follows: "1, 2, 3, 4, 5, 6, 7—all good children go to heaven—Helter Skelter." At the bottom of the writing was the inverted Yoni-sign or peace symbol.

Police reinterviewed Mrs. Nadell-Young-Howard-Conley-Hughes-Williams-Lopez at Sybil Brand Jail and taped it. Police informed Mrs. Nadell that there were perhaps two or three others with whom it would be necessary to share the reward. Ronni asked the cops, or suggested to the cops, that they send her back in to get more information from Sadie, for if Ronni had returned to Sadie's bedside, it would have meant more data.

"You mean to say that you couldn't forget your code of ethics or something like this because this is something out of the ordinary, really."

To which Sergeant Patchett told her, "We have to take this thing to court to prosecute these people and to do so we can't put you back in there; because you will be our agent then."

On November 25 Los Angeles police department took a half dozen prisoners (Clem, Gypsy, Ouish, Brenda, Snake and Leslie) from Independence, California to Los Angeles, on subpoenas from the grand jury. The end was near. Manson was left behind in Independence.

All prisoners were intensively interviewed to attempt to get information incriminating Manson but not even the words "gas chamber" seemed to loosen their tongues. Susan Atkins' confession to her cellmates could only be used to convict Miss Atkins. It could not be used against Watson, Manson, Krenwinkel, Kasabian and the others, because of strict rules pertaining to the admissibility of so-called cellmate confessions.

November 26.

Sadie/Susan had a court hearing in Santa Monica on the Hinman matter.

Richard Condon was relieved of his job as court-appointed attorney and Richard Caballero, a former assistant district attorney, was appointed to represent Miss Atkins, at county expense. Mr. Caballero had a long, lengthy discussion with Atkins. She was evidently confronted with the considerable evidence against her from her cellmates. She was made to believe that the evidence was overwhelming against her, Manson and the others. Somehow she was convinced by her attorney that only if she made a full confession to all the murders and cooperated with the police could she hope to avoid the gas chamber. She did not know that in fact her cooperation would be the evidence-in-chief at that time against the others. Now the case was truly broken.

In the morning of the same day that Susan Atkins agreed to confess, her former cellmate Virginia Graham related to Miss Mary Ann Domn, Graham's counselor at the Corona State Prison for Women, what Miss Atkins had told her about the homicide.

The same day, at 3:15 P.M. Sergeant Mike Nielsen of the Los Angeles police department taped an interview with Miss Graham at the Corona State Prison.

November 28.

Sergeant Mike Nielsen of L.A.P.D. robbery-homicide division, called Joseph Krenwinkel and asked where his daughter Patricia was. He told them that Miss Krenwinkel was to be found in Mobile, Alabama. She would be arrested several days later in Mobile where she was staying with her aunt.

On November 30, Charles Denton Watson was picked up in Copeville, Texas for murder.

At 2 P.M. on December 1, Los Angeles Police Chief Edward Davis held a press conference in an auditorium at Parker Center, the L.A. police headquarters, where he announced the solution of the Tate-LaBianca-Sebring-Folger-Frykowski-Parent homicides.

Facing about fifteen microphones and a knot of jousting cameramen, Chief Edward Davis announced that 8,750 hours of police work brought down the house of Manson.

It was over.

Ahead were the grand jury indictments, the scandals involving the publication of Susan Atkins' confession, the legal maneuvers, the weirdness, the threats, Beausoleil's second trial putting him on Death Row, the Tate-LaBianca trial putting Susan Atkins, Patricia Krenwinkel, Leslie Van Houten and Manson on the Row. Tex Watson's trial, following a period in Atascadero State Mental Hospital, is forthcoming. Also in progress, as of this writing, is the trial of Steve "Clem" Grogan, Bruce Davis and Charles Manson for the murder of Shorty Shea and the trial of Bruce Davis and Charles Manson for the murder of Gary Hinman.

Without a doubt the trials will continue. For justice demands it. And only when all these evil affairs are known and exposed can the curse of ritual sacrifice, Helter Skelter and satanism be removed from the coasts and mountains and deserts of California.